CAMBRIDGE STUDIES IN MUSIC

GENERAL EDITORS: JOHN STEVENS AND PETER LE HURAY

Music and Patronage in
Sixteenth-Century Mantua

I

CAMBRIDGE STUDIES IN MUSIC

Music and patronage in sixteenth-century Mantua

I

IAIN FENLON

CAMBRIDGE UNIVERSITY PRESS

CAMBRIDGE

LONDON   NEW YORK   NEW ROCHELLE

MELBOURNE   SYDNEY

Published by the Press Syndicate of the University of Cambridge
The Pitt Building, Trumpington Street, Cambridge CB2 1RP
32 East 57th Street, New York, NY 10022, USA
296 Beaconsfield Parade, Middle Park, Melbourne 3206, Australia

First published 1980   .

Printed in Great Britain
at the University Press, Cambridge

British Library Cataloguing in Publication Data
Fenlon, Iain
Music and patronage in sixteenth-century
Mantua. – (Cambridge studies in music).
1. Music – Italy – Mantua – History – 16th
century 2. Art patronage – Italy – Mantua –
History – 16th century
I. Title II. Series
338.4′7′78094528   ML290.8.M/   79–41377
ISBN 0 521 22905 7

For
NCF and SMF
in gratitude

Contents

The contents of Appendix II are listed on pp. 166–9.

Illustrations

viii

Preface

The origins of this book lie with my friends in Cambridge, and particularly with my teacher Nigel Fortune, whose friendship, advice and encouragement have been a constant source of support since the afternoon, almost a decade ago, when he first reacted so warmly to my enthusiasm for sixteenth-century Mantuan musical culture. I am grateful to St Catharine's College, Cambridge, for admitting me as a Research Student; but it is to the Provost and Fellows of King's College that I owe my principal debt for conferring upon me the privilege of admission to their own number, and for supporting my work so generously. During a happy and fruitful year as a Fellow of the Villa I Tatti in Florence, I was the fortunate recipient of wise words and great kindness from the Director, Professor Craig Hugh Smyth, and his wife, Barbara. Harvard's support during that year ensured further work in the Mantuan archives, and more work there during 1977–8 was made possible by a grant from the British Academy.

My sincere thanks are due to Professors Denis Arnold, Stanley Boorman, and Howard Mayer Brown for advice in the early stages of the work; to Professor Anthony Newcomb for kindly allowing me to consult a part of his forthcoming book on music in sixteenth-century Ferrara; to Dr Joanna Weinberg, who helped with translations from Hebrew; to Professors William Prizer and Richard Sherr for permission to consult unpublished essays which set me thinking afresh about some problems; to Professor John Stevens, who provided valuable criticism of an earlier draft of part of this study; to Dr Dennis Rhodes for allowing me to consult his unpublished catalogue of books printed in Mantua; to Professor Elizabeth Mahnke, who came to my rescue at a difficult moment; to Mr Andrew Morragh for help with the architectural history of Santa Barbara; to Mme Sylvie Béguin, who arranged for me to examine paintings from Isabella d'Este's *studiolo* now in the reserve collection of the Louvre; to my typist, Ms Barbara Bell, for her achievement in deciphering an often cryptic text; to Dr Nigel Fortune, Dr Pierluigi Petrobelli, and Ms Susan Parisi, who read and criticised the work in its late stages; and to the staff of the Cambridge University Press.

Quite clearly, the work would hardly have been possible without the co-operation and assistance of many librarians in many countries, but I should like to single out a few institutions who have been particularly generous with their help: the Civico Museo Bibliografico-Musicale in Bologna; the Archivio di Stato, the Biblioteca del Conservatorio, and the Biblioteca Nazionale Centrale in Florence; the British Library and the Royal College of Music in London; the Biblioteca Comunale in Mantua; the Archivio di Stato and the Biblioteca Estense in Modena; the Bodleian Library in Oxford; the Biblioteca Apostolica Vaticana; the library of the Accademia Filarmonica in Verona; and the Biblioteca Comunale in Vicenza. Closer to home the task has always been made easier by the unfailing kindness of the staff of the University Library, Cambridge. Above all, my thanks must go to the staffs of the two principal archives in which I have worked, the Archivio Diocesano and the Archivio di Stato in Mantua, and particularly to Dottoressa Adele Bellù and Dottoressa Anna Maria Lorenzoni in the latter, and to Don Giancarlo Manzoli and Dottoressa Donatella Martelli in the former. The greatest debts of all are expressed in the dedication.

King's College, Cambridge
1 March 1979

Abbreviations

AGCAB	Bologna, Archivio Generale Curia Arcivescovile
ASDM	Mantua, Archivio Storico Diocesano
	(Cap.) Archivio del Capitolo della Cattedrale
	(CV) Archivio della Curia Vescovile
	(LM) Liber Massaria
	(MV) Archivio della Mensa Vescovile
	(SA) Archivio della Basilica di Sant'Andrea
	(SB) Archivio della Basilica di Santa Barbara
ASF	Florence, Archivio di Stato
	(AM) Archivio Mediceo
ASL	Lucca, Archivio di Stato
ASM	Mantua, Archivio di Stato
	(AG) Archivio Gonzaga
	(AP) Archivio Portioli
	(D'Arco) Fondo D'Arco
	(Davari) Fondo Davari
ASMod	Modena, Archivio di Stato
BAF	Ferrara, Biblioteca Ariostea
BAV	Vatican City, Biblioteca Apostolica Vaticana
BBV	Vicenza, Biblioteca Comunale Bertoliana
BCM	Mantua, Biblioteca Comunale

Gonzaga of Mantua

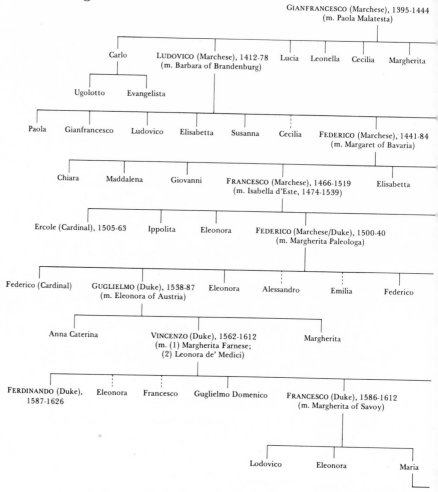

GIANFRANCESCO (Marchese), 1395-1444
(m. Paola Malatesta)

Carlo — LUDOVICO (Marchese), 1412-78 (m. Barbara of Brandenburg) — Lucia — Leonella — Cecilia — Margherita

Ugolotto — Evangelista

Paola — Gianfrancesco — Ludovico — Elisabetta — Susanna — Cecilia — FEDERICO (Marchese), 1441-84 (m. Margaret of Bavaria)

Chiara — Maddalena — Giovanni — FRANCESCO (Marchese), 1466-1519 (m. Isabella d'Este, 1474-1539) — Elisabetta

Ercole (Cardinal), 1505-63 — Ippolita — Eleonora — FEDERICO (Marchese/Duke), 1500-40 (m. Margherita Paleologa)

Federico (Cardinal) — GUGLIELMO (Duke), 1538-87 (m. Eleonora of Austria) — Eleonora — Alessandro — Emilia — Federico

Anna Caterina — VINCENZO (Duke), 1562-1612 (m. (1) Margherita Farnese; (2) Leonora de' Medici) — Margherita

FERDINANDO (Duke), 1587-1626 — Eleonora — Francesco — Guglielmo Domenico — FRANCESCO (Duke), 1586-1612 (m. Margherita of Savoy)

Lodovico — Eleonora — Maria

Gonzaga of Guastalla

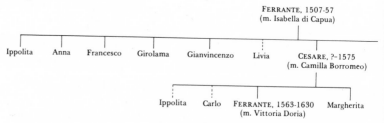

FERRANTE, 1507-57
(m. Isabella di Capua)

Ippolita — Anna — Francesco — Girolama — Gianvincenzo — Livia — CESARE, ?-1575 (m. Camilla Borromeo)

Ippolita — Carlo — FERRANTE, 1563-1630 (m. Vittoria Doria) — Margherita

⁝ = illegitimate

After Litta: *Famiglie celebri italiane*, IV, *Gonzaga*

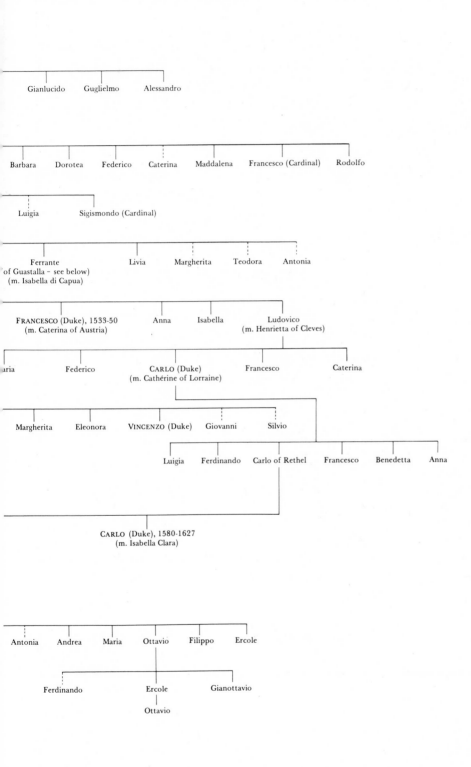

Gianlucido   Guglielmo   Alessandro

Barbara   Dorotea   Federico   Caterina   Maddalena   Francesco (Cardinal)   Rodolfo

Luigia   Sigismondo (Cardinal)

Ferrante
of Guastalla – see below)
(m. Isabella di Capua)   Livia   Margherita   Teodora   Antonia

FRANCESCO (Duke), 1533-50   Anna   Isabella   Ludovico
(m. Caterina of Austria)   (m. Henrietta of Cleves)

aria   Federico   CARLO (Duke)   Francesco   Caterina
(m. Cathérine of Lorraine)

Margherita   Eleonora   VINCENZO (Duke)   Giovanni   Silvio

Luigia   Ferdinando   Carlo of Rethel   Francesco   Benedetta   Anna

CARLO (Duke), 1580-1627
(m. Isabella Clara)

Antonia   Andrea   Maria   Ottavio   Filippo   Ercole

Ferdinando   Ercole   Gianottavio

Ottavio

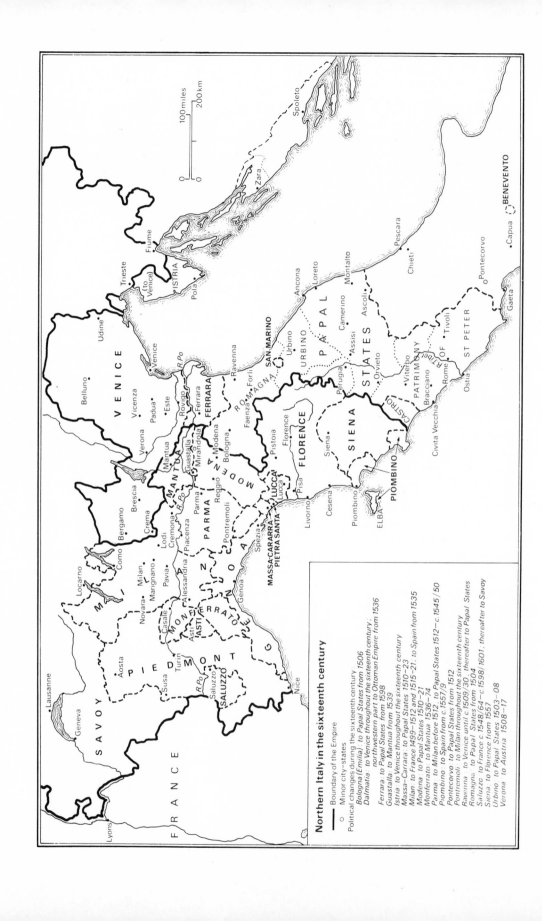

Northern Italy in the sixteenth century

—— Boundary of the Empire

○ Minor city-states

Political changes during the sixteenth century

Bologna (Emilia): to Papal States from 1506
Dalmatia: to Venice throughout the sixteenth century:
    northwestern part to Ottoman Empire from 1536
Ferrara: to Papal States from 1598
Guastalla: to Mantua from 1539
Istria: to Venice throughout the sixteenth century
Massa-Carrara: to Papal States 1510–23
Milan: to France 1499–1512 and 1515–21: to Spain from 1535
Modena: to Papal States 1510–21
Monferrato: to Mantua 1536–74
Parma: to Milan before 1512, to Papal States 1512–c.1545/50
Piombino: to Spain from c.1557/9
Pontecorvo: to Papal States from 1512
Pontremoli: to Milan throughout the sixteenth century
Ravenna: to Venice until c.1509/30, thereafter to Papal States
Romagna: to Papal States from 1504
Saluzzo: to France c.1548/64–c.1598/1601: thereafter to Savoy
Siena: to Florence from 1557
Urbino: to Papal States 1503–08
Verona: to Austria 1508–17

Introduction

A longish title ought to indicate the contents of a book, but 'patronage' is an ambiguous term and its use here needs to be clarified. To state a commonplace, the history of music is organically and dynamically related to the history of society, from which it cannot be isolated without losing its intelligibility. The following pages discuss what seem to me to be the major shifts in Mantuan musical taste during a period of remarkable cultural achievements in relation to the interests and activities of the ruling élite. All the rulers discussed were acutely aware of the Gonzaga dynasty as an independent entity, as a cause, while at the same time they pursued quite different and highly personal styles of government. One area in which music and the arts played an increasingly important role during the period was as an important aspect of despotic mythology, whose primary function was to provide traditional explanations of the nobility, antiquity, and political legitimacy of the dynasty, further encouraged by contemporary theories of magnificence and the tendency of an increasingly professional and bureaucratic court to generate ceremonial. Mythology emphasised traditional virtues, adapting itself to the particular qualities of individual rulers, and since the differences in the qualities, interests, and commitments of the Gonzaga discussed here were considerable, the changes in Mantuan life and culture were dramatic. The extraordinary transformation of Mantua during the period is treated here as an essentially cultural phenomenon, and as a musical one in the way that the changing production of music reflects the activities and interests of the élite. It is in this broad sense that the book is about patronage.

There is another, closely related commonplace. Music has social functions, and changes in social structures and needs bring about changes in the function of music itself. The first chapter gives some account of the social structure of Mantua during the period, the reflection of that structure in its institutional life, and the major changes in society as they relate to the production of music. Findings are necessarily tentative since evidence is scarce and methodology comparatively unsophisticated. One of the most fertile sources of information about the processes of patronage is the dedications to publications of polyphony, but even here the nature of the information is

I

severely limited. The relationships which publication involved were complex, but the specifics of the contacts between patron, printer, composer, poet and, in some cases at least, the hack employed to devise a suitably flattering dedication are unclear. The crude assumption made here, verifiable as a practice from a small number of cases, is that a dedication signed by a composer and addressed to a patron was paid for by the latter, and that the payment represented the composer's major income from the publication. From dedications, contemporary writings, and the few surviving archival records that are known, I have attempted to present an overview of Mantuan society and institutions, and to evaluate the extent to which groups and individuals outside the court commissioned music or employed performers. The results are perhaps unsurprising. Some musical activity did take place outside the narrow confines of the court, particularly in the cathedral but also in academies, churches, and confraternities, and the extent of involvement increased during the century as some of these institutions were revitalised by fresh injections of interest and money from the new merchant and bureaucratic classes. To step outside the period briefly, it was the Accademia degli Invaghiti that sponsored Monteverdi's *Orfeo*, and it was surely in the academies, homes of oratory and versification, that the rhetorically based language of the late madrigal would have been readily appreciated. Certainly the extent to which the base of music patronage had broadened (though hardly beyond the old aristocratic élite) by the early decades of the seventeenth century is evident from the dedications of a popular and established court composer such as Gastoldi, but nevertheless the initial impression of sources of interest distinct from Gonzaga power, interests, and money is deceptive. That is one important general conclusion. Another that emerges strongly from this first chapter is that the system of patronage itself was essentially familial; and both these points are strongly underlined throughout the remainder of the work.

So for the period under discussion Mantuan patronage is practically synonymous with Gonzaga patronage, and inevitably, given its underlying assumptions and objectives, the main part of this study deals with the production of music as it reflects and illuminates the temperaments and activities of successive rulers. This is one form of limitation imposed by the evidence, and at first it might seem that since it is concerned with written musical culture mostly surviving in polyphonic repertories it must necessarily be limited in another way, by being exclusively preoccupied with élite musical culture. Yet the lines of demarcation between popular and learned culture cannot be so confidently drawn, and recent writing has emphasised that there was interaction between the two which proceeded in both directions. The case for learned culture exerting an influence on popular culture is vividly illustrated in painting, where peasant painters often took over the gestures of a new learned style but retained an essentially medieval approach to matters such as perspective; one example from contemporary music history might be the recitation of epic poetry by writers such as Ariosto in the sort of improvised popular performance described by Montaigne. It also needs to be remembered that influences travelled up the social scale. The nobility adapted dance-forms from the peasantry, and the court festival, at least during the earlier part of the period, is often indistinguishable from popular festivals such as Carnival (in which courtiers participated throughout the period) except for the status of the participants. Here, at certain types of state ceremonials, sometimes in church and in the activities of the confraternities, both the ordinary people and the élite observed or participated, and in this simple sense too the two cultures were not so separate as has often been assumed.

The two central chapters are primarily concerned with the musical tastes and activities of Cardinal Ercole Gonzaga and Duke Guglielmo Gonzaga as a reflection of reformist principles. To understand the growth of the reform movement it is necessary to recall the Rome of Leo X, a city not as pagan as it is often portrayed, and a city where a number of prelates prominent in Papal circles understood the need for reform. From 1520–1, sustained by the Erasmian message, reform-seeking Europe was in ferment until the council, announced as early as 1532, finally delivered its verdict thirty years later. In Rome itself the foundation of the Oratory of Divine Love, and even more importantly the Order of Theatines, formed in 1524 with the purpose of improving the education of the clergy and particularly that of the Italian bishops, is symptomatic of the new climate. The Council of Trent finally finished its work in December 1563, after a series of debates spanning twenty years. And in March 1564, when the canons were published, the traditional beliefs which Protestantism had been challenging for the previous half-century were strongly re-affirmed. In addition, the Curia took a number of complementary steps including arrangements for the periodical revision of the *Index librorum prohibitorum*, and for publication (in 1566) of the new catechism composed for the council by Carlo Borromeo and of a new breviary in 1568 and a missal in 1570. Orthodoxy was thus closely defined, but the most important business of the Council concerned the discipline, training, and activities of the clergy, an area where reformers from a variety of backgrounds had been particularly critical for some time. The three main issues were the age at which men might enter orders, the obligation of bishops and priests to reside in their places of jurisdiction, and the establishment of a seminary in every diocese; but a host of other concerns entered the council's vision, including the formulation of a theory of decorum for church buildings, images, and music. Dissatisfaction with sacred polyphony can be traced back to the fifteenth century or even earlier, and in a sense the Tridentine decrees, however vague they might seem, were one result of a good deal of thinking and writing about the issue during the previous decades. Ercole Gonzaga seems to have been sensitive to the need for an intelligible liturgy, and aware of the potential of the arts, particularly music and architecture, in the service of the Church, and the second chapter focuses on the way in which his patronage can be seen experimenting with that potential in the decades before Borromeo's involvement with similar issues at Milan. Guglielmo Gonzaga took the process further by deliberately setting out to organise the Mantuan state as a model Christian enterprise and to project himself as the ideal Christian prince, a timely modification of the dynastic mythology, much as Albrecht V through rather different means set out after the Imperial Diet of 1566 to establish himself as the leader of the German Catholic princes. Indeed, given the strong traditional links between the Gonzaga and the Empire the parallel may not be entirely casual, but Guglielmo's course was different. In an age in which political power existed only with the sanction of the Church, and when secular and ecclesiastical institutions existed in constant symbiosis, it is not surprising to find Guglielmo suspicious of certain aspects of the Counter-Reformation, particularly the Jesuits and the Inquisition, but in some other respects the spirit of Trent was an important influence on the ideology on which the Duchy of Mantua was organised. And the one project which, more than any other, reflects not only Guglielmo's genuinely pious temperament but also his acute recognition of the political advantages to be derived from careful cultivation of the posture of the ideal Christian prince is the construction, decoration, and liturgical arrangements of the ducal basilica of Santa Barbara in the decade immediately following the Tridentine decrees. It also lies at the heart of Guglielmo's patronage of the arts, and the operation of the liturgy, the 'purity' of the chant, the suitability of the polyphony for the specially approved Santa Barbara rite were all matters in which Guglielmo took an intense and increasingly obsessive interest; if the real model for many details of the special character of Santa Barbara is St Peter's in Rome, its true spiritual heir is the Imperial chapel in the Escorial. Nowhere else perhaps in Italy outside Rome and Milan is it possible to find so complete a local interpretation of the spirit of the Counter-Reformation and its effects on the arts, particularly music, at this date; and nowhere else in Italy at this time are the political advantages of adherence to Counter-Reformation ideals so vividly demonstrated. The planning and construction of this remarkable building, part conventional church and part dynastic temple, and the initial operation of the polyphonic liturgy within its walls are the main concerns of the third chapter.

This deliberate concentration on Santa Barbara should not obscure the practice of secular music at court, encouraged by Guglielmo's own interest in composition, or the continuing tradition of ceremonial music specially commissioned for important dynastic and state occasions. Certainly Gugliel-mo's cultural interests were centred on the new ducal basilica, and it is this project which provides the key to the duke's own artistic temperament; but in Mantua, as elsewhere in Italy, the growing importance of the politics of spectacle during the period is reflected in the increased splendour (in the purely technological and artistic sense) of court festivals. Although no music has survived for the occasion, the arrangements for the entry of Henri III of France into the city during his progress through Italy in 1574 seem to have been particularly lavish. But it was with Vincenzo Gonzaga's maturity that the more recent forms of madrigal composition, the new styles of singing described by Giustiniani, and the theatre became focal points of Gonzaga court music patronage, though this is not to deny the considerable expenditure which Vincenzo directed towards the ducal basilica. While Guglielmo's tastes were largely formed in the spirit of the Counter-Reformation and through the training of Ercole Gonzaga, Vincenzo's were matured in the rather more secular atmosphere of Florence and Ferrara. The influence of Este and Medici musical life upon Vincenzo's relations with composers and performers is apparent in the 1580s, but it becomes of overwhelming importance after he assumed control of the duchy in 1587, and its effect on Mantuan musical life during the first decade of Vincenzo's rule is the subject of the final chapter. Ultimately it was Florentine contacts that proved the most important, and after the demise of the Este court at Ferrara in 1598 they became paramount. The results are most noticeable of course in the great theatrical entertainments of 1607–8, but the roots of close Mantuan contact with Florentine (and hence French) as well as Ferrarese musical and theatrical traditions lie in the 1580s. This argument is offered as a counter-balance to what I believe to be recent overemphasis on the importance of Ferrara for changes in Mantuan cultural life during the first ten years or so of Vincenzo's period, and the consequent neglect both of indigenous traditions and of influences from elsewhere.

The conclusions of this study have been reached after examination of a great deal of archival documentation, music, and other types of primary material, and the weight of information has made selective presentation inevitable. Short extracts from documents are sometimes quoted in footnotes, but other material which for a variety of reasons it seemed valuable to make available in a fuller form is given in Appendix II. The principles guiding transcription are described there, and some brief notes about the organisation of some of the less well-known archives that I have used are included in Appendix I, but it might be useful to say a work here about *relazioni*. Despatches are one thing, and *relazioni* another. The most famous of these, the *relazioni* of Venetian ambassadors, have enjoyed a high reputation as informative and reliable sources, and those dealing with Mantua have proved invaluable for this study. Only Venice with its patriciate, and a highly developed bureaucracy expertly qualified for diplomacy, produced documents of this kind, providing a broad and comprehensive synthesis, periodically brought up to date by successive ambassadors, of the political, military, economic, and social conditions of a country. It has occasionally been claimed that other Italian states, including Mantua, produced *relazioni*, but investigation reveals that in all cases these are more properly despatches reporting on the conduct and outcome of a mission. So for Mantua the only known *relazioni* remain those of the Venetian ambassadors.

Rudolf Wittkower's celebrated book *Art and architecture in Italy, 1600–1750* begins with the phrase, 'In all fairness, I feel the reader should be warned of what he will not find in this book', and it remains to follow his example. It will be evident from what has already been said that the book is neither a biographical or bibliographical directory of Mantuan music and musicians, nor an all-inclusive guided tour of the forms and styles of Mantuan music. Rather, I have quite deliberately selected developments which seemed to provide the key to shifts in patronage and taste, and have chosen to discuss these in detail in preference to providing continuous chronological coverage. The terminal dates are dictated by the emergence of Cardinal Ercole Gonzaga as a patron of music and the arts in Mantua after his return from the *Studium* in Bologna, and by the important performance of Guarini's *Il pastor fido* at court in 1598. The latter, a culmination of the changes in musical and theatrical life consequent upon Vincenzo Gonzaga's succession to the duchy in 1587, marks off this first phase of development from the second which, inspired by Florentine ideas and personnel, reached a high point in the spectacles of 1607–8. For purely practical reasons I have decided against discussing that second phase here, though some of the material brought forward in my final chapter is clearly germane to the full-length study which needs to be written. Similarly, although it might have appeared more logical to begin this study with a more detailed account of the patronage of Marchese Francesco Gonzaga and Isabella d'Este, I have not done so in view of the intensive archival work now being done on this subject by William Prizer, and have restricted myself to a brief interpretation of their achievement based for the most part on secondary material. Quite deliberate too is the general avoidance of the sort of detailed stylistic speculation which would immediately undermine the contextual character of the work. Certainly the function of music is of prime concern; the function of music is a determinant of form and style, and when function changes new forms and styles arise while old ones tend to be modified and die out. But by the nature of its language music is rarely expressed in the sort of precise terms that would make the study of the process of its production analogous to, for example, architecture, even less to contemporary painting where contracts and specifications drawn up by court humanists can be seen to determine so much of the final result. Indeed there must be few pieces of music of any period where the direct influence of a patron can be traced and analysed in anything but the most vague stylistic terms. Nevertheless, a definable corpus of Mantuan music was the starting point of the enquiry, and a selection of pieces which illustrate in some way the system which brought them into being and has enabled their survival will be published in a companion volume.

I

The origins of Mantuan
Renaissance culture

Tosto che l'acqua a correr mette co,
  Non più Benaco, ma Mencio si chiama
  fino a Govèrnol, dove cade in Po.
Non molto ha corso, ch'el trova una lama,
  Ne la qual si distende e la 'mpaluda;
  E suol di state talor esser grama.

Dante: Inferno, Canto XX

D'ogni altra città Mantova è meglio,
Mantova ha gente buona, liberale,
Mantova sempre sta spaparanzata,
  Barba Pedralo.
Essa ha prodotto poeti primai:
L'uno s'abbevera al fiume di Febo,
L'altro spesso imbriaga di vin greco,
  Pieno un bigoncio.

Folengo: Maccharonee

7

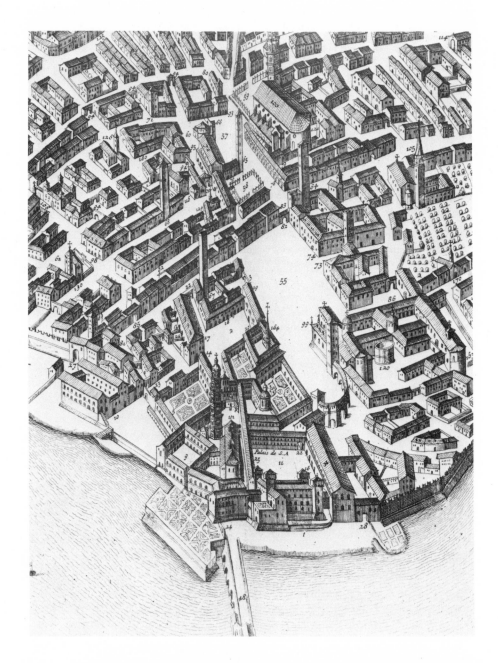

Fig. 1 Pierre Mortier: *La ville de Mantoue*, engraving from J. Blaeu: *Novum Italiae theatrum* (Amsterdam, 1724–5). Detail of oblique view of Mantua (1704)
1: Castello di San Giorgio; 2: Corte vecchia; 55: Piazza di San Pietro;
59: Piazza di Sant'Andrea; 94: Ghetto; 99: San Pietro; 100: Sant'Andrea;
101: Santa Barbara; 116: Santissima Trinità; 164: Santa Croce in Piazza

In his treatise *De l'excellence du gouvernement royal* published in Paris in 1575, the French political historian and theorist Loys Le Roy explains that a country covered with mountains, rocks, and forests, fit only for pasture, and one where there are many poor men, as in most of Switzerland, is best suited for democracy. On the other hand, the lands of the plain, where there are greater numbers of rich and noble men, are better adapted to an aristocratic form of government.[1] This idea is found commonly enough in contemporary writing, for example in Jean Bodin's *Les six livres de la République*, and as a generalisation it is certainly an appropriate and perceptive observation of the historical development of the Northern Italian cities during the late Middle Ages. Mantua is a classic case, moving in the last quarter of the thirteenth century from a system of communal politics to one of despotism, though not from chaos to immediate stability. It was only some fifty years later that the Gonzaga gained control of the city and its region, but once established, their increasing power and wealth were inextricably linked with the development and growth of the city as an important cultural and political centre. Shortly after the family took up the government of Mantua it began to assume a position of considerable significance in the affairs of Italy and of Europe, and after control passed in 1627 from the main branch of the house to its French relations it slowly descended into provincialism. The period discussed in the following pages is only part of some four centuries of Gonzaga rule, properly finishing with the death of Ferdinando Carlo in 1708, but it is a central period, a time when many of the most lasting Mantuan artistic, literary, and musical achievements took place, years when its characteristic forms of social and political organisation were elaborated. It is, moreover, a period of stability when, with Mantua comparatively free from outside threats and confident of its economic resources, the Gonzaga could proceed with the urgent tasks of agricultural production, flood control, and urban construction, in addition to extending their support to the arts as contemporary theories of magnificence required.

The origins of Mantua as a settlement go back to the Etruscan period, a

<hr />

[1] Le Roy: *De l'excellence du gouvernement royal*, p. 37.

fact that already gave it a position of status in the early modern world that was further underlined by its association with Virgil, born in Mantuan territory in 70 B.C.[2] Situated in the southern part of the Paduan plain, on the right bank of the Mincio ten miles north of its confluence with the Po, the city lies twenty-five miles south of Verona and sixty miles from Padua itself. With the increasing economic and strategic importance of the Mincio, the course of the lower part of the river was altered during the medieval period to divert it into the plains around the city where it formed three wide lakes connected to the shore by two moles, and until the eighteenth century Mantua remained entirely surrounded by water. Security was greatly increased by these alterations, while the Mincio itself formed a natural boundary between Lombardy and the Veneto; protectively positioned, the city gradually assumed a degree of economic and strategic importance now difficult to believe and certainly disproportionate to the size and resources of its territory and population. The average population for the years 1496–1560 has been calculated as 21,400 inhabitants – equal, that is, to Parma or Piacenza during the same period.[3] A position on one of the less important north–south trade routes not only brought the city the benefits of commercial traffic and a certain cosmopolitan atmosphere, but also increased the prosperity of its two major industries, agriculture and textiles. In 1531 more than five thousand foreigners visited the city. Most came from nearby centres such as Verona and Cremona on agricultural business, but there were also a large number from Germany, typically soldiers and educated men.[4] Commercial links with the south were modest, and visitors from further afield often did not hold Mantua in the same regard as they did comparable neighbours such as Ferrara, or university cities like Padua or Bologna; Giovanni Botero, Thomas Coryate and William Thomas included it in their descriptions and itineraries of Italy, but Richard Rowlands, John Raymond and Fynes Moryson did not. Land under Mantuan control extended to Mirandola to the south, to Legnano on the Adige to the east, just beyond Canneto to the west, and almost as far as Lake Garda to the north. This territory was bounded by the more powerful states of Milan (which for much of the sixteenth century was under Spanish control) on the west and the Republic of Venice on the east and north, while to the south lay the smaller duchies of Parma, Modena and Ferrara. A number of modest additions were made in the course of the sixteenth century, of which the most substantial was the acquisition in 1539 of Guastalla on the area's southwestern border above the Oglio; but the most spectacular piece of Mantuan territorial expansion during the period was the annexation of Monferrato, which passed from the French sphere of influence to Gonzaga

[2] For the origins of the city see *Mantova. La storia*, I, pp. 3–24.
[3] D'Arco: *Studi statistici*, pp. 36–7. For comparative figures and some useful comments on the inadequacy of the census see Russell: *Medieval regions*.
[4] The documentation on which these figures are based is in ASM (AG) 3070, and is discussed in *Mantova. La storia*, I, p. 451 and Appendix IV.

rule in 1536. This doubled the area under Mantuan control, but the new territory was physically separated from the rest of the duchy and surrounded on three sides by the Duchy of Savoy. The envious eyes which Savoy habitually cast on Monferrato remained the most immediate threat to Mantuan security throughout the period.[5]

Although the inland waterway and the medieval realisation of its commercial and strategic potential was a prime factor in Mantuan security and expansion during the fifteenth and sixteenth centuries, the swampy marshlands which surrounded the city meant that the Mantuan *contado*, in common with all the Mediterranean plains, was extremely susceptible to flooding during the winter rainy season. Despite the vigilance of the inhabitants and the periodic instigation of improvement schemes to drain the marshes and improve crop cultivation, the danger of flooding was (as it still is today) a constant threat. The frequency with which it and its consequences were noted by the Mantuan chronicles during the later sixteenth century supports theories of climatic variation suggesting that around 1600 the weather became colder and wetter and that this change was an important factor in the process of economic decline which characterised Italy at the end of the century. The rains of 1599 which affected the Po valley were so torrential and widespread that even the most unsuperstitious commentators were writing of the 'mutazione di secolo' and the end of the world.[6]

The effects of the Mantuan marshes and waterways, whose importance is suggested by the frequency with which they are highlighted in contemporary gazetteers, extended beyond the purely economic. Flooding produced vast stretches of stagnant water which, in the dangerous humidity of summer, brought malaria (which before the introduction of quinine was often fatal or at least extremely debilitating) as well as swamp fever. Throughout the century, various attempts were made, within the limited means available, to drain the marshes, introduce fresh irrigation and convert the land to crop production, but success was hindered by subsidence, by the return of the infected waters, and finally by the *taglio* of 1604 which gave Venice permission to divert the course of the Po to the south. Flooding also hindered communications, often making roads impassable and carrying away bridges 'to such a degree', as Bandello put it, 'that our Mantuans who have estates on that side of the Po cannot make use of the supplies or goods of their lands'.[7]

[5] For the political boundaries see J. Engel (ed.): *Grosser historischer Weltatlas*, III, p. 118. The addition of Monferrato to Gonzaga territory is discussed in Davari: *Federico Gonzaga e la famiglia Paleologa* and in *Mantova. La storia*, II, pp. 269–372. As far as the period under discussion is concerned, the most troublesome consequences of the acquisition occurred during the 1560s and are best approached through Quazza: 'Emanuele Filiberto di Savoia' and *Mantova. La Storia*, III, pp. 3–28.

[6] Theories of climatic variation and the evidence for increased rainfall are thoroughly explored in Braudel: *The Mediterranean*, I, pp. 267ff. For concise accounts of the economic crisis in Italy at the end of the century see Pullan (ed.): *Crisis and change*, and Braudel and Spooner: 'Prices in Europe'.

[7] Bandello: *Novelle*, I, p. 360. Concern over the ubiquitous mosquitoes of the Po valley is also reflected in the anonymous fifteenth-century verses published in Frati: 'Sonetti satirici contra Ferrara', written in 1494, which capitalise on the rhyme Ferrara–*zanzara*.

The uncertainty resulting from Mantua's geographical position was liable to have damaging effects on its economy, while the rise and fall in Mantuan textile production followed what may have been a general European pattern, rising sharply and then falling just as dramatically. Mantua was not on any of the major Alpine trade routes, but it did attract some passing traffic, and its reputation for liberality and religious tolerance, although ill-founded at some periods in the sixteenth century, attracted permanent residents who often brought new and economically advantageous skills with them.[8]

The works of high quality that arose from Gonzaga artistic patronage, the brilliant legacy of Pisanello, Mantegna, Giulio Romano, Rubens, Giaches de Wert, Palestrina, Monteverdi, Torquato Tasso and Giovanni Battista Guarini, have – in combination with a historiographical tradition which has largely ignored the contexts of that legacy in favour of discussing its content – obscured some important aspects of sixteenth-century Mantuan conditions which bear directly on any consideration of Mantuan patronage. Behind that familiar and imposing façade of artistic brilliance lay a territorially small, politically weak state in a militarily strategic geographical position and with a precarious economic base. Throughout the middle decades of the sixteenth century, stability was achieved by careful administration, avoidance of conflict with neighbouring states, and a strengthening of links with the principal Italian states and particularly with the Habsburg Empire, traditional ally and protector. As will be seen, these attitudes towards foreign states opened up channels of communication which, together with powerful connections within Italy, produced important artistic results; but the system of checks and balances was extremely delicate, as the sack of the city in 1629–30 demonstrated vividly.

During the early medieval period Mantua was dominated by northern invaders. In 1115 it declared itself a free city, and in 1272 Pinamonte Bonacolso took over the government as Mantua's first *capitano*. Later, throughout the period of its greatest prosperity and artistic importance, Mantua was effectively governed as a monarchy by the Gonzaga, whose court functioned as the principal sponsor of learning and the arts. The Gonzaga family, which seems to have originated in the twelfth century, gained control of the city by overthrowing the Bonacolsi in 1328. After a century of control as humble *capitani* they were elevated to the status of *marchesi* by the Emperor Sigismond, who conferred the honour on Francesco

---

[8] De Maddalena: 'L'industria tessile' is now the standard account of the Mantuan textile industry during the sixteenth and early seventeenth centuries, and Brulez: 'Les routes commerciales' is a useful introduction to the trade routes from Italy to the north. Braudel: *The Mediterranean*, I, p. 212 n. 198 cites an undated document claiming that the Mantuan route was used 'al tempo de la peste', and this supports Brulez's view that the route was only of secondary importance. At the same time, the strategic importance of the Po, which flows into the Mincio, should not be underestimated. For the effects of Jewish immigration during the sixteenth century see pp. 39ff below.

II Gonzaga in 1433.[9] It was his successor, Gianfrancesco, who, although clearly a *condottiere* in the family tradition rather than an educated humanist, seems to have been the first member of the family whose conception of princely style extended in any significant way to patronage of the arts. It is symptomatic of this new style that weavers were imported from Flanders to set up the first tapestry factory in Italy, that Pisanello was employed at court from 1425[10] and – most important of all for the propagation of humanist ideas – that Vittorino da Feltre (d. 1446) was appointed ducal librarian. Vittorino's work at Mantua was not principally directed towards building up the Gonzaga collections of 'illuminated codices, but rather towards establishing a court school under Gianfrancesco's patronage. This institution, known as the Casa Giocosa, was initially set up to educate the marchese's children, but it survived their majority and, under Vittorino's direction, earned a contemporary reputation as one of the most progressive of the early humanist schools, a reputation which recent scholarship has emphatically confirmed. Unlike many early humanist educators, Vittorino's own interests were not exclusively literary, and although details of the syllabus at the Casa Giocosa are unclear, it appears that mathematics played a surprisingly large role in his teaching, and that both theoretical and practical music figured among his concerns. One pupil, Francesco Prendilacqua, gives a list of the specialised teachers employed by Vittorino, which includes, together with painters and grammarians, musicians, dancers, singers and instrumentalists: 'Neque deerant grammatici peritissimi, dialecti, arithmetici, musici, librarii graeci latinique, pictores, saltatores, cantores, cithaered, equitatores, quorum singuli cupientibus discipulis praesto erant sine ullo praemio, ad hoc ipsum munus a Victorino conducti ne qua discipulorum ingenia desererentur.'[11]

The achievements of Vittorino's school were largely transmitted through pupils who in turn became humanist patrons. Federigo da Montefeltro, a

[9] For biographies of the Gonzaga I have used Litta: *Famiglie celebri italiane*, IV, Gonzaga, supplemented by Coniglio: *I Gonzaga*. Of works published during the period the most useful are Equicola: *Chronica*, which is effectively a history of the family and a celebration of the Mantuan golden age under Francesco and Isabella, and Possevino: *Gonzaga*. Donesmondi: *Dell'istoria*, though primarily concerned with church history, also includes information about political events. All three are, of course, chronicles rather than interpretations, and belong to the official Gonzaga historiographical tradition. A number of manuscript chronicles in ASM (D'Arco) have also proved useful, in particular MSS 75–9, Amadei: 'Cronaca universale della città di Mantova' (on which the published edition is based); MS 80, Mambrino: 'Dell'historia di Mantova'; and MS 168, Vigilio: 'L'insalata, o storie mantovane'.

[10] See Braghirolli: *Sulle manifatture di arazzi* and, for Pisanello's activities at court, Paccagnini: *Pisanello alla corte dei Gonzaga*, particularly pp. 5–11 and 60–1. Gianfrancesco's building schemes also extended to Florence.

[11] The extract from Prendilacqua's *Dialogus* is taken from Garin (ed.): *Il pensiero pedagogico dello umanesimo*, p. 660, which prints most of the contemporary accounts of Vittorino and his school. A modern bibliography of writings on Vittorino is given in *Mantova. Le lettere*, II, pp. 44–6, and the standard account in English is Woodward: *Vittorino da Feltre*. According to Davari: *Notizie storiche intorno allo studio pubblico*, the school continued until the middle of the sixteenth century. Its importance for the dissemination of humanistic ideas is explored in Baxandall: *Giotto and the orators*, pp. 127ff.

pupil at the Casa Giocosa from 1434 to 1437, is perhaps the most obvious example; another is Lodovico II Gonzaga (d. 1478) who succeeded Gian-francesco in 1444, and who by the end of the next decade was employing both Mantegna and Alberti, two of the ablest humanistically inspired artists of their day. This alone makes Lodovico's cultural tastes comparable in scope to those of Leonello d'Este at Ferrara, educated in the literary-orientated school of Guarino; and it is the same complex of courtly virtues that is extolled in Mantegna's *Camera degli sposi* and in Cossa's frescoes in the Palazzo Schifanoia. Yet these parallels do not, in the current state of knowledge, extend to music, and while its importance at the Ferrarese court during the second half of the fifteenth century is becoming increasingly clear, for Mantua there are only a few scattered notices that do not yet produce a coherent picture of the period before Isabella d'Este's arrival in the city.[12] Under Lodovico and his successor Federico I Gonzaga, who ruled from 1478 to 1484, music seems to have been principally ceremonial, and instrumental; it was performed by players who generally came from the north, particularly Germany, and who were presumably employed only on an occasional basis. It is difficult to know precisely when the players of *pifferi* and *tromboni* who were used on these occasions were formed into an established and permanent group of household musicians with responsibility for ceremonial and dance music at court; but the existence of this *alta cappella* is firmly documented from the 1460s. An early description of one of the functions of this type of ensemble in Mantua is given by the Mantuan chronicler Schivenoglia in his account of the state entry into the city of Margaret of Bavaria, bride of Federico I Gonzaga, on 7 June 1463. Her arrival was announced by 'Bufonij' and 'trombeti', and her entrance was accompanied by '107 trombi, pifari, tromboni, 26 tamburij, pive le quali erano venute con la spoxa et altri instrumenti ge nera senza fine; paria che tuto el mondo sonasse'. These are remarkably large forces, and undoubtedly most of the performers were hired specially for the occasion. It is not until a few years later, in 1468, that the names of the Mantuan court *alta cappella*, a group of four players, are recorded. From its origins as a simple band used on ceremonial occasions, this ensemble seems to have been transformed during the period of Isabella d'Este into a highly skilled and more versatile ensemble performing more sophisticated music. Throughout the sixteenth century frequent references to the *alta cappella* confirm that it remained an important feature of court life and a central institution of court music, performing at banquets, processions and triumphs, at public and private festivals, on major state and family occasions, on the battlefield, and sometimes in church, though presumably not in a

---

[12] Gundersheimer: *Ferrara* is now the standard general account of fifteenth-century Ferrarese court culture. For the musical life of the court during the late fifteenth and early sixteenth centuries see the series of articles by Lewis Lockwood, in particular 'Music at Ferrara', 'Pietrobono', and 'Josquin at Ferrara'; the evidence of musical activity during the period 1420–50 is treated in the same author's 'Dufay and Ferrara'.

liturgical context. Apart from earlier isolated references to individual *pifferi* and the later documentation of the ensemble as established by 1468, there are few references to other musicians at the Mantuan court before Isabella d'Este's involvement, and while it is hazardous to draw conclusions on the basis of such a small number of surviving documents, it seems probable that the *alta cappella* was the principal body of court musicians in the late fifteenth century, and the only group to be permanently employed until Francesco II's foundation of a court chapel in the early years of the next century.[13] This in itself is a useful indication of the increasing importance of ceremonial during the period, and a reflection of how the Gonzaga perceived the function of public music at a time of changing political and social ambitions. Scattered references suggest other functions, mostly in the tradition of courtly education established by Vittorino, though the performance with music, probably in 1480, of Angelo Poliziano's *Fabula d'Orfeo* (usually regarded as the earliest pastoral drama) is indicative of considerable resources.[14]

With the marriage of Isabella d'Este to Francesco II Gonzaga in 1490, the Mantuan court became the focus for a broader and much more lavish style of patronage which encompassed letters, the pictorial arts, and music.[15]

[13] Canal: *Della musica in Mantova* and A. Bertolotti: *Musici alla corte dei Gonzaga*, the two standard general histories of Mantuan music, both devote their opening pages to documentary evidence of musical life there in the pre-Isabellian period, but in neither case does it amount to very much. The same is true of Davari: 'La musica a Mantova', which has now been reprinted (with an appendix of documents not included in the original work) edited by Gherardo Ghirardini. Schivenoglia's 'Cronaca di Mantova', edited by D'Arco, is printed in Müller (ed.): *Raccolta dei cronisti e documenti Lombardi*, II, pp. 117–94; this quotation is taken from p. 137. The development of the Mantuan *alta cappella* has now been exhaustively treated in William F. Prizer's article 'Bernardino Piffaro', which is to appear in the *Rivista italiana di musicologia*. (I am grateful to him for generously sharing the contents of it before publication.) Prizer's study deals with the period 1475–1525, and there are a few notices referring to court *pifferi* earlier in the fifteenth century. The earliest would appear to be the record of 'Maestro Simone, piffaro del Gonzaga' as a Mantuan resident in 18 October 1434 (see ASM (AG) Mandati e Decreti 1434–6, fo. 61), and the same name is also found in later registers (see, for example, ASM (AG) Mandati e Decreti 1444–7, fo. 216). Later *piffero* players include Marco and Giovanni Pecenni, two Germans registered in 1458, and there are also a few notices of instrumentalists of other types, such as Zannino dell'Arpa, who is documented in 1561. See also Bertolotti: *Musici alla corte dei Gonzaga*, pp. 7–8, and Canal: *Della musica in Mantova*, pp. 5–7.

[14] Dates for the composition and performance of *Orfeo* have been disputed, but see now the discussions in Pirrotta: *Li due Orfei*, pp. 5–8, Osthoff: *Theatergesang*, I, p. 9, and Tedeschi: 'La "Rappresentazione d'Orfeo"', pp. 47ff. The year 1480 is now generally accepted as the most likely date for both the composition and the performance of the work. Apart from Vittorino da Feltre, the most important music teacher at court during the pre-Isabellian period was the theorist Franchino Gafurio, who taught and wrote at the court for about two years.

[15] The bibliography of writings about Isabella is extensive, and only a selection can be given here. The most useful general biographies are Cartwright: *Isabella d'Este* and Lauts: *Isabella d'Este*, and there are helpful short sketches in Brinton: *The Gonzaga*, pp. 118–44, and Chiappini: *Gli Estensi*, pp. 172–7. A good impression of her patronage of the visual arts will be gained from Yriarte: 'Isabella d'Este', Wind: *Bellini's 'Feast of the Gods'*, Lehmann: 'The sources and meaning of Mantegna's *Parnassus*', and Verheyen: *The paintings in the 'studiolo'*. Some of the most revealing items from her correspondence with artists are presented in English translation in Chambers: *Patrons and artists*, pp. 126–50. Luzio and Renier: 'La coltura' is the best introduction to her cultivation of letters; C. M. Brown: '"Lo insaciabile desiderio"' deals with her taste for antiquities. The most recent general bibliography is in *Mantova. Le arti*, II, pp. 537–63.

Isabella was raised at Ferrara, where her father had ensured that she received a thorough humanistic education. As a young girl she studied Latin with Battista Guarino, Sebastiano da Lugo, and Jacopo Gallino, and at the age of fifteen she could recite the classics and had studied vernacular verse composition with Antonio Tebaldeo. Her education also developed in her a taste for the visual arts, and her extensive surviving correspondence reveals an informed connoisseur and an autocratic and difficult employer even by the standards of the age, in contrast to the officially fostered image of the 'liberale ed magnanime Isabella'.[16] It is also known from her letters that she was an accomplished musician, could play the cittern, and studied the lute with Angelo Testagrossa about 1495. Towards the end of the fifteenth century she began to study the lira da braccio, an instrument principally associated with the traditions of courtly improvisation, and in addition she sang and could play the keyboards. This is a remarkable list of skills even in a society in which practical musicianship was valued as a necessary part of courtly manners. Her position as an important and musically literate patron of music who consequently understood the technical aspects of composition is unusual, and the quantity of surviving information is particularly revealing about her view of the function of music at court and her perception of the degree of control that she could exercise over its production.[17]

In the first place Isabella considerably enlarged the scope of court music, which previously seems to have been concentrated on the *alta cappella* and the voice and instrument teachers thought necessary for the provision of a decent humanistic princely education. During the first decade of her Mantuan period, the number of singers recorded at court increased dramatically, and many of these, characteristically, were Italians rather than the northerners more usual earlier in the century. Filippo Lapucino, Carlo de Launoy, Don Jacomino di Ostiglia, Jacopo de San Secondo, and Marchetto Cara are all recorded during the early years of her Mantuan period; Bartolomeo Tromboncino is also noted for the first time as a singer and composer, although he had worked at the Mantuan court before Isabella's marriage.[18] Similarly, it was shortly after Isabella's arrival that new instru-

---

[16] Ariosto: *Orlando furioso*, XIII.59.

[17] For music at court during Isabella's Mantuan period see A. Bertolotti: *Musici alla corte dei Gonzaga*, pp. 11ff, Canal: *Della musica in Mantova*, pp. 9ff, and now Prizer: 'Marchetto Cara', particularly pp. 5–61. Rubsamen: *Literary sources*, particularly pp. 9–11 and 24–32, deals with the major literary sources of the Mantuan frottola repertory, those songs written for the most part by native Italians to Italian texts, for the cultivation of which Isabella's patronage was clearly so important. For the most recent additions to Cara's biography see Paganuzzi: 'Notizie veronesi'.

[18] See the tables in Prizer: 'Marchetto Cara' pp. 8–13. It is worth remembering that occasional documentary references to musicians cannot necessarily be taken to indicate permanent employment, and this is particularly important since the change from the casual-labour system to a permanent body of household musicians is obviously a crucial indication of the growth of patronage. Francesco's establishment of a *cappella* is certainly symptomatic of an increased commitment to music for whatever reasons, and despite this fundamental problem of interpreting the documentation of secular music

ments were commissioned in some numbers.[19] The precise significance of the documentation is often obscure: it is difficult to know how many of these instruments were for Isabella's exclusive use and, more importantly, whether the sporadic references to performers and composers reflect occasional rather than permanent employment, but there are other indications of the whole-heartedness with which Isabella's musical interests were indulged. Seen in the context of her Mantuan period as a whole, Isabella's artistic interests were concentrated on two major schemes: the collection of classical antiquities and contemporary works of art for her *grotta*, and the construction and decoration of her private study, described in contemporary documents as 'camerino nostro' or, more usually, as the *studiolo*. More than any of her other enterprises, these two projects, and that of the *studiolo* in particular, provide a detailed and revealing account of the marchesa's conception of the importance and function of both the visual arts and music.[20]

The *studiolo* was by the 1490s a standard fitting in the palaces of north Italian courts, and in installing her own in the tower of the Castello di San Giorgio Isabella was following a tradition which included similar rooms at Urbino, Ferrara, and Gubbio. Work was already in progress in 1491, and by the time the final painting – the *Comos* of Lorenzo Costa the Elder – was completed some time after 1511, the room contained five paintings. Two further canvases by Correggio were added when, as a result of the marchesa's increasing corpulence, both the *studiolo* and the *grotta* were transferred to the more accessible ground floor of the Corte Vecchia in 1522. These paintings are all concerned with classical allegory, and in some cases at least Isabella's part in the *invenzione* (or specifics) of the general theme (*istoria*) was so marked that the artists' freedom was extremely limited. Quite clearly, the cycle of

at court during these years, the cumulative picture of all the available evidence makes some sort of permanent establishment highly likely. This is occasionally suggested also by Isabella's own writings, such as her letter of 8 February 1502 reporting the wedding celebrations of Lucrezia Borgia then taking place in Ferrara: 'Al tertio atto uscì la musica dil Tromboncino, Paulo, Pozino et compagni: cum la quale si fece magior honore ai Mantuani che a' Ferraresi.' The original (in ASM (AG) 2993, Copialettere 13) is part of a series describing the festivities for the benefit of Marchese Francesco, who had remained in Mantua; most of them are transcribed in D'Arco: *Notizie*, pp. 98ff. Three which are not – all of considerable interest for early sixteenth-century theatrical history (including the letter excerpted here) – are given in Appendix II, docs. 1–3.

[19] For some twenty years, from 1496 until his death in 1517, Lorenzo Gusnasco, better known as Lorenzo da Pavia, acted in the dual role of Isabella's principal instrument-maker as well as her artistic agent in her quest for paintings by Bellini, Perugino, and Van Eyck. Working from Venice, Lorenzo supplied instruments not only to the Gonzaga but also to the Sforza, the Este, and Pope Leo X. For Isabella's personal interest in the beauty and quality of the instruments made for her and her specifications to Lorenzo, see Luzio and Renier: 'La coltura', part 1, pp. 48ff, A. Bertolotti: *Musici alla corte dei Gonzaga*, pp. 15 and 17, and Lauts: *Isabella d' Este*, pp. 49ff. See also below p. 19, note 23. The complete correspondence between Isabella and Lorenzo da Pavia, ranging over a wide variety of artistic concerns, is shortly to appear edited by Clifford M. Brown as *Isabella d'Este and Lorenzo da Pavia – Documents for a history of art and culture in Renaissance Mantua*.

[20] The building history of Isabella's rooms has been discussed in Gerola: 'Trasmigrazione e vicende dei camerini', Cottafavi: 'Palazzo ducale di Mantova', and most recently Verheyen: *The paintings in the 'studiolo'*, which I have followed in cases of dispute. Recent examinations and reconstructions which bear upon the history of the rooms are presented in *Gli studioli di Isabella d'Este*.

Fig. 2   Andrea Mantegna: *Parnassus* (1497), oil on canvas. Paris, Musée du
Louvre (photo: Musées Nationaux)

paintings in the *studiolo* should be interpreted as if it were a single work, and
a single work over which the patron exercised a considerable degree of
control. This much seems obvious from the surviving evidence and from
recent reconstructions of the history of the room and the position of the
paintings in it, and whatever the measure of disagreement among art
historians over the interpretation of detail, there exists a certain amount of
common ground concerning the general importance of music in the cycle.[21]

The original conception of the *studiolo* cycle is best seen in the first two works
to be completed, Mantegna's *Parnassus* (Figure 2) and *Minerva*, probably
finished about the same time, *c.* 1497, and then installed opposite each other

[21] The literature on the paintings for Isabella's *studiolo* is extensive. All seven works are now in the Louvre,
whose *dossier*, *Le studiolo d'Isabelle d'Este*, is an excellent guide containing the most recent bibliography
of the subject. Verheyen: *The paintings in the 'studiolo'* also discusses all the paintings, and of the many
treatments of individual works might be singled out Gombrich: 'An interpretation of Mantegna's
Parnassus', Wind: *Bellini's 'Feast of the Gods'*, and, above all, the brilliant essay by Phyllis Williams
Lehmann, 'The sources and meaning of Mantegna's *Parnassus*', to whose interpretation I am heavily
indebted in what follows. The extent of Isabella's own involvement can also be seen particularly clearly
from her correspondence with Bellini and with Perugino, printed in Braghirolli: 'Carteggio di Isabella
d'Este' and Canuti: *Il Perugino* respectively.

in the room. Different formalistic and compositional treatments of Venus in the two works indicate that the author of the *invenzione* – most probably the court humanist Mario Equicola, whose *Libro de natura de amore* was later dedicated to Isabella – adopted the Platonic notion of the two Venuses, terrestrial and celestial. In the *Parnassus*, following this interpretation, the celestial Venus represents *amore honesto*, higher love, as opposed to the mere sensuality presented in the *Minerva*, and one important way in which philosophical and biographical possibilities of this *topos* are explored in the painting is through the use of iconographical traditions derived from classical myths about music. At the centre of the stage are the nine Muses, three singing but all moving to the music of Apollo's lyre. Apollo himself sits to the left, absorbed in his playing, with his right foot resting on a tree stump to support his instrument. Horizontally across from him stands the largest figure in the painting, Mercury, holding his customary caduceus from which his syrinx hangs; one arm rests on the winged horse, Pegasus. Standing on top of a grotto, above all this activity, are the closely linked figures of Mars and Venus, and perched close to them is Amor, holding his bow. But Amor's gaze is directed not at Mars and Venus but at the smallest figure in the picture, Vulcan, who is seen at the mouth of a cave where he has apparently been forging the silver jug in front of him. Work now finished, he has stepped forward towards Amor who is blowing a dart at him through a long cylindrical pipe.

This curious cast of characters has fuelled a variety of interpretations. Some see the work as an allegory of vice, some as an allegory referring to the marriage of Francesco and Isabella, and others as a demonstration, quite free from any personal references, of the harmony produced by the union of these two gods. In the most recent and arguably most thorough attempt to identify Mantegna's sources and clarify the meaning of the painting, music plays a fundamental role.[22] At a basic level, the emphasis on music in the foreground is clear and has often been commented on; it establishes, in the opposition of Mercury's syrinx and Apollo's lyre, reference to classical myths about the superiority of Apollo's instrument and the contest between Apollo and Hermes and its sequel or, as Picard put it, between 'musique citadine et sacerdotale, avec la lyre d'Apollo; musique rustique, avec la syrinx'.[23] This connects Apollo, the singing and dancing Muses, Pegasus (the horse

[22] Lehmann: 'The sources and meaning of Mantegna's *Parnassus*', pp. 164ff.
[23] Picard: 'Andrea Mantegna et l'antique', p. 127. In a recent unpublished paper, 'Isabella d'Este and Lorenzo da Pavia. Musical instruments at a Renaissance court' (summarily described in *Abstracts*, pp. 12–13), William F. Prizer notes that no documentary evidence of Isabella's purchase of wind instruments has so far been found, and suggests that this might be a reflection in life of classical myths about instrument types. Certainly it seems to be a reflection of the widespread theory of courtly decorum which strongly disapproved of women playing instruments with obvious sexual connotations. See Winternitz: 'The knowledge of musical instruments', p. 48, and for a thorough exploration of the *topos* in early-seventeenth-century art, Kettering: 'Rembrandt's *Flute player*: A unique treatment of pastoral'. For further on the Platonic tradition of the flute as a symbol of sensuality and passion, the antithesis of the more sober, rational stringed instruments, see Hollander: *The untuning of the sky*, pp. 34ff and 170ff.

consecrated to the Muses), and Mercury (inventor of the lyre and syrinx). To these can be added Vulcan, specifically identified in Roman legend as an instrument-maker, and operating here through an equivalence with Tubal Cain, who participated in Jubal's discovery of the laws of musical harmony. The stimulus to Vulcan is provided by Amor, the all-powerful Eros of Plato's *Symposium*, 'a composer so accomplished that he is the cause of composing in others', who is 'well-skilled...in all that has to do with music'.[24]

In this way it is possible to relate Vulcan and Amor, and to see their role, like the majority of the mythological characters in the picture, as related to some form of musical activity or invention. But Amor, who inspires Vulcan, has also united Mars and Venus, thus ensuring the peace in which the arts may flourish; and it is reasonable, particularly given the interest in music at the Mantuan court and Isabella's own enthusiasm, to see an implied allusion to the marchesa and Francesco behind the mythological and philosophical content of the painting. In fact, the implication is strengthened by explicit references to both the Gonzaga and Este arms, and to the planetary gods Mars, Venus, and Mercury, in the primary colours of Mars's costume and the draped couch before which the presiding couple stand. Seen in this way Mantegna's work is, among other things, a testimony to the vitality of the arts at Mantua under the patronage of Francesco and Isabella, and in particular the art of music.

None of the other paintings in the *studiolo* cycle refers so precisely to Gonzaga interest in the arts, but most of them are linked to the *Parnassus* not only through common philosophical backgrounds, but also in their employment of classical myths to underline them. Later works in the series make further use of the Apollo–Hermes–Pan legend already present in the *Parnassus* and also present the similar story of the musical contest between Apollo and the Phrygian satyr Marsyas. The dichotomy between instrument types, between the refined and refining character of stringed instruments as opposed to the crude quality of the winds which these fables illustrate, is seen only marginally in Perugino's *Battle between Chastity and Love*, where a group of satyrs playing pipe and drum are associated with the terrestrial Venus. But with the two final paintings, by Lorenzo Costa, who succeeded Mantegna as court painter on the latter's death in 1506, the full force of musical imagery is again felt. This is particularly true of the *Coronation of a lady*, in the centre of which a noblewoman, often taken to be Isabella herself, is about to be crowned as Queen of the Garden of Harmony. The garden is fenced off and guarded by Diana and Cadmus, while within it the major participants in the coronation are surrounded by four musicians playing instruments and two other figures, conceivably a poet composing and an artist sketching.

---

[24] Lehmann: 'The sources and meaning of Mantegna's *Parnassus*', pp. 146ff, quoting from the *Symposium* on p. 157.

Outside the garden a battle rages and there are scenes of sensuality. Some of the details are much debated, but there is general agreement over the autobiographical character of the picture, expressed through the agency of the court humanist Paride de Ceresara. In a general way the *Coronation* forms a pendant to the *Parnassus*; within the garden where Isabella is crowned, a symbol for Mantua itself, the arts flourish and harmony reigns. The musical leitmotif is also carried into Correggio's *Allegories* – the final pair of paintings for the *studiolo*, added after the room had been transferred to the Corte Vecchia in 1522 – where Vice and Virtue are represented through uncomplicated *invenzioni* based on the Apollo–Marsyas legend.

There are indications of Isabella's musical interests elsewhere in her rooms. Little is left of the decorations of her first *grotta* in the Castello di San Giorgio except for the barrel-vaulted ceiling, which is covered with repetitions of Isabella's musical *devisa* consisting of an alto clef, the four mensuration signs, a symmetrical arrangement of rests, and a repetition sign. This was evidently one of her favourite *devise*, occurring elsewhere such as on the ceiling of the second *grotta* in the Corte Vecchia, on one of the walls in the same room, and on some pieces from a set of maiolica plates usually attributed to Nicolo Pellipario.[25] The second *grotta* was also lined with intarsia decorations early in the sixteenth century, and these show a number of architectural scenes and incorporate Isabella's personal *devise*. Two of the panels show contemporary musical instruments, and a third is worked with Ockeghem's puzzle canon 'Prenez sur moi'.[26] In 1542, three years after her death, an inventory was taken of the contents of the *studiolo* and *grotta*: it includes a book of French chansons, a copy of one of Gafurio's treatises, and another volume of French music.[27]

Taken together, the various kinds of evidence of Mantuan court music during Isabella's period present a coherent and remarkable picture of patronage. Her letters are filled with requests for music and for instruments, and are usually quite specific in their demands. Clearly, Isabella had strong views on musical composition, and as a musically literate patron with considerable understanding of performance she was able to exercise some

[25] Isabella's musical *impresa* has been variously interpreted. Scherliess: 'Notizien zur musikalischen Ikonographie (II)' offers a résumé as well as the most convincing explanation. See also *Le studiolo d'Isabelle d'Este*, pp. 8–10 and 26–9, and Lehmann: 'The sources and meaning of Mantegna's *Parnassus*', pp. 164–6 and Plate III, where additional bibliography and illustrations of these items are listed.

[26] See *Le studiolo d'Isabelle d'Este*, p. 29.

[27] The inventory of Isabella's books is printed in Luzio and Renier: 'La coltura', part 9, appendice prima, and includes: [1] 'un libro di musica francesca in carta pegorina coperta di veluto turchino con li fornimenti d'argento'; [6] 'la musica di Franchino [Gafurio] scritta a mano in foglio coperto di rosso'; [80] 'un libro di canzone francese'. The first of these may well be Rome, Biblioteca Casanatense MS 2856, which bears a subsequently altered version of the Este and Gonzaga arms and contains a largely Ferrarese repertory. Llorens: 'El Códice Casanatense' is the standard account but needs revising. To judge from both repertory and palaeography it seems most likely that this manuscript, the only frottola manuscript that can be securely connected with Isabella, was prepared for her betrothal to Francesco Gonzaga in 1480, and that additions were made in the central section of the source during the subsequent decade leading up to their marriage in 1490.

control over the productions of her court composers. Archival records show a steady growth in the number of musicians employed at Mantua during this time, both at court and at the Gonzaga chapel in the Cathedral of San Pietro, founded in 1511 by Francesco (who was also a practical musician, if Castiglione's *Il cortegiano* is to be believed). Whereas one of Isabella's principal concerns in her sponsorship of music seems to have been to encourage native Italian composers and performers in their cultivation of the frottola and related forms, Francesco's attentions appear to have been directed more towards the traditional band of *pifferi* and to the establishment of the chapel choir. And in her patronage of art, in the decoration of her rooms, and above all in the great cycle of paintings commissioned for her *studiolo*, Isabella shows not only her musical tastes and her determination to create a new Parnassus on the Po, but a realisation of the potency of music and harmony as a political metaphor. In musical terms, there is no doubt that Isabella's patronage produced remarkable results, establishing a centre of musical activity where there had apparently been little before; but the quality of her achievement should not cause the activities of other patrons and institutions to be overlooked. Throughout the sixteenth century, music and musicians were sponsored elsewhere in Mantua, in some of the churches, in the ghetto, and by the aristocracy both individually and corporately. The remainder of this chapter examines some of the evidence for that sponsorship.

An essential point about Mantuan society throughout the period with which this study is concerned is that it was divided into recognisable status groups where wealth and power generally followed status. The division is the traditional one into three estates comprising the clergy, the nobility, and the rest, though there were, as elsewhere, important subdivisions within each group.[28] One significant distinction, general throughout Catholic Europe, was between the upper and lower clergy, and in Mantua the upper-status clergy formed a small élite consisting of the bishop, the Abbot of the ducal basilica of Santa Barbara, the Primicerio of Sant'Andrea and, in the other half of the territory, the Bishop of Casale Monferrato. Holders of these appointments were usually local men drawn from the nobility, and were frequently less important members of the Gonzaga clan. To cite the most obvious example, between 1466 and 1566 every Bishop of Mantua came from the ruling house, and at other times the diocese was headed by men from local aristocratic families such as the Andreasi, Cattanei, and Agnelli. There is a similar pattern for the other three major institutions, and it was not uncommon for holders of these posts to move from one to the other, suggesting a hierarchy with the office of bishop as the most prestigious of the four.[29] Speaking of mid-century Venetian society, Campanella remarked that

[28] The typology is taken from Mousnier: *Les hiérarchies sociales*, chapters 1 and 3.
[29] The point is well illustrated by the lists of Cardinals and Bishops of Mantua, *Primicerii* of Sant'Andrea, and Abbots of Santa Barbara, in Donesmondi: *Cronologia*, pp. 8–15.

'the greater part of the nobility live off canonries and bishoprics', and although this is undoubtedly an exaggeration and a specifically anti-Venetian piece of propaganda, the general point is valid for Mantua and is underlined by the manner in which the nobility, primarily members of the ruling house, pooled resources and consolidated their position and power through control of the most wealthy ecclesiastical institutions in the city and at Casale.[30]

Consequently, it is not surprising that the two most lavish music establishments during the sixteenth century outside the court itself were those at the two principal city churches, where wealth and authority were concentrated. Until the construction of Santa Barbara in the 1560s, the Cathedral of San Pietro functioned not only as the principal church of the city but also as the home of the major court chapel. The foundation of a well-endowed private chapel with a permanent establishment was carried out rather late by the Gonzaga, in comparison with other major ruling families such as the Sforza and the Este, although Federico I Gonzaga had contemplated the idea in 1483 and had sought advice from Ferrara.[31] This project died with him in the following year, and even the arrival of Isabella d'Este in 1490 does not seem to have prompted Mantuan emulation of Ferrarese example in this respect, though it clearly did in much else. This is perhaps not so surprising. Neither Isabella's artistic tastes nor her personal life present a particularly strong image of piety, and concern with the foundation of a permanent private chapel and the performance of sacred music at court seems to have come not from her but from her husband. Jachet of Lorraine was invited to organise a Gonzaga *cappella* in 1500,[32] but again nothing seems to have come of the scheme, and it was not until 1510 that Francesco II, prompted perhaps by the availability of talent released by Alfonso I d'Este's temporary disbanding of the Ferrarese court *cappella*, finally established a permanent family *cappella* in the cathedral.[33] It was arranged that this new *cappella* should be housed in the chapel of Santa Maria dei Voti (a choice reflecting perhaps Francesco's devotion to the Virgin), which had been planned in 1477 or 1478 and then constructed between 1480 and 1482. Another influential factor in the choice may have been the presence of an organ, already installed in the chapel by 1491 (and indeed by 1510 Santa Maria dei Voti had an established tradition of chanted offices), though Francesco had already taken steps to replace the instrument in 1511 and a new, larger organ was installed by 1517.

---

[30] Campanella is quoted in Ventura: 'Considerazioni sull'agricoltura veneta', p. 677. For further discussion of this point in relation to Venetian society see Burke: *Venice and Amsterdam*, p. 51.

[31] A. Bertolotti: *Musici alla corte dei Gonzaga*, p. 10.

[32] A. Bertolotti: *Musici alla corte dei Gonzaga*, p. 10, where Jachet's letter is reproduced, Davari: *La musica a Mantova*, p. 64, and Valdrighi: 'Cappelle, concerti e musiche', pp. 421 and 457.

[33] Documents concerning the foundation and early operation of the Gonzaga chapel in the cathedral are now gathered together in Prizer: 'La cappella di Francesco II Gonzaga', where it is also suggested that the Petrucci prints surviving in the Santa Barbara collection in Milan once formed part of the repertory of Francesco's chapel: see also Appendix III below. For further about the organ in the chapel of Santa Maria dei Voti see Levri: *Gli organi di Mantova*, p. 19.

Once established under the direction of Marchetto Cara, Francesco's *cappella* evidently experienced difficulties in retaining singers in the face of competition, particularly from the Papal Chapel, but it did survive until the death of Francesco in 1519 and may have continued to function afterwards.

The cathedral proper, dedicated to Saint Peter, maintained a separate establishment whose early history is less precisely documented.[34] An organ is noted in 1449, and thereafter a number of organists are named: Francesco de Alipradis (1457), Carlo Mainero (1478), and Alessandro degli Organi (1480–1512). A small choir of aspirants (*chierici*) is documented from 1500 to 1511, and again from 1526. By the next year Jacquet of Mantua had taken up residence in the city, and it was under the firm direction of his principal patron Cardinal Ercole Gonzaga that influential traditions of Gonzaga musical patronage in the cathedral were established. Yet despite Francesco's interest, court composers seem to have written little sacred music. Tromboncino composed a set of Lamentations which were published by Petrucci, though there is no evidence that they were written for Mantua; and Ventura detto Musini, a singer in the cathedral in 1509, may be the same as the Johannes de la Venture who composed a Passion setting for the Cappella Sistina in 1507.[35] As for repertory, documents from as early as 1495 concerning Francesco's attempts to acquire sacred polyphonic music for the court, and the Petrucci publications from the years 1502–9 now in the Santa Barbara collection, are probably survivals from the first Gonzaga *cappella*.[36] The foundation of Santa Barbara does not seem to have detracted from the scope of music at the cathedral; following a general pattern, the size of the choir increased as the century drew on, and there seems to have been an atmosphere of co-operation between the two institutions.[37] Some important state and family occasions continued to be celebrated at the cathedral; and although the position of *maestro di cappella* did not attract men of the calibre

---

[34] See Tagmann: *Archivalische Studien*, and Levri: *Gli organi di Mantova*, pp. 18–28, for documents referring to music in the cathedral. Additional material for the period of Cardinal Ercole Gonzaga's episcopacy is given in Nugent: 'The Jacquet motets', pp. 97ff.

[35] Tromboncino's Lamentations are in Petrucci's *Lamentationum liber secundus*, dated from Venice 29 May 1506. For Johannes de la Venture, see Tagmann: *Archivalische Studien*, pp. 32–3.

[36] An undated letter assigned by Davari to 1495 (*La musica a Mantova*, pp. 53–4: original in ASM (AG) 1435, letter of Giovanni Alvise Trombon) encloses a motet by Obrecht. See also Trombon's letter of 27 July 1505, also printed by Davari, which speaks of 'quel moderno moteto a fiauti 8'. For the Petrucci books see Prizer: 'La cappella di Francesco II Gonzaga', pp. 274–6. An inventory of the chapel of Santa Maria dei Voti dated 30 June 1505 lists five missals and 'un libro da cantar in carta bona de messe votive et de la Madona'. See Putelli: *Vita, storia ed arte mantovana*, i, pp. 9–19; the original, in ASDM (Cap.) LM 1505, fos. 59ff. lists additions up to 1510.

[37] For comparative figures see D'Accone: 'The performance of sacred music'. Many documents show that there was a good deal of co-operation between the music establishments at the cathedral and at Santa Barbara; the following is characteristic: 'Il Sig^r Duca Ser^mo mio S^re desidera che M^ro Annibale [Coma] organista di cotesta chiesa Cathedrale vada a servire per questo verno al Sr Prencipe Ser^mo suo figlio et percio mi ha ordinato de scriva...fra tanto che il suddetto Mr Annibale starà assente dal Duomo S.A. darà ordini che Ruggiero [Trofeo] che hora suona in Sta Barbara venga a servire i giorni di capella' (ASM (AG) 2598, letter from Aurelio Zibramonte to a ducal official, 27 November 1576). See also Tagmann: *Archivalische Studien*, p. 41.

of Wert or Pallavicino, it was often filled by able musicians, locally trained men whose compositions were often printed and sometimes attained a modest degree of popularity. Jacquet's successors included Giovanni Contino, Giovanni Maria di Rossi, Ippolito Baccusi, Lodovico Grossi da Viadana, and Giovanni Stefano Nascimbeni, while Annibale Coma and Giulio Cesare Monteverdi each served for a time as organist.[38] After the death of Cardinal Ercole Gonzaga, patronage at the cathedral was next at a height during the episcopacy of Monsignore Francesco Gonzaga, formerly Bishop of Pavia. His restoration and reconstruction of the fabric and the commissioning of the frescoes for the cupola of the cathedral were characteristic of a lavish expenditure on ecclesiastical buildings under his control, which was in turn part of a more general interest in new artistic projects. Undoubtedly influenced by developments in Rome, it received Mantuan expression in the construction and decoration of a number of important new church buildings, notably the Jesuit church of Santissima Trinità and the monastery of Sant'Orsola, and there is some fragile evidence to suggest that there was an accompanying expansion of music establishments in the city churches.[39]

The second church of the city, Sant'Andrea, is a medieval foundation originally built to house a relic of the Blood of Christ allegedly found at Mantua in 804.[40] The largest of the Mantuan churches, its present form is essentially that of the reconstruction begun in 1472 to the designs of Alberti and completed some thirty years later by the addition of Juvara's cupola. Alberti's involvement was prompted by the suppression in the same year of the Benedictine monastery to which the church had been attached, and the re-designation of the church as a basilica under the authority of a *primicerio*. This office was a prestigious one with rights equivalent to that of a Benedictine abbot, and Sant'Andrea itself was independent of the bishop and directly responsible to Rome. The decoration of the interior, mostly carried out in the century after the reconstruction, is certainly on a grand scale, but despite these indications of status and wealth, little can be deduced about provisions for music. An organ was paid for in 1387, and there are a couple of references to its maintenance during the subsequent decade. A new organ is documented in the sixteenth century, one of the organists is known, and

---

[38] For further details see Tagmann: *Archivalische Studien*, to which should be added, for Viadana's brief period at the cathedral, Mompellio: *Lodovico Viadana*, pp. 15–18.

[39] Francesco Gonzaga's achievements during his Mantuan episcopacy are elaborated in Sacco: *Vita e sante attioni*, and there is a good general account of his artistic patronage in *Mantova. Le arti*, III, pp. 458ff. See also the detailed references in Donesmondi: *Dell'istoria*, chapters 9 and 10. A more specialised study of one of the cathedral's major commissions during this period is Askew: 'The question of Fetti as fresco painter'. For Santissima Trinità see Possevino: 'Vita et morte della Serenissima Eleonora' (BCM MS 1216), pp. 27ff, and now the article by Ugo Bazzotti in *Rubens a Mantova*, pp. 28ff. It was for this church that Rubens painted his famous altarpiece showing members of the Gonzaga family.

[40] For a general introduction to Sant'Andrea and its history see Perina: *La basilica di S. Andrea*, and Johnson: *S. Andrea in Mantua*, both of which are essentially concerned with the building history of the basilica. For other information I have used Paolo: *Primiceri di S. Andrea*, and the documents in ASDM (SA): XVI. Documenti compravanti la serie dei Primiceri.

among the few fifteenth-century survivals from the library are a number of handsomely illuminated chant books.[41] Some of the *primiceri* seem to have had musical interests, or at least were prepared to pay for suitabiy flattering dedications in printed music books. Tullio Petrozzani, who held the office from 1591 to 1609, was a member of an old Mantuan family and had served as a ducal minister; he is the dedicatee of Benedetto Pallavicino's *Liber primus missarum* of 1603. Similarly, Marc'Antonio Gonzaga, *primicerio* from 1579 to 1589, was the sponsor of Orazio Vecchi's first book of six-voice *canzonette*, published in 1587.[42] Throughout the century important Mantuan events were often solemnised in Sant'Andrea, and the published account of the inauguration of the Order of the Redentore, which took place in the basilica in May 1608 as part of the arrangements celebrating the marriage of Francesco Gonzaga and Margherita of Savoy, suggests that polyphonic music was performed, but this is hardly proof of a permanent establishment. The most that can be said is that it would have been unusual, from what is known of similar institutions elsewhere during this period, if a foundation with the prestige and resources of Sant'Andrea had not made arrangements for the liturgical performance of polyphonic music.[43]

There are only scraps of evidence about music outside the major churches, precisely as one would expect. The general picture of parochial clergy in Italy, at least before the Catholic Reformation, suggests that the educational attainments of parish priests were often poor if not non-existent. The canonical requirements for ordination, scattered among the *Corpus iuris canonici*, were modest enough, specifying that an ordinand must be able to understand the books necessary for the mass and other offices, and for preaching, but it is clear that even these basic stipulations were often not met. In Italy, as elsewhere, an apprenticeship system was the principal way of teaching priests until seminaries began to be built in large numbers after the Council of Trent,

[41] Gallico: 'Vita musicale in Sant'Andrea' is the only study of the history of music in the basilica, but it has nothing to say about the sixteenth century. This is not surprising, since both the archives and the library were severely damaged during the Austrian occupation, when the church was used as a barracks and stables. Certainly there was an organ in use during the sixteenth century and earlier: see the documentary notices in Muoni: *Gli Antegnati organari insigni*, pp. 9–19, and in Levri: *Gli organi di Mantova*, pp. 29–30. ASM (AG) 3087, one of the necrologies, notes for 8 March 1555 '... mori Pietro Antonio de Benzon, organista in S. Andrea'. Some archival documents, mostly dating from the post-1700 period, and a number of chant books are now in ASDM (SA); and an initial from one of the latter is illustrated and described in *Tesori d'arte*, p. 120.

[42] The dedication of Pallavicino: *Liber primus missarum* is given in *Conservatorio di musica*, pp. 298–9. For further details of Vecchi: *Canzonette a sei voci libro primo* see Vogel: *Bibliothek*, II, pp. 277–8. The extent to which the base of patronage had broadened slightly by the turn of the sixteenth century is suggested by the range of Gastoldi's dedications. In this sense the expansion of patronage among the clergy parallels changes in the social composition and direction of the confraternities.

[43] Among the Gonzaga ceremonies which took place there were the marriage of Duke Francesco Gonzaga to Caterina of Austria in 1549, the funerals of Eleonora of Austria and Leonora de' Medici in 1595, and the funeral of Duke Vincenzo I in 1612. By this time there was certainly some form of music establishment, since in a manuscript dated 1606 (now in the Santa Barbara collection in Milan) Giulio Cesare Antonelli described himself as *maestro di cappella*. See *Conservatorio di musica*, pp. 5–6. For the foundation of the Redentore see Follino: *Compendio*, pp. 19–26.

and few of the parochial clergy would have received a university education. In these circumstances it would be unrealistic to expect performances of polyphonic music in parish churches.[44] Mantua, at least until the episcopacy of Cardinal Ercole Gonzaga, is no exception, and although an improvement in the quality of parochial clergy and churches was a matter of concern to Ercole, the situation must have changed only slowly. A comparison of the visitation reports suggests gradual improvement, but the frequency with which the bishop felt obliged to issue injunctions on the educational and moral condition of parish priests is some testimony to the persistence of old habits. Matters no doubt improved with the foundation of a seminary; a cathedral school had existed for some time, but its effect outside the chapter would have been slight.[45]

Monasteries present a similar picture of changing standards, though the evidence for artistic patronage is rather different. A decline in conscientiousness among the regular clergy was well advanced in most Italian monasteries before the fifteenth century. Claustration was rarely observed, and rules of moderate eating, of chastity, and of obedience were often ignored. Similar problems have been observed among friars, a development of wider significance since their contribution to the general quality of life had been so great and their influence remained so pervasive. The capitular acts of chapters-general suggest how widespread the problem was by the fifteenth century, and sporadic attempts by individual reformers such as Ambrogio Traversari of the Italian Order of Camaldoli could do little to stem the tide. At Mantua itself in 1516, the Dominicans of the Lombard Congregation (Observants) were severely criticised for wearing luxurious linen underclothing and ostentatious headwear, and for cultivating expensive habits. Above all, there was increasing concern throughout the period over the supervision of nunneries and of the moral condition of the inmates, many of whom had forsaken claustration and adopted a style of life which, in the view of some commentators, had brought many convents to the condition of houses of prostitution. These matters were also of great concern to the reform movement, and again the process of reform gradually began to eliminate abuses in the course of the sixteenth century; but the presence of luxury and

[44] For the conditions and duties of the clergy see Thomassin: *Ancienne et nouvelle discipline*, and in particular, Pellicia: *La preparazione ed ammissione dei chierici*. A useful short introduction in English is to be found in Hay: *The Church in Italy*, particularly chapters 4 and 5.

[45] Putelli: *Vita, storia ed arte mantovana* remains the basic source of information about Mantuan pastoral visits during the century, but for the unpublished reports see also p. 164 below. The more important injunctions issued for the Mantuan diocese are E. Gonzaga: *Breve ricordo*, E. Gonzaga: *Costitutioni per il clero*, and Andreasi: *Constitutiones*. Mantuan churches at this period are listed in Donesmondi: *Cronologia*, which also notes (p. 29) the construction of a new seminary in 1594. It is impossible to know if Bishop Francesco Gonzaga was thinking principally of the major churches in the city when compiling the following passage in his *Constitutiones et decreta*: 'che durante la messa non venissero eseguiti nelle chiese canti e suoni eccessivamente vivaci, nei quali il cento e l'organo potessero infondere alcunche di imputo o lascivo' (p. 10). But in general it would be surprising to find any more than, at the most, a polyphonic motet being performed on feast-days in the parish churches.

ostentation among the regular clergy points to social facts which are of some importance for artistic patronage. While many regulars in low positions were, like the run of secular clergy, unable to read or write, a small minority were highly cultivated scholars and writers. This tradition goes back at least to Luigi Marsili and Ambrogio Traversari, both men who came from old and wealthy families, and it was the continued attraction which the monastic life held for the minor aristocracy and the *haute bourgeoisie* that ensured its perpetuation.

So far, evidence of musical activities in Mantuan monasteries is again slight, but probably indicative of much more. The Carmelite Order, one of the largest together with the Augustinians and Dominicans, seems to have included a number of minor composers among the members of its Mantuan congregation. One of these, Ottavio Ragazzoni, probably related to Pietro Paolo Ragazzoni, a singer and composer who served in the Chiesa della Steccata in Parma from 1539 to 1564, subsequently supervised publication of the latter's *Liber primus psalmorum qui in ecclesia decantatur ad Vesperas quinque vocibus*, including Ottavio's own setting of 'Laudate Dominum'. Slightly better documented is another member of the same congregation, Girolamo Bacchini (Fra Teodoro del Carmine), author of a lost treatise on music and composer of a number of works including a book of five- and six-voice masses published in 1589 which place him firmly in Mantuan court and church circles. In the 1590s Bacchini is reported as a castrato performer at court, in 1594 he was in the ducal entourage visiting Regensburg, and in the following year he was in a group of musicians, including Claudio Monteverdi, Giovanni Battista Marinone, and another monk, Serafino Terzi, who accompanied the duke on his first, highly unsuccessful military campaign against the Turks in southern Hungary. Another musician attached to the Carmelites was Neriti da Salò, formerly chaplain and musician to the Emperor Rudolph II, described as 'Capellanus et Sacellanus' at the monastery in the foreword of his first book of four-voice *canzonette* published in 1593, a work sponsored by Enea Gonzaga.[46]

Against the rather dismal picture of clerical life in the pre-Reformation period should be placed the lively religious conditions of many members of the laity as suggested by the proliferation of lay confraternities, one of the most effective channels for the articulation of the views of the bulk of the population, and for the exercise of corporate patronage.[47] Recent writings have attempted, at least for the fourteenth and fifteenth centuries, to

[46] For Bacchini see A. Bertolotti: *Musici alla corte dei Gonzaga*, p. 72. Terzi is recorded as a singer at Santa Barbara from December 1592 to December 1601; see Tagmann: 'La cappella dei maestri cantori', pp. 384–6. He evidently continued in Gonzaga service after then: see Bertolotti: *Musici alla corte dei Gonzaga*, p. 103.

[47] The literature on confraternities is now extensive, though there is still no study of Mantuan ones. The most comprehensive general work remains Monti: *Le confraternite medioevali*, and the remarks in Heers: *L'Occident aux XIVᵉ et XVᵉ siècles*, pp. 305–13, are helpful. This is for the earlier period; for later developments see in particular Meersseman: 'La riforma delle confraternite laicali'.

distinguish between confraternities concerned with penitential discipline, those involved in charitable works, and those primarily concerned with liturgical observance. Sixteenth-century Mantuan confraternities seem to be of the second and third types, though often both these concerns figured in their activities; and the second half of the century witnessed a sudden further growth in the number of confraternities coincident with fresh warnings against heresy and the growing influence of the Jesuits. There is a common pattern in the way the confraternities were organised and how they saw their purpose. Normally they seem to have been founded by members of the laity who then employed priests to perform liturgical services, though it is increasingly common as the sixteenth century wore on to find the confraternities more often composed of the *haute bourgeoisie*, and so more inclined to clerical organisation. The increase in resources which accompanied this development often gave impetus to lavish charitable and religious projects, the provision of funds and services for hospitals, the building and supporting of orphanages, and the construction of churches and oratories. A few examples must suffice. One of the most prominent of the Mantuan confraternities was the Quarant'Ore, which by 1588, when the organisation was under the protection of Carlo Gonzaga, had accumulated sufficient funds to build a new church. In 1574 the Compagnia della Trinità Santissima was founded, so successfully that two years later its activities 'eccitarono una Santa Emulatione in altri gentilhuomini, & mercanti, si che n'instuirono anch'essi un'altra sotto il titolo de' Santi Rocco', and four years later this new confraternity had gathered sufficient funds to put up an orphanage and a church.[48]

So some at least of the Mantuan confraternities were, in the second half of the sixteenth century, comparable in social composition and function – though probably not in wealth – to the Venetian *scuole*; and this raises the question of their role as artistic patrons. Like the confraternities, the *scuole* originated in the thirteenth century and were lay religious societies many of which were formed to encourage mass piety and mutual aid.[49] The fact that many *scuole* originated essentially among groups of merchants partly explains their gradual accumulation of wealth, and although members of the Venetian *scuole* were not individually wealthy enough to commission works of art or to endow charitable institutions, they were prepared to do so collectively, and at the height of their power in the later sixteenth and early seventeenth centuries the results were sometimes spectacular. Music was an important feature of the *scuole*. At San Rocco, the most prosperous, an organist was employed to play at mass on the first Sunday of each month

[48] For further details see Donesmondi: *Dell'istoria*, pp. 229 and 278–9 (for the Quarant'Ore), and pp. 237 and 242–3 (for the Santissima Trinità).
[49] Pullan: *Rich and poor* is the most recent and exhaustive treatment of the *scuole*, and provides a lengthy bibliography.

and on a number of feast-days, while the name-day of the patron saint was celebrated with a festal mass, a procession, and an evening concert.[50] By comparison, the Scuola di Santa Maria della Carità seems to have specialised in dramatic performances, and in the second half of the sixteenth century a number of elaborate presentations were given, some to designs by Andrea Palladio.[51] So far as Mantua is concerned, there is an almost total lack of significant information about the confraternities' musical and artistic activities; nevertheless it is possible to say something, though admittedly speculatively, by comparison and inference. In the first place some of the Mantuan lay confraternities did show some interest in commissioning works of art, though the results were not perhaps of the quality of the *Virgin of the rocks* commissioned by the confraternity attached to San Francesco in Milan from Leonardo and the De Predis brothers, or the patronage as lavish as that of the Corpus Christi confraternity at Urbino, which ordered Justus Ghent's *Institution of the Eucharist* and Uccello's *Profanation of the Host*. Lorenzo Costa the Younger, for example, painted at least two works for Mantuan confraternities: one some time before 1575 for the Compagnia del Preziosissimo Sangue, and another for the Oratorio della Confraternità di San Antonio Abate.[52] Similarly the Mantuan confraternities, like those elsewhere, promoted frequent public processions, demonstrations of collective joy, devotion or commemoration, which often covered long distances starting in the centre of the city, moving to the church of the Madonna delle Grazie outside the city walls, and then returning to visit the major city churches. The desperate condition of Italian church archives probably means that an accurate account of the patronage of the Mantuan lay confraternities cannot be reconstructed, but it seems highly likely that the more elaborate ceremonies in the larger, wealthier institutions would have involved some employment of musicians, if only organists to accompany liturgical ceremonies and the singing of *laude*, and wind instrumentalists to take part in processions.[53] Certainly it is true that in Mantua, as elsewhere in Italy, the number of confraternities increased dramatically after the Council of Trent. In fact, the formation of these societies was an important part of conciliar policy from

[50] Lamberti: *Raccolta degli obblighi e prerogativi*, pp. 293–4, and Arnold: 'Music at the Scuola di San Rocco'.
[51] Selfridge-Field: *Venetian instrumental music*, p. 34.
[52] The painting for the Compagnia del Preziosissimo Sangue is now hanging in the second chapel on the right in the basilica of Sant'Andrea, but that for the Confraternità di San Antonio Abate is apparently lost, though it was described by Cadioli: *Descrizione*, p. 106, in 1763. For both works see now Gozzi: 'Lorenzo Costa il Giovane', pp. 45 and 57.
[53] One such procession is described in a letter written by Luigi Rogna on 24 May, 1568, part of which is given in Davari: *Cenni storici*, p. 66: '...la confraternità delle 40 ore andò processionalmente alle Gratie, poi tornò e visitò S. Pietro, S. Barbara ed altre chiese, portando le pazienze turchine. Domenica si farà quella della compagnia della Crocetta di S. Domenico et quella del Rosario e vi saranno tutti quelli che hanno abiurato con gli abitelli che haveranno là sul pulpito e li dovranno portare per un pezzo...' The best-known depiction of a confraternity procession, Bellini's *Procession of the Reliquary of the Cross*, painted for the Venetian confraternity of San Giovanni Evangelista, shows instrumental musicians: for further discussion see Rosand: 'Music in the myth of Venice', p. 525. There are regular payments for processions on feast-days in ASDM.

the early days, and in 1542 Giberti ordered each parish in the Diocese of
Verona to found a confraternity dedicated to the Body of Christ. By 1540
or so Mantua had a number of such groups, partly through the encouragement
of Cardinal Ercole Gonzaga, and by the end of the century new confraternities
seem to have been founded with great regularity.[54]

The nobility, like the upper clergy, were dominated by the ruling house, itself
arranged hierarchically to discriminate between the main Mantuan branch
of the family and the minor ones at Guastalla, Bozzolo, Sabbioneta, Luzzara
and the towns of Castelgoffredo, Castiglione, and Solferino, each of which
was controlled by yet another section of the Gonzaga clan. Inevitably,
intermarriage between members of the minor branches was a traditional
method of preserving Gonzaga wealth, though marriage into the main
branch of the family was rare. There should probably be a distinction
between even the minor members of the Gonzaga and the rest of the
aristocracy, who were in turn stratified in status groups depending upon
length of lineage. These men, whose economic power was generally derived
from land, often occupied the most important positions in the ducal service
as ambassadors or court secretaries – with the important exception of the
Holy See, where it had long been recognised that a prelate, and if possible
a cardinal, was preferable for such offices. The Gonzaga controlled not just
a city but a small state inconveniently divided into two, and it was generally
members of the local nobility who staffed its bureaucracy, its diplomatic
service, and the upper reaches of the military forces. For these families, too,
wealth was increased by inheritance and consolidated by marriage, while the
rewards of service could, as already noted, include lucrative ecclesiastical
offices and benefices. Evidence also suggests that members of these families
sometimes patronised the arts and that this patronage occasionally extended
to music.

Whatever the recent debates among historians about the relative claims
of the branch (*ramo*), house (*casa*) or the wider clan (*famiglia*) as the most
important unit of family structure among the Italian nobility during this
period,[55] the solidarity of the Gonzaga as a *famiglia* should not be underestimated, and the close relations both among the five minor branches and
between them and the court in Mantua encouraged a circulation of artists,
musicians, writers, and their work which was of some significance for the
artistic development of Mantua itself. At Gazzuolo, Lucrezia Gonzaga,

[54] For Verona see Jedin: 'Il significato del periodo bolognese', p. 13, and for Mantuan information for
the same period, Putelli: *Vita, storia ed arte mantovana*, pp. 37, 44, 48, 51, 56, 62, and passim. General
guidelines for Mantuan confraternities at the end of the sixteenth century are given in F. Gonzaga:
Constitutiones et decrete, pp. 45–50, and Donesmondi: *Cronologia*, p. 29, shows how frequently new
confraternities were founded at that time. Bendiscioli: 'Finalità tradizionali' prints the constitution
of the Confraternity of the Santissimo Corpo di Christo, but the remarks about music are vague and
seem to refer to chanted services. See also *Ordini della compagnia*, fo. [Bvi].
[55] See Cozzi: *Il doge Nicolò Contarini*, p. 6n., and Burke: *Venice and Amsterdam*, pp. 28ff.

praised by many authors for her generosity, gathered around her a small circle of writers; she patronised the popular writer and satirist Ortensio Lando for a brief period from 1548 to 1552, and under his guidance prepared a collection of letters for publication.[56] More extensive were the interests of Vespasiano Gonzaga, Duke of Sabbioneta, whose own enthusiasm for classical antiquity is most vividly seen in the theatre at Sabbioneta, the first to be constructed in Lombardy after the Greek model and clearly indebted to the example of the theatre of the Accademia Olimpica in Vicenza. His biographers provide occasional glimpses of an interest in music; Pallavicino was reputedly in his service when he published his first book of five-voice madrigals, and records occasionally describe performances of plays with music.[57] Rather closer to Mantuan circles was Ferrante Gonzaga (1507–57), co-regent with his brother Ercole Gonzaga and from 1539 the first Gonzaga Count of Guastalla, a title conferred upon him by Charles V. A distinguished career in the Imperial service brought further honours including the Golden Fleece; later he was appointed Viceroy of Sicily and Imperial Supreme Commander. In 1532 the Emperor made him Duke of Ariano in return for his efforts in Hungary against the Turks, but the peak of his career was his appointment as Governor of Milan in 1546 on the death of the Marchese del Vasto. These details nicely underline the strong political and military links between the Gonzaga and the Empire, an association which is so frequently reflected in the artistic atmosphere of the Mantuan court.[58]

As a *condottiere* in the family tradition, Ferrante himself seems to have had only a limited interest in the arts, though that interest apparently did include music. Imperial connections brought him into contact with Gombert, who wrote from Tournai in 1547 enclosing a motet. Orlando di Lasso was apparently taken as a boy to Italy by Ferrante, where he spent some time in his service before going to Naples in 1549; but the composer most consistently associated with Ferrante is Hoste da Reggio. Three of his madrigal books published in 1554 style him as Gonzaga's *maestro di cappella* and are dedicated to Ferrante, to his wife Isabella di Capua, and to Ippolita Gonzaga Carrafa, one of their children, on the occasion of her marriage. A further work published the same year is addressed to Cristoforo Fornari, paymaster of the Imperial armies in Piedmont, who had presumably come to know Hoste through Ferrante. Verses in these publications are mostly taken from conventional sources, but a number refer to Milan where Hoste was presumably based. It seems likely that Hoste was originally introduced to Ferrante by Ercole, the dedicatee of the composer's first book of four-voice

[56] See her *Lettere* and the brief discussion in Grendler: *Critics of the Italian world*, pp. 35 and 74. The contents of Lucrezia's book emphasise her closeness to Mantuan society.

[57] For further details see Affò: *Vita*, p. 96, and for the theatre at Sabbioneta pp. 106ff. Affò also describes (p. 42) celebrations at Bozzolo in 1562 for the marriage of the Prince of Sulmona to a member of the house of Potenza at which a play was given with music. Pallavicino's connections with Sabbioneta are summarised in Einstein: *The Italian madrigal*, II, p. 834.

[58] Biographical details from Ulloa: *La vita*, and Litta: *Famiglie celebri italiane*, IV, Gonzaga *tavola* VIII.

madrigals published in 1547, and although Hoste's association with both patrons seems to have been brief, his presumed transference from one to the other is typical of the contacts between members of the Gonzaga clan over such matters.[59]

Ferrante's successor, Cesare, followed the military traditions of his father, fighting for the Empire in Flanders and against the Barbary pirates. Strong and politically advantageous links were formed between Guastalla and the important Milanese family of Borromeo through Cesare's marriage in 1560 to Camilla, sister of the distinguished reformist churchman Carlo Borromeo. The most far-reaching consequence of his literary and artistic tastes was the foundation and sponsorship of the Accademia degli Invaghiti, installed in the family *palazzo* in Mantua; but he also had a number of contacts with composers, including Matteo Rufilo (whose first published work is dedicated to him), Simon Boyleau, then working in Milan (who composed a piece in honour of Cesare's marriage), and the Roman composer Ippolito Chamaterò.[60] And, as we shall see, the Invaghiti also patronised musicians from early in its history, though it is doubtful whether Cesare was involved in the arrangements. But there can be no doubt of the strength of Cesare's interests in music, nor that those interests were inherited by his successor, Ferrante (another member of the family who wrote and published verse), who assumed control of Guastalla in 1575 and was to direct the state for the next fifty-five years. Giaches de Wert, Annibale Coma, and Ippolito Baccusi all dedicated publications to him in the 1580s, and so did Ippolito Sabino (who spent most of his career at Lanciano catering for the local gentry) and Orazio Caccini. This list emphasises Ferrante's contacts with Mantuan court society, which seem to have been more developed than his father's had been; and his artistic interests in the city included not only the rehabilitation of the Invaghiti, which had fallen on hard times, but also associations with court literary and musical circles patronised by Duke Vincenzo Gonzaga during the 1580s and early 1590s, circles which included Barbara Sanseverina and Agnese Argotta, both of whom were Vincenzo's mistresses: the latter was a crucial influence in the attempts to stage Giovanni Battista Guarini's pastoral play *Il pastor fido* at court in 1591–2. It may well have been through the court

[59] Ferrante's connections with Gombert are noted in Schmidt-Görg: *Nicolas Gombert*, p. 107. The letter from Gombert, Tournai 3 June 1547, to Ferrante is now in the Mary Flagler Cary collection in the Pierpont Morgan Museum, New York. See *The Mary Flagler Cary music collection*, p. 70, and *MGG*, v, cols. 499–500, where it is reproduced. For Hoste da Reggio see the prefaces to his madrigal collections printed in Vogel: *Bibliothek*, I, pp. 320–2, the discussion in Einstein: *The Italian madrigal*, II, p. 479, and Haar: 'A madrigal falsely ascribed', where it is suggested that Hoste is the interlocutor referred to by that name in Doni's *Dialogo*. Lasso's service with Ferrante is fully documented in Leuchtmann: *Orlando di Lasso*, I, pp. 82–7; and Haar: 'A madrigal falsely ascribed' suggests that Hoste may have been Lasso's teacher for a while. Finally, Nugent: 'The Jacquet motets', p. 90, cites a document of 1532 in which singers are asked to entertain Ferrante during an illness.

[60] Boyleau: *Madriali, a IIII, V, VI, VII, et VIII voci* contains 'A cosi lieti' addressed to Camilla and Cesare, as well as a number of other pieces for Cesare, and the volume itself is dedicated to him. So are Chamaterò: *Il quarto libro delli madrigali*, and Rufilo: *Il primo libro de madrigali*.

that Ferrante met Marenzio, a composer whose contacts with Mantua stretched back over several decades, and who dedicated his eighth book of five-voice madrigals to him in 1598 in gratitude for unspecified favours.[61]

The Guastallan Gonzaga provide the best-documented and most impressive example of music patronage among the minor branches of the family, but outside immediate family circles the court of Alfonso Gonzaga, Count of Novellara, is of equal interest. The *Contea* of Novellara, established by Imperial decree in 1501 and then placed under the administration of the Dukes of Ferrara, had previously been the property of one of the branches of the Gonzaga descended from Feltrino Gonzaga (d. 1374), Lord of Reggio. Alfonso, the youngest of three sons born to the second Count Alessandro (d. 1530), was educated in Rome and later became a member of the Papal Court during the pontificate of Julius III. After the death in 1550 of Giulio Cesare Gonzaga, Patriarch of Alexandria, Alfonso inherited the title of Novellara and gradually transferred his interests there, making substantial improvements and renovations to the Rocca and developing the small court as a centre of artistic patronage. As with the Guastallan court, the direction of Alfonso's patronage was partly determined through links with Mantua, as in the case of Lorenzo Costa the Younger, who was commissioned in the 1560s to produce portraits for Novellara,[62] but contacts with Ferrara may also have been important. It has been argued that Wert entered Alfonso's employment in 1553 having previously been at Ferrara where he was taught by Rore; and whatever the merits of the case, Wert was certainly in Novellara by 1558, when he dedicated his first book of five-voice madrigals to Alfonso, opening the work with a piece celebrating Alfonso's marriage. Wert's precise movements between 1558 and 1565 when he took up permanent employment at the Mantuan court are unclear, but he maintained his association with Novellara both during that period and after the move.[63] Giulio Cesare Gonzaga (b. 1532), one of Alfonso's elder brothers, who had renounced his claims to Novellara in 1545 to take up the Gonzaga tradition of military

---

[61] The publications in question are Wert: *Il secondo libro de motetti* (Venice, 1581); Coma: *Il terzo libro de madrigali* (Venice, 1585); Baccusi: *Il quarto libro de madrigali* (Venice, 1587); Caccini: *Madrigali et canzonette* (Venice, 1585); Sabino: *Il settimo libro de madrigali* (Venice, 1589); Marenzio: *L'ottavo libro de madrigali* (Venice, 1598).

Giacomo Moro's *Gli encomii musicali* (Venice, 1585) includes pieces dedicated to Barbara Sanseverina, Agnese Argotta (for further on whom see below, p. 149), and Ferrante. Occasionally too Ferrante's own writings – of which the most substantial is *Eunone* (1593), a *favola pastorale* for which the *intermedii* were written by Torquato Tasso – were set by composers of the Gonzaga circle. See, for example, Wert's setting of Ferrante's 'L'anima mia ferita' in the ninth book of five-voice madrigals (1588).

[62] See Litta: *Famiglie celebri italiane*, IV, Gonzaga *tavola* XIII, and Davolio: *Memorie storiche*, pp. 34ff, for details of Alfonso's biography. His connections with Lorenzo Costa are presented in Gozzi: 'Lorenzo Costa il Giovane', pp. 41–2.

[63] The theory that Wert spent the years 1550–3 at Ferrara was first suggested in MacClintock: 'New light on Giaches de Wert' and then repeated in MacClintock: *Giaches de Wert*, pp. 23–4. It is based upon a single document which speaks of a 'Messer Jacomo', who may or may not have been a musician, and is not supported by the records of the Este *cappella*. There are no records of Wert's activity during the 1550s until the appearance of his *Il primo libro de madrigali a cinque voci*, the dedication of which (to Alfonso) is published in MacClintock: *Giaches de Wert*, p. 231.

employment in the Imperial forces, also seems to have known Wert about this time; Duke Guglielmo Gonzaga's sister Isabella had been married to Don Fernando d'Avalos, Marchese di Pescara e del Vasto, in 1554, and in 1561 Wert's first book of four-voice madrigals was dedicated to Ferrante, apparently at Giulio Cesare's suggestion. Another local composer, Girolamo Carli of Reggio, also addressed a publication to Alfonso in 1567, opening it with an encomiastic piece.[64]

Elsewhere among the minor nobility there are few signs of interest in music, though other less prestigious members of the Gonzaga occasionally put up the money for a dedication or were flattered by single compositions, invariably the work of men already employed at the Mantuan court. Sometimes high-ranking ducal officials also acted in the same way, and from time to time other members of the aristocratic élite figure in dedicatory prefaces; but in general there is little evidence of support for musicians except by the ruling family and its subsidiary branches, and the little that is known of is extremely provincial and inconsequential.[65] If the aristocracy supported the composition and performance of music at all, they were likely to do so corporately, through the confraternities (which the wealthier classes came to dominate during the sixteenth century) and through the academies.

The contribution of the sixteenth-century Italian academies to the culture of their age has not yet been fully assessed. Certainly it is true that under their sponsorship many aspects of Quattrocento scholarship were continued and expanded, and the academies still offered a platform for much new thinking and writing that would otherwise have lacked an outlet. More importantly perhaps, they could be progressive over issues such as the *questione della lingua*, where by championing the cause of the *volgare* and making it their official language they advanced considerably the case for the vernacular as an effective medium for scholarly and poetic discourse. Later they served as models for other learned societies which, though often differently constituted, took up new curricula and adapted themselves to changed intellectual conditions and interests.[66] The earliest recorded Mantuan academy, the Accademia di San Pietro, was a literary society founded

[64] On Giulio Cesare, the second son (also called Camillo), see Litta: *Famiglie celebri italiane*, IV, Gonzaga *tavole* XII–XIII, and Davolio: *Memorie storiche*, pp. 26ff, and for the dedication of Wert's *Il primo libro de' madrigali a quattro voci*, see MacClintock: *Giaches de Wert*, pp. 231–2. Carli: *Il primo libro de madrigali* begins with 'Io canterò te, Alfonso eccelso et chiaro'.

[65] Such as Milleville: *Madrigali...Libro secondo*, dedicated to Prospero Cattaneo and including pieces addressed to members of the Bozzolo Gonzaga. The same also sometimes occurs with important churchmen: I. Baccusi: *Missarum...liber secundus* is dedicated to Mutio Mainoldo. For information about Mantuan families I have relied on Carlo D'Arco's two compilations in ASM (D'Arco): MS 51, 'Alberi genealogia di molte famiglie mantovane', and MS 186, 'Stemme di famiglie mantovane'. There is also useful information in MS 104, Zucchi: 'Genealogia'.

[66] Maylender: *Storia delle accademie d'Italia* remains the standard introduction. Two recent studies of individual academies have been particularly useful: De Gaetano: 'The Florentine Academy' and Samuels: 'Benedetto Varchi'.

in the late fifteenth century, probably along the lines of the so-called Accademia Romana which, having been founded by Pomponio Leto in the 1460s, resumed its gatherings during the pontificate of Julius II and centred its activities in the gardens surrounding the villa of the poet Angelo Colucci. The major concerns of this kind of society were the discussion and promotion of the literature of classical antiquity and the presentation of Latin compositions, on antique models, by its members.[67] The San Pietro, mentioned favourably by Carreto in a letter of 1498 to Isabella d'Este, survived into the early years of the sixteenth century; but more influential, and particularly characteristic of the later academy movement, was the Accademia degli Invaghiti, founded in November 1562 by Cesare Gonzaga of Guastalla, with an initial membership of thirty which included both Scipione Gonzaga and the future Duke Ferdinando, whose influence upon early-seventeenth-century Mantuan musical life was to be considerable. The society met in Cesare's Mantuan *palazzo*, and his proximity to influential circles in Rome acquired special privileges for the academy from Pius IV, including the power to award various professional qualifications. Membership was open to both clergy and laity, and from its inception the Invaghiti was typical of aristocratic and courtly academies in its emphasis on chivalric ceremonial and the arts of oratory and versification. No complete list of the early members survives, but court officials of high standing such as Marcello Donati and Bernardino Marliani were involved and took their turns in the office of *Rettore*, the circulating position of overall director of the academy's regular business.[68] Documentation of the early phases of the Invaghiti's existence is similarly slight, but what does survive suggests that it was organised as a modified version of the Accademia Fiorentina, often claimed to be the prototype of many Italian academies, and it may be significant that Benedetto Varchi, one of the prime movers of the Fiorentina, was involved with the Invaghiti in its early stages. Versification, orations, and learned disputations continued to form the staple fare throughout the patronage of Cesare (d. 1575) and were taken up again when the academy was reconstituted under his son, Ferrante, but theatrical productions were also sometimes given, and on some

[67] For the San Pietro see Maylender: *Storia delle accademie d'Italia*, v, p. 90, and Cian: 'Una baruffa letteraria', p. 387. The Accademia Romana is discussed in Tiraboschi: *Storia*, vii/i, p. 206, Maylender: *Storia delle accademie d'Italia*, iv, pp. 320–7, and Pecchia: *Roma nel cinquecento*, pp. 391ff. Cappellini: 'Storia e indirizzi', p. 202 records an unnamed scientific academy in Mantua in 1518.

[68] The basic account of the Invaghiti is that in Maylender: *Storia delle accademie d'Italia*, iii, pp. 363–4, which should be supplemented by Carnevali: 'Cenni storici' and Cappellini: 'Storia e indirizzi'. There is also some useful information in D'Arco's unpublished notes in ASM (D'Arco) MS 224. Two copies of the Papal Bull bestowing privileges are preserved in ASM (AG) 3368, and the contents are partially extracted in Donesmondi: *Dell'istoria*, p. 216. Some idea of the academy's early membership may be gained from [Castellani]: *Componimenti*, a volume of verses by members issued in memory of Cardinal Ercole Gonzaga. One of the most distinguished members of the Invaghiti at this period was Marcello Donati, a noted doctor, botanist, connoisseur of antiquities, man of letters, and bibliophile, Vice-Rector of the academy in 1566 at the age of 26, and Rector from 1576 to 1599. For further details see Zanca: *Notizie sulla vita*. In addition I have used two manuscripts in ASM (D'Arco): MS 48, Volta: 'Notizie intorno alla Accademia degli Invaghiti', and MS 224, D'Arco: 'Notizie delle accademie'.

occasions at least the general public were admitted.[69] In 1564 a *mascherata* was produced 'quasi all'improvviso' in honour of one of the members, and a letter of 1568 notes payments to 'Leone Hebreo', presumably the Mantuan playwright Leone de' Sommi, author of an important treatise on stage production; he is described as 'nostro scrittore', which may indicate that he had been – unusually for a Jew – elected a member of the academy.[70] As we shall see, de' Sommi was an important figure in court musical and theatrical life during the 1580s and 1590s. Carnival season, the principal feasts in the Church calendar, and important events in the lives of the Gonzaga often prompted the Invaghiti to orate and dispute, and occasionally the fruits of their efforts were published.[71]

The role of music in this is unclear. In the first place discussion of theoretical aspects of music was reasonably common in this type of academy, and this interest could extend to include practical music. One of the earliest societies, the Accademia degli Intronati of Siena, founded about 1527, included all disciplines and the liberal arts among its exercises.[72] But more suggestive of musical interests among members of the Invaghiti is the emphasis upon theatre, and in addition to employing de' Sommi the academy also included another local playwright, Massimo Faroni, whose comedies were quite often performed during the 1570s and 1580s. Sometimes it is overlooked that contemporary dramatic theory consistently specifies musical *intermedi* as a necessary part of comic theatre, and that many plays required music and dance within acts, though customarily at the end. Presentations such as those known to have taken place at the academy would normally have involved music, and it was the Invaghiti who sponsored Monteverdi's *Orfeo* in 1607, to a libretto by one of its own members.[73]

[69] Varchi's work is included in [Castellani]: *Componimenti*. For an account of his involvement with the academy movement, see Samuels: 'Benedetto Varchi'. Information about the Invaghiti's activities is taken from an apparently unnoticed series of letters written by members of the academy and addressed to their patrons Cesare and Ferrante Gonzaga: these letters, now BCM MS 995, cover the years 1563–99. For letters describing theatrical events and occasions when the public were admitted see those of 26 February 1564, 9 February 1568, and 19 January 1569.

[70] BCM MS 995, letters of 4 February 1564 and 30 July 1568. For further on de' Sommi's life and career see now Marotti (ed.): *Leone de' Sommi. Quattro dialoghi*, pp. xv–lxxiii.

[71] [Castellani]: *Componimenti*, the principal publication to reflect the academy's activities, includes verses by Bernardo Tasso, a Mantuan court secretary and father of Torquato, Benedetto Varchi, Giulio Cesare Gonzaga, Scipione Gonzaga, the Ferrarese playwright Giovanni Battista Giraldi, and Giulio Castellani himself. The Invaghiti's meetings are also reflected in two other publications: Bernardino Marliani's *Lettere*, which contains epistles to Annibale Chieppio (pp. 262–3) and to Cesare Gonzaga (pp. 139–40) concerning academy business, and Alessandro Guarini's *Varie compositioni*, which presents (p. 17) an oration presented before the Invaghiti in 1599.

[72] There is a considerable literature on the Intronati, but see in particular Cerreta: *Alessandro Piccolomini*, pp. 10ff, Iacometti: 'L'Accademia degli Intronati', and Mazzi: *La congrega dei Rozzi*. The latter prints the statutes of the academy on pp. 389–90.

[73] One of the most interesting discussions of music and comedy, though one that has generally been overlooked by musicologists, is that in Toscanella: *Precetti*, particularly fos. 14ff and 75. MacClintock: *Giaches de Wert*, pp. 103–4, suggests that 'Qui dove nacque' from the sixth book of five-voice madrigals, a piece praising Virgil and a group of 'novi Cigni', may refer to the Accademia degli Invaghiti. Ascanio de' Mori's *Giuoco piacevole* (Mantua, 1575) includes a *ragionamento* 'ch'egli hebbe in lode delle donne il Carnevale passato in Mantova nell'Academia de' Signori Cavalieri Invaghiti...'

Elsewhere in Mantua a number of other academies were attached to religious houses, such as the Accademia dei Felici, founded in 1583 at the Carmelite monastery, a congregation with strong musical traditions. There may have been others. In Florence, for example, the tradition goes back at least to the fifteenth century, when some religious houses such as Santo Spirito and Santa Maria degli Angeli became the centres for scholarly discussions between their lay friends, and so may have served as precedents and models for more formally organised academies later on. By the sixteenth century such groups were increasingly concerned with practical education, and this was certainly a preoccupation of the Jesuits, whose speciality was to set up secondary schools that offered instruction in all subjects. Although little is known about Mantuan counterparts, they did exist. The most spectacular monastic institution of this kind in Mantuan territory was at San Benedetto Po, which was revitalised around the middle of the sixteenth century through a fresh injection of funds and encouragement by Ercole Gonzaga. And in 1585 the Jesuits opened a *studio* in the Contrada del Griffone in the city to provide basic instruction for the young.[74]

Although no archival evidence has been found of the existence of an essentially practical academy of musicians along the lines of the Veronese Accademia Filarmonica or the academy that met at the house of Goretti in Ferrara, a number of anthology publications of the late 1580s have the air of being produced by precisely such a group of local composers. *L'amorosa caccia*, advertised on its title-page as containing five-voice madrigals by 'diversi eccellentissimi musici mantovani nativi', is dedicated to the 'Ecc^mi Signori Musici di Roma' and edited by Alfonso Preti. Preti does not seem to have been employed by any of the important Mantuan churches or at court and is described in the dedication as a nobleman and virtuoso, a good blend of the practical and social skills necessary for the patron of a small academy. Of the composers represented in *L'amorosa caccia*, a large number were currently employed at the cathedral, and (while there is no evidence to suggest a specific relationship between this Mantuan group and any Roman composers) it is possible that the 'Signori Musici di Roma' were a circle around Marenzio, since he had been known in Mantua since his visit of 1580 and may have lived and worked in the service of Guglielmo Gonzaga in the 1570s.[75] The music of *L'amorosa caccia* is very varied and often undistinguished,

[74] For the tradition in general see Delle Torre: *Storia dell'Accademia Platonica*, and Kristeller: 'The contribution of religious orders'. The Accademia dei Felici is mentioned in Maylender: *Storia delle accademie d'Italia*, II, p. 353, and the Jesuit school in Amadei: *Cronaca universale*, II, p. 853. The original documentation on which Amadei's account is based includes the letters from the Cardinal of Verona, Verona 21, 22, and 27 March 1584, to Duke Guglielmo Gonzaga, in ASM (AG) 3366. For other evidence of musical traditions at the Carmelite monastery in Mantua see p. 28 above.

[75] Preti was also in contact with the Mantuan poet and playwright Muzio Manfredi, who addressed the following letter to him: 'Il Signor Gio. Andrea Robiati mi hà fatte le raccomandationi di V.S. che mi sono state sicare, come la stima ch'io sò di lei, tanto gentile, tanto cortese, e tanto virtuosa; e cento per una le ne vendo. Hammi detto di più, che V.S. desidera qualche mio picciolo Madrigale, da mettere in musica. S'ella mi havesse mandato alcun particular soggetto, ò dell'amor suo, ò, d'altro; mi sarei

a useful barometer of the workaday style of averagely competent craftsmen. The texts are, in their frequent allusions to hunting, an unmistakable piece of Mantuan propaganda, and were presumably also designed to appeal to Vincenzo Gonzaga (soon to become duke), whose obsession with horses and field sports was apparently rivalled only by his enthusiasm for attractive women. Certainly Preti himself had already attempted to attract Gonzaga favour by dedicating his *Primo libro de madrigali a cinque voci* to Duke Guglielmo and by opening the book with a piece deliberately calculated to appeal to Vincenzo's musical tastes. The *Novelli ardori* contains works by many of the composers represented in *L'amorosa caccia* as well as pieces by Gastoldi, Colombano, Masenelli and Pallavicino, at least some of whom were presumably excluded from *L'amorosa caccia* because they were not born in Mantua. So again this anthology is largely drawn from the work of musicians connected with the cathedral, though it was edited by Paolo Bozi, who does not seem to have been employed there but was *maestro di canto* at Santa Barbara from June 1584 until August 1587. Again it is dedicated to an influential local patron, in this case Alfonso Gonzaga, Count of Novellara.[76]

With its lack of substantial industry and only slight importance in banking and finance, it was expedient to the Gonzaga that Mantua should be hospitable to Jews even in the face of considerable ecclesiastical pressure.[77] A Jewish community is first noted in the fourteenth century, and by the middle of the fifteenth the Jewish residents had become a stable and influential section of society at Mantua, as they had in neighbouring Ferrara, Modena, and Reggio. Whilst the occasional anti-Semitic disturbances and punitive measures which affected the Mantuan community during the sixteenth century may have been part of a wider campaign of deliberate persecution, they bear witness to the commercial and financial power which the community had achieved and also, especially in the second half of the century, to the Gonzaga fear of Papal displeasure. A firm attitude towards usury is characteristic of the Catholic Reformation, and given the intensity of Ercole Gonzaga's reformist zeal it is not surprising that his period of administration introduced strict measures directed specifically against the Jews.[78]

ingegnato di farne un paio al manco, per compiacerla: ma non havendo espresso nulla, le ne mando non sò quanti fra molti eletti, ch'io mi truovo; e parrammi di essere avventurato assai, se qualcuno ve ne troverà conforme al voler suo' (Manfredi: *Lettere*, p. 154). I have used Bresciani's manuscript 'Stato del clero' (ASDM) to identify the composers in *L'amorosa caccia*. For further on Marenzio's connections with Mantua see pp. 112ff below.

[76] For Bozi at Mantua see Tagmann: 'La cappella dei maestri cantori', p. 383, based on documentation in ASDM (SB).

[77] Colorni: 'Pressito ebraico' discusses the origins of the Mantuan community in the fourteenth century. For the general background to the Jewish communities in Italy I have used Milano: *Storia degli ebrei*, Roth: *The Jews in the Renaissance*, and Shulvass: *Haye ha-Yehudim be Italyah*. The history of the Mantuan community is best approached through Simonsohn: *Toledòt*.

[78] See below, p. 58.

Guglielmo's government seems to have been characterised by a just attitude, judged by contemporary standards, partly conditioned by a realistic appraisal of the important role of the Jews in his schemes for political stability and economic prosperity. Pius V's banishment of Jews from the Papal territories in 1569, an intensification of a policy inaugurated by his predecessor's notorious bull *Cum nimis absurdum*, was widely opposed in northern Italy and was not imitated at Ferrara, Florence or Mantua, and during 1571 and 1572 the size of the Mantuan Jewish community was greatly increased by an influx of refugees from the Papal provinces and from other territories such as Urbino and Pesaro where Pius V had secured co-operation.[79] Guglielmo seems to have resisted the Papacy successfully until 1576, when an emissary from Gregory XIII secured a compromise arrangement whereby some of the clauses of *Cum nimis absurdum* were published, though probably not conscientiously enforced.[80] Despite Guglielmo's hospitality to the Inquisition and to the Jesuits, who established their church of San Salvatore next to the synagogue in the centre of the Jewish area of the city in 1584, the traditions of comparative liberality continued; and the implementation of Philip II's anti-Semitic measures in Milan, then under Spanish control, in 1596 sent a further wave of refugees to Mantua.[81] Although Vincenzo Gonzaga initially continued the benevolent policies of his father, the combined effect of the Christian reaction to Jewish power and money and the increased pressure of the ecclesiastical authorities culminated in 1602 in a series of disturbances inflamed by the anti-Semitic preaching of Bartolomeo da Salution, which in turn seems to have been the direct cause of the decision to establish the ghetto and to introduce other repressive measures.[82]

It would seem that the Jewish community was important for the theatrical life of the city from the early years of the sixteenth century and perhaps even earlier, and the first recorded example of a Jewish theatrical production in Italy has Gonzaga connections: at Pesaro in 1489, for the marriage of Maddalena Gonzaga, sister of Marchese Francesco, to Duke Francesco Maria of Urbino, a drama based on the story of Judith and Holofernes was staged by and at the expense of the Jewish community.[83] In Mantua itself, Jewish actors were requested from Duke Ercole I of Ferrara for a production celebrating Marchese Federico Gonzaga's accession in 1520;[84] and as early as 1525 the community was obliged to bear the cost of performances by Jewish

---

[79] Simonsohn: *Toledòt*, pp. 22ff.   [80] Simonsohn: *Toledòt*, p. 21.

[81] For the introduction of the Jesuits in Mantua see Donesmondi: *Dell'istoria*, p. 274, and Amadei: *Il fioretto*, p. 91. The effects of the Inquisition of 1568 are mentioned in Donesmondi: *Dell'istoria*, pp. 224–5, and the Inquisition is dealt with in considerable detail in Davari: *Cenni storici*.

[82] See Donesmondi: *Dell'istoria*, pp. 374ff.

[83] Luzio and Renier: *Mantova e Urbino*, p. 49. The history of theatrical life in the Mantuan community would seem to make it an exception to the interpretation in Adler: 'The rise of art music in the Italian ghetto', which argues that in Italy in general the evidence of intense cultural activity coincides with the imposition of the ghetto.

[84] Luzio and Renier: 'La coltura', part 2, p. 9.

actors at the ducal court, a special form of taxation suggesting that their performances were admired by the authorities,[85] while in the same year a letter written by the court secretary Vincenzo de Preti provides the first reference to a Mantuan Jewish acting troupe.[86] Thereafter there is an impressive series of documents suggesting that the Jewish *Università* (the name bestowed on the community when it was reconstituted in 1511) maintained a permanent troupe of actors whose principal function was to present plays at court, particularly during the Carnival season and at special festivities. In August 1549 the marriage celebrations of Duke Francesco and Caterina, the niece of Emperor Charles V, included the performance of two comedies, one given by 'nostri recitanti di Mantova', the other by 'gli Hebrei'.[87] In 1554 the community performed a comedy noted for its lavish spectacle and machines,[88] and in 1563 Ariosto's comedy *I suppositi* was given by the Jews in honour of the visit of the Archdukes Rudolph and Ernst of Austria, with *intermedi* including music and spectacular visual effects.[89] By this time the reputation of the Mantuan Jewish companies and the enthusiasm for their performances had compelled Rabbi David Provenzal to warn the community against the dangers of allowing the tradition to take too strong a hold,[90] but his words seem to have made little impact. A few years later a letter from the ducal secretary Luigi Rogna provides further evidence of the vitality of the Jewish theatre, and a good number of references to Jewish performers survive from the 1580s suggesting elaborate productions including lavish *intermedi* and dance.[91] The Jews performed again for Vincenzo's second wedding in 1584, this time Bernardo Pino's *Gli ingiusti sdegni*, with dances which had been commissioned the previous year from Isacchino Massarano and *intermedi* by Judah Sommi; and in 1587 two comedies were to be given in the court theatre during Carnival – one by the Christians, the other by the Jews – though in the event the Jewish play was not produced because of insufficient rehearsal time.[92] Between Vincenzo's two marriages, in 1582, the community troupe apparently performed Giambattista Cintio's tragedy *Selene*, and in August of that year they gave a comedy at Vincenzo's expense.[93]

---

[85] Roth: 'European Jewry in the dark ages', p. 154.

[86] ASM (AG) 2506, letter of 24 February 1525 to Isabella d'Este. See D'Ancona: *Origini*, p. 398. Roth: *The Jews in the Renaissance*, p. 248, questions whether the play was original or taken from Purim themes; Simonsohn: *Toledòt*, p. 479, n. 272, suggests the former.

[87] Document cited in D'Ancona: *Origini*, pp. 401–2.

[88] Simonsohn: *Toledòt*, citing documents in the Mantuan community archive. The directors of the play, Jacob Sulani and Samuel Shalit, were among the leaders of the congregation.

[89] 'Relazione di un viaggio', p. 83.

[90] Roth: *The Jews in the Renaissance*, pp. 247–8.

[91] For Rogna's letter see D'Ancona: *Origini*, p. 402; it refers to a performance of Massimo Faroni's *Le due fulvie*. Faroni's play was eventually published, with its *intermedi*, at Venice in 1603. One other occasion on which this work was given was during the visit of Maximilian of Austria to Mantua in 1581: see Allacci: *Drammaturgia*, col. 732.

[92] For the first production see D'Ancona: *Origini*, p. 425, and Ademollo: *La bell'Adriana*, p. 51; the expenses are given in Simonsohn: *Toledòt*, p. 482, n. 294. For the second production see D'Ancona: *Origini*, pp. 426–7.　　　　[93] Simonsohn: *Toledòt*, pp. 482–3.

With Vincenzo's maturity and then his accession, theatrical life in general became more vital, and it seems that at least during the 1580s and 1590s the Jewish company's performance during the Carnival season was a regular event,[94] except in 1597 when, in the words of the ducal secretary Annibale Chieppio, 'perchè per la morte del duca di Ferrara, credo che S.A. non avrà voglia di commedie'.[95] In 1591 there were plans to produce Muzio Manfredi's *favola boscareccia Le Nozze di Semiramide con Memnone* during Carnival, with dances by Isacchino Massarano and music by Wert, the enterprise being directed by Leone de' Sommi.[96]

Closely related to the community's interest in theatre was an enthusiasm for formal dancing and choreography. The Jews' activity at court as professional dancing instructors and choreographers stretches back well into the fifteenth century, and Guglielmo Ebreo, author of the important *Trattato del'arte del ballo*, was himself a pupil of Domenichino da Piacenza, one of the most important figures in the development of the new style of complex formal dancing, the contrasting sets of *balletto* measures, which became fashionable at the Ferrarese court of Lionello d'Este.[97] In Mantua, the distinguished choreographer and theorist Leone de' Sommi seems to have had connections with the court from the mid-1560s; and another Jew, Isacchino Massarano, a harpist and singer, was involved in various theatrical productions including the projected performance in 1591–2 of Guarini's *Il pastor fido*.[98] He was apparently still at the court in 1599.[99] As will be seen, Jews were closely involved in the *Pastor fido* productions – the most lavish Mantuan spectacle of the 1590s, and a symbol of the new vitality of Mantuan theatrical life after Vincenzo Gonzaga's accession in 1587.[100]

The Mantuan Jewish community, more than any other in northern Italy, seems to have been highly prized for the quality of its musical life.[101] In 1522 a Jew named Giovan Maria, who was apparently raised to the nobility by Leo X, is recorded as a fine harp-player and as music teacher to the children

[94] Roth: *The Jews in the Renaissance*, p. 251.

[95] Cited in D'Ancona: *Origini*, p. 428.

[96] D'Ancona: *Origini*, pp. 424–5; see also below, pp. 147ff. Letters from Manfredi to de' Sommi, Wert and Massarano are given in Manfredi: *Lettere*, pp. 228–9, reprinted in D'Ancona: *Origini*, p. 428, and translated in MacClintock: *Giaches de Wert*, pp. 176–7. The latter also conjectures that Wert's 'Poi che vuole il ben mio', 'Voi nemico crudele', and 'Amor se non consenti' were all composed for this production. An earlier attempt by Vincenzo to have one of Manfredi's tragedies performed was foiled by his father; on this occasion the community's troupe substituted a comedy by Carlo detto gli Struccione. See D'Ancona: *Origini*, pp. 423–4, and Simonsohn: *Toledòt*, p. 483.

[97] For a general account of the Jewish dancing-master tradition see Roth: *The Jews in the Renaissance*, pp. 275ff. Guglielmo da Pesaro and his work are dealt with in Kinkeldey: 'A Jewish dancing-master', which should be supplemented by Michel: 'The earliest dance manuals'.

[98] D'Ancona: *Origini*, p. 400.

[99] A. Bertolotti: *Musici alla corte dei Gonzaga*, p. 63.

[100] See Neri: 'Gli "intermezzi" del "Pastor fido"', Hartmann: 'Battista Guarini and "Il pastor fido"', and pp. 147ff below. For de' Sommi see D'Ancona: *Origini*, pp. 404ff, and now Marotti (ed.): *Leone de' Sommi. Quattro dialoghi*, introduction.

[101] For Jewish musicians in Mantua see the relevant chapters in Roth: *The Jews in the Renaissance*, Simonsohn: *Toledòt*, and Birnbaum: 'Musici ebrei'.

of Marchese Francesco.[102] Abramo dell'Arpa is mentioned as a participant in a court spectacle as early as 1542,[103] and it was his nephew Abramino dell'Arpa who became one of Duke Guglielmo's favourite performers and who, in 1587, was called to Goito to soothe the duke's last days with his playing. It is presumably to one of these, or at least to members of the same family, that Lomazzo makes reference in his *Trattato dell'arte*,[104] where they are selected in preference to other performers to represent the art of harp-playing in the company of other distinguished contemporary instrumentalists. Other scattered references suggest the liveliness of the Mantuan Jewish tradition during this period: Luigi Groto's *Rime* includes a poem addressed to a Mantuan Jewish musician, and David Sacerdote, a native of Rovere in the Mantuan *contado*, was apparently in the service of the Marchese del Vasto. With the rise to prominence of Salamone Rossi, the importance of Jewish musicians for the musical life of the city seems to have reached a high point; Rossi's name appears in court payment documents, and he seems also to have been in charge of a troupe of travelling musicians with something of a local reputation.[105] Other Mantuan Jewish musicians in the late sixteenth and early seventeenth centuries included Rossi's sister 'Madama Europa', Davit da Civita (whose *Premitie armoniche* was dedicated to the then Duke of Mantua), and Allegro Porto.

The conclusions of this brief survey of such a small, despotically controlled city are not, perhaps, surprising. Musical activity did, of course, take place outside the Palazzo Ducale – in the churches, the academies, the homes of the nobility, and the ghetto. Its extent is difficult to gauge, but the outlines of the system seem reasonably clear. To speak of Mantuan patronage of music and the arts as Gonzaga patronage is not an exaggeration, since such sponsorship as existed elsewhere in the city was supported by Gonzaga interest and Gonzaga money, and is one reflection of the extent to which the

---

[102] Simonsohn: *Toledòt*, p. 488.

[103] Birnbaum: 'Musici ebrei', p. 191.

[104] A. Bertolotti: *Musici alla corte dei Gonzaga*, p. 35, records Abramo dell'Arpa at the Mantuan court in 1566, and Canal (*Della musica in Mantova*) mentions him from 1553. He was also for a time at Vienna and was sufficiently well known to be included by Lomazzo in his list of musicians (see Lomazzo: *Trattato dell'arte*, pp. 347–8, and *Rime*, pp. 163–4). See also Gallico: 'Monteverdi e i dazi di Viadana', p. 243, n. 8. The duke's request for Abramino in 1587 is mentioned in Canal: *Della musica in Mantova*, p. 701, and D'Ancona: *Origini*, p. 400.

[105] Salamone Rossi's name does not appear among the court violists in a salary list of 1559 (see A. Bertolotti: *Musici alla corte dei Gonzaga*, p. 68) but he is registered as a 'musico straordinario' in the early years of the seventeenth century (see Appendix II, doc. 65), and Bertolotti noted a further payment in 1622. His role in providing music for occasional theatrical events is emphasised by his selection as the composer of *intermedi* for the 1608 Mantuan performance of Guarini's *L'idropica* and of incidental music for Andreini's *La Maddalena* given in 1617. In 1612, Alessandro Pico, Prince of Mirandola, the dedicatee of Rossi's third book of five-voice madrigals, requested that Rossi and 'his group of musicians' be sent to Mirandola to entertain the Duke of Modena and other guests, and it is perhaps as the leader of this travelling instrumental group that Rossi made his living. The documentation is in Papotti: 'Annali o memorie storiche della Mirandola', p. 99, n. 2. For a general account of Rossi, see Newman: 'The madrigals of Salamon de' Rossi'.

family dominated local institutions. And as we shall see, the contacts between some of these institutions and the court were often quite close, while outside the city the Gonzaga system ensured contacts with other Italian courts and cities as well as with principal centres abroad. Mantua was an important part of an international political and diplomatic system which incidentally provided the means through which music and musical personnel could be exchanged, and an important question in the following pages is how and why patterns of influence and exchange altered in response to the politically inspired role which successive Gonzaga rulers formulated for music and the arts. Isabella d'Este was the first of the ruling house to make a sustained attempt to realise the potential of culture in the service of the Mantuan state, though this is not to deny either her formidable humanistic education or her apparently genuine interest and accomplishment in music. But the extraordinary achievements of her humanistically orientated patronage, though admired, were not emulated by her successors even within her own lifetime, and already by the middle of the second decade of the century new cultural patterns were beginning to emerge as the balance of power shifted within the family in the direction of her sons. The artistic, and specifically the musical, consequences of that transference of authority, and of the consequent formation of new Mantuan political alignments, are the subject of the next chapter.

2

Ercole Gonzaga and Jacquet of Mantua

Dove voi tu ire adesso? ch'è in disordine tutto il mondo;...Anderò a Mantoa, dove la eccelenzia del marchese Federico non nega el panne a niuno...

Aretino, *La cortigiana*

Fig. 3 Giulio Romano: *Arms of Cardinal Ercole Gonzaga*, modello, possibly
for a tapestry. Chatsworth, Devonshire Collection (reproduced by permission
of the Trustees of the Chatsworth Settlement)

46

Artistic life at Mantua reached a peak during the first twenty years of Isabella and Francesco's period, and by the time of the latter's death in 1519 there were already signs of a declining interest. The succession passed to Federico, the first-born of their nine children, named a captain-general of the Church by Leo X in 1521 and made first Duke of Mantua by Charles V in 1530. Of the other officially recognised offspring Eleonora married Francesco Maria Della Rovere, Duke of Urbino, in 1509, while Ferrante pursued a traditional career, becoming a respected Imperial general and successively Viceroy of Sicily and Governor of Milan. Ercole, who as second son had always been educated for an ecclesiastical career, was in many ways the most talented of the four, intelligent, well educated in the humanist tradition, and with a flair for diplomacy that became the foundation for a highly distinguished career in the service of Church and state. Federico's artistic tastes were mostly confined to the construction and decoration of new palaces (notably the Palazzo del Te designed by Giulio Romano) and to the enlargement of the Palazzo Ducale; and although Ferrante seems to have had broader sympathies for music, the arts, and letters, his career brought him only rarely into direct contact with the Mantuan court. As Isabella's own enthusiasm for artistic projects waned during the last decade of her life, it was the force of Ercole's influence, fuelled by the ideas of the reform movement within the Church, that gradually impressed itself upon Mantuan artistic life. Federico's death in 1540 placed Ercole in a controlling position as co-regent, and it is the stamp of his personality, tastes, and beliefs that characterises Mantuan patronage during the middle decades of the century and, through its powerful influence on the future Duke Guglielmo, remained a crucial factor after his own death in 1563. The process of change, through the half-pagan world of Federico's court to the intensely reformist spirit of mid-century Mantua, and the ways in which it affected and is reflected in Gonzaga patronage of music, form the subject of this chapter.

Federico followed in the *condottiere* tradition of his father, though rather less honourably, pursuing relentlessly opportunist strategies designed to increase the power and territory of the marquisate, seeming to oscillate between the Empire and the Papacy during the conflicts of the 1520s while

47

in reality never abandoning the loyalty to Charles V upon which Mantua's security depended. In the tumultuous events of this decade which brought Pope and Emperor face to face, Federico was able, with Isabella's connivance, to neutralise the effectiveness of the *Cedola secreta* which obliged him to protect the Pope against the Emperor, and his policy of neutrality after the Battle of Pavia extended to allowing the Imperial troops to cross Mantuan territory on their way south. This sudden reversal of roles from Papal protector to Imperial collaborator brought scorn from the Italian states, but recognition and reward from Charles in the form of elevation to the positions of duke and commander of the Imperial forces in Italy. Similarly, during the same period Federico's ambitions were directed towards increasing his status and power through marital politics. Early in January 1515 his marriage to Maria Paleologa, then aged six, had been arranged with the proposal that the wedding should take place in 1524 when the bride reached the age of fifteen. Despite the blessing of the King of France, the arrangement of a formal contract in 1517, and the Emperor's agreement to invest Maria as the heir to Monferrato, Federico not only continued his relationship with his mistress Isabella Boschetti but also began to search for a more prestigious bride. An ingenious series of delays now put off the Paleologa match until 1528 when, in exchange for two prisoners in Federico's charge, Clement VII agreed to issue a *breve* declaring the marriage contract void *causa venedi*. Almost two years later, on 6 April 1530, a new marriage was arranged between the marchese and Giulia of Aragon, who was much older than Federico, and who would bring with her the succession to Cremona. Festivities were arranged to take place in Mantua on 29 June; but hardly had the plans been laid when the death of Bonifacio of Monferrato on 6 June and the succession of the already ailing Gian Giorgio Paleologa prompted Federico to reconsider marriage to Maria, whose control of Monferrato now seemed distinctly more possible than it had earlier. By September Clement VII had been induced to issue a further *breve* declaring the previous one erroneous and now describing the Gonzaga–Paleologa match as 'valido et indissolubile', while Mantuan agents in Augsburg pleaded Federico's case before the Emperor. Again plans were thwarted, this time by Maria's death before the *breve* had been promulgated; but negotiations continued over Maria's sister Margherita, and in July 1530 the Emperor approved the marriage, which took place on 3 October 1531. In the next year Giulia of Aragon was married to Gian Giorgio of Monferrato, who died shortly afterwards, but despite Margherita's legal claim as the rightful heir it was not until 3 November 1536 that Federico was finally able to assume control of the territory with Imperial support. Once acquired by the Mantuans, Monferrato remained a source of concern throughout the rest of the century, coveted by Savoy and fiercely resistant to Mantuan authority.[1]

[1] For further see *Mantova. La storia*, II, pp. 269–372, and Davari: *Federico Gonzaga e la famiglia Paleologa*.

These details of schemes and counter-schemes give some idea of Federico's ruthlessness and skill in the tense game of Italian politics, and emphasise the importance of the Imperial connection for Mantuan stability and, above all, the marchese's preoccupation with Mantuan expansion and enhanced status, an ambition to which all other concerns were subjugated. The climax of his career was Charles V's visit to Mantua in 1530, which lasted from 25 March until 19 April and culminated in the Emperor's proclamation of Federico as first Duke of Mantua. Many of the festivities were centred on the still unfinished Palazzo del Te, not in fact a new building but an enlargement of an existing villa belonging to the family of Isabella Boschetti. More than any other artistic project carried out under Federico's orders, the new palace on the Isola del Te, designed by Giulio Romano and decorated by him and his assistants, gives the measure of the marchese's temperament and provides striking evidence of his conception of the function of art in the service of political ambition.[2]

Initially Federico and his mistress had used the Boschetti villa as a retreat, but then about 1527, coinciding with the marchese's expectation of substantial rewards and increased prestige in return for his encouragement of Imperial objectives, Giulio and his workshop were ordered to expand the existing building to provide a suburban palace. The most obvious addition to the structure was a monumental architectural order, considered essential by contemporary theory for buildings belonging to men of rank. Recent analyses of the iconography of the building have emphasised evidence pointing to Federico's realisation of the potentialities of the Palazzo for expressing both his status and his allegiance to the Empire, and the visit of Charles V provided an opportunity to display the new building and convince the Emperor of Mantuan military and political strength. The detailed account of the visit written by Luigi Gonzaga shows the central role which the new palace played in the arrangements and, quite apart from its value as testimony to the extravagance of the occasion, provides fundamental insights into Federico's conception of the building as a statement of Mantuan power.[3] In iconographical terms the most obvious references in the structure are to the most recently built villas in Rome, allusions which may reflect Giulio Romano's training as much as Federico's wish to rival the splendour of Rome itself, or at least to build in the 'bellissima forma di grandezza'.[4] Similarly, while arguments persist over matters of detail, there is no doubt that the decorations of the Palazzo del Te are a monument to the collaboration of an anonymous humanist and a distinguished architect with the principal purpose of expressing Federico's personal and dynastic ambitions through

[2] There is a considerable literature on the Palazzo del Te. I have relied on Hartt: *Giulio Romano*, 1, chapters 4 and 5, Belluzzi and Capezzali: *Il palazzo dei lucidi inganni*, and Verheyen: *The Palazzo del Te*.

[3] Romano (ed.): *Cronaca del soggiorno*, pp. 239ff.

[4] Hartt: *Giulio Romano*, 1, p. 94; Verheyen, *The Palazzo del Te*, p. 22.

the use of symbolic images.[5] As the Palazzo Vecchio was to be for Cosimo I de' Medici, and Fontainebleau for Francis I, so the Palazzo del Te – the most elaborate and integrated Gonzaga building and decorative scheme since Isabella d'Este's second *grotta* and *studiolo* – stands as an embodiment of Federico's conception of the Mantuan state as well as a monument to his own artistic tastes.

In fact, the decoration of the new building falls into two distinct autobiographical phases. The first campaign (lasting from 1527 to 1529) comprised the three small decorated rooms facing the city in the northwest wing, and the entire northeast apartment centred on the Sala di Psiche. In its consistent use of pagan erotic symbolism, this stage of the decoration is clearly evocative of Federico's well-documented sexual enthusiasms. A second campaign (begun after the Emperor's visit and lasting from 1530 to 1535) is iconographically concerned principally with the new duke's preoccupation with power consequent upon his participation in the siege of Florence, the acquisition of new status at the hands of the Emperor, and the prosecution of an expansionist policy which culminated in the addition of Monferrato to Mantuan territory.[6] Various humanists including Lucas Gauricus, Mario Equicola, and Paolo Giovio have been thought responsible for the programme for the decorations,[7] but study of the iconographical details should not obscure the fact that Federico's personal tastes, similar in some respects to those of Rudolph II, must largely account for the choice and arrangement of some of the strange subject matter shown on the walls. Some, though not all; the placing of the marriage feast, for example, may have been the solution to a purely artistic and representational problem. But certainly the decorations of the Palazzo del Te reveal as much of the personal tastes of Federico as do the *studiolo* and the *grotta* of the predilections of his mother.

Given the small number of surviving archival or literary references to music at Federico's court, it is not surprising to find so few iconographic references to musical legends in the decorative schemes in this central monument to Federico's patronage of the arts. Above the entrances to the Sala del Sole and the Sala dei Cavalli are shown the Gonzaga coat of arms and two lunettes portraying the river Hippocrene, which as a source of poetic inspiration is connected with two wall frescoes showing incidents from the lives of Orpheus and Eurydice and exemplifying the power of music. Ovid's version of the origins of Hippocrene describes the visit of the goddess Urania, who praised it as the place of the Muses and declared the daughters of Mnemosyne to

[5] Principally Hartt: 'Gonzaga symbols in the Palazzo del Te', Gombrich: 'The Sala dei Venti', and Guthmüller: 'Ovidübersetzungen und mythologische Malerei. Bemerkungen'.

[6] Hartt, *Giulio Romano*, I, pp. 106ff.

[7] Wind: *Bellini's 'Feast of the Gods'*, p. 14, n. 20. The view expressed there that Equicola devised the programme is contested in Hartt: *Giulio Romano*, I, p. 139. For the tentative suggestion that Gauricus may have advised, see Gombrich: 'The Sala dei Venti', pp. 116–18.

be happy there. Quite clearly the principal purpose of these frescoes is to emphasise the character of the new palace as a place of happiness, and contemporary architectural theory underlines the appropriateness of the entrance to a ruler's country villa being dedicated to the Muses.[8] The other references to musical mythology are in the decorations of the Sala di Ovidio, which include frescoes showing the contest between Apollo and Pan, Orpheus before Pluto and Proserpina, and the flaying of Marsyas.[9] Two of those incidents are central concerns of the musical symbolism of Isabella d'Este's decorative schemes; but, unlike Isabella's use of these *topoi*, their significance in the Sala di Ovidio is subordinated to the more obvious meaning of the cycle as a whole as an outspoken celebration of erotic pleasures. Finally there are the metopes which run round both the outside and the inside of the central courtyard, and which consist of a non-repetitious pattern of military emblems, suits of armour *all'antica* and so on, interspersed with musical instruments. Some of the latter are fantastic and others simply a continuation of the imagery of war, but others again are accurate representations of contemporary refined courtly instruments. Here too the context is clear. This is no humanistically inspired portrayal of music as one of the liberal arts, but merely the other half of an equation. Overwhelmingly, the architectural and decorative schemes of the converted Boschetti villa proclaim it as a temple to the gods of love and war, and it is as adjuncts to both these activities that music is portrayed. For Isabella d'Este the heavenly harmony which she sponsored was not only a refining force, but a symbol of the earthly harmony over which she and Francesco presided; but at the Palazzo del Te the satyrs were welcomed within the walls.

The few scattered documentary references to the employment of musicians during Federico's period do suggest a continuation of Mantuan musical traditions after Francesco's death both at court and in the ducal chapel of Santa Maria dei Voti, though it is not always clear whether this was due to Isabella's continued interest or to the enthusiasm of the new marchese. A number of musicians who are recorded for the first time during Francesco's period continue to appear in documents throughout the 1520s – for example, Narciso de Mainardi, Giacomo di San Secondo and Roberto di Rimini.[10] Similarly, the court continued to be an important patron of instrument-builders, and there is some evidence that Federico himself took part in these

---

[8] See *Publius Ovidius Naso. Metamorphoses*, ed. F. J. Miller, 2 vols. (London, 1916), I, pp. 256–7. The frescoes are discussed in Verheyen: *The Palazzo del Te*, pp. 24–5 and 114–15, and are illustrated there as Figs. 24 and 25.

[9] Discussed in Hartt: *Giulio Romano*, I, pp. 111–12, and more fully in Verheyen: *The Palazzo del Te*, pp. 110–12.

[10] Narciso de Mainardi was active in Mantua at least from 1492 and died in 1529: see ASM (AG) Reg. nec. Giacomo di San Secondo, who served the court as early as 1501, was granted a pension in 1523; and Roberto di Rimini, noted in 1512, was paid as late as 1522: for both these two, see ASM (AG) Lib. Mand.

negotiations, operating through ducal agents, though the most celebrated addition to the ducal instrument collection during this period – that of an organ in a carved alabaster case – was made not at the marchese's instigation but at Isabella's.[11] And as a matter of course the court *pifferi* and *tromboni* continued to be maintained.[12] Most of these documents date from the first years of Federico's period, and it is only from the early 1520s onwards that anything survives to suggest renewed Gonzaga interest in new musical compositions. On 13 October 1520 Giulia Gonzaga, then only eight years old, wrote to Federico enclosing a newly composed motet by Sebastiano Festa, described in her letter as a servant of her uncle, the Monsignore of Mondoví; and almost three months later a further letter followed enclosing a second motet.[13] The only other possible references to new contacts with composers – concerning Alessandro Agricola and Andrea de Silva[14] – again come from the early years of Federico's rule. Giulia Gonzaga's letters are particularly interesting since they amplify the impression of Federico's interest in liturgical music gained from other documents, and it is at least theoretically possible that some of Jacquet of Mantua's compositions were written for the marchese rather than for Ercole – possible but unlikely, since during the 1530s, arguably the most productive period of Jacquet's Mantuan career, there is almost no evidence of musical activity at court.

Indeed, after the mid-1520s, musical life seems to lose a good deal of its earlier vibrancy and brilliance, and between then and Isabella's death in 1539 the traditions which she established – indeed, fashioned almost single-handedly – slowly disintegrated. In 1525 Cara still had Mantuan connections and was granted citizenship, and Tromboncino continued to work in Mantua, Vicenza and Venice until 1535, though Testagrossa had already transferred his allegiance to the court of Urbino where he died about 1530. The major expansion of the music establishment came with Isabella's arrival at Mantua in 1490 and then with Francesco's foundation of the *cappella* in San Pietro in 1510, and although a number of new musicians are recorded in the documents between 1512 and 1525 their numbers decrease and they are not of the stature of Cara or Tromboncino. This is equally true of the few fresh arrivals noted after 1525, men such as Pizanfora, Pre Michele di Verona and Alessandro de Folengo, as well as the small number of existing

---

[11] For the alabaster organ, see A. Bertolotti: *Musici alla corte dei Gonzaga*, pp. 32ff, and Levri: *Gli organi di Mantova*, pp. 55ff. For Federico's interest in musical instruments, see Appendix II, doc. 4.

[12] See for example the letters in A. Bertolotti: *Musici alla corte dei Gonzaga*, pp. 35–6.

[13] Variously published in Benrath: *Julia Gonzaga*, p. 109, Lowinsky: *The Medici codex*, III, pp. 59–60 (first letter only), and Gallico: *Un canzoniere musicale*, pp. 35–6. The originals are in ASM (AG) 1803; for my transcriptions see Appendix II, docs. 5–6.

[14] For the Agricola documentation, dated after the composer is usually thought to have died, see the *copialettera* of 17 March 1521 printed in A. Bertolotti: *Musici alla corte dei Gonzaga*, p. 32, and the payments to 'Alexandro Agricola cantore' in 1522 and 1523 registered in ASM (AG) Lib. mand. De Silva, recorded at the Papal Chapel in 1519, was paid by the court in 1522 (ASM (AG) Lib. mand.): see also Bertolotti: *Musici alla corte dei Gonzaga*, p. 34.

musicians who continued in service throughout the period, of whom the most popular were Pozino, who was associated with the court from 1501 until at least 1532, and Roberto Avanzini, who was probably a pupil of Cara in 1512.[15]

It may be indicative that the talented Mantuan composer and lutenist Alberto da Ripa (d. 1551) chose to leave his native city about 1528 to find work elsewhere, eventually finding a position with the French royal household;[16] and it is noticeable that the most important stylistic changes in Italian music during the 1520s and 1530s seem to have left Mantua almost untouched. Recent work has shown that madrigals were being composed and circulated in manuscript from the mid-1520s, that is, in many cases some considerable time before they found their way into print. Moreover, in its initial stages this development was an essentially Florentine phenomenon – not connected with the frottola tradition, as the historicist tradition stemming from Einstein would prefer – and only rather later was it taken up by composers elsewhere, principally in Venice and Ferrara.[17] Mantua was later still in cultivating the form: Jacquet of Mantua, the principal composer there before the 1560s, apparently wrote almost no secular music, and it is not until Giaches de Wert's arrival that a madrigalist was employed at Mantua on a permanent basis, though starting with Ercole there was occasional sponsorship of madrigalian publications produced by composers working elsewhere. So in the light of current archival evidence and of the surviving sources it would seem that Isabella's own involvement waned towards the last decade of her life, owing to a complex of reasons which probably included the hardships she underwent during the sack of Rome in 1527 as well as changes in musical fashions; similarly, what is known about Federico's court suggests a continuation of previous traditions of patronage. Moreover, the necrology for the plague years 1527–8 suggests a severe impact on musical life in Mantua at a time when, as we have seen, Federico's attention was firmly engaged elsewhere.[18] And as interest at court waned, the centre of musical patronage seems to have shifted from the court to the bishop's residence.

Ercole was born in 1505, and in 1520 succeeded his uncle Cardinal Sigismondo as Bishop of Mantua, with the reluctant consent of Leo X.[19] On

---

[15] Pizanfora is mentioned in a letter of Mario Equicola, Mantua 4 August 1521, to Marchese Federico: 'Il Pizanfora è malato, subito che serà megliorato V.S. l'haverà col cytharino' (original in ASM (AG) 2500). For Folengo and Michele di Verona see A. Bertolotti: *Musici alla corte dei Gonzaga*, p. 34.

[16] Vaccaro (ed.): *Oeuvres d'Albert de Rippe I: Fantasies*, introduction.

[17] Fenlon and Haar: 'Fonti e cronologia'.

[18] ASM (AG) Reg. nec. for 1527–8 records the deaths of Polonia, wife of Jacquet of Mantua, Gilio Fiammengo 'Cantore de Mons. Cardinale' (i.e. Ercole Gonzaga), Fra Francesco 'cantore in San Pietro', Rossino 'cantore', Sebastiano 'maestro delli organi dell'Ill. S.', and Bernardino Piffero.

[19] The most useful general accounts of Ercole's career are Donesmondi: *Dell'istoria*, pp. 197–206, Pastor: *History of the Popes*, XI, pp. 505–8, Litta: *Famiglie celebri italiane*, IV, Gonzaga *tavola* V, and Montesinos: *Cartas inéditas*, pp. xxi–liv.

his mother's advice, he was sent to further his education at the *Studium* at Bologna, not only because of its fame as the oldest centre of learning in Italy, but principally because of the presence there of the Mantuan philosopher Pietro Pomponazzi. Pomponazzi's teaching exerted a profound effect upon Ercole, as he later acknowledged himself, and although his letters from the Bologna years do not suggest an enthusiasm for music, they clearly indicate a serious-minded approach to Latin, Greek, and Arabic studies.[20] By the time of Pomponazzi's death in May 1525, which prompted Ercole's return to Mantua, Isabella had already begun to press his claim to be raised to the cardinalate. Negotiations continued into 1526, but finally in the autumn of that year Clement VII acceded to the Gonzaga request secretly, while withholding an official announcement of the elevation until only three days before the sack of Rome in the hope of extracting a larger financial contribution from Isabella. From this new position of power, Ercole quickly established himself as a skilful diplomatist in Church affairs, intervening successfully in the difficulties caused by the Protestant sympathies of Renée, daughter of Louis XII of France and wife of Ercole II d'Este; subsequently he was appointed Pontifical Legate to Charles V, though this is perhaps not surprising in view of the traditional Gonzaga allegiance to the Empire.[21] These were the first major involvements in a Church career which was to bring him close to the triple crown on two occasions, but his abilities were not solely directed to the execution of Papal policies. In 1536 he was despatched to Casale as the first Governor of Monferrato, which came under Gonzaga control in that year; and with the death of Federico in June 1540 the duchy passed to his first-born son Francesco, then aged seven, while the government was effectively administered by a regency consisting of Federico's wife the Duchess Margherita, Ferrante (then Viceroy of Sicily), and Ercole.

The death of Francesco on 21 February 1550, less than a year after his installation as duke in his own right, again placed state affairs in Ercole's hands. It was decided that the regency should be reconstituted until it had become clear whether Francesco's recent bride, the Archduchess Caterina, would have any issue by her marriage; meanwhile Ercole was urgently sent for from Rome, where the conclave was in the process of electing Pope Julius III. When Caterina was returned childless to Germany, it became clear that Federico had always intended that Guglielmo, the eldest surviving son, should pursue an ecclesiastical career; both Cardinal Ercole and the Duchess Margherita now suggested that he abandon his rightful claims to the duchy

[20] Luzio: 'Ercole Gonzaga allo studio di Bologna'. Later Ercole had Pomponazzi's profile incorporated in his seals of office; see Luzio and Torelli: *L'Archivio Gonzaga*, II, pp. 271–3. Little is known about Ercole's library. On becoming Bishop of Mantua he inherited the well-known missal executed by Belbello of Pavia for Gianlucido Gonzaga during his student days in Pavia, and now kept in ASDM (Cap.).

[21] On Ercole and the cardinalate see Pastor: *History of the Popes*, IX, pp. 384–5, and for Renée of France Luzio and Torelli: *L'Archivio Gonzaga*, II, p. 199.

in favour of his brother Ludovico. This idea Guglielmo spiritedly rejected, but in practical terms he did not take over the government until 1558; meanwhile Cardinal Ercole continued to exercise a strong control over the business of state and began the task of grooming Guglielmo in the religious and humanistic ideals which would best fit him for his future role.

Ercole's fourteen-year period of effective control was conducted in stark contrast to the profligacy of Federico's rule. Extravagance, corruption and political dishonesty were now firmly discouraged, the ducal finances were strengthened, and above all a workable and efficient system of bureaucracy was introduced. Ercole's own humanistic background found firm expression in the education of his nephews, whilst his own position as an advocate of reform, together with his scholarship, experience and considerable reputation for piety and good works, made his choice as a candidate for the Papacy in the conclaves of 1549 and 1555 highly likely. Finally, in 1559, his third attempt seemed almost certain of success, despite Farnese opposition, until Philip II, by withdrawing his support, ensured the election of Pius IV.[22] In these circumstances it was both a politic step and a recognition of Ercole's skills as a mediator that the new Pope, in attempting to resolve the problems that arose between Philip II and the Papacy over the convocation of Trent in 1560–1, appointed two conciliar legates, Cardinal Puteo as an acknowledged canonist and Gonzaga himself as a diplomatist; and Ercole's subsequent appointment as president of the third session of the council which opened in November 1561 seems to have been generally and warmly applauded. By some at least he was considered not merely a wise and astute administrator but – together with Cardinal Seripando – the hope of Trent itself; but during the course of the session Ercole contracted fever, and it was there that he died on 2 March 1563.[23]

The conventional image of Ercole makes it tempting to view him as more a prince than a prelate, concerned more with weighty affairs at Rome or with diplomatic missions than with the business of the Mantuan duchy or his diocese, but this is to miscalculate the character of his position as regent and to underestimate his commitment to ecclesiastical reform at a local level. The first major practical demonstrations of his interest in reformist ideals were his institution of the pastoral visits which took place in 1535 and 1538, and his close supervision of the running of his own diocese after his return from

---

[22] The conclave of 1559 is discussed in Pastor: *History of the Popes*, xv, pp. 1–65. Further information on Ercole's relationship with Pius IV is given in Drei: 'La politica di Pio IV'. There is a considerable literature on Ercole's role at the Council of Trent, but see in particular Amadei: *Cronaca universale*, ii, pp. 731–2 and Drei: *La corrispondenza*.

[23] Jedin: *Papal legate*, pp. 578–9, quotes Vergerio's remark about Seripando and Ercole at Trent: 'I know of no-one who has loved or favoured me more; perhaps God has brought them to Trent to bring about reconciliation with the Protestants.' [Castellani]: *Componimenti* is a volume of verses in memory of Ercole, compiled by the newly formed Accademia degli Invaghiti and prefaced by the customary eulogistic essay. Among the contributors are Bernardo Tasso, Benedetto Varchi, Giulio Cesare Gonzaga, Giovanni Battista Giraldi, and Scipione Gonzaga.

the *Studium* in Bologna, both measures which show an appreciation of the views of Gasparo Contarini and Gian Matteo Giberti, Bishop of Verona, who placed great stress on the controversial question of the observance of residence by bishops and parish priests as a necessary preliminary to the strengthening of orderly pastoral activity. Later it became one of the great issues of Trent itself, though it was not until May and June 1546 that the matter was accepted for debate on the conciliar agenda.[24] The Mantuan pastoral visits – repeated at intervals, and concentrating upon the moral and educational condition of the clergy, the physical layout and decoration of churches, and the operation of services – are a clear indication of Ercole's allegiance to reformist ideals in the 1530s, and there are other signs to confirm it.[25] After attempts to convoke councils at Mantua and subsequently at Vicenza in 1537 had miscarried, the advocates of change argued that spontaneous personal action by prelates committed to reform would be the only viable alternative to the grim prospects of either conciliar authority or schism. Encouraged by Paul III, Ercole played a distinctive role in the attempts to reform the old monastic and mendicant orders through his position as protector of the Lateran canons, and it was Paul III who also provided a firmer base for the reform movement by raising the layman Contarini to the College of Cardinals. After his creation on 22 December 1536 a small nucleus of like-minded cardinals gathered round him, including Gonzaga, Carafa, Sadoleto, and Pole, and it was this group which, in the years between the abortive attempt to convoke a council at Mantua and the convocation of Trent by a bull of 22 May 1542, resolved to pursue reform through personal intervention at the diocesan level. The campaign proceeded with difficulty, and suspicions of heresy were voiced by some members of the Curia; but the reformers had Papal support, and the appointment of Contarini to the Legation of Bologna, the second city of the Papal States, in January 1542 provided the group with greater powers. From Milan, Contarini was able to supervise the campaign through his connections with the leading prelates in the northern dioceses and his supporters in the Curia: Sadoleto at Carpentras, Cervini at Reggio–Emilia and later at Gubbio, Pole and his supporters at Viterbo, Giberti at Verona, and Morone, who became involved in the diocese of Modena through his position as Nuncio of the Romagna. In Mantua Gonzaga lent his weight through personal involvement, preaching, pastoral visits, and the encouragement of new lay confraternities; and by 1540, the year of Federico's death, Ercole had achieved sufficient impact to have attracted the attention of the Venetian ambassador.[26] These were the first steps in a policy which after 1540, with

[24] Jedin: *A history of the Council of Trent*, II, pp. 317–69.
[25] Ercole's institution of pastoral visits is discussed in Putelli: *Vita, storia ed arte mantovana*, II.
[26] See Friedensburg: 'Der Briefwechsel Gasparo Contarini's mit Ercole Gonzaga', Alberì: *Relazioni degli ambasciatori veneti*, II/ii, p. 16, and Segarizzi: *Relazioni degli ambasciatori veneti*, I, p. 56. On the progress of reform in general, see now D. Fenlon: *Heresy and obedience in Tridentine Italy*.

Fig. 4   Giulio Romano: Remodelled interior of the Cathedral of San Pietro,
Mantua (begun 1545). View from the west end (photo: Giovetti, Mantua;
reproduced by permission of the Ente Provinciale per il Turismo)

57

Ercole's assumption of greater political control, became increasingly rigorous. Although the bureaucratic reforms of the regency undoubtedly benefited administrative organisation particularly in the chancellery, and restored Gonzaga finances severely depleted after the profligacy of the late duke, Ercole's vision proved a mixed blessing for the general population. Efforts to improve social conditions included the reconstruction of the Ospedale Grande in 1545, but the Catholic Reformation also brought with it a flood of repressive measures against certain groups such as heretics and Jews, and against specific activities such as bigamy and clandestine marriages, which in turn presaged the more severe restrictions of the Inquisition.[27] As the pressure for reform gathered momentum and as Gonzaga began to achieve greater prestige within the deliberations of the *spirituali*, the spirit of the reform party was translated into practical terms by the increasing use of force within the Mantuan diocese. Quite clearly, Ercole's vision of reform was not confined to the spiritual but encompassed all aspects of Mantuan life, and his own strong position as a patron of the arts at personal, state, and Church levels made him a focal point of emerging ideas about the function of the arts in the service of the Catholic Reformation. And not surprisingly, the focal point of Ercole's artistic patronage lay not at the court but in the cathedral.

If Vasari is to be believed, one of Ercole's principal reasons for retaining Giulio Romano in court service after the death of Federico II was to use his expertise in reconstructing the Cathedral of San Pietro (Figure 4).[28] Under Federico, Giulio had been principally occupied since his arrival from Rome in 1524 with palace-building, firstly on the villa at Marmirolo, but from 1526 on the Palazzo del Te, that extraordinary synthesis of Giulio's ideas about architecture, interior decoration, and pictorial composition that was his preoccupation until the mid-1530s. For the remainder of Federico's life Giulio produced in quick succession the new rooms in the Castello and the Palazzina della Paleologa, the Appartamento di Troia, and the Rustica, as well as numerous public works and temporary decorations for pageants, plays and festivities; and when the age of gold came to an end, Giulio attached himself to Ercole as readily as he had done previously to his brother. The artist had executed religious commissions before, notably the Nativity and its accompanying frescoes for the Chapel of the Sacred Blood in Sant'Andrea in Mantua, and the frescoes in the apse of Verona Cathedral executed in

[27] The Ospedale Grande replaced the earlier building of 1449 which by 1545 had become hopelessly inadequate; see the documentation in ASM (AG) 3358 and the remarks in Donesmondi: *Dell'istoria*, p. 204. Donesmondi also notes (pp. 205–6) that Ercole left money to the Monte della Pietà for distribution to the poor, and praises his concern for the physical as well as the spiritual condition of the Mantuans. The introduction of repressive measures under Ercole is described in *Mantova. La storia*, II, pp. 448–9.

[28] Vasari–Milanesi: *Le vite*, v, p. 552. See also the brief accounts in Hartt: *Giulio Romano*, I, pp. 243–5, and *Mantova. Le arti*, II, pp. 212–13. For one contemporary Mantuan, Giovanni Battista Vigilio, the reform of San Pietro was Ercole's greatest achievement: see ASM (D'Arco) MS 168, Cap. 3.

1534, but during the final six years of his life which Giulio spent in Ercole's service, the building and decoration of churches became the artist's main work. Chief among the projects of these last years were the abbey church of San Benedetto Po begun in 1539 and left unfinished at Giulio's death, and the reconstruction of the cathedral started in 1545.

According to Vasari, Giulio was initially commissioned to prepare a drawing of a scheme and to calculate the cost with the master mason Battista da Covo.[29] By April 1545 the expenses of 16,000 *scudi* had been tabulated and the cost divided between the young duke (3,000), the male co-regents Don Ferrante and Cardinal Ercole (7,000 between them), and the clergy of the cathedral (2,000). The remainder was to be raised through a salt tax levied on the citizens, 'which will be paid with such ease that there will be no one who will even notice having paid', and on 15 April the duke issued a declaration stating his intention to rebuild and requesting the civic authorities to raise the levy. Work itself had apparently already begun, prompted by an extensive fire in the early part of the same month which made some demolition inevitable anyway, and by the end of the year the main parts of the interior were established and the organ put in place. With Giulio's death in November 1546 and Covo's demise shortly afterwards the reconstruction entered a period of uncertainty that was only resolved in 1549 when Bertani, who had come to prominence through designing the *apparato* for the entry of Philip II into Mantua in January of that year, took on the cathedral project as part of his new responsibilities as director of ducal building and architectural advisor to the cardinal. Bertani's main task was to complete the decoration of the interior started in 1547 and to supervise the arrangements for the side chapels, and as part of that work he commissioned nine altarpieces, designing three of them himself. The painting was assigned to artists from the Mantuan area or close to it, four being Veronese, and some had been placed in position by 1552. But work progressed slowly after this; in 1599 the cathedral was still unfinished, and it was Bishop Francesco Gonzaga who brought Giulio's scheme to its conclusion.[30]

[29] Gaye: *Carteggio*, II, pp. 326–9.

[30] The building history is described and documented in *Mantova. Le arti*, I, pp. 78–9, and II, pp. 212–13. For the paintings see Vasari–Milanesi: *Le vite*, VI, pp. 488–9, and Perina: 'Bertanus invenit'.

    Francesco was most actively concerned with the appearance of the cathedral from 1593 to 1609. In 1593 he renovated the façade; in 1594 he consecrated the building; in 1595–6 he began the construction of the cupola and the choir; in 1598 he ordered tapestries from Paris to hang on the piers of the crossing; in 1599 he presented cloth of gold to the sacristy, embellished the main altar, built two new side altars, frescoed the walls of the transepts, and made alterations to the high altar. In 1600 a marble balustrade was built at the entrance to the choir; in 1605 'seguitava tuttavia con nuovi ornamenti d'abbelire la sua Cattedrale'; and in 1600 a new altar was dedicated to San Luigi Gonzaga. In 1607 he gave seven silver candlesticks and a cross for the high altar; and the next year the eight large tapestries from Paris were finished and placed in the Cappella Grande. See Donesmondi: *Dell'istoria*, pp. 308f, 321, 332, 341, 350, 358, 361f, 402, 411 and 432ff. The completion of the project is thoroughly dealt with in Askew: 'The question of Fetti as fresco painter'.

The Council of Trent's views on reform, published in 1564, sensibly laid down the most general of guidelines, leaving bishops to interpret them in more precise terms suitable to local contexts. For the most part, the large body of sixteenth-century literature produced to propagate and clarify the Tridentine attitude towards the arts focused on moral and doctrinal concerns, and inevitably, reformers were more interested in piety than in aesthetic quality, though the pursuit of the former obviously involved a serious consideration of the latter.[31] In its attempt to find art that would 'educate' and inspire devotion, the Church required works that spoke a plain and simple language with conviction, relying on an accepted and orthodox iconographical tradition, and in the most general terms it is this simple principle which lies behind Tridentine thinking about all the arts. In practical terms, this attitude paid special attention to instances of iconographical licence or impropriety in the representation of religious subjects; Veronese's indictment by the Inquisition for the genre elements in his *Supper in the house of Simon*[32] and the strong objections to the nudity in Michelangelo's *Last Judgement* are the most celebrated cases of these fundamental aspects of Counter-Reformation criticism in action. So in stylistic terms these requirements involved a reaction against central Italian mannerism with its emphasis on sophistication and intellectualism, and this much is clear from the critical stance of the theologian Gilio da Fabriano, one of the earliest writers to translate the Tridentine decree into practical terms, and from the well-known later treatise of Gabrielle Paleotti, Archbishop of Bologna.[33] In architecture it was mainly due to Cardinal Borromeo, Archbishop of Milan from 1566, that the ideals of Trent became influential in Lombardy, partly through the now official policy of pastoral visits, but also through his *Instructiones* on church building and decoration first published in 1577.[34] Here, in the most practical and comprehensible way, Counter-Reformation principles are applied to themes which, since Alberti, had been left to the tastes of individual patrons and architects. It has been claimed that some aspects of the *Instructiones* embody architectural types that had already been used in some Milanese churches of the 1560s such as Sant'Angelo, the Olivetan church of San Vittore al Corpo worked on by Galeazzo Alessi, and SS. Paolo e Barnaba which the same architect designed for the new Counter-Reformation order of the Barnabites.[35] This has been held to be particularly true of the disposition of the choir and transept and the placing of the choir stalls behind the altar, points on which Borromeo's treatise is particularly specific. What is interesting about the arrangements at San

---

[31] Blunt: *Artistic theory*, chapter 8.
[32] Fehl: 'Veronese and the Inquisition'.
[33] Fabriano: *Dialogo degli errori*. For Paleotti see Prodi: *Il Cardinale Gabrielle Paleotti*, and the same author's 'Ricerche sulla teorica'.
[34] Borromeo: *Instructionum fabricae*, Barocchi: *Trattati*, III, pp. 9ff, and Blunt: *Artistic theory*, pp. 127–32.
[35] Heydenreich and Lotz: *Architecture in Italy 1400 to 1600*, pp. 293–6.

Pietro in Mantua is that in a number of details such as the placement of the stalls, the arrangement of the high altar and its relation to the side altars, and the connections between the sacristy and the high altar, Giulio's design again anticipates later Counter-Reformation practice, and in its creation of a large interior space San Pietro is again close to Tridentine views. Moreover, it seems highly likely that Ercole played a considerable role in the design of the cathedral; Vasari strongly implies that the renovation was the Cardinal's own idea, and the ducal patent of 15 April 1545 no doubt represents Ercole's views to a considerable extent.[36] The old structure was unsatisfactory, the document claimed, because 'one cannot find a cathedral smaller and uglier than ours, and so badly constructed that very few people can hear, let alone see, when the divine offices are celebrated, especially on holy days'. Mantua deserved something better 'so that it should not be inferior in this respect to the other cities of Italy'. In fact, Giulio was almost certainly presented with a Romanesque basilica with five aisles which had been rebuilt and decorated in the Gothic style in 1403 to produce a seven-aisle structure. This no doubt presented certain restrictions on the arrangement of the interior space, but it can hardly account for the correctness of so much of the decorative detail, which is in such startling contrast to the fantasy of Giulio's earlier works that one historian has suggested it to be Bertani's work. But in its sober classicism San Pietro is not alone among Giulio's late works, the most important of which were all ecclesiastical commissions, and it is not fantastic to suggest that this new sobriety in the work of one of the most fantastical and unorthodox artists of the age was conditioned by what his principal employer thought was appropriate. Interestingly, the final result has been compared to an early Christian basilica,[37] precisely the model that Borromeo was later to commend to architects in the *Instructiones*. It may also be that Ferrante Gonzaga, the other co-regent named in the patent, was influential since he too seems to have sponsored the construction of churches with Tridentine tendencies, principally the Franciscan monastery of Sant'Angelo in Milan, designed by Ferrante's personal architect Domenico Giunti da Prato (1506–60) who had been employed by Ferrante in Sicily and had then been brought by him to Milan in 1546 where Ferrante had been appointed viceroy.[38]

An interpretation of the reconstruction of San Pietro as a product of Ercole's reformist principles applied to ecclesiastical architecture may find some support from the little that can be inferred about the arrangement of the altarpieces. Four of the artists commissioned were from Verona, an important centre of reformist thought during the episcopacy of Ercole's close friend Giberti, and one where particular attention was paid to the function

[36] The patent is printed in Gaye: *Carteggio*, II, pp. 326–9.
[37] Hartt: *Giulio Romano*, I, pp. 235, 244–5.
[38] Heydenreich and Lotz: *Architecture in Italy 1400 to 1600*, pp. 292–3.

and style of the arts in the service of the Catholic Reformation. And, as noted already, Verona was probably influential in some of the practical details of reform at a local level which were subsequently taken up in Mantua. Vasari emphasises in his account of Michele Sanmichele that the artists for the San Pietro altarpieces were chosen by Ercole,[39] and it seems most likely from the surviving documentation that the choice of artist and subject matter was made by the cardinal, leaving technical details to be managed by Bertani.[40] Unfortunately none of the paintings is known to survive, but certainly Ercole seems to have had some interest in devotional painting. In May 1546, during the important debate at Trent concerning the Bible, one of his protégés, Bishop Bertano, took time off to gratify one of Ercole's enthusiasms by acquiring from Cardinal Pole a *Pietà* by Michelangelo in which Ercole had shown an interest.[41] And of course Giulio Romano designed many objects of a private nature for Ercole, though few of them indicate any particular depth of religious feeling so much as the Cardinal's taste for luxury. As we have seen, Giulio's ecclesiastical buildings are more reminiscent of the palace or the temple than of the Christian church, and it was the dramatic rather than the spiritual aspects of religious subjects that engaged him. A single remark by Vasari allied to some ambiguous documents is not hard evidence, but the central point is clear and well supported. From the third decade of the century, Ercole Gonzaga, established by the mid-1530s as an influential and prestigious member of the central group of reformers within the Italian Church, was putting the ideals of that group into practice at Mantua where his positions as co-regent and cardinal–bishop placed him in an unusually strong position to carry through reform in the civil, ecclesiastical, political, social, and cultural spheres of Mantuan life. As far as religious conditions are concerned, many of the central ideas of Trent itself are anticipated through Ercole's firm belief in residence, institution of pastoral visits, and general supervision of the moral and religious condition of both clergy and laity; and as Bishop of Mantua Ercole took particular care of the operations at the Cathedral of San Pietro, which functioned as a focal point and symbol of renewal.

After his return from the *Studium* in Bologna in 1525, Ercole took an interest in music which seems to have revitalised the musical activities at the cathedral, which had apparently deteriorated since Marchese Francesco's death in 1519. Francesco, it will be remembered, was originally responsible for the foundation of a Gonzaga *cappella* in the Chapel of Santa Maria dei Voti in 1510, and it was Francesco rather than Isabella who appears to have sponsored religious art including music. A little is known about the operations of the *cappella* in its first years. By February of 1511 the new singers were

[39] Vasari–Milanesi: *Le vite*, vi, pp. 367–8.
[40] *Mantova. Le arti*, iii, pp. 340–4.   [41] Jedin: *A history of the Council of Trent*, ii, p. 473.

present at a number of offices attended by Francesco and Isabella; and the sometimes sudden documented contractions and expansions of the group in the next few years testify to its continuation. Six singers left to join the Papal Chapel in 1514 and others returned to Ferrara about the same time, but the *cappella* survived these difficulties and the death of Francesco himself. The repertory of the *cappella* is not definitely known, though it has been suggested that the ten Petrucci publications surviving in the Santa Barbara collection, and mostly devoted to masses by Josquin, Obrecht, and other composers of the same generation, were originally acquired for Francesco's foundation rather than for Santa Barbara, and although the books may have been acquired by Ercole it is noticeable that they include a good deal of music written by composers associated with Ferrara, where Francesco acquired other music and singers for his foundation. Polyphonic music continued to be performed after Francesco's death, and in 1521 (one year after the beginning of Ercole's episcopacy) a letter from Giovanni Arcario speaks of a solemn mass of the Virgin sung in *canto figurato* with organ accompaniment.[42] But the next major phase of interest in music at the cathedral follows hard upon Ercole's return from Bologna, and although detailed records of the size of the choir have not yet come to light for the whole of Ercole's period as bishop, the few that have survived suggest a steady growth in size comparable to that noted elsewhere. In 1528 there were eighteen men (and about twelve boys), while in 1565 the choir clergy stood at thirty-two,[43] though some caution must be exercised in interpreting the documents, which do not necessarily include under a musical heading men who are known from other contexts to have had considerable musical abilities, while some of the singers clearly held only temporary appointments. From 1521 until his retirement in 1556, the organist at the cathedral was 'Girolamo Organista' – sometimes thought to be the distinguished organist Girolamo Cavazzoni, but in reality a younger man, Girolamo de Araldis.[44] He was succeeded by Giovanni Battista Recalco, presumably the composer of the same name, who is recorded for the first time in 1564.[45] Apart from Jacquet of Mantua, who is noted for the first time in 1527 but who probably arrived in the city earlier, the only other known composer in the *cappella* during Cardinal Ercole's episcopacy was Pre Lauro, mentioned by the cardinal in a letter of 1532 as a chaplain and apparently, judging from the context of the letter, then functioning as *maestro di canto*, a post which had previously been held by Don Francesco da Ostiglio (1526–7) and Don Pietro da Candia (1528–33). Pre

---

[42] For details of the early history of Marchese Francesco's *cappella* see Prizer: 'La cappella di Francesco II Gonzaga'. For Arcario's letter see Appendix II, doc. 7.

[43] Tagmann: *Archivalische Studien*, pp. 32 and 35–6.

[44] The belief that Cavazzoni worked at the cathedral has now been disposed of in Tagmann: *Archivalische Studien*, pp. 38–40 and 82. See also George Nugent's review of the book, and his communication in the *Journal of the American Musicological Society*, xxv (1972), pp. 492–3.

[45] Tagmann: *Archivalische Studien*, pp. 41ff.

Lauro may in turn be the tenor Don Hieronymo recorded at Mantua in 1509 and 1526,[46] the composer Laurus whose work appears in manuscript collections, and the frottolist Hieronimo de Lauro known from a number of printed collections.[47] Equally he may be the Pre Lauro placed in the company of Willaert, Cavazzoni and Francesco da Milano, amongst others, in Pietro Aretino's *Il marescalco*, which has a Mantuan setting.[48]

In so far as any conclusions can be drawn from incomplete data, it would seem that the number of adult singers of polyphony at San Pietro, which by the mid-1520s seems to have stabilised at about fifteen, is quite large by contemporary standards. Of the chapels for which reliable statistics are available, the Sistine Chapel maintained the largest establishment, which varied between sixteen and twenty-one singers in the first decade of the sixteenth century and – after an expansion during the Papacy of the music-loving Leo X – settled at twenty-two to twenty-four singers during the late 1520s under Clement VII. Mantua Cathedral's complement makes it comparable with the larger Italian institutions such as Siena Cathedral, while the cathedrals at Milan, Florence, Padua and other large towns in the north rarely employed more than a dozen singers.[49] Unfortunately there is never sufficient information about the distribution of voices in the choir; but a little is known about its duties and operations. The liturgy called for a daily low mass, when motets could be performed, as well as Vespers and Benediction; on Sundays and feast-days solemn high mass was celebrated at the high altar; and on Saturdays the choir sang mass in the Chapel of the Madonna. Rehearsals took place in a sacristy beneath the cathedral tower, and the singers sometimes entered the church in procession. The organ in the Gonzaga chapel continued to be used as well as the instrument in the main chapel, and there was also a portable organ for rehearsals, but otherwise no other type of instrumental accompaniment is noted until 1588.[50]

Similarly, the employment of a composer of Jacquet's ability at an institution outside the five most important political centres (Rome, Naples, Milan, Florence, and Venice) is another indication of a keen interest in polyphonic music, and the fact that Jacquet was paid by the cardinal rather than the cathedral chapter underlines Ercole's personal interest in the music arrangements at the cathedral, an interest which is also revealed in correspondence. The abiding problem of finding and training new singers

---

[46] Ercole's letter of 11 April 1532 is summarised in Bautier-Regnier: 'Jachet de Mantoue', p. 106; the original is in ASM (AG) 1946 fasc. 7. For the tenor known as Don Hieronymo see Tagmann: *Archivalische Studien*, pp. 33 and 65–77.

[47] Compositions by Laurus appear in RISM 1517², 1520⁵, 1526⁵, 1530¹, 1542¹⁶, and in Perugia, Biblioteca Augusta MS I.M. 1079, Bologna Conservatorio MS Q21, and Bergamo Cathedral MS 1209 D (for the Bologna manuscript see Gallico: *Un canzoniere musicale*, and for the Perugia source Fenlon and Haar: 'Fonti e cronologia', pp. 226ff). The situation is further complicated by the fact that Verdelot was occasionally known as Laurus: see Jacobs (ed.): *Miguel de Fuenllana*, p. lxiii.

[48] Aretino: *Il marescalco*, Act V Scene iii.

[49] D'Accone: 'The performance of sacred music'.

[50] Tagmann: *Archivalische Studien*, pp. 36ff and 70, and Nugent's review of the book.

was one in which Ercole sometimes became personally involved, and there are indications too of his concern over the domestic problems and conditions of the singers employed by the cathedral (cf. Figure 5).[51] Ercole had some contacts with composers elsewhere. In 1547 Hoste da Reggio dedicated his first book of madrigals to the cardinal, a gesture which may have helped him secure a position with Ercole's brother Ferrante, whose musical interests are known from other sources. Fourteen years later the Parmesan Paolo Clerico dedicated to Ercole two madrigal books including settings of texts by Scipione Gonzaga; and the cardinal's letters occasionally contain requests for music by other composers.[52]

As Bishop of Mantua, Ercole maintained a private household in the Bishop's Palace. Few documents survive referring to the arrangements there, and it is only for the years 1537, 1547, and 1561 that they exist in any quantity, but a good proportion of this rather small corpus comprises references to musical activities. The most frequent references are payments to singers and instrumentalists: in 1537 there are payments to the court trombone and *piffero* players as well as to a group of visiting *pifferi* and the ducal drummers, probably for services during the carnival, and at the end of 1547 there are payments for the purchase of violin and viol strings, suggesting perhaps that the cardinal maintained a permanent ensemble. Some of the musicians paid from the household accounts are named in the few surviving registers: a 'M^ro Jacheto Musico' is presumably Jacquet of Mantua, and Giovanni Battista Fachetto may be the Brescian organ-builder who worked on a number of projects for the Gonzaga, principally at the monastery at San Benedetto Po, the other major reconstruction undertaken during Ercole's regency, where he was employed in 1552.[53] A last group of payments comes from 1561, the year in which Ercole was appointed president of the third session of the Council of Trent. Despite the cardinal's injunction against luxury issued to the diocese in 1551,[54] his own life style at Mantua does not seem to have been particularly abstemious, and Trent itself was evidently used as an opportunity for display by some of the delegates. French and Spanish bishops for example were generally accompanied by suites of twenty-five or thirty people, but Ercole had a following of 160.[55] There was an acute shortage of accommodation during the sessions, but the two most

---

[51] A selection of letters demonstrating Ercole's personal concern for the welfare of musicians at the cathedral is given in Appendix II, docs. 8–12.

[52] See Hoste: *Primo libro de madrigali*, Clerico: *Li madrigali a cinque voci libro primo*, and Clerico: *Li madrigali a cinque voci libro secondo*. Writing to Ercole II d'Este in April 1532, Ercole expressed a high opinion of the music of Maistre Jhan, remembering in particular a (now lost) seven-voice mass performed with voil accompaniment, and requesting copies of all his compositions. See ASMod Carteggio con i principi esteri, Roma 1373, excerpted in Segre: 'Un registro di lettere', p. 411. In 1549 Ercole was in correspondence with Adriano Willaert, *maestro di cappella* at St Mark's in Venice, in a search for singers: see Appendix II, doc. 13.

[53] Original documents in ASDM (MV); a selection is presented in Appendix II, docs. 14–20.

[54] The injunction is printed in Amadei: *Cronaca universale*, II, pp. 657–64.

[55] Sickel: *Römische Bericht*, I, p. 21.

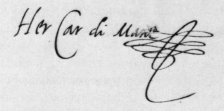

Andreasio: ogni uolta che a M.ro Piachetto mio Maestro di
capella accascara bisogno alcuno di far notar, o, spender
in cosa che appertenga alla musica, vi cōmetto per Virtù
di questa mia et voglio che gli prouediate di qlli denari
ch'egli vi ricercara, senza aspettar da me cōmissione
più particolar di questa, La quale intendo et serua
adesso perche gli habbiate a dare il modo di farmi notar uno libro di motetti, et nell'auenir fin'a tanto et
da me vi sara cōmesso altro in contrario, state sano
Di Roma il · x · di decembre · M · xxxv.

Her Car di Mant

Fig. 5   Letter of Cardinal Ercole Gonzaga, Rome 10 December 1535, to
Francesco Andreasio (Appendix II, doc. 11)

66

spacious residences in the town, the two connected houses of the influential Thun family which are now the town hall, were used as a base by Ercole, and later by Morone during the last phase of the council.[56] Evidently the entourage at Trent included musicians, and the 1561 documents include disbursals for putting instruments in order and for the travelling expenses of singers. It is clear that the cardinal's principal agent in these arrangements was the Brescian Giovanni Maria di Rossi, *maestro di cappella* at Mantua Cathedral from 1563, and that some members of his music establishment were moving with him between Mantua and Trent at this time. But perhaps the most intriguing documents among these few survivals are those that give a glimpse of music being copied. In April 1538, and again in 1547, the documents register payments for binding music books. The usual practice was for unbound books to pass via one of the cardinal's stewards to the bookbinder and to return the same way, but the 1538 payment specifies that the bound volume of ruled paper should return to 'M^ro Jachetto' (undoubtedly Jacquet of Mantua) who was yet to enter compositions in it. The 1547 documents name both Pre Lauro and another musician at the cathedral, Paolo Campora, so that again Ercole's personal subsidy of the cathedral music is emphasised.[57]

Records of secular music at court during Ercole's regency are sparse. Amongst occasional notices of other singers and instrumentalists, Abraam de Louin (Abramo dell'Arpa) is noted from 1542;[58] and of the few musicians known to have served Duke Federico, only the singer and lutenist Roberto Avanzini seems to have been active during the regency (born in Mantua in 1480, and recorded as a pupil of Cara in 1512, Avanzini continues to appear in court records until a few years before his death in 1560).[59] Apart from

---

[56] Jedin: *Papal legate*, p. 565.

[57] See Appendix II, docs. 14 and 16. There are more of Cardinal Ercole's household receipts in ASM (AP) 5 (1549–50), 6 (1539, 1553), and 7 (1559–61). They include further payments for instrument strings in large numbers (ASM (AP) 7 fasc. 1559, nos. 43, 125, and 166), for instrumentalists (ASM (AP) 7 fasc. 1559, no. 126), and for having instruments made (ASM (AP) 6 fasc. 1553: payments of 15 December and 6 February to 'Zoan dale viole cremonese'). The agent in many of these arrangements was Giovanni Maria di Rossi. There are further payments to Jacquet of Mantua (ASM (AP) 5 fasc. I, fos. 5v and 14v), and a payment was made in 1539 (ASM (AP) 6) 'per aver ligato li motetti di Jachetto ha cinque libri', presumably one of Scotto's two publications of that year. A number of other payments to musicians are recorded including one to 'R^do Fra Pietro Musicho' (ASM (AP) 6, 1 March 1553), and another to 'M^ro Cipriano Musico'. In view of the size of the latter disbursement, 25 *scudi d'oro in oro*, it is possible that 'M^ro Cipriano' was Rore. The receipt is in ASM (AP) 7, no. 126.

[58] For dell'Arpa, who died in 1566, see A. Bertolotti: *Musici alla corte dei Gonzaga*, p. 35, and the original documentation in ASM (AG) 401, p. 40, and ASDM (Cap.) LM 2897 (1552) fo. 172.

[59] Avanzini is noted in A. Bertolotti: *Musici alla corte dei Gonzaga*, pp. 21–2, Canal: *Della musica in Mantova*, pp. 674–5, and Tagmann: *Archivalische Studien*, pp. 65–6. There is a good deal of additional material, not referred to in these studies, which shows that Avanzini was a permanent resident, notably ASDM (MV) Sezione II Registro 60 (*olim* 58). Investiture di terre appartenenti all'episcopato mantovano 1527–1530, fos. 148–9, and ASDM (MV) Sezione II Registro 64 (*olim* 62). Investiture di terre appartenenti all'episcopato mantovano 1533–1539, fo. 187; also ASDM (MV) Sezione III – Registri. Serie Licenze dell'episcopato, Registro 5 "Licenze" 1533–38 parte II, fo. 7v, and ASDM (MV) Sezione

dell'Arpa and Avanzini, there seem to have been no other musicians in regular court employment except the *alta cappella*. The *memoria* drawn up in 1554 by the President of the Ducal Treasury, Giulio Cavriani, for the information of Duchess Margherita, mother of the young Duke Guglielmo, lists only 'Roberto [Avanzini] cantore' as a salaried courtier, while dell'Arpa appears in the 'nota di tutte le bocche che si trovano in corte'.[60] As in earlier years, additional musicians were probably employed and the resources of court and cathedral merged for ceremonial occasions, state visits, and festivities. During the course of the regency a number of state visits and dynastic marriages were elaborately celebrated, notably the visit of Charles V to Canneto in 1543,[61] the visits of Maximilian of Austria in 1548 and 1551,[62] the visit of Philip II in 1549,[63] and the marriage of Duke Francesco to Caterina of Austria in 1549,[64] yet although quite precise accounts survive of some of these occasions they do not mention music. Similarly, although some contemporaries claim Ercole as an enthusiastic patron of the theatre, and although it was he who commissioned Bertani's new court theatre (constructed between 1549 and 1551), no music has so far come to light that can be associated with productions there.[65] This is not surprising; the only composer of any consequence resident at Mantua was Jacquet, and his activities as Ercole's private musician were directed almost entirely towards the composition of liturgical music.

To speak of Jacquet of Mantua is immediately to confront the problem arising out of the contemporary habit of referring to composers and musicians by their Christian names only. The first attempts to deal with the difficulties of confused biographies and conflicting attributions that have resulted were made towards the end of the nineteenth century, when the Mantuan Jacquet was distinguished from other Flemish musicians of the same name on the basis

III – Registri. Serie Licenze dell'episcopato, Registro 6 "Licenze" 1541–46 parte I, fo. 14 – all referring to legal transactions. Avanzini's death on 22 January 1560 is recorded in ASM (AG) 3089. The other principal court musician of Federico's time was Pozino, active from 1501 until at least 1532. See Bertolotti: *Musici alla corte dei Gonzaga*, pp. 21 and 26, Frey: 'Michelangiolo und die Komponisten', p. 153, and Tagmann: *Archivalische Studien*, p. 13. See also Appendix II, doc. 2.

[60] The *memoria* is preserved in ASM (AG) 401 and records dell'Arpa and Avanzini together with 'Isabella ballarina' as the only musicians in the permanent household of the court (see pp. 34, 40, 41, and 43 of the document). The *memoria* itself has now been published in De Maddalena: *La finanze del ducato di Mantova* as Appendix 1.

[61] Amadei: *Cronaca universale*, II, pp. 609ff, the documentation in ASM (AG) 199, and the letter of L. Zaffanto, 25 June 1543, in ASM (AG) 2533.

[62] Donesmondi: *Dell'istoria*, and Possevino the Younger: *Gonzaga*, p. 750.

[63] Ulloa: *La vita*, Lib. IV, pp. 256ff.

[64] The best general account of entries and celebrations for the period after 1549 is now Fabbri: *Gusto scenico*, which gives (pp. 107ff) a useful list of primary and secondary source material, though there is still much valuable material in Intra: 'Nozze e funerali'.

[65] In addition to the material listed in Fabbri: *Gusto scenico*, p. 108, the references to Ercole's patronage of the theatre in [Castellani]: *Componimenti*, fos. 12–12v should be noted.

of archival evidence which showed that he was born in Brittany.[66] Subsequently, efforts were made to resolve cases of doubtful or conflicting attributions on stylistic criteria, and there the matter rested until further archival work revealed additional biographical details.[67] In the last twenty-five years a number of attempts have been made to clarify the issue through both stylistic analysis and archival work, but it is only recently that any generally agreed view of the main outlines of the composer's life and his authorship of motets has emerged, while the number of masses that should be attributed to him is still in dispute.[68] According to the latest résumé of biographical information Jacquet, the composer most widely known by this single unqualified name during the period, was born Jacques Colebault in 1483, probably in Vitré in Brittany; this much is evident from documents.[69] He was perhaps related to the singer Antoine Colebault (Bidon), and by the end of the second decade of the sixteenth century, when his compositions began to be copied into north Italian manuscripts, he had probably travelled to Italy where he attracted the patronage of a number of élite families. It has recently been suggested that he may be the 'Jacquet' referred to in a letter of 5 July 1516 from Jean Michel, then in service at the Ferrarese court as principal music copyist and ducal singer, to Sigismondo d'Este. If this is correct, Jacquet was apparently then in Ferrara.[70] He may be identifiable with a 'Giachetto cantore da Spilamberto' paid from Pope Leo X's private accounts in 1519 and 1520, in which case he was then in the service of the Modenese branch of the Rangoni family, neighbours of the Este.[71] His next move may have been back to Ferrara itself, where a 'Iachetto' is recorded in a list of payments to musicians in 1525; but at some time in 1526 he had probably arrived in Mantua, since the death of his thirty-year-old wife

[66] Haberl: 'Das Archiv der Gonzaga in Mantua', p. 40, and the same author's *Die römische 'Schola Cantorum'*, Eitner: 'Jachet da Mantua', and Haberl's review of A. Bertolotti: *Musici alla corte dei Gonzaga*.

[67] Huber: 'Die Doppelmeister' attempts to resolve the difficulties through stylistic analysis. Further archival information was subsequently presented in Bautier-Regnier: 'Jachet de Mantoue'.

[68] Widmaier: 'Jachet von Mantua', Tagmann: *Archivalische Studien*, Jackson: 'The masses of Jacquet of Mantua', and particularly Nugent: 'The Jacquet motets'.

[69] Jacquet is called 'Collebaudi' in the decree of 1534 granting him citizenship. See Haberl's review of A. Bertolotti: *Musici alla corte dei Gonzaga*, p. 114, and my own transcription in Appendix II, doc. 21. Similarly, in the registration of his death in ASM (AG) 3088, Affari di Polizia III: 'M. Jac° di Cholebaudi in contrada leon vermilio morto di febra infermo giorni 10 di eta anni 76' (2 October 1559).

[70] The letter, in ASMod Ambasciatori, comments on music copying by Jacquet and later advises: '... ne laissez point perdre le temps a notre maistre Jacquet qu'il ne compose aulcune foys et qu'il ne soit point amouroulx de faulcons flacons et de se qui est dedans, qu'il ya oste l'entendement...' Lewis Lockwood, who first discussed this letter in 'Jean Mouton and Jean Michel: New evidence on French music and musicians in Italy, 1505–1520' (*Abstracts*, p. 13; for a revised version see Lockwood: 'Jean Mouton and Jean Michel', listed in my bibliography, below), is of the opinion that 'Jacquet' is Jacquet of Mantua. (I am grateful to Professor Lockwood, whose transcription I quote, for permission to cite his work prior to publication.)

[71] The possible relationships are suggested in A. Bertolotti: *Musici alla corte dei Gonzaga*, pp. 27–8, Bautier-Regnier: 'Jachet de Mantoue', p. 43, Tagmann: *Archivalische Studien*, p. 16, n. 4, and Nugent: 'The Jacquet motets', p. 60; Nugent concludes that Jacquet and Antoine were brothers or cousins. For the suggestion that Jacquet may have worked for Leo X see below, p. 72, note 77.

Apollonia is recorded there in January 1527.[72] Although his association with Cardinal Ercole is firmly documented only from 1534, the year in which he was also granted Mantuan citizenship, it is reasonable to assume that Jacquet was brought to Mantua by Ercole in late 1525 or 1526 and remained in his employment throughout the rest of his career until his death in the city on 2 October 1559. His presence and responsibilities in Mantua are frequently documented in the intervening years, and it seems from the records that Jacquet was paid by the cardinal rather than the cathedral, despite his official title; the payments themselves were inadequate and he died in debt.[73]

Jacquet's contemporary reputation owed a great deal to the growth of music printing during his lifetime, though his work was also widely disseminated in manuscript. Scotto was Jacquet's principal publisher, and the first to issue publications devoted exclusively to his work – the two motet publications of 1539, both dedicated to Ercole Gonzaga. Between then and 1567 Scotto produced nine further volumes devoted exclusively to Jacquet's compositions. Gardane also issued a considerable amount of Jacquet's music, including three volumes of motets published in 1540, but none carries a dedication and the first two volumes follow suspiciously close on the heels of Scotto's volumes and duplicate large portions of their contents. Gardane can on the other hand be convincingly shown to have been Jacquet Berchem's official publisher; and the close connection of each composer with one publisher increases the value of their printed attributions. In general, Scotto is quite careful to identify Jacquet as 'de Mantova' in publications devoted entirely to his own work, no doubt as a way of associating the composer with Ercole's patronage, while in collections of pieces by several composers he refers to Jacquet by his Christian name only but distinguishes his namesake as Jacquet Berchem. The logical conclusion – though it still leaves some difficulties of conflicting attributions unresolved, particularly when the inconsistent practices of scribes are introduced into the relatively consistent picture presented by printing-house practices – is that the unqualified attribution 'Jacquet' normally refers to Jacquet of Mantua, and that after 1540 when Jacquet Berchem's work began to appear in print his place of origin (near Antwerp) was appended to his Christian name as a way of distinguishing the two men. Moreover, the same usage was adopted by

[72] The Ferrarese lists are in ASMod Bolleta de li saliarati de la camera ducale, and were first noted in Nugent: 'The Jacquet motets', p. 74. What is usually taken to be the first indication of Jacquet's presence in Mantua is the registration of his wife's death, first given in Widmaier: 'Jachet von Mantua', p. 9, n. 1; the original is in ASM (AG) 3068, Affari di Polizia III: 'Polonia uxor de m. Jachet cantoris in contrada griffonij morta est ex fabera et gelibus fuit infirma per mesi cinque aetatis anni 30' (29 January 1527).

[73] The important point that Jacquet was employed by Ercole rather than directly by the chapter is argued in Nugent: 'The Jacquet motets', who notes that Jacquet received only occasional payments for special duties from the chapter, in contrast to the rest of the *cappella* who were paid regularly as recorded in the accounts in ASDM (Cap.). Many of these occasional payments are given by Nugent (pp. 41–54): my own transcriptions of a selection, giving some idea of Jacquet's duties and his relations with Ercole, are presented in Appendix II, docs. 8ff.

theorists, and the general currency of the practice (especially since so few pieces survive only in manuscript copies) alleviates considerably the problem of attribution.[74]

This is equally true of masses and of motets. In the case of the four-voice motets, for example, the sources ascribe forty-three pieces to either Jacquet of Mantua, Jachet de Berchem, or merely Jachet, thirty-nine in printed collections and four only in manuscripts. Difficulties of missing or conflicting attributions are helped considerably by the three large Venetian anthologies devoted to Jacquet: Scotto's first volume of 1539 which contains twenty-four pieces, his second collection of twenty-two motets published in 1544 which duplicates some of the contents of the first but also contains some new pieces, and Gardane's anthology of one year later which includes some further new works but is heavily dependent upon Scotto's second collection. Seventeen compositions are common to all three publications, which between them establish a hard core of thirty-four motets for which Jacquet's authorship is, with one exception, generally accepted. Of the remainder, Scotto published 'Nos pueri' twice with clear attributions to Jacquet of Mantua, and 'Levavi' and 'Praeparate' were printed in an anthology published in Lyons by Moderne, whose other ascriptions to 'Jacquet', verifiable from concordant sources, apply without exception to the works of Jacquet of Mantua. This leaves in doubt a number of works in Bologna Q19, and a handful of pieces with conflicting attributions.

The important problem of dating sources and compositions, and attributing authorship of works, is raised here not in its own right but because it is a necessary part of another question, the extent to which this process can provide additional information about Jacquet's activities and patrons in the crucial first decades of his career. Secure evidence of his connection with Ercole exists only for the period after 1534, and while it is traditionally assumed that Jacquet came to Mantua about 1526 there are no hard facts to support it. Beyond that there is only speculation about his early years, but the view that he may have been connected with the Este court at Ferrara as early as 1516 and is perhaps identifiable with the 'Jachetto' noted there in 1525 is supported by evidence from the sources themselves. Although none of Jacquet's four-voice motets appeared in print until Scotto's first collection of 1539, some of them were composed as early as the final years of the second decade of the century and then circulated in manuscript. The earliest source for any of them is Bologna Q19, a choirbook whose small dimensions and unsophisticated calligraphy suggest that it was compiled for private practical use. It is largely devoted to compositions by French composers, headed by Mouton. The name Sebastiano Festa and the date '1518 adi 10...zugno' which appear on fo. [2v] in a contemporary hand have led one historian to

---

[74] This conclusion is reached in Nugent: 'The Jacquet motets', pp. 359ff, the most searching and authoritative attempt to establish a corpus of Jacquet's works.

suggest that Costanzo Festa edited the manuscript, and to assert that the manuscript was probably copied by Festa in France for presentation to Diane de Poitiers. His principal evidence for this interpretation is the presence of an *ex libris* bearing a stag chained to a tree (an emblem known to have been used by Diane), flanked by the initials DP on one of the opening leaves.[75] But the *ex libris*, a collage, is later work, part of an attempt to give Bologna Q19 a more elaborate appearance; and in any event the emblem was not exclusive to Diane, and the version of it presented in Q19 is significantly different in both character and execution from the examples in books and manuscripts which she is known to have owned. In addition, the paper on which Q19 is copied carries a watermark most frequently associated with mills in the Venetian area, and the compelling evidence for Italian origins which these facts taken together provide is strengthened by further paleographical and other details. There can be little doubt that Bologna Q19 was copied in northern Italy, most probably in the Emilian region.[76]

The arguments are of obvious importance in the context of Jacquet's life and works, since his pieces in Bologna Q19 are the earliest traces of his career. The source contains seven compositions ascribed to 'Jacquet', of which the paired responsories 'O vos qui transitis' and 'Cogitationes meae' later appeared in Scotto's 1544 collection and Gardane's 1545 anthology, and since these are consequently undoubtedly Jacquet's work it has been reasonably assumed that the remaining compositions are also his. Certainly it is not surprising to find Jacquet's earliest known works in an Emilian manuscript of this date into which a good deal of local repertory is copied. It has been argued that the earliest records of Jacquet's employment date from 1519, and that he was then in the service of the Rangoni family of Modena, most probably under the personal patronage of Cardinal Ercole dei Rangoni (1491–1527), Bishop of Adria in 1519 and Bishop of Modena five years later.[77] It is also with that area that Bologna Q19 is most firmly connected, since before its acquisition by what is now the Civico Museo in Bologna it belonged to the Rusconi family, one of the prominent aristocratic families of the area, whose name is inscribed on the spine of the present binding. North Italian associations are also underlined by other manuscript sources. Bologna Q20, usually thought to have been copied about 1520, contains five works, two of which also appear in Q19, and the latter also shares one composition with

[75] Bologna, Civico Museo Bibliografico-Musicale MS Q19. For this view of the origins and provenance of the manuscript see Lowinsky: *The Medici codex*, 1, pp. 52–60, and the same author's 'On the presentation and interpretation of evidence'.

[76] This interpretation, based on detailed first-hand examination of the source, agrees with the evidence and conclusions reached in Leeman L. Perkins's review of Lowinsky: *The Medici codex*, in Crawford: 'A review of Costanzo Festa's biography', and in Finscher: 'Der Medici-Kodex'.

[77] See Frey: 'Regesten' (1956), p. 143, where Leo X's private accounts record payments in January 1519 to 'Maestro Giachetto cantore da Spilamberto', and in May 1520 to 'Maestro Giachetto cantor servitore de la casa de Rangoni'. Nugent: 'The Jacquet motets', pp. 70–2, argues that these records refer to Jacquet of Mantua, and that his patron was Cardinal Ercole dei Rangoni, whose musical interests are documented.

Bologna Q27 II.[78] Three of Jacquet's pieces are also included in Padua A17, a choirbook copied in 1522 by Giordano Passetto, *maestro di cappella* at the cathedral from 2 May 1520 until his death in 1557, so that taken together these five sources present a small corpus of works which must date from the period up to 1522 and emphasise Jacquet's connections with north Italy at that time.[79] Similarly, 'Omnes sancti' was composed before *c.* 1530, when it was copied into Florence II.I.350 and Modena IX; and four works of which two were certainly composed before 1522 appear in Cividale LIX dated no later than 1537.[80] It is possible in this way to suggest *termini post quem* for a small number of compositions, though it is hardly possible with a composer of Jacquet's versatility to proceed to a chronological account of stylistic change, not even when the impression of the four-voice motets is enlarged by other datable works.

Similarly, it is possible to suggest *termini* for a number of the early five-voice motets and the few that Jacquet composed for larger forces. Again the earliest source is Bologna Q19, which contains two pieces, while the lament 'Ploremus omnes' comes from the same period. As has been pointed out elsewhere, the text of 'Ploremus' refers to the death of Prince Cesare of Aragon, third son of King Federico of Naples and the youngest brother of Don Fernando, Duke of Calabria. This means that the piece must have been written about 1519, and it is worth noting that Jacquet's connection with the family, exiled in the Mantua–Ferrara region after the death of Federico in 1504, is further confirmation of the composer's connection with the Emilian region about this time.[81] The next datable sources for the five-voice motets come from the late 1520s and early 1530s and include manuscripts originating in Florence and Rome as well as one with strong Ferrarese connections copied by a scribe from Forlì.[82] A rather neglected source from the early 1530s, bound and

---

[78] Bologna, Civico Museo Bibliografico-Musicale MS Q27. For the most authoritative inventory see Lowinsky: *The Medici codex*, I, pp. 114–15.

[79] Padua, Biblioteca Capitolare MS A17. See Rubsamen: 'Music research in Italian libraries', pp. 80–6, Garbelotto: 'Codici musicali', pp. 297–8, and Perkins (ed.): *Johannes Lhéritier. Opera omnia*, I, pp. xlii–xliii.

[80] Florence, Biblioteca Nazionale Centrale MS II.I.350. See Becherini: *Catalogo dei manoscritti musicali*, pp. 91–2, for a rather imperfect inventory. Modena, Archivio Capitolare MS IX is described in Rubsamen: 'Music research in Italian libraries', pp. 77–80. It appears that Cividale del Friuli, Museo Archeologico Nazionale MS LIX was compiled about 1534–7, but then re-arranged about 1545: this dating emerges from watermarks and their presence in contemporaneous local archival registers. The source originally came from the collegiate church of Santa Maria Assunta in Friuli. (I am grateful to Lewis Lockwood for information on Cividale LIX.)

[81] Nugent: 'The Jacquet motets', pp. 215ff.

[82] Namely the much-discussed source Rome, Biblioteca Vallicelliana s¹.35–40 (*olim* S. Borr. E.II.55–60); Vatican City, Biblioteca Apostolica Vaticana MS Cappella Giulia XII.4 (dated 1536); and Treviso, Archivio Musicale del Duomo MS 36, respectively. For the latter see Dunning: *Die Staatsmotette*, pp. 269–71.

The 'Vallicelliana partbooks' have been thought to have originated in either Florence or Rome; for the arguments see Lowinsky: 'A newly discovered sixteenth-century motet manuscript', Bragard: 'Étude bio-bibliographique', and Slim: *A gift of madrigals and motets*, I, pp. 55–60. My own view is that the books were copied in Florence by Antonio Moro, scribe of a number of sources in a central complex of related Florentine manuscripts of the period, for a member of the Pucci family, most probably Roberto di Antonio Pucci. For the evidence see Fenlon and Haar: 'Fonti e cronologia', pp. 216–17.

presumably copied for the Roman patron Antonio Massimo, contains six motets by Jacquet.[83] In addition, 'Inclita sanctae Virginis' exists in a source which might have been copied about 1530; one further piece, the Marian antiphon 'Alma redemptoris mater', was published for the first time in 1532; and 'Plorabant sacerdotes' was already known to Giovanni del Lago in October 1529, when he mentioned it in a letter to Giovanni Spartaro.[84] Thereafter a trickle of compositions reached print before the major publications of 1539 and 1540.

Finally there are the masses, but here there are no early sources and the principal material is printed. It reveals that of twenty-five 'Jacquet' masses twelve are clearly assigned to Jacquet of Mantua and two to Jacquet Berchem, while eleven carry conflicting or inconclusive attributions. Recent writing has produced two very different accounts of. Jacquet of Mantua's share of this production, one arguing for his authorship of probably eleven and possibly thirteen masses, another tentatively advancing the proposal that he could have written twenty-three.[85] For present purposes only two masses are of interest, both indisputably the work of Jacquet of Mantua: the *Missa Ferdinandus dux Calabriae* and the *Missa Hercules dux Ferrariae*, both based on laudatory tenor *soggetti* around which the remaining voices are given the usual texts of the Ordinary. The 'Hercules' Mass, one of at least five written by various composers in honour of Ercole II d'Este, may have been composed for his succession to the Duchy of Ferrara in 1534; it is almost certainly the 'messa nocta in canto figurato' for which the Este archives record a payment to Jacquet in October 1536.[86] The second mass cannot be dated so precisely. Don Fernando of Aragon (1488–1550), Duke of Calabria and Prince of Taranto, deprived of the throne of Naples after the abdication of his father Federico in 1501, was taken prisoner by Spanish troops in 1502 and exiled to Spain. Here he was kept until 1523, when he was released on Imperial orders, and subsequently it was arranged that Fernando's marriage to

---

[83] Rome, Library of Count Leone Massimo, two partbooks without shelf-marks, briefly described in Lippmann: 'Musikhandschriften und -Drucke', p. 267. They contain the following pieces by Jacquet (folio references are to the Cantus book): 'Descendi in ortum meum' (fo. 34v), 'Aspice Domine' (fo. 37v), 'In die tribulationis' (fo. 40v), 'Surge Petre' (fo. 54v), 'Salve Regina' (fo. 57), and 'Sancta Trinitas' (fo. 77v). The name 'Antonius Maximus' is stamped on the covers of the bindings of both Cantus and Tenor partbooks, and the bindings themselves seem very close in style to those of the Vallicelliana partbooks. Should the binding of the Massimo books be Roman, this would strengthen the argument in Fenlon and Haar: 'Fonti e cronologia', pp. 216–17, that the Vallicelliana books were copied in Florence for a patron (Roberto di Antonio Pucci) who spent most of his later career in Rome (see also above, note 82). (I am grateful to Friedrich Lippmann of the German Institute in Rome for information about the Massimo partbooks.)

[84] Bologna, Civico Museo Bibliografico-Musicale MS R142 contains 'Inclita'. The manuscript is the work of six scribes and was compiled over a period of years, but is sometimes thought to have been begun about 1530. Osthoff: *Josquin Desprez*, II, p. 17, suggests that it was written out between 1515 and 1530: but for convincing evidence of a later dating see Blackburn: 'Josquin's chansons', pp. 50–4. 'Alma redemptoris' is included in Moderne's *Secundus liber*. For Giovanni del Lago's letter to Spartaro see Nugent: 'The Jacquet motets', pp. 41–2.

[85] Jackson: 'The masses of Jacquet of Mantua'; Nugent: 'The Jacquet motets'.

[86] Jackson: 'Two descendants of Josquin's "Hercules" Mass', pp. 192–3.

Germaine de Foix should be solemnised at the same time as the Emperor's own wedding to Isabella of Portugal in 1526. Fernando spent the remainder of his life as Duke of Valencia, collecting about him a cultured court noted for its humanistic leanings, and since he did not return to Italy after 1502 his connections with Jacquet were probably made through the agency of his mother Isabella who, after the death of her husband in 1504, went into exile first at Mantua and afterwards, from 1508 until her death in 1533, at Ferrara. On this assumption the date of composition of the *Missa Ferdinandus dux Calabriae* can be narrowed down to the period 1508–33, and to speculate further that Fernando would have preferred to use his new title after 1526 would place it in the early 1520s, perhaps as a work celebrating the duke's release after twenty-one years. This would date the piece within three or four years of the five-voice motet 'Ploremus omnes', written for the death of Fernando's brother, Prince Cesare of Aragon.[87]

The overwhelmingly liturgical character of Jacquet's output while in Ercole's service is already suggestive of the cardinal's musical priorities. In fact, with the exception of the Latin song 'Canamus et bibamus' and a couple of four-voice chansons, all his surviving compositions are masses and motets, albeit in some cases with unmistakable secular functions, and the majority of these were presumably written for performance in San Pietro. On this assumption it is possible to draw up a calendar on the basis of feasts for which Jacquet evidently wrote specific motets, and no doubt at Mantua, as elsewhere, these pieces could also be sung on other occasions, perhaps explaining the absence of motets for major feasts such as the Annunciation, the Nativity of the Virgin, and All Saints. As far as questions of liturgical function are concerned, Jacquet's music indicates regular use of polyphony for the Ordinary and at Vespers, at least for major feasts, and polyphony was also used at daily mass at other times. For Holy Week Jacquet composed not only settings of the Ordinary, but also the Lamentations of Jeremiah and a Passion. In short, while the precise duties of the cathedral choir are undocumented, as we have seen, the liturgical texts which Jacquet set suggest that the choir's role was similar in scope to that of similar institutions elsewhere in Italy whose functions are more accurately recorded.[88] The same point might be argued by considering the repertory acquired, most probably, by the cathedral during Ercole's period as bishop. Quite clearly, the composition of liturgical music was the primary occupation of a composer

[87] McMurty: 'Ferdinand, Duke of Calabria' provides a good résumé of Fernando's life, speculates about a number of possible dedicatees of the *Missa Ferdinandus dux Calabriae* (on the assumption that the original text was different), and concludes that it seems likely that the work was originally written for Fernando. Jackson: 'Two descendants of Josquin's "Hercules" Mass', pp. 193ff, suggests that the mass might have been written in the first instance for one of the Gonzaga, probably Ferrante. He also hypothesises that Jacquet's *Missa Hercules dux Ferrariae* was originally composed to honour the visit of Charles V to Mantua in either 1530 or 1532. Neither case is strong.

[88] See, for example, the information in D'Accone: 'The musical chapels at the Florentine Cathedral', pp. 3 and 37.

who, as the documents reveal, was effectively employed as Cardinal Ercole's personal *maestro di cappella*. These pieces emphasise Jacquet's relationship both to the cathedral and to Ercole, while also reflecting the cardinal's conception of the role of music in the service of the Church, a Church whose stirrings for reform Ercole was intimately and crucially involved with. As we have seen, the cardinal took a strong personal interest in reform at a local level despite his absences from Mantua (when he worked through a deputy), and tangible traces of that concern are apparent in the decorative and structural alterations to the building which functioned as the focal point of reformist ideals in the diocese, as well as in the maintenance of a music establishment and the operations of the liturgy. It is not an exaggeration to claim that Ercole's patronage represents a local and early attempt to implement an integrated approach to the arts in the service of a reforming Church, and it may be no accident that the appearance of Jacquet's first published works, with dedications to the cardinal, coincides approximately with Ercole's campaign to remodel the cathedral itself. These publications are also an indication of Jacquet's reputation, the rapid growth of which can be traced through manuscript sources starting with the Emilian compilation Bologna Q19, and continuing through Paduan and Ferrarese manuscripts to reach Florence and Rome by the early 1530s. At the same time, the evidence of the manuscript sources confirms what is known of Jacquet's early biography, and it is worth noting that both archival and musical sources suggest that Jacquet was connected with the Este court at Ferrara immediately before his arrival at Mantua. For a complex of political, economic and geographical reasons, Ferrara was more a part of an international system which incidentally could be used for the exchange of music and musicians, and Mantua's continued reliance on the example and expertise of the Este *cappella* during the first decades of the sixteenth century is not surprising. The tradition extends back as far as Marchese Francesco's first attempts to found a Gonzaga *cappella*, and in general cultural terms the relationship is much older but, as will be seen, it is a tradition that was radically modified in the second half of the century.

San Pietro was not only a showpiece for the practical application of Ercole's emergent reformist ideals, but the dynastic church of the ruling family, and a number of Jacquet's motets underline the political aspects of his employer's activities. In the first section of 'Cantemus Domino', the text notes that 'tristitia nostra versa est in gaudium' since the Lord 'fecit mirabilia super principem nostrum', while the second half calls upon the aid of the Virgin and eventually all the saints to intercede for the protection and preservation of Giulio Boiardo. Boiardo, who controlled Reggio as an Este fiefdom from 1530, entertained Jean Calvin at Scandiano after the reformer's refuge at Ferrara under the protection of the Duchess Renée in 1536, an episode which lowered the Este stock considerably in the eyes of the rest of the Italian nobility. The motet celebrates Boiardo's return to the fold after what was evidently considered to be a grave heretical lapse, and in composing it Jacquet was, as one commentator has put it, 'the instrument of his master, Ercole Gonzaga, who had both an official and a personal concern in Renée's religious activities'.[89] There is nothing else in Jacquet's work which alludes so directly to the political character of Ercole's activities as a reformer, although 'Jam nova perpetuo' emphasises his close contacts with Cardinal Cristoforo Madruzzo (1512–72), Prince–Bishop of Trent. After this there are pieces which reflect Ercole's position as co-regent, such as 'Quis incredibili', which may have been written for a Mantuan celebration of the Treaty of Bologna, and the state motet 'Hesperiae ultimae invicto regi'. In the second week of January 1549, Charles V's son Philip (later Philip II of Spain) made an impressive entry into Mantua, an event later commemorated by Tintoretto on Guglielmo Gonzaga's instructions, and by 'Hesperiae', one of two tribute motets by Jacquet published in Scotto's fourth book of *Motetti del laberinto*.[90] It has been convincingly argued that 'Nos pueri tibi principi' is a celebration of the coronation of the young Francesco Gonzaga in 1540; and both 'O angele Dei' and 'O Domine Jesu Christe' could refer to the elevation of Ippolito d'Este, Ercole's first cousin, to the cardinalate.[91] 'Plorabant sacerdotes' and 'Salvum me fac Domine' may refer to a different facet of Ercole's political role, since both seem to refer to the devastation which Mantua experienced during the severe flooding and consequent plague of 1527–8, and 'Estote fortes' was conceivably written in connection with some Mantuan military campaign. At a less elevated level 'Enceladi coeique soror' clearly alludes to the Gonzaga and their legendary fondness for horses.[92]

The essential points are the extent to which liturgical compositions predominate in Jacquet's *oeuvre*, presumably as a reflection of his employer's concerns, and the degree to which the texts of this small corpus of motets reflect the variety and character of Ercole's political activities as ruler, reforming churchman, and diplomatist. It was almost exclusively in fulfilling these varied but inseparable roles that Jacquet was employed, it seems, as the potential of music in the pursuit of policy was explored on a broad front.

[89] Nugent: 'The Jacquet motets', pp. 175–6.

[90] For 'Jam nova' see Dunning: *Die Staatsmotette*, pp. 255–9, and for 'Quis incredibili' Nugent: 'The Jacquet motets', pp. 177ff. Dunning: *Die Staatsmotette*, pp. 265–7, discusses 'Hesperiae'. The other tribute motet in the *Motetti del laberinto* is 'Dum vastos', a commemoration of Josquin incorporating quotations from five of his best-known motets; for further details see Dunning: 'Josquini antiquos'.

[91] For 'Nos tibi' see Widmaier: 'Jachet von Mantua', pp. 40–1, and for 'O angele Dei' and 'O Domine' Dunning: *Die Staatsmotette*, pp. 248–51. Dunning: *Die Staatsmotette*, pp. 247–8, suggests autobiographical references in Jacquet's 'Jucundum mea vita' and 'Si vera incessa', both of which Nugent: 'The Jacquet motets' associates with the theatre. The latter also suggests that the canonic motet 'Repleatur' may have been written for the Imperial coronation in Bologna in 1530, and that 'Si bona' may have been composed when Ercole became co-regent in 1540.

[92] In addition, 'Formoso Vermi' has been variously put forward as a commemoration of the story of the love of Camilla, daughter of Valente Valenti of Mantua for Giacomo Michele Dal Verme, and of the betrothal of Caterina of Austria to Francesco Gonzaga announced by Charles V in 1543. See Dunning: *Die Staatmotette*, pp. 259–62, and Nugent: 'The Jacquet motets', pp. 221–4.

In terms of style, it is tempting to argue that some of Jacquet's maturer work prefigures certain later composers' responses to the Council of Trent's vague edict about sacred music. From payment documents it seems that the Vespers hymns, published posthumously, were among his last works, and these are generally written less elaborately than the motets. Nevertheless even here there is considerable reliance upon counterpoint, as there is even in the Passion setting from St John. In fact, it would be quite misleading to project this kind of argument, partly because of the lack of a satisfactory chronology for Jacquet's work, but in any case because to do so requires accepting certain historicist assumptions. Jacquet's most productive years seem to have been the third and fourth decades of the century, precisely the period when Ercole's interests in formulating reformist policies at a local level were at their height, but a time when serious questions about the role of music in the liturgy had yet to be formulated. Even after Trent there was a great variety of approaches to the Commission of Cardinals' general pronouncement on the reform of sacred music, as might be expected from any such deliberately vague statement, and (as a number of studies have shown) scholarly concentration on Carlo Borromeo and Milan has tended to obscure the activities of contemporary reformers elsewhere.[93] In Mantua the issues of reform seem to have been most favourably taken up by Duke Guglielmo, and it is to his interpretation of the spirit of Trent as revealed in Gonzaga patronage of the arts and music that we shall now turn.

[93] See in particular Prodi: *Il Cardinale Gabrielle Paleotti* and Prodi: 'Lineamente dell'organizzazione diocesana' for discussions of Bologna, and Cairns: *Domenico Bollani* for Brescia.

3

Guglielmo Gonzaga and the Santa Barbara project

...Al servitio di Dio Nostro in quella officiare di quella dolcissima ed copiasissima musicha de diversi cantori per li quali non restava di spender denari ne gli sparagnava a fargli cercare per havergli, pur che fossero perfetti in detta professione. Si come face, per quel gran compositore di musica Jaches Vuert fiamengo per ottenerlo il quale puoi per un gran tempo gli e stato mastro di capella...

Vigilio: 'L'insalata'

'...Su via, facciamo un Papa di Santa Barbara.'

Pius IV

Fig. 6 Frans Geffels: *View of the high altar of Santa Barbara during the obsequies of Carlo II Gonzaga* (1666), engraving. Mantua, Biblioteca Comunale

In August 1587, on the eve of the feast of the Assumption of the Virgin, Guglielmo Gonzaga, Duke of Mantua and Monferrato, reached the end of more than thirty years devoted to transforming the duchy into a model Catholic state based on reformist principles according to a personal and highly detailed vision. After four days' journey from Guglielmo's favourite residence at Goito, the funeral cortège reached Mantua on the evening of the eighteenth, and throughout the next day while his body lay in the ducal basilica of Santa Barbara the solemn rites were recited. Finally, after the last mass had been sung and the funeral oration delivered, the duke was buried in the crypt of Santa Barbara, the church whose construction, liturgy, decorations, and minute arrangements had occupied him so fully for a quarter of a century.[1]

Undoubtedly impressive and successful though the execution of Guglielmo's plans had been, it is important to realise his indebtedness to his uncle for a training which had developed considerable political and administrative skills, religious ideals and humanistic values. Initially it might have seemed as though he would be unable to continue Ercole's skilful policy of preventing Mantuan involvement in the numerous conflicts which frequently engaged their neighbours. The principal difficulty concerned Monferrato (the other half of the duchy but physically separated from Mantua), which had come to the Gonzaga as part of Margherita Paleologa's dowry when she married Federico Gonzaga in 1531. Monferrato's strong traditions of autonomy and self-government, which its former masters the Paleologi had respected, were clearly inimical to the new brand of fierce absolutism with which Guglielmo intended to strengthen and consolidate the economic and political achievements of the regency. The decision taken in 1565 to construct a fortress at the gates of Casale was seen by Mantua as a revolt generated by the long-standing territorial ambitions and personal hatred of Emanuele

---

[1] For accounts of Guglielmo's death and funeral see Comanini: *Oratione*, Follino: *Descrittione dell'infirmità*, Amadei: *Cronaca universale*, II, pp. 871–84, and Vigilio: 'L'insalata' (ASM (D'Arco) MS 168), Cap. 82. Gregorio Comanini's remarks on Guglielmo's musicianship and his patronage of musicians are given in Appendix II, doc. 22. Follino: *Descrittione dell'infirmità*, p. 5, notes that the Duke 'è tanto versato nelle arti liberali...ma in particolare, tanto e di tempo, e di fatica spese nelle sagre lettere, e nella musica...', and L. Arrivabene: *Vita*, pp. 10–11, makes similar comments.

Filiberto of Savoy, and was ruthlessly countered. Although the difficulties over Monferrato were not finally resolved on this occasion, and the attempted assassination of Guglielmo himself in the cathedral at Casale in 1567 evidently remained fresh in Mantuan memories, the Monferrato question was the only serious external threat to Mantuan stability during Guglielmo's period.

Thus in the tumultuous politics of northern Italy during the second half of the sixteenth century Mantua was able to play a relatively cautious role, characterised by a realistic appreciation of the advantages of a basically defensive strategy for a second-class power surrounded by more impressive neighbours. Mantuan concern over Casale, and particularly over Emanuele Filiberto's designs on it, continued throughout the 1570s and 1580s, expressed mostly in further repressive measures to deprive it of the few remaining vestiges of independence; but in general, Guglielmo's efforts were directed towards the continuation of the administrative reforms begun by Cardinal Ercole, rather than towards aggression. In turn, this firm control over the workings of the duchy, and in particular its economic operations, allied to a relatively strong awareness of the security brought about by the years of peace, led to greater industrial and commercial prosperity; the deterioration in both is not really perceptible until the years of Vincenzo, whose own incredible extravagance could only hasten the economic decline that seems to have been general throughout Italy.

Encouraged by these favourable conditions, and despite the effects of plague and famine, the population of Mantua expanded from about 43,000 in 1560 to 46,000 in 1587, though some of the increase is accounted for by Jewish immigration. In general, Guglielmo proved to be an able ruler who avoided serious conflict with Savoy, subjugated Casale, extended the duchy by the addition of Luzzara, Gazzuolo and Dosolo, created improved commercial conditions, and consolidated his economic resources. The political position of the Gonzaga was further strengthened by the carefully arranged marriages of his three children: Margherita married Alfonso II d'Este in 1579; on 30 April 1581 Prince Vincenzo, heir to the duchy, took as his bride Margherita Farnese, daughter of Alessandro, Governor of the Low Countries; and one year later Guglielmo's third-born, Anna Caterina, married Archduke Ferdinand of Austria. If the second of these arrangements was to put the family at the centre of one of the most celebrated and undignified scandals of the century as well as incurring the animosity of the Farnese, the third reconfirmed traditional links with the Empire. Margherita's marriage did not bring the Este the necessary heir; but this match, together with Vincenzo's second marriage, to Leonora de' Medici in 1584, brought the Gonzaga closer to two of their more powerful neighbours with, as will be seen, important cultural consequences during the 1590s. Elsewhere Guglielmo trod with caution, supporting his subjects against the excesses of the Inquisition, and adopting a policy of tolerance towards the Jewish community in the city despite the persecutory measures of Pius V. Nevertheless, a spirit of devotion and piety was encouraged through the duke's own example as well as by the construction of new churches, donations to existing ones, and the encouragement of new confraternities. During his final years Guglielmo's personal religious practices took on an obsessive fervour; he must have felt, as he lay on his deathbed at Goito, that as a model Christian prince he could face the judgement of posterity with equanimity.[2]

Guglielmo's attitudes towards personal expenditure were characterised by notable stringency towards his own family – particularly Vincenzo, whose extravagances were legion – but considerable generosity towards projects which would advance the image of the Gonzaga in the eyes of other Italian princes. It is interesting to note that many artistic projects seem to have been designed to demonstrate the distinction and stability of the Gonzaga, with a use of symbolism and mythology that can reasonably be compared with Cosimo I's skilful use of classical allusions to enforce the re-establishment of the Medici by cultural means. Cultural patronage was one field in which pious, political and personal motives often overlapped, so that it is entirely consistent that, despite Guglielmo's well-documented scrupulousness in matters of administrative efficiency, his careful accountancy and bureaucratic honesty, vast sums were spent on favoured prestige projects. A good example is the construction and decoration of the suite of rooms dedicated to the achievements, military in particular, of previous Gonzaga, which were then adorned with four large oil paintings, the *Fasti gonzagheschi*, commissioned from Tintoretto and similar in function to Vasari's paintings for Cosimo I in the Sala del Cinquecento of the Palazzo Vecchio in Florence.[3] Another, the most important in the context of his patronage of music, was the planning, construction and final arrangements of the ducal church of Santa Barbara.

Before looking at this central question – the key to an understanding of Guglielmo's interest in music in his inseparable and overlapping roles of private individual and ruler–patron – it is worth recalling that there is an impressive body of evidence pointing to a wide variety of musical activities

[2] The Casale Monferrato question is discussed in Quazza: 'Emanuele Filiberto di Savoia', *Mantova. La storia*, III, pp. 20–8, and Coniglio: *I Gonzaga*, pp. 320–30. Guglielmo's administrative reforms and fiscal policies are best approached through De Maddalena: *Le finanze del ducato di Mantova*. A good general survey of the history of Monferrato is Di Ricaldone: *Annali del Monferrato*. The changing political character of Monferrato during the sixteenth century is, of course, reflected in its culture, and some approach to the effects of Gonzaga domination on musical life is offered in Crawford: *Sixteenth-century choirbooks*, pp. 41ff and 64ff.

[3] Tintoretto's relationship with the Gonzaga is documented in A. Bertolotti: *Artisti*, pp. 57, 156. The *Fasti gonzagheschi* are discussed in Bercken: *Die Gemälde des Jacopo Tintoretto*, pp. 116–17, and the drawings for the paintings in Tietze and Tietze-Conrat: *The drawings of the Venetian painters*, pp. 279, 283–4, and 289–90. For Cosimo I de' Medici's patronage, see Forster: 'Metaphors of rule' and the bibliography cited there; and for Vasari's work in the Palazzo Vecchio, Rubenstein: 'Vasari's painting'.

at court throughout the period. Through his agents both in Italy and elsewhere, the duke was constantly in search of good singers (particularly, it seems castrati) and instrumentalists and performers who could bring a wide variety of skills were especially sought after. In a world where cultural achievements, magnificence, and splendour were seen as essential parts of the courtly image, it is not surprising to find Mantuan agents reporting on the musical life of other courts, acting as intermediaries in negotiations with performers, and sometimes displaying a virtuosic command of subterfuge and double-dealing in their attempts to secure vocalists and instrumentalists for Gonzaga service. From references in letters and the few surviving pay rolls from these years it seems that the Gonzaga maintained a permanent establishment of musicians at court, unlike the Medici, for example, who seem to have employed performers on any scale only on an occasional basis, for *feste* and other large-scale spectacles. This collection of frequently changing personnel entertained at court, playing before visiting dignitaries and at banquets, and also provided music during state ceremonies, the entries of distinguished visitors, and the public ceremonies which accompanied the funerals, the baptisms, and particularly the marriages of the principal members of the ruling house. Such events were not as lavish at this period as the similar festivities at the Medici court in Florence (though as we shall see they became so, partly under Florentine influence, during the rule of Vincenzo Gonzaga). Nevertheless, the main dynastic occasions of these years, the marriage of Guglielmo himself to Eleonora of Austria in 1561,[4] and those of his eldest son and heir Vincenzo, first to Margherita Farnese in 1581, and then more successfully to Leonora de' Medici in 1584, were extravagantly celebrated in a series of entertainments, some of which involved music. Similar arrangements were made for the celebration of significant political events, such as the visit of Henri III of France in 1574, or the Venetian victory over the Turks at the Battle of Lepanto in 1571.[5]

There can be little doubt of the interest in musical entertainment at

---

[4] Accounts of these occasions are distressingly uninformative about the music involved. Thus the published description of the festivities makes quite frequent mention of instrumental music, presumably performed by the *alta cappella*, but names no composers. The mass itself was 'cantata da Reverendissimo Soffraganeo et dei Musici del Duomo'. See [A. Arrivabene]: *I grandi apparati*, sig. [Cii].

[5] See ASM (D'Arco) MS 168, Cap. 12, which notes that for the entry of Henri III in 1574 'stava l'Arco di detta porta [Pusterla] della guardia stava una musica de suoni & canti de diversi instromenti et massimamente una cornetta, la persona della quale la sonava fu giudicata suprema'. The Mantuans sent a contingent to fight at Lepanto, as the anonymous author of the *Invito* colourfully relates (fo. [Aiv]v):

> E tu Mantova bella, e ornata
> Di honorati Cittadini,
> So che non far ai ingrata
> Contra questi can mastini
> Se Christiani ancor minazza
> Ogn'un crida guerra amazza
> Questi Turchi falsi cani.

Mantua presumably celebrated the victory, but no polyphony can be definitely associated with it, though Wert's 'Le strane voci' is undoubtedly a celebration of the outcome.

court – vocal, instrumental, and theatrical – during Guglielmo's period. That much is clear from documentary sources, and from the surviving secular music of composers known to have been employed by the Gonzaga during these years. Admittedly, the precise significance of music publications in any study of sixteenth-century Italian patronage is difficult to estimate, since so little is known about the function of the contents, and even less about the crucial relationships between composer, patron, printer–publisher, and poet. Nevertheless, proceeding by analogy with the few scraps of information that survived about some of these relationships as they operated outside Italy, it is reasonable to assume that a dedication signed by composer or publisher was paid for by the patron, and it seems unrealistic to argue otherwise. Similarly, it would be perverse not to believe that the large body of published madrigals written by Wert, for example, after his arrival at Mantua, does not to some degree reflect both the musical life and the musical tastes of the court. Yet the surviving products of this side of Gonzaga patronage and the documentation which relates to it are easily surpassed in both extent and quality by the impressive body of surviving material relating to the focal point of Guglielmo's cultural patronage – the ducal church, or more correctly the palatine basilica, of Santa Barbara.

In the published tributes and books of commemorative verses which followed hard upon Guglielmo's death, a consistent theme is his devotion to the art of music. Comanini's oration, for example, delivered during the final solemnities in Santa Barbara, praises his learning, magnanimity, and religious zeal, and then launches into an extended eulogy of him as a Maecenas of musicians comparable to Alexander.[6] Similar sentiments were expressed by other contemporaries, and the theme persisted well into the seventeenth century as a leitmotif of official Gonzaga historiography. Guglielmo's musical training and interests as a patron who was also a published composer, and who corresponded with his fellow-composers, are indeed very unusual. It is true that there is a tradition of dilettante artists, composers, and poets among rulers, stretching from the Emperor Nero, who reputedly not only sang, played and composed music but also acted, painted, modelled (*finxit*), and worked in metal, to Guglielmo's contemporary Francesco I de' Medici, who showed a lively and catholic taste for various arts and crafts.[7] But in general, those who did try their hand were usually attracted by the more mechanical arts rather than by musical composition, a skill which requires early training in musical language as well as the unteachable talent of original musical thought. Unfortunately nothing is known of Guglielmo's musical training, but by a comparatively early age his interest and ability in composition were appreciated outside Mantua, and he had begun the exchange of ideas and opinions with other composers which

[6] See Appendix II, doc. 22, and cf. p. 81, note 1 above.
[7] The tradition is discussed in Middeldorf: 'On the dilettante sculptor'.

remained a feature of his correspondence throughout his life. The earliest of these contacts seems to have been with the theorist and composer Nicola Vicentino, then at the Ferrarese court, and dates from 1555. Guglielmo, nineteen years old and shortly to take official control of the Mantuan duchy in his own right, was evidently already known to have musical interests, while Vicentino had previously sent one of his published works, presumably a copy of the first edition of his controversial treatise *L'antica musica ridotta alla moderna prattica*, printed that year by Antonio Barrè in Rome, together with ten five-voice madrigals. These gifts had remained unacknowledged, but nevertheless the composer was now sending other works presumably in manuscript and now lost: ten five-voice madrigals, one for six voices, a twelve-voice dialogue, and a motet for seven voices. Vicentino's covering letter emphasises that these pieces were easy to perform, 'almost as if they were composed [in the tradition] of *musica communa*'.[8]

From the 1560s, when Santa Barbara was being completed and its *cappella* established, there is better documentation of contacts of this kind; the *maestro di cappella* of the Governor of Milan sent a mass in 1564, and Guglielmo's own work was published for the first time in 1567 with the appearance of one piece in Wert's *Quarto libro*.[9] Contacts with Ferrara and Milan are not surprising, and neither is Joanelli's presentation in 1569 of his *Novus thesaurus musicus* (Venice, 1568), a collection of 257 motets mostly by composers in the Imperial service, dedicated to the Emperor Maximilian II, and clearly intended as testimony to the brilliance of musical life at the Imperial court.[10] Traditional Gonzaga links with the Empire had been strengthened by Guglielmo's marriage to Eleonora of Austria in 1561, and the exchange visits of members of the Imperial and Gonzaga courts which occurred quite frequently during Guglielmo's period often included musical events, such as Wert's skilled keyboard improvisation at Augsburg in 1566, when a meeting had been called by the Emperor to propose measures against the Turks. There were also contacts about this time with Stefano Rossetto in Florence, who wrote to the duke asking for advice about musical matters.[11]

Guglielmo's contacts with Florentine musicians may have been encouraged

---

[8] Letter of Don Nicola Vicentino, 15 December 1555, to the Duke of Mantua: the original is in ASM (AG) 1252. Canal: *Della musica in Mantova*, p. 730, claims that the ten madrigals mentioned in the text are from Vicentino's *Madrigali* of 1546 but offers no proof. Kaufmann: *The life and works*, p. 33, is misguided in his belief that Vicentino was taking advantage of the good relations established between Mantua and Ferrara by the marriage of Guglielmo's daughter Margherita to Alfonso II d'Este: that event did not take place until 1579.

[9] Letter of 1 December 1564, noted in Canal: *Della musica in Mantova*, p. 76: the original is in ASM (AG) 2947 lib. 359. Guglielmo's piece, 'Padre che'l ciel, la terra e'l tutto regi', is in Wert: *Il quarto libro de madrigali a cinque voci*, p. 1. This publication is also dedicated to Guglielmo.

[10] Letter of 12 March 1569; see Canal: *Della musica in Mantova*, p. 77. The copy may well be that which survives in the Santa Barbara collection with the shelf-mark s.b.58; see *Conservatorio di musica*, pp. 82–95, and Appendix III below.

[11] Straeten: *La musique aux Pays-Bas*, I, p. 174, and MacClintock: *Giaches de Wert*, p. 31. For Rossetto's letter see Appendix II, doc. 23. There is also a letter of 8 December 1565 from Rossetto, which speaks of 'queste opperette mie fatte segondo il piacer di Sua Sta': the letter, in ASM (AG) 2573, lacks indication of the intended recipient.

by Alessandro Striggio, a member of the Mantuan aristocracy, who served as a musician at the Medici court from the end of the 1550s; and, indeed, Striggio may have written one of his most impressive works for the Duke of Mantua. In a letter of 21 August 1561, Striggio claimed to have composed 'una musica a quaranta voci' on a text honouring Guglielmo's marriage to Eleonora of Austria, which had taken place the previous April; he remarked on the size of the forces required, and enclosed both words and music. Regrettably, neither has survived among the Gonzaga papers, but given the highly unusual scoring of the piece it seems likely that Striggio's wedding motet for Guglielmo has been preserved (presumably with different words) as his forty-voice motet 'Ecce beatam lucem', known from a Zwickau manuscript dated 1587. This is usually thought to have been performed in 1568, at a banquet celebrating the marriage of Duke Wilhelm of Bavaria with Renée of Lorraine when, according to Massimo Troiano's account, a forty-voice motet composed by Striggio was played and sung under the direction of Lasso. The matter is yet further complicated since the Florentine diarist Agostino Lapini, in his description of the entry of Cardinal Ippolito d'Este into Florence on 13 July 1561, noted 'una canzona a 40 voci, composta per messer Alexandro Striggio musico del principe Francesco, che fu tenuta cosa bellissima'. Though it is conceivable that Striggio composed more than one forty-voice piece – particularly since he is known to have written other works, no longer extant, for even larger forces – it seems more likely that the one composition, first recorded in connection with Cardinal Ippolito d'Este's entry, later served to honour the marriages of Guglielmo Gonzaga and Wilhelm of Bavaria, and was subsequently copied into the Zwickau source.[12]

It is from the end of the 1560s that the first traces survive of Guglielmo's celebrated correspondence with Palestrina, and there are occasional hints, during that decade, of Gonzaga patronage of less able composers such as Dominico Magiello, Orazio Faa, and Paolo Isnardi. For the early 1570s there is comparatively little information about Guglielmo's contacts other than those with court composers and the continuing correspondence with Palestrina, though Ippolito Baccusi, a native Mantuan who later held appointments at Mantua Cathedral, dedicated his *Primo libro de madrigali* to him in 1570, and David Sacerdote, a local Jewish composer, also addressed a piece to him in his six-voice madrigal book of 1575.[13] A significant increase, at least in Guglielmo's sponsorship of music publications, came in the last decade of

---

[12] Letter of Alessandro Striggio, Florence 21 August 1561, to Duke Guglielmo Gonzaga. Original in ASM (AG) 1112: see Appendix II, doc. 24. Striggio was paid as a member of the Medici court from 1 March 1559, when he is first recorded with the high salary of 257 *scudi* (see ASF Depositeria generale 1515, fos. 58v–59). For the Munich celebrations see Troiano: *Dialoghi* (mentioning the motet on p. 146, and describing the instruments used on that occasion); and for Cardinal Ippolito d'Este's entry into Florence, Lapini: *Diario*, p. 132. Further details of Striggio's career as it was involved with Mantuan musical life are given on pp. 140–2 below and note 50, where documents recording his compositions for forty and sixty voices are also cited.

[13] Information from the dedications of Magiello: *Il primo libro di madrigali*, Faa: *Il primo libro di madrigali*, Isnardi: *Il primo libro de madrigali*, and Baccusi: *Il primo libro de madrigali*; see the entries in Vogel: *Bibliothek*. For Sacerdote's dedication see I. Fenlon: 'A supplement', II, pp. 326–7.

his life, the period when strenuous efforts were made to entice composers of the distinction of Marenzio and Palestrina to enter Gonzaga service, as well as men such as Filippo Nicoletti. The latter was recommended in October 1579 as a chaplain to the duke by Alessandro Nodari, who noted Nicoletti's good voice and compositional abilities, but despite Nodari's enthusiasm Nicoletti seems not to have gone to Mantua.[14] Two years later Vincenzo Galilei presented a copy of his *Dialogo* to Guglielmo, following it a year later with a set of responds and lamentations 'after the manner of the ancient Greeks'; and in November 1581 Francisco Guerrero wrote asking permission to visit the duke: it was, he claimed, one of the principal reasons he had come to Italy, and to emphasise his regard he sent a copy of his *Missa 'La bataille'* and a motet.[15] A few years later Giovanni Maria Nanino also sent copies of his works to Guglielmo, and the many composers whose publications were dedicated to him during the 1580s included not only men employed locally at the cathedral and at court, such as Benedetto Pallavicino and Paolo Cantino, but composers working elsewhere, such as Francesco Soriano and Girolamo Belli.[16]

It is a token of the ambitious nature of Guglielmo's plans for the basilica and of the prestige which the institution had achieved that attempts were made during the 1580s to attract both Marenzio and Palestrina to Mantua. According to the reports of Scipione Gonzaga, who sometimes during this decade assisted Guglielmo's efforts to recruit singers and instrumentalists working in Rome, Marenzio had already spent some time in Gonzaga service, and if the Brescian historian Ottavio Rossi is correct in describing Giovanni Contino as Marenzio's teacher that might help to explain the earlier association.[17] Rossi's claim is supported by Marenzio's brief appointment to Contino's sometime employer and patron Cardinal Cristoforo Madruzzo, and this too brings Marenzio close to Mantua, where Madruzzo was an influential and frequent visitor. Marenzio subsequently spent the period between 1578 and 1586 in the service of Cardinal Luigi d'Este, brother of Duke Alfonso II of Ferrara, at the Cardinal's principal residence, the

[14] Letter of Alessandro Nodari, Ferrara 23 October 1579, to the Duke of Mantua. The original is in ASM (AG) 1254.
[15] Letters of Vincenzo Galilei, Florence 2 January 1581 and 13 March 1582, to the Duke of Mantua. The originals are in ASM (AG) 1112; the contents are summarised in A. Bertolotti: *Musici alla corte dei Gonzaga*, pp. 60–1, and transcribed in A. Bertolotti: *Artisti*, pp. 195–7. For Guerrero's letter see Sherr: 'The publications of Guglielmo Gonzaga', p. 118; the original is in ASM (AG) 929, and Guglielmo's reply in ASM (AG) 2954 lib. 386. Presumably the Guerrero mass was his *Della batalla escoutez*, later published in his *Missarum liber secundus* (Rome, 1582).
[16] For Nanino see the letters of Scipione Gonzaga, Rome 18 January and 1 February 1586, both in ASM (AG) 941. They are excerpted in A. Bertolotti: *Musici alla corte dei Gonzaga*, p. 66, and given in full in A. Bertolotti, *Artisti*, p. 117. The dedications to Cantino: *Il primo libro de madrigali*, Pallavicino: *Il primo libro de madrigali a sei voci* and *Il secondo libro de madrigali a cinque voci*, Soriano: *Il primo libro de madrigali*, Belli: *I furti* and *I furti amorosi* are all noted in Vogel: *Bibliothek*.
[17] Letter of Scipione Gonzaga, Rome 31 May 1586, to Federico Cattaneo in Mantua. The original is in ASM (AG) 947 and is partly given in H. Engel: *Luca Marenzio*, p. 218. Rossi's remarks are in *Elogi historici*, p. 493.

Villa d'Este at Tivoli near Rome. In August 1580 Luigi moved to Ferrara where he stayed until June 1581, and it seems likely that Marenzio accompanied him. It has been proposed that circumstantial evidence suggests that Marenzio heard the Ferrarese *concerto delle donne* during this visit, and a number of archival references underline his association with Ferrara, an association which received clear musical expression in *Il primo libro de madrigali a sei voci* (Venice, 1581), which is dedicated to Alfonso.[18] Certainly there can be no doubt of Marenzio's associations with Mantua at this time. In September 1581 the Mantuan agent Annibale Capello sent a copy of the composer's first book of five-voice madrigals from Venice and reported that Marenzio himself was then at Padua with his family, and later the same month Marenzio visited Mantua.[19] During the summer of 1582 Giaches de Wert became ill with malaria and had to be replaced by Gastoldi, and this may have prompted Guglielmo to look for another *maestro di cappella*. Marenzio's name was suggested but rejected on the advice of Palestrina, who compared Marenzio unfavourably to Soriano and recommended his own pupil Annibale Zoilo. Three years later, quite extended negotiations to secure Marenzio's services for the Mantuan court finally foundered over the question of money.[20]

In many cases the contacts between Duke Guglielmo and composers working both in Mantua and elsewhere, as revealed in documents and suggested by the dedications of printed works, indicate little more than the usual relationships between composers and patron, though the quantity of material suggests a high degree of interest on Guglielmo's part. His support for the composers working at court and at the local cathedral was quite extensive, though sponsorship of this kind was also, of course, a piece of cultural propaganda. The more interesting aspect of these connections is that some composers were sending unpublished works in manuscript, suggesting that Guglielmo was being consulted in his capacity as a fellow-composer rather than simply being presented with the finished product as a patron or prospective employer. What makes Guglielmo's case so unusual is the combination of a powerful patron who not only had genuine musical interests but was also musically literate, since it is only when these two conditions obtain that there can be any basis for postulating a direct influence of patron upon style, and only then that there could have been detailed consultation between patron and composer about specific technical aspects of musical

[18] Details of Marenzio's career come from Ledbetter: 'Luca Marenzio', pp. 1ff. For his connections with Ferrara see also Newcomb: 'The musica segreta', pp. 370ff.

[19] Letters of Annibale Capello, (1) Venice 10 and 17 September 1580, to Aurelio Zibramonte in Mantua, and (2) Venice 24 September 1580, to the Duke of Mantua. All three are in ASM (AG) 1115 and are partly transcribed in H. Engel: *Luca Marenzio*, pp. 215–16.

[20] Letters of Aurelio Zibramonte in Rome to the Duke of Mantua, 26 March, 9 and 13 April 1583, all in ASM (AG) 934 and partly given in A. Bertolotti: *Musici alla corte dei Gonzaga*, p. 53. For the 1586 negotiations between Marenzio and the Gonzaga court see pp. 112–14 below.

language. For this reason alone Guglielmo's patronage of music is of particular interest, but that interest is magnified by its extent and by the clarity with which the evidence suggests his own highly developed vision of the place of music within a Catholic state serving the ideals of the Catholic Reformation. The focal point of that argument, as will be seen, is his personal involvement in the Santa Barbara project.

Some conception of Guglielmo's ideas about musical style can be derived from details of his relationships with other composers, particularly Palestrina. Palestrina's personal connections with Guglielmo seem to have begun in 1568 and lasted until the duke's death, and a series of letters, apparently Palestrina's only surviving correspondence, show something of both composers' attitudes to aspects of composition. The first, dated 2 February 1568, concerns a mass which the duke had evidently commissioned through Wert in Mantua, and through the ducal agent Annibale Capello, a friend of Palestrina's, in Rome. In it Palestrina asked Guglielmo to be more specific about the commission, whether it should be 'short, or long, or written so that the words can be understood'.[21] Unfortunately Guglielmo's reply is not known, and the work itself cannot be securely identified, though it is particularly interesting that Palestrina should have been concerned about textual audibility; but by December of the same year a further letter from Palestrina reveals him at work on motets for which the duke had supplied the words.[22] There is then a two-year gap in the correspondence until March 1570, when Palestrina wrote to the duke about a madrigal and a motet which Guglielmo had sent to him for criticism. Palestrina had put the motet in score, commended it for 'the vital impulse given to its music, according to its words', made alterations to the arrangement of the parts though not to the harmony itself, and noted that 'because of the dense interweaving of the imitations, the words are somewhat obscured to the listeners, who do not enjoy them as in *musica commune*'.[23] Later letters help to fill out details of the relationship between the two. On one occasion Palestrina presented a copy of one of his publications, and on another there was an attempt to find one of Palestrina's sons, Rodolfo, an appointment at Santa Barbara, shortly before the latter's death on 20 November 1572.[24] In May of the same year the two

---

[21] Letter of Giovanni Pierluigi da Palestrina, Rome 2 February 1568, to the Duke of Mantua. Original in ASM (AG) 6, no. 652; transcription in A. Bertolotti: *Musici alla corte dei Gonzaga*, p. 47. See also the *copialettera* of 19 April 1568 in ASM (AG) 2950 lib. 368, fo. 130v: 'A M[r] Gio. Pietroluigi da Palestrina. Se bene non v'ho prima d'adesso ringratiato della messa, che mi mandaste di passato non resta per questo ch'io non l'habbia havuta cara, anzi ella mi e piacciuta assai et me la tengo molto cara.'

[22] Letter of Giovanni Pierluigi da Palestrina, Rome 13 December 1568, to the Duke of Mantua. Original in ASM (AG) 6, no. 654; transcription in A. Bertolotti: *Musici alla corte dei Gonzaga*, p. 48.

[23] Letter of Giovanni Pierluigi da Palestrina, Rome 3 March 1570, to the Duke of Mantua. Original in ASM (AG) 6, no. 655; transcription in A. Bertolotti: *Musici alla corte dei Gonzaga*, p. 49.

[24] See the letters from Annibale Capello, Rome 24 September 1572, and from Bishop Odescalco, Rome 3 January 1573, both to the Duke of Mantua. The originals are in ASM (AG) 907 and 909, and both are transcribed in A. Bertolotti: *Musici alla corte dei Gonzaga*, pp. 49–50.

may have met in Rome when Guglielmo went to attend the coronation of Gregory XIII, and later in 1572 Palestrina's second book of five-voice motets, which also contains pieces by his sons Angelo, Silla and Rodolfo, was published with a dedication to Guglielmo expressing the devotion and gratitude of the whole family. The second book, of which two sets survive in the Santa Barbara collection, also contains the motets 'Gaude Barbara' and 'Beata Barbara', which were probably written for the ducal basilica. In an exchange of correspondence in 1574 Guglielmo sent one of his own masses to Palestrina for criticism.[25] But the most specific information about compositions comes from two letters of 1578. The first, sent to the duke in October by Capello, describes the re-arrangement of the Cappella Giulia choir into two choirs of twelve singers and then continues 'If with the gracious permission of Your Highness it may be so, Palestrina also wishes to have the second parts and to use them in the church in question [St Peter's] instead of the organ on occasions of high solemnity. For he affirms that Your Highness has truly purged these plainsongs of all the barbarisms and imperfections that they contained. I trust that he will not do this [i.e. perform the finished work at St Peter's] without your permission, and as soon as his infirmity permits he will work out what he has done on the lute with all possible care.'[26] This passage has been variously interpreted, but it now seems generally agreed that the 'second parts' are the non-polyphonic sections of an *alternatim* setting composed on chants taken from the Santa Barbara liturgy which specified *alternatim* practice.[27] The point becomes clear from Palestrina's own letter of 5 November, which requests the chants with some urgency, a request which is gently supported by Capello's covering note.[28]

From this it seems clear that these letters refer to the 'Mantuan' masses, one of which had already been finished, perhaps specifically to the *Missa in duplicibus minoribus* in the fourth mode and a *Missa della Madonna* in the authentic seventh mode, both of which survive in the Santa Barbara manuscripts.[29] Palestrina's nine five-voice *alternatim* masses composed for the

[25] The dedication of Palestrina: *Motettorum...liber secundus*, which includes works by Rodolfo, Angelo, and Silla Palestrina, is printed in *Conservatorio di musica*, p. 292, recording one of the Santa Barbara copies. The 1574 letters are from Annibale Capello, Rome 17 April 1574, in ASM (AG) 912, and from Giovanni Pierluigi da Palestrina, Rome 17 April 1574, in ASM (AG) 6, no. 656; both are transcribed in A. Bertolotti: *Musici alla corte dei Gonzaga*, p. 50.

[26] Letter from Annibale Capello, Rome 18 October 1578, to the Duke of Mantua. The original is in ASM (AG) 943; the transcription in A. Bertolotti: *Musici alla corte dei Gonzaga*, p. 52, is now superseded by that in Strunk: 'Guglielmo Gonzaga', where an English translation is also provided.

[27] For the debate see Strunk: 'Guglielmo Gonzaga', pp. 100ff, Jeppesen: 'The recently discovered Mantova masses', pp. 40–2, and Jeppesen: 'Pierluigi da Palestrina'.

[28] Letter from Giovanni Pierluigi da Palestrina, Rome 5 November 1578, to the Duke of Mantua. Original in ASM (AG) 6, no. 658; transcriptions in A. Bertolotti: *Musici alla corte dei Gonzaga*, p. 52 (where the date is incorrectly given as 1 November), and in Strunk: 'Guglielmo Gonzaga', pp. 100–1, which also provides an English translation.

[29] Santa Barbara MSS 164 and 166 contain Palestrina's 'Mantuan' masses. See the descriptions in *Conservatorio di musica*, pp. 276–8 and 312–13, and Casimiri et al.: *Le opere complete di Giovanni Pierluigi da Palestrina*, XVIII and XIX.

exclusive use of the ducal basilica were, then, composed on chants selected by the duke and at least in some cases revised by him; and this procedure is confirmed by a comparison of the chants of the Santa Barbara liturgy with Palestrina's *cantus firmi*. The revisions themselves, as might be expected, mostly consist of changes made to assist declamation of the text; and perhaps the most significant aspect of the arrangement – with obvious implications for that part of the basilica's polyphonic repertory similarly composed on Santa Barbara chants – is that Guglielmo effectively instigated the compositional process while imposing constraints upon a composer's freedom of action.[30] The remaining letters reveal the size of the commission and the speed with which Palestrina completed it. On 15 November a second mass was sent by Capello, and another on 10 December; finally the composer himself sent off the last three in March 1579, with a note acknowledging the generous payment of one hundred *scudi d'oro*.[31] A tenth mass, for four men's voices, is probably the earliest one referred to in the correspondence, composed before the Santa Barbara plainsongs had been revised.

Apart from Palestrina, Duke Guglielmo also had an apparently fruitful series of detailed exchanges over musical matters with the Ferrarese composer Don Lodovico Agostini (probably the nephew of Agostino Agostini), who was associated from 1572 with the *cappella* of Ferrara Cathedral, where other members of his family had worked, and who from 1578 until his death in 1590 was employed at the Ferrarese court. By the time of his first letter to Guglielmo, dated 9 February 1575, Agostini had already published three collections of pieces, and he now embarked on a correspondence with the duke that seems to have lasted until July 1586, just over a year before Guglielmo's death. Quite frequently Agostini sent his own compositions to Guglielmo both in manuscript and after publication, and in 1581 his *L'echo et enigmi musicali a sei voci*, whose opening piece is addressed to Guglielmo, appeared with a dedication to the duke.[32] Shortly afterwards, in November 1582, Agostini sent copies of one of his publications, almost certainly the *Madrigali... libro terzo a sei voci* published that year in Ferrara, which includes pieces individually dedicated to both Guglielmo and Vincenzo Gonzaga, as well as to members of the Este family, two of the Ferrarese court *concerto delle donne* Anna Guarini and Laura Peperara, and Luzzasco Luzzaschi.[33] In

---

[30] For the surviving chant manuscripts from Santa Barbara, see Appendix III below. The revisions to the *Missa dominicalis* are discussed in Strunk: 'Guglielmo Gonzaga', pp. 104–7.

[31] See the letter of Annibale Capello, Rome 15 November 1578 beginning 'Mando a V. Alt^{za} la seconda messa del Palestrina...' (original document in ASM (AG) 943). Also a further letter from Capello to Duke Guglielmo, Rome 10 December 1578: 'Mando a V. Alt^{za} la quarta messa fatta dal Palestrina della quale egli molto si compiace' (ASM (AG) 943). Palestrina's note of 21 March 1579 is in ASM (AG) Raccolta d'autografi 6.

[32] The correspondence is noted in A. Bertolotti: *Artisti*, pp. 114–15, and has now been transcribed in full in Cavicchi: 'Lettere', pp. 191–9. The originals are in ASM (AG) 1254–7; my transcriptions are presented in Appendix II, docs. 25–40.

[33] Letter of Lodovico Agostini, Ferrara 20 November 1582, to the Duke of Mantua: Appendix II, doc. 29.

January of the next year Agostini sent Guglielmo a madrigal in score, and then on 23 July 1583 wrote thanking the duke for sending a copy of his own recently published book of madrigals. Seven days later these pieces had been tried out at Ferrara, and Agostini's report to the duke praised the pieces highly, claiming that they should be not only admired but imitated.[34] Already, it seems, Agostini had in mind his own madrigals parodying and imitating some of Guglielmo's pieces which appeared in his *Le lagrime del peccatore* (Venice, 1586), whose dedication to Guglielmo recalled the duke's gift of three years earlier. October 1583 brought another present, this time copies of Guglielmo's motets which Agostini then had bound for presentation to Alfonso II d'Este, and subsequently these too were performed and apparently admired, at least by Agostini who confessed to being so impressed with their art and invention that he felt intimidated at the idea of writing motets again himself.[35]

Indeed, although Agostini had a distinguished ecclesiastical career which culminated in appointments as monsignore and Protonotary Apostolic, and was the author of popular religious writings, he composed little sacred music: the *Canones et echo sex vocibus* (Venice, 1572), which contains liturgical settings, and his last publication, *Le lagrime del peccatore*, a set of spiritual madrigals based on texts by Tansillo. The *Canones* contains a prose for Saint Barbara, but there is no evidence that this piece, published three years before Agostini's correspondence with Guglielmo began, has any connection with the ducal basilica, and the Santa Barbara collection does not contain any of Agostini's music. Yet the association of the two composers may have involved not only the exchange of each other's work and mutual admiration, but also genuine criticism. On at least one occasion Agostini sent his work in score, and it is clear from contemporary theoretical writing and some surviving sources that one of the common uses of this format was to facilitate analysis and discussion of compositional techniques. We have seen that Palestrina transcribed one of Guglielmo's motets into score to do this; and in 1585 when Costanzo Porta sent two motets for the duke's opinion they were already in score.[36]

Guglielmo was evidently already composing by 1567, when his madrigal 'Padre ch'el ciel' was published in Wert's fourth book of five-voice madrigals; but it was only towards the end of his life that steps were taken to publish his works, 'not out of ambition, but simply in order that his former labours

[34] Letters of Lodovico Agostini, Ferrara 5 January, 23 July, and 30 July 1583, to the Duke of Mantua: Appendix II, docs. 31, 34 and 35.

[35] Letter of Lodovico Agostini, Ferrara October 1583, to the Duke of Mantua: Appendix II, doc. 32. Agostini's *Le lagrime* includes two madrigals 'sopra Padre del ciel del Serenissima Duca di Mantova', and one, 'Tu vedi ben', 'ad imitatione del Serenissima & Invitissima Signor Duca di Mantova'. For further on these pieces by Guglielmo see p. 94 below.

[36] Letter of Costanzo Porta, 19 January 1585, to the Duke of Mantua. Original in ASM (AG) 940; transcription in A. Bertolotti: *Artisti*, pp. 115–16. The duke's reply is in ASM (AG) 2954 and is dated 25 January 1585.

may not be lost entirely, some of them having already gone astray, and that he may enjoy from time to time the fruits of his past studies'.[37] In 1583, Antonio Gardane published a volume of five-voice madrigals by an anonymous composer. Anonymity was most frequently reserved in music publications for works of aristocratic authorship; and these pieces can be identified as Guglielmo's not only because the opening setting of 'Padre ch'el ciel' is an elaboration of *soggetti* shared with the setting of the same text ascribed to him in Wert's fourth book of 1567, but because the same model was used as the basis for two pieces published by Agostini in his *Le lagrime del peccatore* of 1586, where he revealed the composer of the original. Further quotations from the anonymous madrigals of 1583 can also be found in the second edition of Girolamo Belli's *I furti amorosi* (Venice, 1587), which is dedicated to the duke, and Belli's preface acknowledges that he used Guglielmo's pieces.[38] Agostini's letters from Ferrara in late July 1583 reporting the performance of some of Guglielmo's madrigals presumably refer to this publication, and about the same time Muzio Gonzaga presented 'a copy of the books of music composed by His Highness and recently printed to the Archduke Karl in Graz'. The anonymous *Sacrae cantiones quinque vocum in festis duplicibus maioribus ecclesiae Sanctae Barbarae* also published by Gardane in the same year is also certainly Guglielmo's, not only because of the associations with the basilica, but also because the copies surviving in the Santa Barbara collection are inscribed 'Motetti di S[ua] A[ltezza] a 5'. These are perhaps the works which Agostini performed in Ferrara and admired, and which Pallavicino praised, together with Guglielmo's magnificats, in the dedication of his *Il primo libro de madrigali a sei voci* (Venice, 1587).[39] The appearance of these two anonymous volumes, both published in 1583 by Gardane, raises the possibility that the (now incomplete) *Villotte mantovane* which he brought out in the same year is also Guglielmo's work.[40] Surviving letters and contemporary printed works refer to two books of magnificats composed by the duke, and although no copies survive of the publication, their contents may be duplicated in two manuscripts in the Santa Barbara collection containing anonymous magnificats.[41] Other pieces also survive attributed to him in manuscript: three five-voice masses, of which one is

[37] Minute di lettere della cancelleria ducale: letter of Duke Guglielmo Gonzaga, Mantua 27 July 1583, to Muzio Gonzaga in Graz. The original is in ASM (AG) 2215, and is reported in Canal: *Della musica in Mantova*, p. 685, and Strunk: 'Guglielmo Gonzaga', p. 96.
[38] [G. Gonzaga]: *Madrigali a cinque voci*, Wert: *Il quarto libro de madrigali a cinque voci*, p. 1 and dedication, Agostini: *Le lagrime*, and Belli: *I furti amorosi*.
[39] For the Santa Barbara copies of the *Sacrae cantiones* see *Conservatorio di musica*, p. 42, and Appendix III below. The dedication of Pallavicino's first book of six-voice madrigals is excerpted in Vogel: *Bibliothek*.
[40] A suggestion first made in Einstein: *The Italian madrigal*, II, pp. 751–4.
[41] Letter of Angelo Gardane, Venice 12 July 1586, to Giaches de Wert in Mantua. The original is in ASM (AG) 1571. The transcription in A. Bertolotti: *Musici alla corte dei Gonzaga*, pp. 45–6, is now superseded by that in Sherr: 'The publications of Guglielmo Gonzaga', pp. 124–5, where it is suggested that the duke's magnificat settings survive as Santa Barbara MSS 9 and 16.

presumably the work submitted to Palestrina for criticism, and a setting of the Te Deum.[42]

Enough has already been said about Guglielmo's contacts with composers outside Mantua, particularly Palestrina and Agostini, to suggest the very special character of his patronage of music. As a wealthy patron who not only took a keen interest in music but had published compositions of his own, the duke was in the very unusual position of being able to specify in precise and technical terms the style or content of a piece of music. It is clear that many of the composers with whom he corresponded, and who were presumably looking for sponsorship, were sending compositions in study form and were receiving critical replies. Unfortunately few of Guglielmo's answers to his musical correspondents have survived; but the cumulative evidence of his few documented remarks about musical style and his own pieces suggest that he took a consistently conservative position, greatly admiring contrapuntal skill, and placing a high value on clarity of text, at least in liturgical works. It is also clear that the composers employed at Mantua were involved in advising Guglielmo over compositional matters, and later helped to prepare his works for the press. In August 1586, for example, when Wert wrote to a ducal official asking for permission to visit Ferrara he demonstrated the urgency of his request by saying that otherwise he would not have left the court while the duke was composing; and later in that same year Pallavicino acted as a proofreader for a volume of the duke's magnificats which had apparently been printed by Gardane. Both Wert and Pallavicino were deeply involved in the musical arrangements for Santa Barbara, and a combination of documents and the surviving music suggests that a great deal of their time was spent composing for the basilica and that Guglielmo himself took a strong interest in their work. Indeed, the growth and operation of liturgical music at Santa Barbara is important to an understanding of the duke's conception of this quite extraordinary Counter-Reformation institution, and it is the foundation and construction of the basilica and the role of music in its rite that will now be considered.

More than any other single artistic project carried out during his time as Duke of Mantua, the construction, special liturgical arrangements and general operations of the palatine basilica of Santa Barbara, devised as a ducal chapel on a grand scale, occupied Guglielmo almost to the point of obsession. There had been a number of previous Gonzaga chapels, some of which remained in use after Santa Barbara had been completed, including two small family chapels in the old Castello di San Giorgio, Marchese Francesco's chapel of Santa Maria dei Voti in the cathedral, and the small church of Santa Croce in Piazza within the confines of the Palazzo Ducale. Reports of the pastoral

[42] See Gallico: 'Guglielmo Gonzaga' for an almost complete list of Guglielmo's musical compositions.

visitation of 1575 noted (in addition to Santa Barbara itself) Santa Croce, the two chapels in the *castello*, and three other chapels one of which at least contained an organ.[43] Nevertheless, by the early 1560s the arrangements then in operation were thought to be insufficient for a court which had increased in size and was extending its use of ceremonial in proportion to its ambitions. This much is clear from an anonymous account of Guglielmo's wedding to Eleonora of Austria in April 1561, when mass was said in the 'cappelletta vecchia di sopra' (presumably the chapel in the Palazzo del Capitano), while the duke was in the Sala dei Cavalli and the singers in the Sala Grande.[44] In July of the same year a new or refurbished chapel in the *castello* was completed, but the first steps in the direction of Guglielmo's more ambitious schemes were taken in November when plans were laid to construct a new church in the *Gioco della Palla*, the area reserved for ball games within the confines of the *fabbrica nuova*.[45] The new building was to consist of six side chapels and a main altar, was to be large enough to accommodate a college of canons, and was to supersede the functions of Santa Croce. Under pressure from Guglielmo matters proceeded quickly, and by 19 November excavations for the campanile were already in hand. About the same time, the duke applied to Pius IV through the Mantuan agent Tonnina for permission to transfer to the new foundation the ten chaplaincies established in the cathedral under the terms of Duke Federico's will with an endowment of 10,000 *scudi*; and with the help of Cardinal Ercole's influence the request was quickly considered by the Curia and acceded to in a Bull of 2 September 1562, *Sincerae devotionis affectus*. One tradition claims that the removal of benefices from the cathedral and the cost of Guglielmo's ambitious plans were disapproved of by Ercole, whose pastoral directive of 1551 had criticised the kind of superfluous spending and ostentation which Guglielmo's plans eventually involved; but by April 1562 the new church in the *Gioco della Palla* was practically completed, and in May it was consecrated by the suffragan bishop and dedicated to Saint Barbara.[46] Just a few months later, perhaps in gratitude for the safe birth of his son and heir Vincenzo on 22 September 1562, Guglielmo had already instructed the overseer of the ducal fabric,

[43] AGCAB MS H 492, Visitacio Mantua 1575, fos. 519ff, gives the Visitors' reactions after their inspection of Santa Barbara on 3 February 1576. The report makes special mention of the music at the basilica, singling out Wert and Gastoldi for special mention. The Bologna volume is the companion volume to ASDM (CV) Visite pastorale 1575 II, which describes the court chapels on fos. 651ff.

[44] ASDM (SB) Diario di Mantova 1561–1601, unfoliated. The description helps to identify the chapel as that on the first floor of the Palazzo del Capitano, the Sala dei Cavalli presumably being the nearby room in which Pisanello's frescoes depicting a tournament have recently been uncovered, and the Sala Grande the main chamber which lies between the two. The chapel was still in use in 1575 when it was described by the Visitors in ASDM (CV) Visite pastorale 1575 II, for 652v ff. For photographs of the chapel see Paccagnini: *Il palazzo ducale*, pp. 14–18.

[45] Letter of Baldassare de Preti, Mantua 9 July 1561, to Cardinal Ercole Gonzaga: 'la chiesola che ha fatto far Sua Ecc.za in Castello sarà finita fra due giorni'. Original in ASM (AG) 1935. See also the letter of Ercole Gonzaga, 9 November 1561, to the Castellano. The original is in ASM (AG) 2141, and is partly transcribed in Gozzi: 'La basilica palatina', p. 39 n. 11.

[46] Gozzi: 'La basilica palatina', pp. 8–9, where the necessary source material is cited.

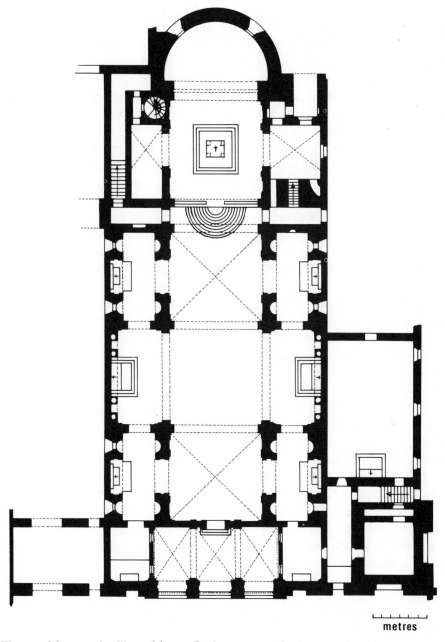

metres

Fig. 7   Mantua, basilica of Santa Barbara, ground plan

Giovanni Battista Bertani, to draw up plans for a larger and more impressive structure on the same site. The Mantuan ecclesiastical historian Ippolito Donesmondi interestingly says that the inadequate space for musicians in the first building was the principal motivation for the new project, and while

there may be some truth in this it is certainly significant that the planning
and construction of this second church coincides with Guglielmo's reorganisation of the state.[47] During the 1560s there was a considerable development
of Guglielmo's personal style of government and his presentation of a
Gonzaga image quite different from that associated with Cardinal Ercole,
and many of the most distinctive features of the building are best explained
by reference to the elaborate state and religious functions that were to take
place inside (cf. Figure 7).

There is some confusion about when work began on the new basilica, but
it was certainly in progress by February 1563, and by October of the
following year the altars and the crypt were consecrated. This completed the
first phase of construction, but even the main outline of the church had not
reached its final shape, and only two years later the main chapel was enlarged
by demolishing the east wall and adding a semicircular apse and a passage
connecting the choir with the Sala di Manto in the *fabbrica nuova*. Work began
in January 1569 and was finished by late 1572, and while the reasons for
the alterations are unclear they do underline the special character of
Guglielmo's conception of Santa Barbara, and probably affected the performance conditions of the liturgy.[48]

There is some doubt as to how the basilica looked in October 1564 when
it was virtually completed and the first consecration took place, partly since
rearrangements in 1724 destroyed some of the original planning of the
interior, and partly because of the modifications of 1569–72. From the
documents it is clear that there were then eight altars, a main chapel and
two cupolas, and that the crypt had been finished. A letter from Giulio
Bruschi to the duke in October 1564 in connection with the consecration
ceremonies describes the altar as being in the middle of the church beyond
the balustrade of the choir, and this has been interpreted to mean that the
permanent position of the high altar was in the middle of the nave. Viewed
in this way, the remodelling of the main chapel involved not merely a change
in the shape of the east end, but a radical reorganisation to accommodate
the high altar in its new position. But against this interpretation is the
evidence of a letter from the ducal secretary Luigi Rogna written in April
1568, some nine months before any alterations to the main chapel are
recorded. According to Rogna the changes were to allow the high altar to
be placed in the middle as in St Peter's in Rome and the abbot's chair to
be placed where the altar had previously been.[49] This more likely arrange-

[47] Donesmondi: *Dell'istoria*, p. 206, ASDM (SB) MS 1760, p. 4, and Amadei: *Cronaca universale*, p. 726.
[48] Gozzi: 'La basilica palatina' gathers together most of the documentation concerning these first two
phases of the building history of the basilica. As will become clear, I believe Gozzi's explanation of
the alterations of 1569–72 to be questionable.
[49] Letter of Giulio Bruschi, Mantua 5 October 1564, to the Duke of Mantua: 'tutto apparato sin alla
porta, lo altare [è] nel mezzo della chiesa, fuori dalle balustre del coro, Mons^re Illmo ha fatto l'ufficio,
la sedia di S. Ecc^za Illma è ala prima colona da presso lo pilastro del choro, li canonici vi erano

ment fits well with the earliest view of the interior of Santa Barbara (Figure 6), engraved by Frans Geffels for the official account of the obsequies for Carlo II in 1666: this shows the altar in its present position in the centre of the sanctuary, with the officiating clergy ranged around the apse.[50] But whichever solution is preferred, both underline the special character of the basilica in two ways. First, the alterations of 1572 seem to be clearly motivated by an attempt to increase the prestige of the Santa Barbara clergy and to emphasise both their hierarchical structure and that of the court itself by a physical arrangement that was more imposing, discriminatory, and theatrical. Secondly, the new placing of the altar allowed the celebrant to face the congregation, a rarely granted Papal privilege which not only makes Rogna's comparison extremely apposite but lends some truth to Pius IV's reported comment on the Santa Barbara project, 'facciamo un Papa di Santa Barbara'. The result, if the 1666 engraving can be taken as an indication of earlier practices, was a characteristic and convenient merging of earthly and celestial deities within the sanctuary gates.

At the same time, the placing of the choir behind the altar was a common interpretation of Tridentine attitudes as they affected church architecture, and was propagated and enforced later in the century through pastoral visits and episcopal letters in Mantua as elsewhere. Perhaps the most interesting aspect of Santa Barbara in general terms is that here, only shortly after the Council of Trent had issued its directive about sacred building, is an attempt to construct and decorate a church in a manner loyal to the spirit of the council, a highly personal interpretation of its deliberately vague pronouncements about sacred art and ecclesiastical architecture, which also emphasised the power and dignity of the Gonzaga and provided a suitable setting for state and family ceremonial.[51] Bertani's restrained classicism speaks the same language as Giulio Romano's style during the last years of his life, and indeed some details of Santa Barbara can be traced directly to Giulio's example, particularly to his alterations to the monastery church at San Benedetto Po, begun in 1539. Similarly, the arrangement and the decoration of the side altars demonstrate a sobriety which is appropriate to the general theme, while showing some sympathy for Ercole's decorative schemes in the cathedral. The dedications of the altars were determined by their relics: each contained the remains of three saints, the most important of which according to the Church's classification was selected for depiction in the altarpiece. The earliest letters about these paintings date from October 1564, when Bertani

dietro...' Letter of Luigi Rogna, Mantua 26 April 1568: 'S. Ecc^za stà per agrandir la capella grande si Sta Barbara mettando l'Altare in mezo, come e quello di San Pietro, et mettando la sedia dell'Abbate, dove hora è lo Altare.' The originals are in ASM (AG) 2572 and 2579 respectively.

[50] See D'Arco: *Delle arti*, ii, pp. 183 and 185, Thieme and Becker: *Allgemeines Lexicon*, xiii, pp. 334–5, A. Bertolotti: 'Architetti', pp. 117ff, and *Mantova. Le arti*, iii, pp. 516–17.

[51] For the Council of Trent and architecture see Schroeder (trans.): *Canons and decrees*, session xxv, tit. 2, Blunt: *Artistic theory*, chapter 8, and Schlosser: *La letteratura artistica*.

was negotiating with Lorenzo Costa the Younger for the Saint Barbara altarpiece, with Fermo Ghisoni for the pictures of the Virgin and Saint Adrian, and with Domenico Brusasorci for the altarpiece for the main altar.[52] Of the three the most prestigious was Costa (the son of the Ferrarese painter who had become the principal artist at the Gonzaga court after the death of Mantegna), who was already known to the Gonzaga through his work at the cathedral and perhaps through a number of other commissions including those executed in the early months of 1564 for Alfonso Gonzaga, Count of Novellara. According to Vasari, the choice of Brusasorci as the artist of the main altarpiece was Guglielmo's, impressed with the picture of Saint Margaret that he had executed for the cathedral. Four years elapse before anything further is recorded about the altarpieces, and in the event, Costa painted two of them, the *Martyrdom of Saint Adrian* completed during 1569–70, and the *Baptism of Constantine* finished in January 1572. Together with the crucifix for the main altar, worked by Anteo della Mola in July 1570, these were the first decorations to be put in place.[53]

Guglielmo's founding of the basilica, and his subsequent concern for the details of its management, may have been motivated by genuine piety or by the simple desire to convince his subjects, if not the rest of Christian Europe, that he possessed the qualities necessary in a God-fearing ruler; at the same time he was evidently aware of the propagandistic possibilities of the Santa Barbara project. Whether or not the initial decision to construct the basilica was directly inspired by the birth of his son and heir, the choice of patron saint may also have been prompted by dynastic motives, since Barbara was not only the patroness of the house of Gonzaga but also recalled Barbara of Brandenburg, the Hohenzollern wife of Marchese Ludovico Gonzaga (1444–78); moreover, Guglielmo's second daughter was baptised Margherita

[52] The relics for the altars are listed on a single sheet preserved with a letter of 14 October 1564 in ASM (AG) 2572:

S. Barbarae	S. Crucis
S. Martae	S. Catherinae
S. Lazari	S. Galli
S. Magdalenae	S. Margaritae
S. Eucarij	S. Blasi
S. Damiani	S. Valerij
S. Adriani	S. Silvestri
S. Mauritij	S. Martini
S. Cristiantiae	S. Anastasiae
Gloriosae Virginis Mariae	S. Johanis Baptistae
S. Simeonis	S. Cosmae
S. Debeon	S. Luciae

This iconographical scheme is also reflected in a number of books of motets written for the basilica, notably Duke Guglielmo's own *Sacrae cantiones*. It is also very common to find the liturgy for the name-days of these saints occupying a prominent position in the work of composers associated with the basilica.

[53] See Gozzi: 'La basilica palatina', pp. 28ff, and Gozzi: 'Lorenzo Costa il Giovane', pp. 41–2. For Brusasorci see Vasari–Milanesi: *Le vite*, VI, p. 367.

Barbara on 17 May 1565, only a few days before the new basilica was consecrated.[54] There are other ways, too, in which Saint Barbara fitted neatly into Guglielmo's vision of a dynastic church. According to legend, Barbara was extremely beautiful and for this reason was imprisoned by her father Dioscurus at the top of a high tower at Heliopolis in Syria. During her father's absence she became converted to Christianity and was baptised, and it was this which prompted her to persuade some workmen who were building two windows into her tower to add a third in honour of the Trinity. Dioscurus, a fanatical pagan, was unimpressed by her readily confessed reasons for this architectural modification and attempted to kill her, but she was miraculously transported to a nearby mountain summit. Nevertheless, her place of refuge was eventually discovered, and she was taken before the magistrates, who condemned her to death for her religious beliefs; Dioscurus carried out the sentence himself but was subsequently struck down by lightning, presumably in divine retribution.

Despite the obvious weaknesses of the myth, even by the standards of the genre, Barbara was an extremely popular object of devotion throughout medieval Europe. The cult seems to have begun in the seventh century, and by the ninth her name appears in an English calendar; the story is related in countless martyrologies, is the subject of a considerable body of literature including Caxton's *Golden Legend*, and generated a fertile iconography. This popularity is partly a reflection of the multitude of occupations and human conditions over which she was reputed to exercise protection, as the patron of architects, artillery-founders, prisoners, and stonemasons, and as the protector against thunderstorms, fire, and sudden death. She is generally represented in paintings and miniatures in one of two ways, either with a miniature tower in her hands, or else with a tower behind her and a crown on her head, holding either the palm or the sword of martyrdom as well as a chalice surmounted by a radiant sun. But Barbara was appropriate as the patron saint of the new basilica not only because of her secure position in the calendar and a tradition of devotion in the Gonzaga family, but also because she was principally thought of as the patron saint of war.[55] It is, then, not surprising that she became the dedicatee of a church which served as a visual symbol of Gonzaga wealth, power, and authority; nor is it remarkable that the tower which was the scene of her martyrdom was taken by Bertani as a cue for one of the building's most striking features, the tall and architecturally unconventional campanile which dominates both the city and the surrounding *contado*.

According to the *Constitutiones* drawn up in 1568, the establishment of the new basilica consisted of nine ordinary canons and six supernumeraries, four

[54] Bautier-Regnier: 'Jacques de Wert', p. 47, and Donesmondi: *Dell'istoria*, p. 207.
[55] Kirschbaum: *Lexicon der christlichen Ikonographie*, v, pp. 304–11.

mansionarii, a variable number of chaplains, two *maestri di ceremonie* and a sacristan; in addition there were usually twenty or so aspirants (*chierici*), two deacons, two subdeacons, an organist, and a *maestro di cappella*. At full strength the institution employed sixty-four people, presided over by an abbot and six dignitaries.[56] As a specially constituted and privileged institution, Santa Barbara was responsible not to the local diocesan authorities but to the Holy See, and a further indication of exclusiveness was the development of a distinctive Santa Barbara rite with its own separate missal and breviary, based on reformist principles. The Santa Barbara liturgy, which was to some extent Guglielmo's own work, did not come into immediate operation but was the subject of long negotiations with Rome, conducted between the duke and Cardinal Sirleto from 1568 to 1579. From the Vatican's point of view the arrangements over Santa Barbara were merely one aspect of a process of liturgical reform begun in earnest by Pius V and continued under Gregory XIII.[57] The breviary was finally published with Papal approval in 1583 in two formats: a small pocket version put out by Giunta in Venice, presumably for use by the Santa Barbara clergy, and a larger edition printed by Nicolini. In the same year the basilica's own missal was published, and two years later the ducal printing-house Osanna brought out the *Officium defunctorum*. This was done partly for the sake of prestige, since for practical purposes the plainsong repertory continued to be copied into choirbooks, more than twenty of which survive containing mass chants, propers, hymns, psalms, antiphons and responses.[58] And, as has already been stressed, the 'reformed' Santa Barbara chant, partly the work of the duke himself, lent a particular stamp to polyphonic works using the chants as *cantus firmi*.

The operation of the liturgy is reasonably unambiguous in the documents. The celebrant and his assistants faced the congregation, and the rest of the clergy, including those responsible for the performance of the chant, were ranged around the apse behind the celebrant.[59] On feast-days, when polyphony was performed, the musicians were placed in the gallery at the west end, and since one account mentions both clerics and musicians it is perhaps reasonable to assume that chanted and polyphonic sections of *alternatim* settings were sung from there rather than from the east and west

[56] Donesmondi: *Dell'istoria*, p. 209. The 'Constitutiones Capituli S. Barbarae Mantuae', dated 1568, are preserved in ASDM (SB). Lists of the clerics and other related material are in ASM (AG) 3294: for extracts from one pay list, see Appendix II, doc. 41. See also Bresciani: 'Stato del clero', a manuscript compilation of 1901 in ASDM (SB), and the remarks on the arrangement of the archive in Appendix I.

[57] See the general account of the reform of service books in Jedin: 'Das Konzil von Trient'. The correspondence between Guglielmo Gonzaga and Cardinal Sirleto is preserved in BAV Cod. Vat. Lat. 6946, 6182, and 6183.

[58] For the printed books from Santa Barbara in ASDM (SB) see Appendix III below. A great deal of recopying was carried out by the Santa Barbara scribes, particularly Vicentini, shortly after the new missal was published: see the payment documents in ASDM (SB) Filcia LXXVII. Mandati di spesa del 1579 et 1580.

[59] See the description, closely related to Donesmondi's account, in ASM (AG) 3294: 'L'Altar grande e posto nel mezo [of the main chapel] sotto un cupola alta havendo di dietro in figura di mezo tondo spatio competente per il choro.' Cf. Donesmondi: *Dell'istoria*, pp. 211ff, and see Appendix II, doc. 42.

ends of the basilica alternately. Small galleries high up on the north and south walls accommodated the organ and members of the court respectively. There is no room in the organ gallery for performers, other than the organist, and no evidence that the instrument was ever placed elsewhere. The small gallery on the north side originally connected with the palace, and two connecting corridors linked the palace with vantage points overlooking the high altar. Most probably these were reserved for high-ranking ladies of the court, who were excluded from the sanctuary, and this is the arrangement shown in Geffels's engraving (Figure 6), which also shows the duke and some male courtiers sitting within the sanctuary.[60]

It was the duty of the Prefect of the Chorus to ensure that the correct chant was used as laid down in the liturgy, to teach the chant to other clerics, and to rehearse the celebrants who were to sing mass and the other services.[61] The Prefect was assisted in these duties by two canons who also taught chant, while the *mansionarii* were primarily responsible for the chanting of offices and giving intonations. Constitutionally four *mansionarii* were required, and this strength seems to have been maintained a good deal more consistently than some of the other appointments. The *maestro di cappella* was responsible for the polyphony required by the *Constitutiones* on feast-days, bringing in singers from the court if necessary.[62] As with polyphonic music, the occasions on which the organ was required are specified, in such a way that there is no reason to believe that the organist accompanied either chant or polyphony at this date. Neither is there any indication in the Santa Barbara manuscripts of an organ being used, and the lack of payments to instrumentalists further suggests *a cappella* performance, as might be expected in an institution so strongly influenced by Tridentine thinking. It is difficult to know when the arrangements for the performance of polyphonic music in Santa Barbara were first considered. Though writing at some distance from events, Donesmondi claimed that the basilica was constructed so that elaborate music could be performed as part of the liturgy.[63] Certainly Bertani's original plan, as executed between early 1563 and March 1567, included provision for a large gallery for the musicians running the entire length of the west wall, and it may be that negotiations about the organ (which is still standing, though in a much restored condition) may have been started as early as August 1563 when Giulio Bruschi, who was acting for the duke in many of the internal arrangements of the basilica, had dealings with Girolamo da Urbino

---

[60] Gozzi: 'La basilica palatina', p. 32, proposes that the organ was originally placed in one of the lateral chapels of the main altar. Her view, presumably based on the assumption that polyphony was always accompanied, is that the present location is disadvantageous. This is not supported by documentary or iconographical evidence, and both Donesmondi and the account in ASM (AG) 3294 seem perfectly unambiguous: 'sopra le capelle picciole ad alto sono altri luoghi di dove si può veder in chiesa, et in uno di questi spatij e situato l'organo'.

[61] For the relevant excerpts from the 'Constitutiones' on which the following discussion is based see Appendix III, doc. 43.

[62] ASM (AG) 3294: 'e se bene i cantori sono pochi suppliscono i cappellani, ordinati et chierici, che tutti cantono per ragion di musica'.   [63] Donesmondi: *Dell'istoria*, p. 201.

(i.e. Girolamo Cavazzoni). The instrument was largely constructed in June and July of 1565 by the distinguished Brescian builder Graziadio Antegnati, but it was finally finished only in September of that year. Originally planned to have eight registers, it was finally completed with twelve, and Girolamo himself spoke warmly of the instrument and estimated its value at 600 *ducati*.[64] In 1570 Costanzo Antegnati, the son of the builder, was called to Mantua to repair damage to the instrument evidently caused by the reconstruction of the east end of the basilica, and in March 1572 the paintings were attached to the organ shutters. These paintings, traditionally attributed to Lorenzo Costa the Younger, showed the Annunciation with the shutters open, and (interestingly, in view of Pius IV's reported remark) Saint Peter as well as Saint Barbara when closed.[65]

In considering the formation of a nucleus of performing musicians at Santa Barbara, a distinction must be made between those canons of the basilica whose official duties included musical responsibilities, and court musicians who took part in performances in Santa Barbara on feast-days and important ceremonial occasions. Reconstruction is further complicated by the almost complete lack of records for the basilica before 1573. The earliest list of the clergy, dated June 1565, notes archpriest, archdeacon, provost, deacon, and sixteen other clerics of whom half were canons; another list, undated but probably copied about the same period, omits five of these sixteen but includes four new *ordinati* including Giulio Guarnero and Gioseffo Vicentini. The former is recorded together with Gastoldi as a teacher of plainsong, polyphony and counterpoint to the aspirants (*chierici*) from September 1579, when reasonably complete documentation begins; and Vicentini is entered in the *provisione* from the same date and was the principal scribe of the basilica's choirbooks until Francesco Sforza began work towards the end of the century.[66] Both men clearly had musical skills and would have been able to participate in the musical aspects of the liturgy even though not holding the position of *mansionarii*, whose primary duty, as laid down in the *Constitutiones*, was to ensure that the chant was correctly and efficiently performed. In other words, it is as difficult to estimate the size of the choir at Santa Barbara as it is at the cathedral, since even where records exist some men with musical skills are not recognised as such, while on some occasions performers from outside the basilica were used.

[64] For the early references to Bruschi see ASM (AG) 3124, payment of 23 August 1563. For the construction of the organ see the letter of Giovanni Battista Bertani, Mantua 9 June 1565, to the Duke of Mantua, in ASM (AG) 2573. The originals of Graziadio Antegnati's letters are kept in ASM (AG) 1498 and 1509 and are transcribed in A. Bertolotti: *Musici alla corte dei Gonzaga*, pp. 37–8. The account in Levri: *Gli organi di Mantova*, pp. 31–2, is based not on the original documentation but upon summaries of the correspondence in ASM (Davari) 16. See also Mischiati: 'I cataloghi di tre organari bresciani'.

[65] Gozzi: 'La basilica palatina', p. 88 doc. 222. The attribution to Costa has been questioned: see *Mantova. Le arti*, III, p. 384, and Gozzi: 'Lorenzo Costa il Giovane', p. 53.

[66] The undated list and that of June 1565 are in ASM (AG) 2573. The post-1579 documents are summarised in Tagmann: 'La cappella dei maestri cantori'. For Guarnero and Gastoldi see ASDM (SB) Filcia LXXVII. Mandati de spesa del 1579 et 1580. For Vicentini and for Sforza, see Appendix III below.

It is clear from the documents that many of the original ideas about the detailed working of Santa Barbara were formulated by the duke and then translated into practice by court officials. Among these was Giulio Bruschi, a Piacenzan composer of modest abilities whose position as Guglielmo's *maestro di cappella* in the years just before Giaches de Wert's arrival at the Mantuan court has caused some confusion. Many of the first clerics to be employed at Santa Barbara had previously been at the cathedral, and were no doubt attracted to the basilica by the more favourable conditions and prestige of the new posts, a pattern of transfer between the two institutions that continued throughout the century. An early reference to Bruschi comes from 1552–3, when he received payments as the *Mansionario di Santa Speciosa* in the cathedral, and his name continues to appear in the annual records until 1560, though since the character of the records changes so drastically from that year with the list of the chapter clergy now omitted, it cannot be assumed that Bruschi left the cathedral in that year or indeed at all.[67] Certainly receipts for occasional payments suggest that he maintained contact with the cathedral while taking up new responsibilities in connection with Santa Barbara. Bruschi's earliest recorded dealings with the court seem to have been in 1561, when in return for some unspecified service the duke rewarded him with rights to some land.[68] In general, he acted in two capacities at Santa Barbara: as Guglielmo's *maestro di cappella* for a brief period, and as an adviser on some of the arrangements of the interior of the basilica and its operations. In October 1564, for example, when the initial soundings over the Santa Barbara altarpieces were being made, Bruschi was sent to Verona to discuss matters with Domenico Brusasorci, and as already noted he may have been involved in negotiations over the organ. His name appears most frequently in connection with the arrangements for polyphonic music before the basilica became fully operational in October 1564. When Guglielmo sent him to the Prior of San Savino in August 1563 he was described as 'il Brusco mio maestro di cappella', though this is sometimes such an unspecific description of any musician of higher status than 'musico' that it cannot be necessarily taken to mean that Bruschi was Wert's predecessor in status. About this time Bruschi was also involved in attempts to hire new singers, and in June 1565 he sent a lengthy report to Guglielmo assessing the abilities of singers who had been brought to Italy in the entourage of the Cardinal of Augsburg.[69] Other letters, including a number which contain early descriptions of the

[67] See ASDM (Cap.) LM 1552–3 fos. 21v and 30v, and LM 1552 fos. 25v and 41v for the first entries. Thereafter LM 1553 fo. 107v, 1554 fo. 109v, 1555 fo. 128v, 1556 fo. 131v, 1557 fo. 120v, 1558 fo. 114v, 1559 fo. 282v, 1560 p. 285.

[68] There are occasional payments in ASDM (Cap.) Filza: Rendiconti Sec. xvi(1) [actually 1539–97] Distribuzione: 1556, 1557, 1561, 1563, 1565, 1566. See also, in the same *busta*, the list of 'Dinari distribuiti alli S^ri Canonici che intravvenero alla Processione della Translatione della Reliquie che sonno a Sta Barbara a di 26 Novembre 1564', which also includes Bruschi. His earliest dealings with the court are noted in ASM (Davari) 16, fo. 300.

[69] The *copialettere* of the duke's notes to the Prior of San Savino, dated 19 August 1563 and 18 January 1564, are in ASM (AG) 2646 lib. 355, fos. 93v and 103v. Bruschi's report on the Cardinal of Augsburg's singers, in a letter of June 1565, is in ASM (AG) 2573: see below, p. 114 note 98.

performance of the Santa Barbara rite, place special emphasis upon music, and Bruschi was among the first to compose polyphony for the basilica's liturgy. It is not clear when Bruschi's association with Santa Barbara stopped, but he may have been involved as late as 1569.[70]

Another composer who was concerned with the early arrangements for polyphony was Giovanni Contino. Born in Brescia about 1513 and trained at the school attached to Brescia Cathedral where he was a chorister, he was employed about 1541 as a household musician by the Archbishop of Trent, Cardinal Cristoforo Madruzzo,[71] but ten years later returned to Brescia to take up a five-year contract as *maestro di cappella* at the cathedral, a contract which was apparently renewed for a further five years in 1556. It used to be thought that Contino's involvement at Mantua was restricted to a brief period after 1561, but recent documents establish him at both San Pietro and Santa Barbara at later times, including the period from August 1573 until his death in March 1574; he is recorded during this period as 'Mons. Giovanni Contino Decano' at Santa Barbara.[72] Another musician who continued in this tradition of dual service was Giovanni Maria di Rossi, also of Brescia, who was apparently curator of the ducal instrument collection during the regency, *maestro di cappella* at the cathedral between 1563 and 1576, and organist there from 1582 to 1585; he seems also to have been a singer at court.[73]

The extra documentation concerning Contino reinforces what might have been inferred from other evidence which has always suggested a deeper involvement at Mantua than a brief spell in the early 1560s. His five-voice *Missa dominicalis* was one of several works based on chants drawn from the Santa Barbara liturgy.[74] Three other five-voice works survive only in Santa Barbara sources, and the 1611 inventory of the basilica's music holdings

---

[70] See Bruschi's letters, Mantua 28 June 1565 and 12 May 1566, in ASM (AG) 2573 and 2575. What may be a late reference to him comes in a letter from the Bishop of Verona, Verona 17 August 1569, to the duke: 'Ho sentito molta consolatione intendere col testimonio di V. Ecc^tia la buona prova che fa D. Giulio in quella sua chiesa di Sta Barbara.' The original is in ASM (AG) 1501. Two letters of October 1564 speak of his compositions: (1) letter of 5 October 1564, to the Duke of Mantua, in ASM (AG) 2572: 'Con tutta la Ecc^tia mia in musica, mi rompo il capo intorno alli salmi'; (2) letter of 18 October 1564, to the duke, in the same *busta*: 'Penso che questa mattina saranno finiti li salmi della Vig^a di Sta Barbara, se non mi vien male come ho havuto da Domenica in qua.' If Bruschi was writing polyphonic psalms, they have not survived. (See below, p. 114 note 99).

[71] Madruzzo was an important patron of music, a reforming churchman, and a close friend of Ercole Gonzaga's; he continued to make quite frequent visits to Mantua after the latter's death. These contacts are underlined by close musical relations between Trent and Mantua. Contino's 'Austriae stirpis' was written for the entry of Caterina of Austria and Francesco Gonzaga into Trent in 1549 (see Dunning: *Die Staatsmotette*, pp. 308–16), and Contino's own choir apparently performed at the Council of Trent.

[72] Guerrini: 'Giovanni Contino di Brescia', pp. 130ff, Tagmann: *Archivalische Studien*, pp. 17–19, and Tagmann: 'La cappella dei maestri cantori', p. 379. It is also worth noting that Contino's first book of magnificats, published in Ferrara in 1571, of which a set of parts survives in the Santa Barbara collection, is dedicated to Guglielmo, and that Contino's music was being extensively copied into the basilica's manuscripts about the same time.

[73] Tagmann: *Archivalische Studien*, pp. 17ff, and MacClintock: *Giaches de Wert*, p. 31.

[74] Masses by Contino, Gastoldi, Palestrina, Rovigo, Striggio, and Wert, on Santa Barbara plainsongs, are in Pellini (ed.): *Missae dominicales quinis vocibus* (Milan, 1592).

included a representative selection of his published works. Contino's presence at Mantua from about 1568 until 1574 does not materially affect the general impression of musical conservatism which characterises the city churches and which emanated from Santa Barbara; but it does raise the intriguing possibility that Marenzio may have spent some time at Mantua during that period, since Marenzio's career was apparently bound up with that of Contino at a number of points.

But the major figure associated with the first arrangements for polyphony at Santa Barbara was Wert, who was probably born at Wert near Antwerp about 1535, and who was brought to Italy as a child and placed as a choirboy in the *cappella* of Maria di Cardona, Marchesa of Padulla, at Avellino near Naples. It has been suggested that Wert spent some time at Ferrara about 1550, but the evidence is not conclusive, and nothing further is definitely known about his career until 1558 when he is firmly recorded in the service of Alfonso Gonzaga at Novellara, where he may have been since 1553. This appointment provides the obvious link with Mantua, but Wert evidently had other connections as well: in 1561 he may have been in the Farnese chapel at Parma under the direction of Rore, and the dedication of his third book of five-voice madrigals of 1563 indicates that he had been in the service of Consalvo Fernandes di Cordova, Duke of Sessa and Governor of Milan. Wert was thus established in print by the time he entered Gonzaga service, probably in 1564 but certainly by February 1565, some five months after services began in the basilica.[75] He is referred to as *maestro di cappella* from the start, and although the initial status of his appointment is unclear in respect of the position of Bruschi, who continued to compose music for Santa Barbara after Wert's arrival, he seems to have rapidly assumed a position of ultimate responsibility to Guglielmo for polyphony at Santa Barbara and music-making at court. A handful of references to his activities in these early Mantuan years survive. In 1566 he accompanied the Gonzaga retinue on a visit to Augsburg, where he was tempted with Imperial offers of employment, and during the Carnival season of the following year he travelled to Venice, providing entertainment together with other court musicians. In this same year occurs the first of a series of references to the hostility which Wert's appointment apparently caused among other members of the *cappella* – particularly Agostino Bonvicino, who had hoped to be preferred – and Wert's early years were clouded by rivalries and attempts to discredit him, culminating in the exposure of Bonvicino's adultery with his wife in 1570.[76]

[75] Bautier-Regnier: 'Jacques de Wert', MacClintock: 'New light on Giaches de Wert', and MacClintock: *Giaches de Wert*, pp. 19ff. Discrepancies between the account in the latter and that given above are explained by a more cautious attitude here towards the documentation, particularly with respect to Wert's alleged training at Ferrara. The first concrete evidence of Wert's presence at Mantua comes in a letter of Giulio Cesare Tridapoli, 19 February 1565, to a ducal minister: 'con la venuta di Mr Jacomo, maestro di cappella, mando a V.S. una lettera'. The original is in ASM (AG) 2944.

[76] For Wert at Augsburg see p. 86 above; for his trip to Venice in 1567 see Appendix II, doc. 44. The most important letters concerning Bonvicino's attempts to displace Wert are (1) Wert's letters of 27 August 1567 to the Duke of Mantua and to Federico Cattaneo (originals in ASM (AG) 2578,

Despite these manoeuvres, Wert remained securely in the position of *maestro* throughout Guglielmo's period, only occasionally being replaced, during periods of illness, by Gastoldi, who was eventually to succeed him in 1592.[77]

Although a great deal of circumstantial evidence suggests that polyphonic music figured in Guglielmo's ambitious original conception, and was performed there from the start, it is not until April 1582 that the Santa Barbara records specify payments to professional singers, first to Giovanni Grosser, and from December 1583 to Pompeo Tarabuzzi as well.[78] Both these singers remained at Santa Barbara until Guglielmo's death in August 1587, and were presumably supplemented by other singers from court when polyphony was required. During Guglielmo's period the teaching of music at Santa Barbara was divided between two men, a *maestro di canto* who was presumably responsible for teaching basic techniques, and a *maestro di contrappunto* who taught musical theory ('canto figurato e contrappunto'); again, both these appointments are documented only from 1579 but were probably in existence earlier. Similarly, although the *Constitutiones* lay down the organist's duties quite specifically, it is only in 1573 that the surviving records explicitly refer to Francesco Rovigo as organist of the basilica, although he is probably identical with the 'Franceschino' who was sent to Venice to study with Claudio Merulo in 1570.[79] From other documents it is possible to build up some sort of picture of the music establishment at court during the 1560s, an establishment which includes musicians who undoubtedly had contacts with Santa Barbara. The most important is Bonvicino, who was in service at court before Wert's arrival, and whose two surviving masses were presumably written for performance at Santa Barbara. He left his post in 1570 but seems to have remained in Mantua, probably employed at the cathedral, until 1576 when he died possibly as a result of injuries sustained during Carnival celebrations.[80] Another possible composer at court during the first years of Santa Barbara was Guglielmo Fordo (or 'Fordosio'), a French castrato, who is recorded in Mantua for the first time in 1565, and who may be identifiable with the 'Fortio' whose psalms are preserved in manuscript

transcriptions in A. Bertolotti: *Musici alla corte dei Gonzaga*, pp. 40–1); (2) Wert's letter of 21 September 1568 to the Duke of Mantua (original in ASM (AG) 2579); and (3) Wert's letter to the Duke of Mantua, 22 March 1570 (original in ASM (AG) 2584, transcriptions in Bertolotti: *Musici alla corte dei Gonzaga*, p. 42, and Straeten: *La musique aux Pays-Bas*, VI, p. 334).

[77] Tagmann: 'La cappella dei maestri cantori', p. 380.

[78] Tagmann: 'La cappella dei maestri cantori', pp. 385ff. From references elsewhere it seems that professional singers for Santa Barbara were being sought earlier. See for example the letter of Pompeo Strozzi, Rome 5 March 1570, to the Duke of Mantua, in ASM (AG) 907.

[79] Tagmann: 'Le cappella dei maestri cantori', pp. 383ff and 394ff.

[80] Bonvicino's possible death is reported in a letter of Lodovico Maggio, Capitano di Giustizia, Mantua 24 February 1576, to a ducal official, thus highlighting the dangers of Carnival: 'Questa notte passata alle cinque ore è statto ferito, l'una ferita in testa pericolosa de morte, Don Augustino Bonvicino altrevolte cantore di V.A., mentre esso Don Augustino andava a piacere in mascara.' Original in ASM (AG) 2597. It would seem that after he left the court Bonvicino worked at the cathedral: his name is registered in ASDM (Cap.) Rendiconti sec. XVI. Distributione...del agnello paschali for 1571–75, where he is described as *mansionario*.

in the Santa Barbara collection.[81] Both these men are listed as 'musici' in an account thought to be for 1566–70, together with eight others including Guglielmo Testore, another composer, whose two five-voice masses preserved in the Santa Barbara collection were presumably written for the ducal basilica,[82] and who was probably involved in searching for singers for the Gonzaga court in the summer of 1566.[83] Rare glimpses of some of these musicians at work at court and elsewhere during the late 1560s are occasionally provided by letters. During the Carnival season of 1567, for example, a party of Mantuan courtiers travelled by barge to Venice for the festivities, taking with them a group of musicians including Wert; and another letter written a year later by Giulio Aliprandi describes a concert performed by Wert, Bonvicino, Giovanni Maria di Rossi (then *maestro di cappella* at the cathedral), Valeriano Cattaneo, and others.[84]

As already noted, the organ in Santa Barbara was constructed in 1565 by Graziadio Antegnati, and the subsequent maintenance of the instrument by either him or his son Costanzo is documented.[85] Occasional advice about musical matters also came from Claudio Merulo, one of the organists of St Mark's in Venice, whose correspondence with the duke seems to have begun in January 1566 shortly after the instrument had been completed. Later

---

[81] Fordo, one of the earliest examples of Duke Guglielmo's interest in castrati, is documented for the first time in a letter of G. P. Conegrani, Mantua 15 August 1565, to a ducal official, in ASM (AG) 2573: 'Si raccomanda la speditione del Cattaneo per la sua pensione et non meno quella di Guglielmo Fordo castrato francese.'

[82] The list, in ASM (AG) 3146, is undated but must come from the period 1566–70, since Testore's *Il primo libro de madrigali* (Venice, 1566) does not describe the composer as a Gonzaga employee, and in 1570 Bonvicino is thought to have been dismissed.
[fo. 8v]:

Mastro di Cappella	
A m. Giaches de Wert	duc. 9 - 63 - 0
Musici	
A m. Livio Martinelli	duc. 3 - 0 - 0
A m. Guglielmo Testori	duc. 3 - 0 - 0
A m. Guglielmo Fordosio	duc. 3 - 0 - 0
A m. Tassino Gallo	duc. 3 - 0 - 0
A m. Claudio Borgognone	duc. 3 - 0 - 0
A m. Agostino Buon Vicino	duc. 3 - 0 - 0
A m. Garcia Spagnuolo	duc. 3 - 0 - 0
A m. Antonio Bressiano	duc. 3 - 0 - 0
A m. Don Giuglio Brusio, il quale non leva più le sue paghe	

A slightly earlier payment document records occasional payments to other musicians who were presumably not permanently employed at court. See ASM (AG) 2573, Entrata e uscita 1562–1565:
June 1565:

A Mr Erasmo cantore	L54 - 0 - 0

July 1565:

Mr Hiero d'Urbino	L216 - 0 - 0

August 1565:

Mr Hiero Zanacho per libri di musicha	L133 - 6 - 0

[83] For further on Guglielmo Testore's activities see the letter of 7 August 1566 in Appendix II, doc. 45.
[84] See Appendix II, doc. 46.
[85] See above, p. 104 note 64 for Antegnati's letters concerning the organ. For additional correspondence see Appendix II, docs. 47–49.

Merulo advised about an organ and in 1570 undertook to teach Rovigo, who was presumably being trained for service in Santa Barbara.[86] Throughout his career Rovigo maintained an ambiguous relationship with Mantua, after showing a preference for Imperial employment at Graz, but he is the first clearly documented organist at the basilica. He too was a composer, and among his largely liturgical output survives a *Missa dominicalis* on Santa Barbara plainsongs.[87] The search for new singers was constant, and to find them Guglielmo operated through established Gonzaga diplomatic channels using ambassadors or agents, sometimes assisted by musical advisers. An early example of the system is illustrated by a letter from Bruschi, then at Mantua, to the duke at Casale. Bruschi reported the abilities of singers in the *cappella* of the Cardinal of Augsburg, laying particular emphasis on the number of castrati and discriminating between a *cappella* voice and a *camera* voice.[88] This is reminiscent of a slightly earlier description of the cardinal's musicians prepared for the duke, clearly as part of enquiries aimed at securing the services of some of them for the Mantuan court. Reports from elsewhere often contain equally detailed characterisations of musicians. A letter of 1570 from Francesco Fullonica, one of the clerics at the cathedral, notes that musical life in Rome was then at a low ebb because all the best singers were employed by the Cardinals of Ferrara and Trent, who spent much time away from Rome with their households; Fullonica advises the Mantuan court secretary Aurelio Zibramonte of the presence in Rome of a tenor 'con voce gagliarda et piena, bellissimo cantante et di buon contrapunto'.[89] Throughout Guglielmo's period strong contacts with Rome were maintained, partly through Gonzaga cardinals (particularly Scipione Gonzaga) who had households there, partly through the usual diplomats, and partly through Guglielmo's own contacts first with Palestrina and later with Marenzio, Nanino, and Soriano. Later Paolo Faccone, a singer in the Papal Chapel, functioned as a Mantuan agent recommending new singers as they came to his notice.[90] Negotiations between ducal representatives and musicians were often protracted, and not infrequently collapsed altogether over the matter of money. From the large body of material which survives, it seems that Mantuan agents were always conscious of the need to attract musicians to Mantua and were well equipped to provide useful and detailed reports. There is also some consistency about Guglielmo's requirements as inferred from these reports. In the first place musicians were admired for versatility, and a good performer was able to sing as well as play instruments. This was of course an economic consideration as much as an artistic one. A singer was expected to be able to sing from memory, sight-read, and improvise embellishments,

[86] See Appendix II, docs. 50–52.   [87] See above, p. 106 note 74.
[88] See Appendix II, doc. 53.   [89] See Appendix II, doc. 54.
[90] On Faccone see A. Bertolotti: *Musici alla corte dei Gonzaga*, pp. 67ff, 82ff, and 90ff, A. Bertolotti: *Artisti*, pp. 118ff.

and certain voice types were expected to have a *cappella* voice and a *camera* voice. In one case a performer is described as singing falsetto *in camera*, and contralto *in cappella* where falsetto singing was presumably discouraged. Quite unusually for Italy at this time, castrati were always being sought for the court, and some of the lengthier negotiations were concerned with attempts to hire them not only in Italy but elsewhere. Often Guglielmo was looking for fully trained performers with established reputations who would add lustre to the court establishment, but Mantuan agents were also alerted to the need for finding boys who were relatively untrained and comparatively much cheaper to employ.[91]

Many of these points are vividly illustrated in Scipione Gonzaga's letters from Rome. Scipione, made Patriarch of Jerusalem by Sixtus V in 1585 and two years later raised to the cardinalate, was born in 1542, and as a young man was sent to study Latin, Greek, history, mathematics, and philosophy, principally at Padua with Marcantonio Genova. While at Padua, he founded the Accademia degli Eterei, possibly reformed from the membership of the Accademia degli Elevati, whose *maestro di musica* was the composer Francesco Portinaro, who dedicated to him his first book of four-voice madrigals, published in 1563. It was also during this Paduan phase of his career, spanning the years 1558–66, that Scipione formed a close friendship with Torquato Tasso, who lived with him after being expelled from the University of Bologna in 1564, and was later to return to his protection after being released from seven years' incarceration in the Ospedale di Sant'Anna in Ferrara. After completing his studies at Padua, Scipione spent some years as Mantuan ambassador at the Imperial court before moving to Rome in 1572. There he continued his activities as a literary patron, as a connoisseur of wood and copper engravings, particularly those by Dürer, and as a patron of musicians.[92] Since the 1560s he had not only sponsored composers but had also maintained connections with Mantuan cultural life, particularly through the Accademia degli Invaghiti, of which he was a founder member; and

[91] These general conclusions are based on a great many surviving letters. An early group dates from late 1565 and is spread among ASM (AG) 593, 2573, 1209, and 1211. There is an important series of letters from Ferrante Ghisoni in Paris to the duke between December 1582 and November 1584 in ASM (AG) 660; properly speaking, this series begins with Ascanio Andreasi's letter of 16 July 1582 in ASM (AG) 659, and includes the four letters written from Mantua on 4 May 1583, three from Teodoro San Giorgio in ASM (AG) 2621, and one from the duke in ASM (AG) 2214. The largest number of letters concerning singers were written by Mantuan agents from Rome. The 1571 correspondence between Aurelio Zibramonte and the Castellano of Mantua is in ASM (AG) 905, and 2950 lib. 370. The longer series of letters stretches throughout 1586 and can be traced in ASM (AG) 941, 943, and 944; it consists mostly of letters from Scipione Gonzaga to Federico Cattaneo, and it was as part of this exchange that negotiations were carried on with Luca Marenzio. These major groups of letters have all been partly explored by Canal, Bertolotti, and Engel, and they are mostly transcribed in ASM (Davari) 15. More recently, a number of those dealing with castrati have been discussed by Richard Sherr in an unpublished paper: see *Abstracts*, p. 14. Five typical examples from this correspondence are given in Appendix II, docs. 55–59.

[92] For details of Scipione's biography see Prinzivalli: *Torquato Tasso*, pp. 223–38, and the remarks in Pastor: *History of the Popes*, XXI, p. 236, and XXIV, p. 507.

during the 1580s both these interests were combined in his negotiations with composers, singers, and instrumentalists on behalf of the Gonzaga court. The most substantial documentation of his efforts on behalf of the Gonzaga *cappella* dates from the period from January to November 1586 and begins with a note from Scipione to the ducal secretary Federico Cattaneo enclosing published madrigals by Nanino dedicated to the duke. Later, towards the end of March, a fresh spate of letters begins over singers and instrumentalists and continues until the early days of November. Apart from the usual Gonzaga requests for castrati, three performers occupy most of the attention in this correspondence; Giovanni Luca Conforto, the composer and castrato, another castrato identified simply as the eunuch of Aquila, and a violinist, Giovanni Battista Giacomello. The length and quantity of these letters are testimony to the obstacles which the most sought-after musicians could place in the path of prospective employers over questions of pay and conditions, as well as to the duke's parsimony, while the descriptions of the singers in particular consistently emphasise the employer's demand for versatility.[93]

But the most prestigious of the negotiations which Scipione carried out on behalf of Guglielmo during these months were with Luca Marenzio. Marenzio may well have had connections with Mantua during his early career and was certainly in contact with the court by 1581; Scipione may have come to know him through musical acquaintances in Rome such as Nanino or Faccone, or perhaps through his visits to the Villa d'Este at Tivoli, the home of Marenzio's employer Cardinal Luigi d'Este. In January 1585 Marenzio dedicated his first book of four-voice motets, the only surviving book of his sacred music to have been published during his lifetime, to Scipione, with a preface which strikes an uncharacteristically personal note and emphasises Scipione's thorough understanding of music.[94] It was, then, only natural that in May 1586, at a time when Guglielmo Gonzaga was evidently making strenuous efforts to recruit new musicians and when Cardinal d'Este seemed close to death, it was Scipione who was requested by Cattaneo to obtain details of Marenzio's status, conditions, and possible willingness to leave Rome.

In his reply of 3 May, Scipione wrote that Marenzio still served Luigi d'Este, who was treating him quite well, and that there was no longer any

---

[93] Originals in ASM (AG) 941, 943, 944: Appendix II, docs. 56–59. Giacomello, described in the correspondence as a highly talented performer, may be identical with the instrumentalist of the same name who played in the celebrated *intermedi* given with the play *La Pellegrina* in Florence in 1589. For further on these *intermedi* and their music see pp. 128ff and 158ff below, and for Giacomello see [Malvezzi]: *Nono parte*.

[94] Marenzio: *Motecta festorum totius anni*: '& haec ex artificio musico deprompta munuscula nullam sibi patronum adoptare libentius poterant, quam eum qui in ipso Musarum sinu ita altus atque aspectu ipso spirare videatur...Equidem & ad illud expoliendum, quicquid potui, contuli: ut aliquid effecisse me sperem, tu facis, qui plerunque illorum, quae hoc libro continentur, & audisti iam & probasti.'

possibility of sending him to France as had been rumoured earlier, but that there was a chance that he would enter the service of Luigi's brother Alfonso II d'Este, Duke of Ferrara. Other patrons seemed to be interested in employing the composer, particularly the Duke of Gioiosa. Finally, it seemed quite clear that Marenzio was inclined to leave Rome provided that he was offered a position that was both very honourable and very useful.[95] A week later Scipione wrote again confirming his original reply. Marenzio himself was against working in France, but might consider 'alcuna honorata servitù, che gli si offerisse'. Luigi d'Este's permission for a move did not seem difficult to obtain, though he was opposed to the composer going to Ferrara, a point on which his earlier report had been misleading. Scipione was unable to find out Marenzio's terms, since he was unwilling to discuss them before knowing who he was being asked to serve and what would be his conditions. In other words, Marenzio was being quite selective about his possible new patron, an attitude which impressed Scipione together with his courtesy, modesty and 'spiriti molto nobili'. In the following days Scipione was again in contact with Mantua to report that Marenzio would not accept the conditions that were being proposed, which were indeed poorer than others had offered him. Then at the end of May he wrote with Marenzio's own conditions: two hundred *scudi* per annum as salary, with expenses for himself, for his servant, and for a horse, and an advance of one hundred *scudi* to cover the expenses of moving. Previously, it seems, the negotiations had been conducted in such secrecy that the composer had not been told who Scipione was acting for; but by now he had become convinced that he was working for the Duke of Mantua whom, he had commented to Cardinal Vincenzo Gonzaga, he would serve more willingly perhaps than any other prince, having already spent some years in the same service. But Marenzio's conditions remained, since if he accepted a lower salary he would neither give nor receive satisfaction. It was a fortnight before Scipione wrote again, after further instructions from Cattaneo on 7 June, but only to report that further attempts to talk to Marenzio had been frustrated. Nevertheless, Scipione promised to see Marenzio as soon as possible, and to instruct another Mantuan official, Annibale Capello, to advise the composer to accept, but he was not sanguine about the prospects of success. The final letter was written on 21 June. Capello had indeed spoken to Marenzio, after which Scipione himself had tried a new assault; discussion had gone on for some time, but the only practical result had been that the composer had reduced his demand to one hundred and fifty *scud d'oro in oro* together with the agreed expenses. Yet this too seems to have been more money than Guglielmo intended, and the subject was not raised again for almost six months.

[95] All the letters of Scipione Gonzaga that are used for the following discussion are in ASM (AG) 941. They have been transcribed in H. Engel: *Luca Marenzio*, pp. 216–19, and now, more accurately, in Ledbetter: 'Luca Marenzio', pp. 187–91.

Cardinal Luigi d'Este died on 30 December 1586. Marenzio received a bequest of fifty *scudi*,[96] but this hardly compensated for a regular income, and his new situation brought renewed approaches from Mantua. This time it was not Scipione who conducted the negotiations but another Mantuan agent in Rome, Attilio Malegani, who was written to on 9 January 1587 by Cattaneo.[97] Guglielmo Gonzaga was evidently in a hurry. No doubt there will have been considerable competition to secure the services of such a prestigious composer, whose reputation had recently been enhanced by the appearance of a further book of six-voice madrigals dedicated to the Marchese di Pisani, an ambassador to the King of France; but Malegani seems to have taken his time. Four days after receiving the letter on 17 January he had still not managed to see Marenzio, but on the 24th he was able to report the results of their meeting. The news was not encouraging. Marenzio's reply was unchanged from his discussions with Scipione Gonzaga: he needed a salary of two hundred *scudi* per annum, estimated on the basis of his living expenses in Rome; moreover, now that his patron was dead he was once again under the authority of his father, whose permission had to be sought in any new arrangements. Malegani had urged acceptance, pointing to the gifts which the duke gave to 'Signor Giaches [de Wert], et à tanti altri cantori minimi'. Guglielmo took immediate steps to secure the support of Marenzio's father through a Brescian monk referred to simply as Frate Cesare, as Malegani reported to Cattaneo in a letter of 10 February. There the matter seems to have rested for some weeks, and it is not until 13 May that a further note from Malegani provides the sequel. Marenzio had received the necessary paternal permission, but only on condition that his terms were met; for his part, the composer would be obliged to the duke and his family for life. Again, it seems, Guglielmo balked at the price.

As with so many other matters surrounding the first musical and liturgical arrangements at Santa Barbara, it is Bruschi who provides the earliest reports of polyphony being performed there. A letter of June 1565 describes two masses being sung – that is chanted – the second 'con l'organo sonato per Mes[r] Girolamo' (i.e. Cavazzoni), and notes that 'tutti li salmi sono finiti di scrivere'.[98] These were presumably the works that Bruschi had written about in October of the previous year,[99] but it is unclear whether he was responsible

---

[96] ASMod Amministrazione dei Principi, non-regnanti. 1393: Libro de' legati del Card. d'Este.

[97] Malegani's letters are transcribed in H. Engel: *Luca Marenzio*, pp. 219–20, with the exception of those of 17 and 21 January 1587. All the originals are in ASM (AG) 947. The letter from Frate Cesare, Brescia 10 February 1587, to Federico Cattaneo is in Engel: *Luca Marenzio*, p. 220; the original is in ASM (AG) 1519.

[98] Letters of Giulio Bruschi, 28 June 1565, to the Duke of Mantua, in ASM (AG) 2573: '...Il Caldora ha cantato la missa della Croce, Mes[r] Gio. Maria ha contato quella dell'ottava con l'organo sonato per Mes[r] Girolamo dopo prima. Hora che a terza, scrivendo io questa s'incomincia l'ufficio di morti e cantera la messa Mons[r] Arcidiacono...tutti li salmi sono finiti di scrivere.'

[99] See above, p. 106 note 70.

for the words or the music, or even if the pieces were polyphonic, and no psalm settings by him survive. But certainly he was among the first composers to write polyphony for Santa Barbara, and a letter written in May 1566 describes him at work on a mass, presumably one of the two attributed to him in the Santa Barbara manuscripts.[100] Bruschi's work, together with that of Testore, Bonvicino and Fordo, and the first of the Palestrina commissions, is probably the earliest corpus of specially composed polyphony for the basilica, to be followed by the efforts of later members of the *cappella* such as Rovigo, Contino and Gastoldi, and other outsiders including Paolo Isnardi, Alessandro Striggio, Nicola Parma, Paolo Pezzani, and Vincenzo Suardi. The most prolific of these was Wert, though it is impossible to know how much of his output was composed for Santa Barbara or when. Some of the contents of his first motet book published in 1566 and dedicated to Guglielmo may have been composed for the basilica, and presumably the remaining two volumes of sacred works published in 1581 reflect Santa Barbara practice. Apart from the printed works, eight masses, eighteen psalms, two magnificats, one Te Deum, a Passion setting, and twelve hymns survive only in the Santa Barbara manuscripts; and his *Missa dominicalis* was one of a group by various composers, all based on the same Santa Barbara plainsongs.[101] All these compositions of Wert are *alternatim* settings except the *Missa 'Transeunte Domino'* based on his own motet on that text, and the texts of three of the hymns are from a set of twenty-seven specially written for the Santa Barbara liturgy by Marc'Antoine Muret.[102] There can be little doubt that the majority of Wert's sacred works, and certainly those pieces which survive only in Santa Barbara and related manuscript sources, were written for the basilica; and taken together with the information in the *Constitutiones* and the *Ceremoniale* they help to clarify when polyphony was used in the liturgy, how the practice of *alternatim* settings imposed restrictions upon the composers' freedom of action, and how the results were performed. The Santa Barbara manuscripts are also testimony to the isolation and persistence of the repertory, being copied and recopied well into the seventeenth century (first by Giuseppe Vicentini and later by Francesco Sforza), by which time their contents had sometimes been in circulation for over fifty years, an extraordinary length of time in a world of rapidly changing musical fashions even within the Church.[103]

[100] Letter of Giulio Bruschi, 12 May 1566, in ASM (AG) 2575: 'intorno la missa, ho fatto il Kyrie primo per esservi il canto firmo, la Gloria et il Credo, se vi fossero stati li altri canti firmi del Christe et Kyrie ultimo et Sanctus col resto l'havirei anchor fatti, fu fatta tanto a tempo che fu cantata il giorno deputato da Sua Ecc.ª...' Two masses by Bruschi survive among the Santa Barbara manuscripts, as MSS 34 and 174: see *Conservatorio di musica*, pp. 121–2.

[101] See above, p. 106 note 74.

[102] A. Bertolotti, *Lettres inédites*. Wert refers quite explicitly to his work for Santa Barbara at Duke Guglielmo's instigation in a letter of 12 March 1587 (ASM (AG) 2638): '...cominciaro dunque dal primo tono seguitando il comandamento di S.A. nel nome de la Santissima Trinità, pregando humilissimamente la Maesta Sua concedermi tanto spirito ch'io possa laudare in musica questa santa gloriosa...'   [103] See Appendix III below.

In addition to the unique survival among the Santa Barbara manuscripts of works by composers associated with the basilica, some idea of growth and change in its repertory can be gained from the printed books in the collection. As suggested elsewhere, the collection as a whole falls into chronological groupings which coincide with the foundation of the first Gonzaga *cappella* in San Pietro, the growth of Ercole Gonzaga's patronage, and the foundation and development of Santa Barbara itself; and while it is possible that the whole collection was formed after the basilica had been established, it seems more probable that it represents the repertory of the Gonzaga *cappella* from its inception. The music published and presumably acquired during Ercole's period is predominantly the work of northern composers, with Jacquet of Mantua taking pride of place, and includes a large series of Attaignant motet books. After the foundation of Santa Barbara the printed repertory is dominated by the published works of composers associated with the institution or having contacts with Guglielmo, particularly Contino, Wert and Palestrina. Lasso is the only significant exception, and even he made a short if unremarkable visit to Mantua in 1574.[104] Seen as a whole the repertory performed at Santa Barbara during Guglielmo's period is an inward-looking and to a large extent private and unpublished one, much of it reserved for exclusive use at the basilica in a way analogous to the jealously guarded repertory of the Ferrarese court *concerto delle donne* during the 1580s.[105] Indeed this characteristic, common to much court art of this period, is symptomatic of a conception in which the arts are seen, at least in part, as a way of presenting and extending a particularly distinctive image of the prince.

This idea lies at the heart of the Santa Barbara project. The new church was planned as a dynastic temple, a theatre for Gonzaga politico-religious ceremonies, as well as a highly individual interpretation of Counter-Reformation attitudes towards sacred art. Its special character, expressed through extraordinary Papal privileges including a separate rite and prestigious positions for its clergy, is unprecedented outside Rome itself; the foundation Bulls of Pius IV automatically conferred a status upon the institution which made it the envy of other Italian princes. And since the

---

[104] See Leuchtmann: *Orlando di Lasso*, II, p. 78, giving Lasso's letter from Mantua of 2 April 1574.

[105] There are dozens of documentary references to the high quality of music at the basilica. One of the earliest is in a letter from Annibale Cavriani, Podestà of Ostiglia, of 9 March 1566, to Duke Guglielmo: '...alle 23 hore e arrivato il R^{mo} Monsr Cardinale d'Augusta et m'ha pregato che voglia avisa V^{ra} Ecc^{tia} come hoggi al non potuto venir a Mantoa ma el vi sarà dimani fra le 19 et 20 hore et prega V^{ra} Ecc^{tia} che voglia far intratenir il vespero in Santa Barbara sino alla sua venuta et somamente desidera d'haver questo favor da V^{ra} Ecc^{tia}...perche desiderà di venir al vespro per sentir la bella musica di V^{ra} Ecc^{tia}...' (ASM (AG) 2574). Nevertheless, things could go wrong, as on one occasion described by Federico Follino (in ASM (AG) 2638): '...Il disordine dell'essersi mancato in Santa Barbara di cantar alcuni salmi al vespro in canto figurato il giorno di S. Giovanni, nato per l'haver noi prestati quei libri ad altri, e causa ch'io d'ordine di S.A. con questa mia vi dichi che l'errore è stato grande per se, ma molto più per esser intravenuto quel di et a quell'hora nella quale vi era il concorso di tutto il popolo...' (ASM (AG) 2638).

building was the particular brainchild of Duke Guglielmo Gonzaga, music-lover and amateur composer, it is not surprising that the recruitment of musicians and the composition of polyphony to conform with the special requirements of the Santa Barbara rite played an important part in the initial conception and were a major preoccupation during the early stages of planning, construction, and operation. More than that, it is clear from Guglielmo's correspondence with composers both in Mantua and elsewhere, from his own compositions, and from works commissioned for Santa Barbara that he maintained a consistently conservative taste in music. Indeed, his pieces, and works written for Santa Barbara by others, are consistent in their constraint, their use of *cantus firmi* taken from plainsongs, their concern for clarity of text, their emphasis upon old-fashioned contra-puntal skills, their avoidance of extravagant representational devices and adventurous 'harmonic' effects. There can be no doubt that Guglielmo Gonzaga's patronage of music and musicians through the Santa Barbara project is the most singular and best-documented example anywhere in sixteenth-century Italy of the extent to which a musically literate patron could influence the style of musical composition; but the effect upon composers such as Wert, who was clearly alive to new musical techniques, was evidently stifling. In fact, during the 1580s Wert's affiliations with Ferrara strengthened considerably, not only (one suspects) for personal reasons but for artistic ones as well, and Guglielmo's attempts to secure Marenzio's services in 1586–7 may well have been prompted by the fear that his *maestro di cappella* was about to be lured into the employment of Alfonso II d'Este. Nor was Wert the only 'Mantuan' to prefer the cultural climate of Ferrara to that of the Gonzaga court during this decade. In training and temperament, Vincenzo Gonzaga, Duke Guglielmo's son and heir, was closer to the courts of Florence and Ferrara than he was to his father's, and when he inherited the title it was his experiences outside Mantua that were to form his own approach to the arts. The radical changes in the cultural and specifically musical climate of the Gonzaga court in the first years of his rule are the subject of the final chapter.

4

Vincenzo Gonzaga and the new arts of spectacle

Quando Amarilli bella
De l'invitto Vincenzo in dolci modi
Fà risonar le lodi
Par che 'l Mincio con l'onda
Soave le risponda:
Deh ninfa vaga, e snella,
Poi ch'io non posso à paro
Di te cantare il nome eccelso, e chiaro;
Fussero l'onde mie tutte, e l'arene
Cantatrici Sirene.
                    Grillo: *Rime*

Fig. 8   Peter Paul Rubens: *The Gonzaga adoring the Trinity* (1604–5), oil on canvas. Detail, showing Duke Vincenzo I Gonzaga and his father, Guglielmo. Mantua, Palazzo Ducale (photo: Scala)

The death of Guglielmo Gonzaga placed in charge of the duchy a young man who was temperamentally almost the exact opposite of his father. On 22 September 1587 Vincenzo's accession was marked by celebrations of extraordinary ostentation even by the standards of the age, including a sacred ceremony in San Pietro, a banquet, and fireworks. The apparent munificence towards the people on this occasion is prophetic of an attitude to money and luxury that within a few years was to drain the Gonzaga treasury of much of the resources so carefully acquired by Cardinal Ercole and Duke Guglielmo.[1] In terms of foreign policy the contrast between Vincenzo's approach and the guiding principles of his immediate predecessors is equally severe. Initially it seemed as though Vincenzo was to pursue a statesmanlike course, particularly in his benevolent gestures towards the Casalese nobility which compare favourably with Guglielmo's asperities; but in 1595 Rudolph II, preoccupied with the Turkish advances against the Empire, appealed to the Italian princes for aid. No doubt it would have seemed effective for the protector of the author of *Gerusalemme liberata* to respond so readily, nature in this case almost imitating art, but Vincenzo was the only Italian ruler to do so, and in both military and economic terms the three campaigns of 1595, 1597, and 1601 were a catastrophe.[2] Such examples could be multiplied to present an image of Vincenzo in which personal ambition and vanity aided by accumulated financial reserves, and encouraged by the military traditions of the Gonzaga, combined in a vision of the potentialities of the Mantuan state which recognised only too fully its strategic importance but grossly

[1] The principal account of Vincenzo's coronation is Follino: *Descrittione dell'infirmità*, but see also Amadei: *Cronaca universale*, III, pp. 7–9, which notes that Follino himself assisted at the ceremonies, and Follino's own letters in ASM (AG) 2638. Having described the decorative arrangements inside San Pietro, Follino notes (fo. A4): '...Preparate dunque tutte queste cose, posti all'ordine gli cantori con suoi concerti di tromboni, cornette & voci...' This is before the celebration of the mass itself, and the next mention of music comes at the end of the ceremony (fo. B1v): '...Finita la messa, la quale fù di musica perfettissima, composta per questo effetto, dell'eccellentiss. musico & mastro di cappella di S.A. il Sig. Giaches Vuert, huomo per l'eccellenza dell'opre sue, assai famoso al mondo: & spediti i concerti d'organo, voci, cornette, e tromboni, si cominciarono tutti ad incominare per una sbarra...' Later there was also vocal and instrumental music performed outside the cathedral (fo. B3).
[2] For Vincenzo's part in the Imperial campaigns against the Turks see *Mantova. La storia*, II, pp. 42ff, Errante: 'Forse che sì, forse che no', Coniglio: *I Gonzaga*, pp. 363–78, and the documentation in ASM (AG) 388. For Vincenzo's foreign policy in general see *Mantova. La storia*, II, pp. 37ff.

overestimated its resources and capabilities. Historians have traditionally
dated the origins of the political and economic decline of Mantua and the
Gonzaga from the early years of Vincenzo's period, and the evidence for that
interpretation seems overwhelming, though the excesses of Vincenzo's
personal style of government may not be entirely responsible. Other
contributory factors include the decline of the textile trade on which
Mantuan wealth partly depended, and the general collapse of the north
Italian economy, which seems to have been most severe during the 1590s.[3]

As so often, the years of decadence and decay also witnessed extraordinary
cultural achievements, though again the contrast between Vincenzo's taste
and that of his father is striking. Certainly Guglielmo had commissioned the
Fasti gonzagheschi from Tintoretto in 1579 and the altarpiece for San
Benedetto Po from Veronese in 1561, but in general both the permanent
establishment of architects and artists and the recipients of occasional
commissions were local men, spiritual disciples of Giulio Romano such as
Lorenzo Costa the Younger, Ippolito Costa, Fermo Ghisoni, and Ippolito
Andreasi.[4] Vincenzo's principal architect and advisor, Antonio Maria Viani,
was also a local man in the sense that he was born at Cremona, but his style
was partly formed at Munich in the school of Friedrich Sustris and Peter
Candid, and indeed Viani collaborated with Candid over the decoration of
the Aquarium in the Residenz. Viani's principal task, as Prefect of the Ducal
Fabric, was to design and supervise the extensive alterations and extensions
to the Palazzo Ducale which are the most tangible remains of Vincenzo's
grandiose vision of Mantuan status and power, including the Galleria della
Mostra, the Loggia di Eleonora, the shell of the Galleria degli Specchi, and
the Teatro Ducale. Viani was not the only 'northern' artist to be imported.
Probably in 1599, during a journey in Flanders, Vincenzo encountered the
work of Frans Pourbus the Younger, already established in his own country
as a portrait-painter, and by the next year the artist was in residence at the
Gonzaga court where his time seems to have been mostly spent executing
portraits of the ruling house until his departure to serve Maria de' Medici
in 1609. Vincenzo's greatest acquisition in this field occurred in 1600.
According to a contemporary account, when on 9 May 1600 Peter Paul
Rubens rode southwards from Antwerp intent on a personal exploration of
Italy, he headed for Venice. Conveniently for himself he arrived there during
Carnival, made the acquaintance of the Mantuan ducal secretary Annibale
Chieppio, if not of Vincenzo himself, and by October at the latest had entered
the duke's service. In fact, Rubens was entrusted with only one major
Gonzaga commission during his Mantuan period, the three vast canvases

---

[3] For the textile trade see De Maddalena: 'L'industria tessile'; and among the many treatments of
the general collapse, see Luzzato: *Studi di storia economica*, Stella: 'La crisi economica', Sella: 'Il declino
dell'emporio', and Cipolla: 'Il declino economico'.

[4] See the survey in *Mantova. Le arti*, III, pp. 361ff, and Susanna Muliari Moro's article 'Mantova e la
corte gonzaghesca alla fine del secolo XVI' in *Rubens a Mantova*, pp. 18–27.

executed for the Jesuit church of Santissima Trinità in Mantua in 1604–6, and his most important work during these years was done for patrons in Rome and Genoa. But his very presence at the Gonzaga court, like that of Viani and Pourbus, is symptomatic of two important characteristics of Vincenzo's cultural patronage: its expansion, fuelled by Vincenzo's money, personal tastes, and notion of appropriate *splendeur*, and its cosmopolitanism.[5]

It would be easy to demonstrate the quite dramatic effect of Vincenzo's accession on all aspects of Mantuan cultural life, but this final chapter is principally concerned with the radical changes in the court music establishment during the first decade or so of Vincenzo's control of the duchy, and the implications which those changes held for the compositional techniques of some of the court musicians. In general terms the permanent music establishment at court seems to have been greatly expanded during these years, and among the new arrivals was the young Claudio Monteverdi, who was probably established in the ducal service by 1590.[6] A similar increase in numbers also took place at Santa Barbara, whose range of activities as a dynastic and state church was broadened.[7] It is perhaps not surprising, in view of Vincenzo's reputation as a patron, well established by the time of his succession, that the early years of his period saw new publications by Mantuan composers, many bearing dedications to the new duke, but the sheer quantity of new published work is impressive and, as we shall see, it is often quite different in character from music by the same men written at Duke Guglielmo's court.[8] Seen as a whole, three new interests are noticeable in the works of court composers published or written during the 1590s: a new taste for the lighter secular forms, perhaps encouraged by the success of Marenzio's *villanelle* and most vividly shown by the even greater popularity of Gastoldi's *Balletti*; an enthusiasm for the new virtuoso styles of singing as cultivated at Ferrara and Florence; and an interest in new stage works, of which the most prominent example is the attempt to stage Giovanni Battista Guarini's pastoral drama *Il pastor fido* at court. The delineation of the last two of these developments occupies this chapter, and the origins of both clearly lie in the contacts which Vincenzo had as a young man with the Este and Medici courts, where the cultural atmosphere was markedly different from the Counter-Reformation gloom of his father's.

After his sister Margherita married Duke Alfonso II d'Este in 1579, Vincenzo became in effect a child of the Ferrarese court. The young prince was now

[5] For a general account of the activities of Flemish artists at Mantua I have used Mattioli: 'Fiamminghi a Mantova tra cinque e seicento' in *Rubens a Mantova*, pp. 68–86, and for Rubens at Mantua Jaffé: *Rubens and Italy*. For a general survey see also *Mantova. Le arti*, III, pp. 419ff.

[6] In a letter of 2 December 1608 (ASM (AG) Raccolta d'autografi 6) Monteverdi claimed that he had served Vincenzo Gonzaga for 'dieci nove anni continui'.

[7] See Tagmann: 'La cappella dei maestri cantori', pp. 385ff.

[8] See below, pp. 135ff.

at an impressionable age, and while his frequent visits to Ferrara were partly
a response to the legendary charms of Barbara Sanseverina, Countess of Sala,
there can be no doubt that in any event Vincenzo found the gaiety of the
Este court preferable to the rather austere atmosphere at Mantua. This in
itself was a cause of dissension between Vincenzo and his father, intensified
by Guglielmo's dislike of his son's extravagant tastes, by the apparent
encouragement of Alfonso, and finally by the scandal caused by the collapse
of his first marriage to Margherita Farnese. Nor did his remarriage to
Leonora de' Medici in 1584 cure him of his hedonistic inclinations as
Guglielmo had hoped, and as the decade wore on the duke's almost morbid
jealousy increased, finding a practical outlet only in attempts to deprive his
sons of funds. It would be quite wrong, though, to cast Vincenzo in the same
half-pagan mould as Duke Federico; and just as it was at Ferrara and, after
1584, at Florence that Vincenzo gained a command of the basic acquirements
of court life, so it was there too that he received a grounding in music, poetry,
and theatre, all of which became strong interests. At Ferrara he cultivated
the friendship of Torquato Tasso and Guarini; and, as we shall see, it was
at Ferrara that his musical tastes were largely formed. Contemporary
chroniclers often place Vincenzo in Ferrarese court musical circles during the
1580s, but among the composers there his closest contacts were with Wert,
spiritually and sometimes physically another refugee from the constraints of
Duke Guglielmo's Mantua. Florence also played a part in shaping Vincenzo's
musical tastes. Leonora de' Medici is recorded as an admirer of dancing and
music, particularly the lighter styles, and it was to her that Wert dedicated
his book of *canzonette villanelle* in 1589; the noticeable enthusiasm for the
canzonetta style in the years just after Vincenzo's accession may well reflect
her influence. But the most marked effects of Florentine and Ferrarese
influence in Mantuan court music of the 1580s are to be found in Mantuan
cultivation of new styles of singing and theatre.

During the 1580s, when Vincenzo Gonzaga spent much of his time at the
Este court at Ferrara, Ferrarese musical life seems to have been dominated
by the *concerto delle donne*. The importance of this ensemble and the music that
was composed for it is well established, and since Einstein's lengthy discussion
of the 'Three Ladies of Ferrara' in his study of the Italian madrigal,[9] most
historians of music have included some reference to them when discussing
Italian vocal music of the late sixteenth century. Although this revival of
interest in these virtuoso performers and the music that was composed for
them can be largely attributed to Einstein's writing, his own work owed a
great deal to the documentary evidence and archival material that had been
assembled in the nineteenth century by Angelo Solerti,[10] and within the last
decade other scholars have separately re-examined the available evidence

[9] Einstein: *The Italian madrigal*, II, pp. 825–35.
[10] Solerti: *Ferrara e la corte estense*, pp. cxxix–cxl.

and discovered that Einstein's interpretation of Solerti's documentation is seriously at fault.[11] Two crucial points in Einstein's presentation are wrong: the explicit statement that the *concerto delle donne* consisted of only three female performers, and the inference that these three – Tarquinia Molza, Lucrezia Bendidio and Laura Peperara – always sang together. Although Solerti devotes much of his discussion to these particular singers, he also mentions other female performers, and it is now clear from re-appraisal of the documentary sources that there were two *concerti* at Ferrara of different natures and with almost completely different personnel, and that Einstein's 'Three Ladies' are drawn from both groups.

The earliest reference to the first of these ensembles appears in a letter written by Canigiani, the Florentine ambassador to the Este court.[12] The courts of Mantua and Ferrara had gathered at Brescello, near Parma, to meet two of the sons of the Emperor Maximilian II. Canigiani accompanied the Ferrarese contingent, and his letter, dated 14 August 1571, describes the musical entertainments, which included dancing in the German and Italian styles, a performance of the famous Ferrarese *concerto grande* (which on this occasion numbered about sixty instrumentalists and vocalists), and some songs given by Lucrezia and Isabella Bendidio singing both separately and together to the harpsichord accompaniments of Luzzasco Luzzaschi.

By 1577 the performances of female singers seem to have enjoyed greater prominence in the social life of the court. There were now four ladies who regularly sang together, and a distinguished professional singer, the Neapolitan bass Giulio Cesare Brancaccio, had joined the ensemble; performances were often given in the rooms of one of the Este princesses. The fullest description of the first *concerto* comes from shortly before its dissolution in 1579. On 4 February Leonardo Conosciuti, a courtier who kept Cardinal Luigi d'Este in Rome informed of events in Ferrara, wrote of a private performance, from which many courtiers including himself had been excluded, given by five women singers who had been previously rehearsed by Luzzaschi.

The formation of the more prestigious second *concerto delle donne* seems to have been inspired by Margherita Gonzaga, the daughter of Duke Guglielmo of Mantua. Her marriage to Alfonso II d'Este, by which Alfonso hoped to produce the male heir which had so far eluded him, was lavishly celebrated during the Ferrarese Carnival season of 1579. Margherita was keenly interested in music, dancing and the theatre, and her influence on the social activities of the Este court seems to have been considerable. Partly at her instigation, four sopranos – Laura Peperara, Tarquinia Molza, Anna Guarini and Livia d'Arco – were attracted to Ferrara during the next four years. These ladies replaced the existing members of the ensemble while Brancaccio

---

[11] Cavicchi (ed.): *Luzzasco Luzzaschi*, pp. 7–23, and Newcomb: 'The musica segreta'.
[12] The following account is based on Newcomb's exhaustive study of the two Ferrarese *concerti delle donne*, which also presents all the major documents.

was retained, and this second *concerto* rapidly acquired a reputation throughout Italy for its brilliantly executed florid singing. What had been in 1571 merely an incidental feature of court entertainment seems to have been cultivated almost obsessively after 1580, as the Florentine ambassador Urbani complained.[13] But the chronology of the two groups is important, since the difference between them is not simply one of personnel but of essential character. One member of the first *concerto*, Brancaccio, continued to sing with the second, but otherwise the change was from an ensemble of aristocratic amateurs performing for their own pleasure to one of professional virtuosos who rehearsed and performed for an audience in a more formal sense.

It was during the early 1580s, when the *concerto delle donne* was at the height of its fame, that Vincenzo Gonzaga became a frequent visitor to Ferrara; and after his sister married Alfonso II in 1579, he seems to have identified himself more with the Este court than with his father's.[14] Consequently, it is hardly surprising that when Vincenzo assumed control of the Duchy of Mantua in September 1587 he substantially changed the social character of the court by installing some of the traditions, and indeed some of the musicians, of the Este court. He was evidently an admirer of the Ferrarese *concerto delle donne*, since shortly after his accession he formed a similar group in Mantua, described in detail in Vincenzo Giustiniani's 'Discorso sopra la musica':

But as the Villanellas acquired greater perfection through more compositional artifice, so also every composer, in order that his compositions should satisfy the general taste, took care to advance in the style of composition for several voices, particularly Giaches Wert in Mantua and Luzzasco in Ferrara. They were the superintendents of all music for those Dukes, who took the greatest delight in the art, especially in having many noble ladies and gentlemen learn to sing and play superbly, so that they spent entire days in some rooms designed especially for this purpose, and beautifully decorated with paintings. The ladies of Mantua and Ferrara were highly competent, and vied with each other not only in regard to the timbre and training of their voices but also in the design of exquisite passages [*passaggi*] delivered at opportune points, but not in excess. (Giovanni Luca of Rome, who also served at Ferrara, usually erred in this respect.) Furthermore, they moderated or increased their voices, loud or soft, heavy or light, according to the demands of the piece they were singing; now slow, breaking off sometimes with a gentle sigh, now singing long passages legato or detached, now groups, now leaps,

[13] This celebrated letter from Urbani, dated 14 August 1581, is given by both Solerti and Newcomb, and also in Arnold: *Monteverdi*. Both Livia d'Arco and Laura Peperara came from Mantua. Laura, the daughter of a wealthy merchant in the city with strong court connections, seems to have been the leading member of the second *concerto*, and was evidently a performer of great talent. A number of poets dedicated verses to her, the most prominent being Torquato Tasso (see the index of names in Maier (ed.): *Torquato Tasso. Opere*), and she was the dedicatee of three important music anthologies of the 1580s, *Il lauro secco* (Ferrara 1582), *Il lauro verde* (Ferrara 1583), and the manuscript compilation Verona, Accademia Filarmonica MS 220. For further on her and the other members of the second *concerto* see Solerti: *Ferrara e la corte estense*, pp. cxxixff, and Newcomb: 'The musica segreta', particularly Appendix I, pp. 253–63; and for the anthologies dedicated to her, Kenton: 'A faded laurel wreath', and Newcomb: 'The three anthologies for Laura Peverara'.

[14] See Intra: 'Una pagina', pp. 197–212, Ronchini: 'vita', and for a technicolour view of Vincenzo's youth Bellonci: *Segreti*, pp. 11–111.

now with long trills, now with short, or again with sweet running passages sung softly, to which one sometimes heard an echo answer unexpectedly. They accompanied the music and the sentiment with appropriate facial expressions, glances and gestures, with no awkward movements of the mouth or hands or body which might not express the feeling of the song. They made the words clear in such a way that one could hear even the last syllable of every word, which was never interrupted or suppressed by passages and other embellishments. They used many other particular devices which will be known to persons more experienced than I...[15]

Giustiniani's treatise is usually believed to have been written about 1630, and it can be definitely placed between December 1628 and May 1631 on the evidence of one passage in particular.[16] Because of its date, the value of Giustiniani's account for musical practices during the second half of the sixteenth century may seem suspect; and his description of a group of virtuoso female singers at the Mantuan court may be doubted for the same reason, but there is a sound body of documentary evidence to support it. A list of payments made in the very first years of the seventeenth century includes four women singers, Lucia Pellizzari, Isabella Pellizzari, Lucrezia Urbana, and Caterina Romana.[17] Two of these, the Pellizzari sisters, whose brother Antonio was a musician and a custodian of the Accademia Olimpica in Vicenza, were probably heard by Duke Guglielmo during a visit to the academy in 1582. Lucrezia Urbana, who also played the harp, came from Naples, and is otherwise recorded in Mantuan documents only for the years 1603–5. Caterina Romana is almost certainly Caterina Martinelli, known from other letters as 'La Romanina', the young singer who later prepared the title role of Monteverdi's *Arianna* under the composer's guidance but who died shortly before the first performance. This suggestion is supported by the absence of a payment against her name in this list, since at the time it was compiled she could have been no older than fifteen, and may well not have been eligible for a salary.[18]

---

[15] MacClintock (trans.): *Hercole Bottrigari: Il desiderio...Vincenzo Giustiniani: Discorso*, pp. 69–70: cf. Appendix II, doc. 60. 'Giovanni Luca of Rome' is presumably Giovanni Luca Conforto, a virtuoso falsettist who worked primarily in the Papal Chapel but who also served the Duke of Sessa and was at San Luigi dei Francesi in Rome during the 1580s. He was still at the Papal Chapel when his *Passagi sopra tutti li salmi* appeared in 1607. Although strenuous attempts were made by Scipione Gonzaga and Nanino to persuade him to accept employment at Mantua in 1586, there is no evidence that he worked either there or at Ferrara.

[16] Namely: '...from this it may be seen that the maestri di cappella of the principal churches [in Rome] are young men; the oldest among them is Vincenzo Ugolino, who is about 40 years old. He was Maestro di cappella in San Pietro for some years and is now in Parma, called there upon the occasion of the marriage of that Most Serene Duke with the Most Serene Margarita de' Medici, sister of the Grand Duke of Tuscany...' (MacClintock (trans.): *Hercole Bottrigari: Il desiderio...Vincenzo Giustiniani: Discorso*, p. 77). The marriage of Odoardo Farnese and Margherita de' Medici took place on 11 October 1628, and the festivities in Parma began on 13 December with a performance of Tasso's *Aminta*: see Nagler: *Theatre festivals*, pp. 139–61, Reiner: 'Preparations in Parma', and Lavin: 'Lettres de Parme'. By 1 May 1631 Ugolino had returned to Rome to take up the post of *maestro di cappella* at San Luigi dei Francesi.

[17] See Appendix II, doc. 64, and the footnote to doc. 61.

[18] For Lucrezia Urbana see Ademollo: *La bell'Adriana*, p. 28. For the latest résumé of Caterina Martinelli's involvement in the theatrical and musical life of Mantua see Reiner: 'La vag'Angioletta', pp. 53ff.

Antonio Pellizzari is first mentioned in the records of the Accademia Olimpica as a singer in connection with the installation of Giulio Pogliana as 'Prince' of the academy on 9 January 1582, when he and two of his sisters were responsible for providing music during the ceremonial mass which was done 'con somma soddisfatione, anzi stupore di tutti'. In August of the same year Guglielmo Gonzaga visited Vicenza, and although the Pellizzari are not specifically mentioned, it is reasonable to assume that they were present during the musical performances that were given then, since by this time Antonio had been officially recognised as custodian and musician to the academy with responsibility for all the music given there, at a salary of twenty *ducati* per annum.[19]

The next record of the family dates from 1585. On Sunday 6 March, the last day of the Carnival, the new Teatro Olimpico, designed for the academy by Palladio, was inaugurated with a production of Sophocles' *Oedipus Rex* in a vernacular translation by Lionardo Giustiniani, with choruses by Andrea Gabrieli. It would appear that some of the Pellizzari women were particularly admired on this occasion, not for their singing but for their performance on the cornetto and trombone.[20] The documents leave it unclear whether these Pellizzari were Antonio's sisters or his daughters; but it seems highly likely that a Pellizzari ensemble can be identified with 'la musica vicentina' who were paid the impressive sum of 3,000 lire in 1588. Certainly by 1592 at the latest, Antonio, Lucia, and Isabella Pellizzari had entered Gonzaga service.[21]

Evidence from a different direction indicates that the three 'Mantuan' Pellizzari were an established attraction there by April 1589, and also includes music that was almost certainly performed by them as part of a court entertainment of unparalleled opulence, the festivities designed to celebrate the marriage of Christine of Lorraine, the favourite granddaughter of Caterina de' Medici, to Grand Duke Ferdinando of Tuscany.

On 23 April 1589, the flotilla bringing Christine from Marseilles to Tuscany for the marriage arrived at Livorno. The new grand duchess disembarked

[19] For accounts of these occasions see Appendix II, docs. 66–67.

[20] Gabrieli's music survives in Gabrieli: *Chori* and is transcribed in Schrade: *La représentation*, which also includes a lengthy preface. The gestation of the first production in the new theatre of the Accademia Olimpica is now more thoroughly and accurately discussed in Gallo: *La prima rappresentazione*. A number of contemporaries praised the performance of the Pellizzari sisters on this occasion. Gallo: *La prima rappresentazione*, pp. li–lii, prints the remarks of Dolfin and Pigafetta; but the most precise account is in BBV MS Ziggiotti Gonzati 21-11-2 and has been published in a number of places, notably Magrini: *Il Teatro Olimpico*, p. 63. The original runs: 'Ebbe massima parte nell'apprestamento degli abiti Giambattista Maganza, nelle musiche M. Pordenone, nei cori M. Andrea Gabrieli organista di S. Marco. Fecero specialmente attoniti gli ascoltanti col suono del cornetto e del trombone due giovinette figlie del Pellizzari custode dell'Accademia...'

[21] The 1588 payment is in ASM (AG) 410b (43), fo. 16: '...Adi 14 Agosto dati alla musica vicentina... L3000.00.' For further documents listing the Pellizzari sisters see Appendix II, docs. 62 and 65, and the footnote to doc. 61 concerning the dating of these records. The second of these two lists also includes Antonio Pellizzari, and some of the later documents include Annibale and Bartholomeo Pellizzari, who may well be further members of the family.

and continued her journey via Pisa to Poggio a Caiano, where she met Ferdinando for the first time, and then to Florence, where she arrived on 30 April. The nuptial entertainments began the next day and continued until 15 May: along with the traditional game of *calcio* in the Piazza Santa Croce, jousting and animal-baiting, they included three plays of which the most lavishly produced was Girolamo Bargagli's *La Pellegrina*, which was given on 2 May, together with six *intermedi*, by the Intronati of Siena in the theatre on the first floor of the Uffizi. According to Settimani's 'Diario', the performance was repeated on 15 May for the benefit of the Venetian envoys and others who could not attend on the first occasion. It is the *intermedi* that concern us here: Count Giovanni de' Bardi had been commissioned to devise them, Emilio de' Cavalieri was entrusted with organising and directing the spectacle, and Bernardo Buontalenti was responsible for executing the sets.

The novelty and opulence of the occasion is indicated by the unusually large number of contemporary accounts that were published, of which the most important are Bastiano de Rossi's *Descrizione*, and the extensive references to the musical items and performers given by Cristofano Malvezzi in the *Nono parte* of his edition of the music, which appeared in 1591. In addition, Barthold von Gadenstedt, a German observer who travelled through Italy between 1587 and 1589, recorded his impressions of the event in his journal.[22] Rossi's sophisticated description of the *intermedi* is principally concerned with explaining the complex humanistic and classical allusions of Bardi's conception; Malvezzi's object was to present the music and to extol the achievements of the highly distinguished musicians who took part. But their accounts differ in several significant respects, and one of these differences is crucial for the present discussion.

The list of the musicians who took part in the *intermedi* is impressive. The major composers were Malvezzi himself and Marenzio, but music was also provided by Antonio Archilei, Giovanni de' Bardi and Jacopo Peri, while Cavalieri supplied two items in the sixth *intermedio* including the final *ballo*. The aria 'Io che dal cader' from the fourth *intermedio* was composed by Giulio Caccini but was not printed in the original edition. The singers and

[22] The principal sources are [Rossi]: *Descrizione*; Pavoni: *Delle feste*; Cavallino: *Raccolta*; and *Li sontuosissimi apparechi*. Excerpts from Settimani's 'Diario', which is preserved in ASF, are given in Solerti: *Gli albori*, II, pp. 17–18. Nagler: *Theatre festivals*, pp. 70–92, is a translation and conflation of contemporary accounts. The fundamental account of the event is that in Warburg: 'I costumi teatrali' (in *Gesammelte Schriften*, I, pp. 259–300, with important addenda and excerpts from the 'Memorie e ricordi' of Girolamo Ser Jacopi, the engineer in charge of the machinery, on pp. 394–422 of the revised version edited by Gertrude Bing). Walker (ed.): *Les fêtes du mariage* is a complete edition of the music and includes important prefatory essays by Ghisi and Walker himself. The most recent discussions of the music composed for the *intermedi* are those in Osthoff: *Theatergesang*, I, Kirkendale: *L'Aria di Fiorenza*, and Pirrotta: *Li due Orfei*, pp. 234–56. Barthold von Gadenstedt's journal is in the Herzog August Bibliothek in Wolfenbüttel, with the shelf-mark Cod. Guelf. 67.6. Extrav. fol. A transcript of the portion of the diary that describes the Florentine *intermedi* is given in Kümmel: 'Ein deutscher Bericht'. Information about additional source materials, particularly pictorial, will be found in Berelà and Petrioli Tofani: *Feste e apparati medicei*, pp. 67–85, and *Il luogo teatrale*, pp. 110–16.

instrumentalists who are known to have taken part were equally distinguished. In the fifth *intermedio* Peri sang his own composition 'con maravigliosa arte sopra del chitarone & con mirabile attentione de gli ascoltanti', and Lucia Caccini performed in the fourth to the accompaniment of 'lire grandi' and in the *terzetti* of Cavalieri's *ballo* together with her sister Margherita. The highest praise is reserved for Vittoria Archilei, who appeared as Armonia Doria in the first *intermedio* and who also sang in the *terzetti* of the final item. What is particularly noticeable for the present discussion is that a large number of musicians came from outside Florence, and the majority of these were provided by Vincenzo Gonzaga. The best-known was Alessandro Striggio, whose participation in the *sinfonia* of the first *intermedio* is mentioned enthusiastically by Malvezzi; although Striggio had been connected with Medici court festivals for the previous quarter-century, he had never severed his links with the Gonzaga, and had by this date returned to his native Mantua and was taking part in the music at court. In addition, his son Alessandro, who was later to be Monteverdi's librettist for *Orfeo*, may have taken part in the fourth *intermedio*. The Mantuan contingent was particularly prominent in the fifth *intermedio*, where, according to Malvezzi, the first item, the five-part madrigal 'Io che l'onde raffreno', was sung by Vittoria Archilei to an accompaniment of lute, chitarrone, and an 'arciviolata lira toccata dalla maestrevol mano del famoso Alessandro Striggio'. In the next item, the sectional madrigal 'E noi con questa bella diva', two Mantuan court musicians are named, Paolo Basso and the harpist Giulio Cini.[23] It is this background of borrowed Mantuan talent that helps to illuminate the significance of the second *intermedio* in terms of cultural politics.

This *intermedio* was set in a garden in the centre of which stood a mountain on which sixteen nymphs disported themselves – an effect which seems deliberately reminiscent of the rock which supported the sixteen provinces of France in the entertainments that were given in Paris before visiting Polish dignitaries in 1573.[24] On each side of the mountain there were moss-covered grottoes. On the right hand sat the nine daughters of Pierus, and on the left hand the nine Muses. This was the setting for a song contest between the Muses and the Pierides, in which the nymphs officiated as judges. According to Rossi's *Descrizione*, the Pierides sang first, followed by the Muses. Both pieces had been composed by Marenzio to texts by Rinuccini and, according to Malvezzi, were accompanied by the same instrumental forces: 'un Leuto grosso, un Chitarrone, un Basso di Viola'. The nymphs declared in favour of the Muses in the dialogue for three choirs 'O figlie di Piero', and the unfortunate Pierides were spectacularly transformed into chattering magpies

---

[23] For details see [Malvezzi]: *Nono parte*, pp. 7 and 11–12. Malvezzi's account of the fourth *intermedio* refers to 'una violina sonata da detto Alessandrino', and this diminutive is often used by Striggio himself to refer to his son. See for example his own letters from Ferrara (which also indicate his son's musicality) in Gandolfi: 'Lettere inedite', pp. 527ff, and Appendix II, doc. 68, which Gandolfi overlooked.

[24] For the 1573 spectacle, see below, pp. 154–5.

in accordance with the original classical story. The mountain then vanished and the garden dissolved.[25]

All the published accounts, together with Gadenstedt's diary, agree on this outline of the scene, though they differ significantly in detail. Thus Rossi's *Descrizione* mentions sixteen nymphs and the anonymous chronicler eighteen, whilst Buontalenti's pen-and-ink wash drawing shows only twelve, and the engraving by Epifanio d'Alfanio which was published in 1592 depicts only ten.[26] Elsewhere, discrepancies between published accounts and pictorial evidence need not arise only from inexact observation, but can also result from unfamiliarity with the involved classical philology upon which the scenes were based, much of which was clearly unnoticed or misinterpreted by the spectators. In the first *intermedio*, for example, one commentator (Pavoni) did not recognise the central figure of Armonia Doria (the Dorian mode), but saw only 'una donna' sitting upon a cloud and singing 'molto soavemente'. The anonymous chronicler described the same character as an 'Idra...quale canta sola eccellentissamente', and Simone Cavallino da Viterbo noticed only 'una donna da angiola vestita' and was evidently unimpressed by Vittoria Archilei's vocal powers. As Warburg has remarked, the symbolism of the costumes was probably unappreciated by even the most cultivated observers, and Rossi's erudite commentary did not appear until after the first performance, though it could conceivably have been published in time for the second one.[27]

Against this background of varying interpretations, omissions and incomprehensions, it is perhaps not surprising that Malvezzi's edition of the music should include a short scene which is not described or depicted in any other source. Between Marenzio's opening *sinfonia* and the song of the Pierides, Malvezzi published a short *canzonetta*, also ascribed to Marenzio, which is written in the fashionable light style, very much in the manner of Marenzio's own *villanelle*. The *Nono parte* gives the following account of the piece:

[25] [Malvezzi]: *Nono parte*, p. 8. In Greek mythology the nine maidens of Pieria in northern Thessaly were so proud of their vocal skill that they challenged the Muses to a song contest on Mount Helicon. River nymphs were selected as impartial judges. When, not unexpectedly, the Muses won, the Pierides hurled abuse at them, and it was for this reason (rather than for their arrogance in issuing the challenge) that they were transformed into magpies and condemned to a life of chattering and scolding. The Pierides were so named and the incident thus reported by Nicander of Colophon, a poet of the third century B.C. Although Nicander's works were printed in the sixteenth century, it is more likely that Rossi derived the scene from Ovid's *Metamorphoses*.

[26] [Rossi]: *Descrizione*, p. 38, *Li suntuosissimi apparechi*, as given in Nagler: *Theatre festivals*, p. 80 n. 34. The Buontalenti drawing and the d'Alfanio engraving are also reproduced in Nagler as Figs. 48 and 51 respectively. For further pictorial sources see *Il luogo teatrale*.

[27] Pavoni: *Delle feste*, p. 15, Cavallino: *Raccolta*, and the synthesis in Nagler: *Theatre festivals*, p. 36. Similarly, Barthold von Gadenstedt also failed to identify the Doric mode in his account. The dedication of Rossi's *Descrizione* is dated 14 May 1589, one day before the second performance. It may be that some of the commentators are reporting different performances, or even conflating their impressions of more than one. The *intermedi* were performed a number of times with various plays during the celebrations themselves, and were also rehearsed before the court before Christine of Lorraine's arrival in the city on 30 April. For details of these rehearsals see the despatches of the Ferrarese ambassador in Florence, Ercole Cortile, in ASMod Ambasciatori (Firenze) 29.

Il seguente Madrigale cantorno con esquisita maniera, & arte due giovine, che servono il Serenissimo Duca di Mantova con invidia più che mediocre de gl'amatori di cosi nobil virtù: e da un putto lor fratello accompagnata dal suono di un'Arpa, e due Lire...[28]

It seems reasonable to suggest that these 'due giovine' were the Pellizzari sisters, and it should be noted that here they sang not with their father but with a young brother. Despite the lack of consistency in either published accounts or pictorial documentation, it seems justifiable to rely upon Malvezzi's description. Although particulars can be omitted or misunderstood, it is unlikely that such a detailed description of a musical performance together with music would have been published if the item had not been performed. The suggestion that performers of the trio were the Pellizzari sisters and their brother is supported by the knowledge that a large Mantuan contingent was involved in the *intermedi*, by the voice ranges of the piece itself, and by Malvezzi's description of the singers as 'giovine' which agrees with other impressions of their youthfulness.

One clue to the discrepancy between source materials over this trio may be revealed in one final contemporary description of Vincenzo Gonzaga's *concerto delle donne*. On 14 April 1589, Horatio della Rena, the Medici resident in Ferrara, wrote a report which describes a visit to the Este court by Vincenzo and his retinue. This despatch not only fits well with what we already know of the Pellizzari sisters' musical abilities, but suggests that the girls were unknown to the Medici resident and thus probably to the Medici court as well. Rena's letter is dated only eighteen days before the first performance of the *Pellegrina intermedi*. It is therefore conceivable that the Pellizzari's short and mythologically unnecessary scene in the second *intermedio* was hurriedly interpolated into Bardi's scenario and thus was omitted from published accounts, some of which may have been prepared in advance:

For entertainments that were rich banquets and hours of exquisite music-making ...with the Duke of Mantua came four ladies from Vicenza who sing very well and play the cornetto and other instruments. The Duke of Ferrara gave them a chain worth 100 *scudi* and a purse of 100 *scudi* besides to share among themselves. His wife the duchess gave another chain worth 50 *scudi* to each one.[29]

Thus by April 1589 the Mantuan musical establishment was sufficiently accomplished for some of its members to be exhibited in the prestigious Florentine entertainments of that year. Moreover, this exercise in cultural politics probably involved the Pellizzari sisters, who as we have seen were among the first female virtuosos to be employed at the Gonzaga court, and who were undoubtedly members of Vincenzo Gonzaga's *concerto delle donne*

---

[28] [Malvezzi]: *Nono parte*, p. 8. The piece is printed in Walker (ed.): *Les fêtes du mariage*, pp. 37–8.

[29] Original document published in Newcomb: 'The musica segreta', Appendix V document 60. In view of the information assembled above, it seems likely that the 'four ladies from Vicenza' were in fact two from Vicenza, one from Rome, and one from Naples: the Pellizzari sisters, Caterina Romana, and Lucrezia Urbana.

which he formed in obvious imitation of the Florentine and Ferrarese models shortly after his succession to the title in 1587.

However, Vincenzo's attempts to introduce the Ferrarese taste for female singers can be traced to 1581, shortly after the formation of the second Ferrarese *concerto*, and arose out of the arrangements that were made to celebrate his politically significant (though personally disastrous) first marriage.

On 30 April 1581, Vincenzo was married to Margherita, daughter of Alessandro Farnese, Governor of the Netherlands. Unfortunately the only account of the festivities known to have been published is not extant; nevertheless, it is reasonable to suppose that the arrangements were lavish. The match was of considerable importance for Guglielmo Gonzaga's astute political policies, which were brought closer to fruition precisely one year later with the celebration of another dynastic marriage: on 30 April 1582, Guglielmo's strategy and the traditional Gonzaga links with the Empire were strengthened by the union of his third child, Anna Caterina, with Archduke Ferdinand of Austria. Some of the preparations for the celebration of Vincenzo's wedding were made well in advance. In October 1580, for example, Guglielmo arranged that Vittoria Pilissima and her company of actors were to perform at Mantua both during the Carnival season and later as part of the wedding festivities. The first of these performances may have been the *pastorale* with musical *intermedi* that Francesco Borsati reported as part of the entertainments given in honour of the visit of the Bishop of Osimo in February 1581.[30] For a glimpse of the dramatic productions that enlivened the wedding festivities in April, we have the description of Reale Fusoritto da Narni, who remarks on 'una comedia, con un bellissimo parato et una sontuosissima scena, con vari e bellissimi intermedi apparenti'.[31]

Vincenzo's wedding also seems to have inspired his father to attempt to recruit new singers of considerable reputation, initially one must suppose as participants in the entertainments. Certainly it would appear that Guglielmo pursued the idea seriously, since two important ducal agents, Aurelio Zibramonte and Antonio Rizzi, were engaged in the negotiations. Other members of the Mantuan court and *cappella* were also employed in the quest for musical talent, and the documents indicate a considerable increase of activity at the end of 1579 and in the early months of 1580, some of which involved Giaches de Wert.

---

[30] See ASM (AG) 2615, Letter of Francesco Borsati, Mantua 4 February 1581.

[31] Cervio: *Il trinciante*, p. 88, and Mambrino: 'Dell'historia di Mantova' (ASM (D'Arco) MS 80) for reports. Canal: *Della musica in Mantova*, p. 68, notes that Paolo Cantino composed the music for *intermedi* given at court in 1581, and this may have been the same occasion. Archival records show that Cantino was organist at Mantua Cathedral in 1580–1 and 1601–8, and that he served as *maestro di cappella* there in 1589–90 (see Tagmann: *Archivalische Studien*, pp. 44ff and 84ff). His music for the 1581 *intermedio* does not survive among his printed works. For further documents concerning the performance see D'Ancona: *Origini*, I, pp. 479–80.

On 2 March 1581 Guglielmo informed Zibramonte that a musically accomplished young member of the Mezzovillani family – Laura Bovia, a niece of Monsignore Bovio – was then in Bologna and would make a suitable companion for Margherita Farnese. Guglielmo's description was based on details provided by Annibale Capello, a former ducal chaplain subsequently in the service of Cardinal Luigi d'Este, and an important figure in the attempts to persuade Marenzio to enter Gonzaga service five years later. Capello, it seems, had heard the girl sing and play a number of instruments, and recommended her for the job. Nevertheless there were difficulties, since Bovio was reluctant to give his permission, and Guglielmo enlisted the help of some cardinals to add weight to his request as well as sending Antonio Rizzi to report on her abilities.[32] Margherita's father was also kept in touch with the progress of negotiations through Cardinals Cesi and Paleotti, both of whom were evidently involved in the discussions.[33] A letter from Federico Pendaso written towards the end of the month describes Laura's talents, and notes that she was then in the convent of San Lorenzo, where many people came to hear her sing and play during the Holy Week services. Subsequently she did work at Mantua, though briefly, and by 1582 she was apparently back in Bologna, where the local composer Camillo Cortellini dedicated his *Primo libro de' madrigali a cinque voci* to her with a eulogistic preface extolling her fame as a virtuoso among both musicians and nobility.[34]

There is nothing to suggest that Guglielmo intended to employ Laura Bovia as a member of a *musica secreta* on the Ferrarese model, but subsequently she did join an ensemble of this kind in Florence. From Striggio's letters of 1583–4 it is clear that a group of three sopranos had been formed at the Medici court under the direction of Giulio Caccini; and a description of the festivities in Florence celebrating the marriage of Vincenzo Gonzaga and Leonora de' Medici in April 1584 mentions music performed by two women and other musicians – one of the two being Vittoria Archilei, and the other a Bolognese in the service of the grand duchess. Certainly Laura Bovia was

---

[32] See ASM (AG) 2952 lib. 379, fo. 42, *copialettera* of Duke Guglielmo Gonzaga, 2 March 1581, to Aurelio Zibramonte, and Teodoro San Giorgio's *copialettera* to Federico Pendaso, dated from Mantua the same day, in ASM (AG) 2952 lib. 381, fos. 9–9v. An extract from the latter is in Appendix II, doc. 69. Zibramonte's reply of 5 March, in ASM (AG) 201, includes the passage: '...S. Ecc^za ha scritto all Ill^mi Sig^ri Cardinali che sono a Bologna per disponer con la loro autorità Mons. Bovio à mandar sua nipote, chiamata dal Vescovo d'Osimo figliuola, al servitio della Signora Sposa...'

[33] Letters from Cardinal Cesi to the Duke of Parma, Bologna 11 March 1581, from Cardinal Paleotti to the Duke of Parma, Bologna 10 March 1581, and from Cardinal Cesi to the Duke of Mantua, Bologna 11 March 1581. All three are in ASM (AG) 1161, and the last two are given in Appendix II, docs. 70–71.

[34] The letter from Federico Pendaso to Aurelio Pomponazzi, Mantua 27 March 1581, is in ASM (AG) 1161 and is given in Appendix II, doc. 72. See also the subsequent correspondence between the two reporting on the progress of the negotiations. Pendaso's letter of 11 April 1581 notes 'la moltitudine et qualità de musici chiamati da Monsr Bovio per fare insegnare a questa figliola...' (ASM (AG) 1161). Appendix II, doc. 73 presents a minute from Teodoro di San Giorgio to Pirro Malvezzi in Bologna, also connected with the negotiations, which gives a useful picture of the state of the ducal music establishment. Cortellini's remarks are in his *Il primo libro de' madrigali*, fo. 1.

employed by the Medici that year, and seems to have remained in service until early 1589 when, as a result of changes introduced by the new Grand Duke Ferdinando, the Florentine *concerto* was disbanded.[35] Surprisingly, although Vincenzo Gonzaga was then expanding the Mantuan music establishment and had formed his own *concerto*, Laura did not return to Mantua but seems to have moved next to Parma. The last trace of her occurs in Claudio Merulo's *Canzoni d'intavolatura d'organo* published in Venice in 1592. After a distinguished career at St Mark's in Venice, Merulo moved to Parma in 1587 and was appointed organist at the ducal chapel of the Steccata in 1591. The volume, dated from Parma and dedicated to Ranuccio Farnese, contains nine pieces each addressed to a Parmesan lady, beginning with a 'Canzon a4 dita La Bovia'.[36]

It is not known when either the Mantuan or the Ferrarese *concerto* was disbanded. Archival references to the Ferrarese ensemble are scarce in the later period, but it is usually assumed that the group was dispersed shortly after the Este territories were handed over to Cardinal Aldobrandini as a Papal fief in 1598. At Mantua, Vincenzo Gonzaga's interest in Laura Bovia and his employment of the Pellizzari girls together with the other virtuoso singers are the first indications of an enthusiasm for virtuoso singers that continued throughout his rule. In the 1590s and the early years of the seventeenth century, Mantua and Florence acquired Ferrara's former reputation for vocal performances, and the beginnings of this process can be traced to the interest of both courts in the early achievements of the second Ferrarese *concerto*. The new importance and artistic status of the Gonzaga court is symbolised for the first time by the involvement of the Mantuan *cappella* in the 1589 Florentine *intermedi*, and re-emphasised ten years later by Vincenzo Gonzaga's success in attracting Francesco Rasi to Mantua, to the great envy of the Florentines. But the first indications of the influence of the Ferrarese virtuoso style upon composers of the Mantuan court occur at the end of the 1570s.

The obvious agent for communicating Ferrarese musical styles to Mantua during the late 1570s and early 1580s is Giaches de Wert. For one thing, he was probably the most renowned and admired composer at either court; moreover, his own connections with the Este household stretch back to the mid-1560s and possibly even earlier. His first proven associations with the Este court date from shortly after his arrival at Mantua to take up his post at Santa Barbara, and the first secular publication of his Mantuan career, *Il quarto*

[35] Newcomb: 'The musica segreta', pp. 163ff, and Ledbetter: 'Luca Marenzio', pp. 109ff.

[36] Merulo: *Canzoni d'intavolatura d'organo*, fo. 1. All these *canzoni* together with six further pieces by Merulo, Crecquillon, Guami and others are contained in Verona, Biblioteca Capitolare Cod. MCXXVIII. In this version 'La Gratiosa' is called 'La Zerata', and 'La Cortese' is 'La Sussona', while two of the additional pieces by Merulo are called 'La Basa' and 'La Rosa'. See Turrini: *Il patrimonio*, pp. 27–9, and Disertori: 'Le canzoni strumentali'.

libro de madrigali a cinque voci of 1567, contains three items which can be associated with Alfonso d'Este's marriage to Barbara of Austria which was celebrated in December 1566: the dialogue madrigal 'Cara Germania mia'; 'Di cerchio in cerchio', which praises Alfonso's sister Lucrezia d'Este; and 'Donna de la real stirpe', which is evidently addressed to Queen Renée of France, Alfonso's mother. After this there is little information about his contacts with Ferrara until ten years later, though in the interim he was involved in litigation which may have taken him there several times. His sixth book of five-voice madrigals of 1577 is dedicated to the fifteen-year-old Vincenzo Gonzaga and contains a setting of Torquato Tasso's 'Tolse Barbara gente', addressed to Barbara Sanseverina, which must have been composed shortly after Tasso had completed the verse.

The largest body of evidence for Wert's involvement with Ferrara comes from the 1580s. There seem to have been three principal reasons for his interest in the Este court: his love affair with Tarquinia Molza, the greater musical opportunities and more progressive cultural climate at Ferrara, and his close relationship with Vincenzo Gonzaga, who, as we have seen, spent a good deal of time there during the same period.

Tarquinia Molza, niece of the poet Francesco Maria Molza, was born into an important Modenese family in 1542, and in 1560 was married to Paolo Porrina, who died tragically nine years later. She was an accomplished poetess and a skilled performer on the viol and the lute, and Alfonso d'Este himself fought a joust in her honour. She is known to have visited Ferrara on a number of occasions in 1582, and final arrangements for her to join the court as a *dama d'onora* to Margherita Gonzaga were completed by 25 April 1583. Provost Trotti is the first Ferrarese chronicler to mention her participation in the *concerto della donne*. Her affair with Wert seems to have begun in 1584, and was finally exposed in October 1589 as a result of enquiries that had been ordered by Alfonso d'Este. It was unpardonable in such a highly structured society that a well-bred lady should associate in this way with a court official: as Laderchi's report to the duke stressed, 'Jaches era povero fiammingo, stato ragazzo da cantar della Marchese della Padulla, et poi lungo tempo servidore del Conte Alfonso di Nuvolara...'[37] No doubt Wert was encouraged to visit Ferrara during the 1570s and early 1580s both by Vincenzo and by Alfonso d'Este himself. The four surviving documentary references to his visits there undoubtedly represent only a few of the trips that he made, and Laderchi's report of Wert's affair with Tarquinia Molza refers to the frequency with which he appeared at court. The first notice occurs in a letter of 15 October 1583, written by the composer Lodovico Agostini, which mentions that Wert had been present at a musical evening

[37] Biographical details on Tarquinia Molza from Vandelli: *Opusculi inediti*, Ramazzini: 'I musici fiamminghi', and Newcomb: 'The musica segreta', pp. 260–1. Laderchi's report is given in Ramazzini's article.

in Ferrara earlier in the month.[38] In the next year Wert seems to have spent the period between 14 September and 22 December there, as a result of which Guglielmo Gonzaga felt obliged to write to Alfonso d'Este with the request that Wert be sent back to Mantua. Nevertheless, within a few weeks Wert had returned for the Carnival season, and this second visit prompted Duke Guglielmo to enquire via his secretaries whether Alfonso was attempting to lure Wert to a permanent position in Ferrara.[39] A final indication of Wert's Ferrarese connections is a letter written by the composer and dated from Ferrara on 8 November 1586.[40]

Wert's *Settimo libro de madrigali a cinque voci* is dedicated to Vincenzo Gonzaga and Margherita Farnese on the occasion of their marriage in 1581 – an event which, as we have seen, may have stimulated Vincenzo to persuade his father to engage a group of virtuoso singers which included Laura Bovia – and the book follows an arrangement traditional in such publications by opening and closing with encomia. As has recently been emphasised, stylistically the *Settimo libro* is extremely varied, almost as if it were a conscious attempt to compile a compendium of contemporary madrigal styles.[41] The second, fourth, fifth and seventh items in the book are in the tradition of the brief, largely homophonic, and by this date rather old-fashioned type of madrigal that Giustiniani speaks of in the 'Discorso'. Another traditional style that is well represented in the publication is that of the brightly textured festive piece in the 'Venetian' manner of Andrea Gabrieli. As one might expect, the opening and closing items adopt this style, and the final section of 'Sorgi et rischiara' is rather reminiscent of Gabrieli's music in its use of clear diatonicism, short phrases, and a final sequential climax. Wert's setting of Guarini's pastoral dialogue 'Tirsi morir volea' reveals a third current style while establishing a method of dealing with the text that was to exert a considerable influence on many other composers during the subsequent quarter-century. Although the piece is laid out as a large-scale dialogue on a conventional plan, in its vital rhythms, short phrases and predominantly homophonic texture it still preserves the spirit of the *canzonetta*. This modification of the dialogue style also affects the setting of 'In qual parte', though because of its contrapuntal elaboration, long phrases and thicker textures, this piece rarely displays the lightness of touch that characterises the Guarini setting.

While these compositions in established genres all display Wert's individuality and competence, important and radical changes in Wert's musical language can be seen in the three remaining items in the book, which taken together represent two fresh styles of writing that are of fundamental

[38] See Appendix II, doc. 36.
[39] MacClintock: *Giaches de Wert*, p. 79 no. 81.
[40] Original document in ASM (AG) 1217.
[41] See MacClintock: *Giaches de Wert*, pp. 106ff, and Newcomb: 'The musica segreta', pp. 158ff.

importance for the later madrigal. Both the third item, a setting of Torquato Tasso's sonnet 'Donna, se ben le chiome', and the ninth madrigal, 'Giunto alla tomba' (a five-movement setting from Canto XII of *Gerusalemme liberata*) are the first examples of a declamatory style whose relationship to early monody has probably been exaggerated. The remaining item is the most startling, a setting of a traditional madrigal text, Petrarch's 'Solo e pensoso', which is genuinely experimental in its uneven melodic outlines, disjointed textures and unexpected changes in the pulse of the harmonic rhythm. It is not surprising to find Ferrarese tendencies in the two declamatory madrigals on Tasso texts, particularly in the textural contrasts which the largely homophonic medium produces. There is some motivic diminution in all three, particularly in 'Giunto alla tomba', requiring more advanced vocal skills than anything in the sixth book; and it is the technical difficulties of some of the other pieces in the volume which mark them off from Wert's earlier vocal writing. It is also significant that the two declamatory pieces are the only settings in the book of Tasso's verse and that one of these, 'Donna, se ben le chiome', was originally composed by the poet at the instance of Cornelio Bentivoglio for his bride Isabella Bendidio, one of the members of the first Ferrarese *concerto*. Wert must have set this text before it had been officially published. Consequently, the texts, the virtuoso style in general and simultaneous diminution in particular, and the simple, homophonic harmonic framework of these two pieces suggest that they, and perhaps other compositions in the seventh book, were composed with Ferrarese forces in mind and under the influence of the progressive poetic and musical impulses at the Este court. The case is strengthened by one other piece in the volume, the setting of Petrarch's sonnet 'Gratie ch'a pochi il ciel'. This, the only composition in the book to use a pair of upper voices in G2 clefs, employs considerable stretches of intrinsic florid writing – that is, thematic rather than purely decorative – and is also indebted to the homophonic texture of the lighter styles. The text itself, in praise of female charms, has been assumed to have been chosen with Vincenzo's bride Margherita Farnese in mind, but it is equally appropriate to the special character of the Ferrarese *concerto*.

If the Ferrarese traits in the seventh book have been underestimated, writers since Einstein have not neglected to underline their presence in the eighth book, which appeared (with an undated dedication) in 1586.[42] Many of the pieces are suffused with the mature Ferrarese virtuoso style, and the dedication to Alfonso d'Este and Margherita makes it clear that the contents were composed for the Ferrarese women. A number of pieces had been composed by November 1583. On the sixth of that month Vincenzo Gonzaga wrote to Wert asking for his setting of Tasso's 'Qual musico gentil ch'al canto snodi' together with any other recent compositions, and on the fifteenth Wert

[42] Einstein: *The Italian madrigal*, II, pp. 831ff, and MacClintock: *Giaches de Wert*, pp. 110ff.

replied complying.[43] Indeed, the importance of the eighth book lies not only in its demonstration of the Ferrarese style but also in its highly influential propagandising on behalf of Tasso's verse. Six of the texts are taken from *Gerusalemme liberata* (four of them from Canto XVI alone), and 'Non sospirar pastor' is taken from the third Eclogue – a preoccupation with Tasso which is foreshadowed in the *Settimo libro*. Similarly, the predominant musical style of the eighth book is clearly an outcome of the previous one and is a style that is of obvious importance for contemporary composers. Einstein recognised the work as a crucial document, though his enumeration of the pieces within it in which the Ferrarese influence is indisputable is conservative. In addition to the three that he mentions ('Si come ai freschi matutini rai', 'Non è si denso velo', and 'Vener' ch'un giorno havea'), three more display all the characteristics of motivic diminution, *concertato* groupings and high tessitura: 'Usciva homai', 'Sovente alhor' and 'Misera non credea'. One feature which is now developed much further is the *concertato* treatment of the three upper voices. In Wert's earlier works there are often passages for paired upper voices against a third which acts as a harmonic support, but in the eighth book the three upper voices sometimes predominate in a five-voice texture, and also frequently insert short (usually virtuoso) passages, in which the diminution is more equally shared, without the lower parts: for instance, at the opening of 'Si come ai freschi' or that of 'Fra le dorate chiome'.

It would seem, then, that Wert thoroughly mastered the mature Ferrarese manner between 1581 and 1586, the years when his personal and professional contacts with the Este court were closest. Once established, it remained a predominant feature of his secular writing up to and including the final *Undecimo libro* of 1595, though rarely was the diminution as elaborate as in the eighth book or the *concertato* separation as well defined. Nevertheless, the essentials of the Ferrarese manner are clearly present in much of the ninth book of 1588. Whereas the eighth book is a product of Ferrarese experience, is dedicated to Alfonso II, and contains pieces tailored to the vocal techniques of the Ferrarese *concerto delle donne* as Wert himself stated in the preface, the ninth book has a distinctly Mantuan flavour. It is dedicated to Vincenzo, commemorates his coronation in 1587, and opens with 'Hor si rallegri il cielo', a setting of a poem published on that occasion by the Mantuan court chronicler Follino.[44] There is a significant shift in poetic taste too, away from the dramatic intensity and impassioned gloom of many of the texts in the eighth book and towards light occasional verse and pastoral lyrics. This is also symbolic of the new Mantuan enthusiasm for the pastoral which characterises the early part of Vincenzo's period, reaching a climax in the *Pastor fido* production of 1598. Admittedly, two pieces in the collection,

---

[43] See Appendix II, docs. 74–75.
[44] For the text see *Componimenti volgari et latini...nella coronatione*, sig. [D1]v.

'Mesola il Po' and 'Ha ninfe adorn'e belle', are on Tasso texts with specific Ferrarese references; but these references are to an event in 1583, and the music was probably composed for that occasion. The two encomia are here strategically placed so that the volume opens with one in praise of Vincenzo and concludes with another in honour of his sister Margherita and her husband Alfonso – musical testimonies to the political unity and apparent personal amity of the two houses.

In short, the ninth book is a Mantuan product; and it would be difficult to imagine that Wert's first publication after the accession of Vincenzo, with whom he seems to have had a particularly close relationship, could have been anything else. The style of the contents is unmistakably that of the Ferrarese virtuoso manner, modified (it could be suggested) to take account of the particular temperaments and vocal abilities of the Mantuan *concerto*. In general these pieces are more strongly homophonic than any of Wert's earlier publications, and there are long stretches of thematic motivic diminution, often in paired equal high male or female voices, and also passages reminiscent of the *concertato* style of the eighth book. The Mantuan *concerto* was formed between Vincenzo's accession in September 1587 and April 1589, when some of its members travelled with Vincenzo to Ferrara and subsequently performed in Florence, and it seems probable that much of the music in Wert's ninth book was composed with Vincenzo's new performers in mind. This suggestion can be supported, as will be seen, by other musical evidence; if it is correct it would date the establishment of the Mantuan ensemble quite precisely.

Wert's close connections with the Este court between the years 1581 and 1586 are symbolised not only in his own music, but also in the rather curious *Il nuovo echo a cinque voci* by the Ferrarese composer Lodovico Agostini, which was published in 1583 with a dedication to Alfonso d'Este, and which includes one madrigal 'Ad imitatione del S. Giaches Wert'. Interestingly, the same book contains three pieces (two vocal and one instrumental) which parody compositions by Alessandro Striggio, and it is significant for the present discussion that during the period when Wert seems to have been most influenced by Ferrarese practice, another distinguished Mantuan composer witnessed the performances of the *musica secreta* and may have adjusted his style of composition in response to the experience.

Although Striggio was a member of the Mantuan nobility, his principal connections appear to have been with the Medici court at Florence, where he was admired as a string-player and was occasionally employed as a diplomatic agent. Together with Corteccia he provided much of the music for the spate of important ceremonial and theatrical festivals that marked the last decade of the rule of Duke Cosimo I. Nevertheless, he maintained close relations with the Gonzaga court throughout his career. His wife, the distinguished singer and lutenist Virginia Vagnoli,[45] probably lived there, and their three children Francesca, Giovanni, and Alessandro were born and educated there. Striggio spent most of his time after 1586 at Mantua, though both he and his son returned to perform in the *intermedi* that were given in Florence in 1589 as part of the production of Bargagli's *La Pellegrina*.[46] It was in his native Mantua that Striggio died in 1592.[47] Although he was probably not part of the permanent music establishment there, it is interesting that Monteverdi associates him with three prominent members of the Santa Barbara *cappella* in a letter of 28 November 1601, and towards the end of his life he entered the service of Duke Guglielmo Gonzaga as 'musico straordinario'.[48]

Striggio's early work was extremely popular among contemporaries. The *Primo libro de madrigali a sei voci* of 1560 was reprinted eight times in a little over thirty years, and the *Madrigali a cinque voci...libro primo*, which first appeared in the same year, ran to seven editions.[49] 'Nasce la pena mia' seems to have been particularly admired: it was used by Philippe de Monte as the basis of a six-voice parody mass, and was disseminated in numerous printed and manuscript collections of the period. Striggio's contemporary reputation as a composer seems to have largely rested on these early works and on his frequent contributions of new works to anthologies. His last three madrigal books were assembled by his son Alessandro and published posthumously. Those later books must be compilations of works that had been composed at various times during the previous fifteen years, since the texts of two or possibly three items from *Il quinto libro de madrigali a cinque voci* were composed to celebrate the public marriage of Grand Duke Francesco I and Bianca Cappello, which was celebrated in Florence in October 1579.[50] Each of them

[45] The standard accounts of Striggio's early career are Einstein: *The Italian madrigal*, II, pp. 761–8, and Tadlock: 'Alessandro Striggio'. For Virginia Vagnoli see Saviotti: 'Un'artista del cinquecento'.

[46] [Malvezzi]: *Nono parte*, p. 10.

[47] ASM (AG) Reg, nec. 1592.

[48] Monteverdi's celebrated latter is given in Malipiero: *Claudio Monteverdi*, p. 127; an English translation is provided in Arnold and Fortune: 'The man as seen through his letters', pp. 22–3. The original is in ASM (AG) Raccolta d'autografi 6. For documentation of Striggio's last years at Mantua see Appendix II, doc. 65.

[49] Einstein: *The Italian madrigal*, II, p. 761, suggests that the first book for five voices was originally published in 1557, and Tadlock: 'Alessandro Striggio' assigns it to 1558. This is presumably prompted by the announcement on the title-page of the 1560 edition that that is a reprint, but commercial statements of this kind cannot be taken at face value, and there is good reason to believe that this was a common way for publishers to create an audience for a publication, particularly the first publication of an unknown composer.

[50] See Schrade: 'Les fêtes du mariage', Ghisi: *Feste musicali*, pp. xxxv–xl, and Solerti: *Musica, ballo e drammatica*, pp. 9ff. It is worth noting that a previously unnoticed *intermedio* setting by Striggio, 'Ecco che fa' for eight voices, is in the Vincenti and Amadino anthology *Musica de diversi auttori illustri* (Venice, 1584). This was written for the 1565 *feste* in Florence; for the texts see Ghisi: *Feste musicali*, p. xxvi. Striggio also seems to have experimented with solo song. The index to Florence, Biblioteca Nazionale Centrale MS Magl. XIX.66 records his setting of Rinuccini's 'Se più del pianto', but the music does not survive: see Becherini: *Catalogo dei manoscritti musicali*, p. 33. In addition to the celebrated forty-voice motet 'Ecce beatam lucem' (see above, p. 87) Striggio may have written a mass for large forces. This is suggested by a letter from the Mantuan agent at the French court to Duke Guglielmo Gonzaga dated

is known in only one edition; for only one do all the partbooks survive.

There are clear indications that Striggio was deeply impressed by the Ferrarese *concerto delle donne* and that he experimented with elements of the virtuoso style both during and after a visit that he made to the Este court in 1584. In July of that year he was invited, together with his wife and his son Alessandro, by Alfonso II d'Este to stay for twenty days. The visit was to 'Sentire il suo concerto di donne', but it is also clear from Striggio's letters to the grand duke and from the *copialettere* of the grand duke's replies that the composer had been commissioned to set some madrigals in the Ferrarese style. On 29 July Striggio wrote two letters to Florence, one to the grand ducal secretary Belisario Vinta praising the ladies of the *concerto*, the other to the grand duke mentioning his four-voice madrigals with three ornamented soprano lines and noting that 'these ladies sing excellently and are confident both in their *conserto* and from partbooks without rehearsal'. Certainly the Ferrarese experience seems to have exerted a profound influence on Striggio, as local observers noted, and on 24 August, after his return to Mantua, he sent two further pieces to the grand duke, 'Cor mio mentr'io vi miro' and 'Per voi, lasso, conviene', expressing the hope that 'they will go well when they have been memorised, and when the words are well enunciated and sung to the accompaniment by Master Giulio Caccini'. Caccini was dissatisfied, however, and in December Striggio sent four further attempts on texts which had been sent from Florence.[51] Whilst these facts emphasise the associations between Striggio and the Medici, the possibility cannot be ignored that Striggio also contributed to the rise of the Ferrarese style amongst members of the Mantuan *cappella*. He was obviously known and admired there, as Monteverdi testified, and became a colleague after 1586. His ties with Ferrara continued after this visit: together with Luzzaschi and Wert he is praised in Tasso's *La Cavaletta*, which was published in 1584, and his posthumous publications include settings of Tasso's verse. It is difficult to resist the inference that Striggio's part in the adoption of the Ferrarese vocal style at Mantua, by virtue of his rank, experience and reputation, may have been considerable. Regrettably, none of the pieces mentioned in the correspondence have survived; there are no hints of the Ferrarese style in the works which have survived complete; and his only known essay in the monodic style (which may well have provided further proof of his interest in new vocal writing) has unfortunately not survived.

11 May 1562: '...Egli e arrivato qui alla corte il Striggino musico...Sua Maestà l'ha sentito sonare et di viola et di lira et hoggi...ha sentito la sua messa a 40 et l'agnius a 60' (original in ASM (AG) 653).

[51] For the texts of Striggio's letters see Gandolfi: 'Lettere inediti', pp. 528ff. To these I have added a further one: see Appendix II, doc. 68. For further on Caccini's reaction to the Ferrarese concerto see Ledbetter: 'Luca Marenzio', p. 116.

From a slightly later period comes additional proof of the attractions of the Ferrarese style for composers at the Gonzaga court. Now that the last three madrigal books of Pallavicino are partly rescued from the obscurity which formerly surrounded them, it is generally accepted that they were heavily influenced by Wert's late madrigals, and that they in turn played a (perhaps crucial) role in impressing Wert's later style upon the early works of Monteverdi.[52] Of greater importance here is the transition from the conventionalities of Pallavicino's early writing to something more akin to his mature manner.

By training and experience Pallavicino was provincial in comparison with Wert and Striggio. He may have been born in Cremona, was perhaps connected with the Accademia Filarmonica in Verona, and was almost certainly employed for a time in Sabbioneta by Vespasiano Gonzaga. According to documentary evidence he may have been in Mantua by 1582, and certainly he was there by 18 December 1584, the date of a letter which refers to him as being in the ducal service. In 1586 he was involved with Gardano in arrangements to publish some of Guglielmo's compositions; another member of the ruling house, Alfonso Gonzaga, was the dedicatee of his *Terzo libro*.[53] These works were competent and imaginative within the limitations of the conservative musical styles in vogue at the Mantuan court.

The sudden, striking change of direction which can be seen in Pallavicino's secular compositions with the publication of the fourth book of madrigals was such that contemporaries could cite his music in support of either side in the debate which grew up about dissonance and expression. Artusi placed him in a conservative context together with Merulo, Porta, Andrea Gabrieli, Palestrina, Gastoldi, Giovanelli, and Nanino, while Banchieri saw him as a progressive along with Gesualdo, Fontanelli, and Cavalieri. It is easy to see how such conflicting views might be justified. Pallavicino's earliest madrigal publications, the four-voice book, the first three five-voice books, and the six-voice book, display a competent but essentially conservative manner. The very choice of a four-voice medium for his first book – published in 1579 and dedicated to the *ridotto* of the Accademia Filarmonica at Verona – was itself a cautious move, since the four-voice madrigal had by this date virtually moved into the realm of didactic literature. In the first five-voice book, published two years later, there is great reliance upon imitative entries quite strictly carried out throughout all the voices, and preoccupation with complex rhythmic interplay between the voices which thickens the texture and tends to obscure the words. Of the five identifiable texts in the volume, two are from Ariosto's *Orlando furioso*, one from Caporali's *Rime*, and one by

[52] See Einstein: *The Italian madrigal*, II, pp. 833–4, Arnold: '"Seconda pratica"', and Arnold: 'Monteverdi: some colleagues and pupils'.
[53] The most complete résumé of his career is Flanders: 'The madrigals', chapter 1.

Guarini. *Il secondo libro*, probably published for the first time in 1584, is the largest of his madrigal books and includes considerable use of consciously archaic devices, particularly paired imitative entries and canonic writing. In 'Misero te, non vedi' the words 'Son di varii color' are represented by notating each of the voice-parts in a different mensuration; and in the setting of Petrarch's 'Passa la nave mia' the text 'che son d'error con ignoranzia a torto' is set in parallel fifths and 'root-position triads'. Representational wit of this kind, which has a distinguished ancestry in the madrigal, stretching back to Arcadelt and Verdelot, continues to be a vital aspect of the later development of the genre despite Einstein's censure.[54] It is perhaps significant that Pallavicino's writing should expand to accommodate gestures of this kind in the one book amongst his early publications that shows any definite tendency to emulate Wert's music, the dominating influence of his later works. Stylistically there are echoes of Wert's personal manner in chains of parallel 'first-inversion chords' or in the use of archaic 'double leading-notes'; but of equal interest is the choice of two texts, 'Destossi fra il mio gelo' and 'Ninfe leggiadre'. Both refer to 'Laura', who must be Laura Peperara, one of the members of the second Ferrarese *concerto*, since 'Ninfa leggiadre' appeared for the first time in a setting which Wert contributed to *Il lauro verde*, an anthology produced in Ferrara on the occasion of her marriage. Pallavicino's choice of these verses does not necessarily indicate any links with Ferrara, but does help to confirm the impression that it is in this book, the first to be produced after Pallavicino's move to Mantua, that Wert's influence can first be seen.

The major stylistic shift in Pallavicino's work comes with the fourth book of 1588. It is dated 9 August and is dedicated to Vincenzo Gonzaga, now Duke of Mantua. In the opening piece, 'Mentre che qui d'intorno', the concentrated use of an initial motif which is subsequently inverted and then augmented harks back to the contrapuntal technicalities of the second book; but elsewhere in the volume there are completely fresh approaches to the use of dissonance. Slow-moving dissonant passages now suddenly intrude to contrast quite violently with the surrounding brisk polyphony, and this dissonance involves third-related chords, irregular suspensions and frequent cross-relations. One piece in particular, 'Perfida, pur potesti', is almost a continuous exercise in concentrated dissonance, similar in mood and technique to Pallavicino's later compositions such as 'Cruda Amarilli'. A second novel feature in the fourth book – one which, interestingly, also reveals an attention to vertical sonorities – is the new emphasis on diminution. Many of the pieces contain extended passages of thematic embellishment of a virtuosity which leaves little doubt that these works were intended for professional performers, while the dedication makes clear that they were

---

[54] Einstein: *The Italian madrigal*, I, pp. 229ff. Einstein's disapproval of certain types of connection between words and music, particularly *Augenmusik*, is more a reflection of nineteenth-century aesthetics than of sixteenth-century sensibilities.

composed at the Mantuan court. In the course of the volume diminution
occurs in all voice-parts, but generally it is more noticeable in the soprano
and bass lines. The opening piece – otherwise somewhat conservative –
includes some elaborate passages for tenor and bass within a simple
'harmonic' framework; and in 'Tutti eri foco, Amore' there is a sequence
for soprano and tenor in which the soprano line incorporates a written-out
trill, in the manner of Luzzaschi's *Madrigali*. The fifth voice in this book is
usually a second soprano, and the sopranos sometimes use G2 clefs. As with
Wert, so with Pallavicino: once mastered, the fully mature virtuoso style
remained an important aspect of his writing throughout the rest of his career.

Archival evidence, contemporary printed sources, and the evidence of
stylistic change in the music of Wert and Pallavicino all suggest that
Vincenzo Gonzaga's *concerto delle donne* was formed between 1587 and 1589,
and that by April 1589 some of its members performed in Florence. The
formation of the ensemble was symptomatic of the fundamental alteration
in attitudes that took place at the Mantuan court with the passing of Duke
Guglielmo. Conservatism, piety and moderation now gave way to a
preoccupation with the latest fashions and the pursuit of pleasure. Composers
with court connections seem to have found this new climate stimulating;
between 1588 and 1591, Gastoldi and Wert each published three books of
secular music, and during the same period Pallavicino, Rossi, Baccusi and
Trofeo produced volumes of madrigals and *canzonette*. Once established, the
mature virtuoso style retained its importance throughout Wert's last works,
as pieces such as 'Scherza nel canto' from his eleventh book demonstrate
clearly. Interestingly, too, the crucial connections between the serious
polyphonic madrigal and the lighter styles which, according to Giustiniani,
provided the basis for the Ferrarese manner are emphasised by the presence
of the developed virtuoso style in Wert's *canzonette villanelle* and in the
light-hearted tenth book. Similarly, the new technique is an essential in
Pallavicino's later works, especially the sixth and seventh madrigal books.
Its importance for minor composers working at Mantua seems to have been
slight, as is evident from the conservative tone of anthologies such as *L'amorosa
caccia*, but its effect on the finest of the court composers during Vincenzo's
period is indisputable. Although the precise date of Monteverdi's arrival at
Mantua is unclear, by 1590 at the latest he had been taken on there as a
violist. His adoption of the virtuoso manner in *Il terzo libro de madrigali a cinque
voci* of 1592, the first of his works to be published after his arrival at the
Gonzaga court, has been remarked upon by nearly every writer who has
discussed the book. It is usually assumed that pieces such as 'O come è gran
martire' from this book and 'Quel augellin che canta' from *Il quarto libro* of
1603 were originally written for and in admiration of the Ferrarese *musica
secreta*, since Monteverdi acknowledged his debt to the performers and
composers of the Este *cappella* in the preface to the latter publication; but
it is evident that during the period when at least the third book was being

written, the Gonzaga court employed not only a virtuoso ensemble of its own but also a small circle of distinguished composers who had thoroughly mastered the Ferrarese manner.

The primary influence on Vincenzo's decision to establish a *concerto delle donne* at Mantua was clearly the example of Ferrara; but he may also have been impressed with the attempts to found a similar ensemble at the Medici court, where he was also a frequent visitor after his marriage to Leonora de' Medici in 1584.[55] The question of the influence of Florentine culture at Mantua is even more crucial for the development of theatrical life at court after Vincenzo's accession. By the time of the first production of Monteverdi's *Orfeo* during the Carnival season of 1607, and of the lavish celebrations which accompanied the marriage of Vincenzo's son Francesco to Margherita of Savoy in the following year, the importance of Florentine example and participation for court theatre at Mantua is inescapable. This was partly due to the interest of Cardinal Ferdinando Gonzaga, who had close associations with Medici musical and theatrical circles, but the impact of Florentine musical theatre is noticeable from the early years of Vincenzo's period, long before Ferdinando's tastes had matured, most prominently in the attempts made during the 1590s to produce Guarini's *Il pastor fido* at court.[56]

Against the rich background of almost continuous popularity and influence which *Il pastor fido* has enjoyed since the early seventeenth century, it comes as a surprise to realise that the play was the object of fierce debate and criticism even before it had been published.[57] Composed probably between 1580 and 1585 and then circulated in manuscript, it was not published until 1590.[58] Shortly after it was finished, Guarini began a subtle and successful campaign to cultivate the friendship of the distinguished philologist Lionardo Salviati in Florence, apparently with the aim of persuading him to 'correct' the manuscript. By the beginning of October 1586 Salviati had read the pastoral through and, following Guarini's instructions, had also shown it to other members of the Accademia degli Alterati. Salviati's comments, diplomatically conceived, talked of finding the work excellent in every respect but nevertheless, in response to the author's request, pointed out faults

[55] For further details see Newcomb: 'The musica segreta', pp. 181ff.

[56] The documentation of the Mantuan performances of *Il pastor fido* is presented and discussed in D'Ancona: *Origini*, II, pp. 535–75. See also V. Rossi: *Battista Guarini*. For further on Vincenzo's enthusiasm for the theatre, and for his contacts with Florentine theatrical life, see Ledbetter: 'Luca Marenzio', p. 113.

[57] For the development of the controversy up to 1600 see Weinberg: *A history of literary criticism in the Italian Renaissance*, II, pp. 1074–1105, and for a shorter account extending beyond 1600 Perella: *The critical fortunes*.

[58] There is some discussion over the long gestation of the work. Some commentators have suggested that it was conceived as early as 1569. A more commonly accepted view is that Guarini began the work in earnest at the end of 1580 or the beginning of 1581, prompted perhaps by the appearance of Tasso's *Aminta* in the 1581 Aldine edition. For the various arguments see D'Ancona: *Origini*, II, pp. 535ff, and V. Rossi: *Battista Guarini*, pp. 55ff.

in it: 'Inconsistencies, a failure to develop any single passion, a suspicion of contrivance in the ending, all kinds of doubts about character, decorum and verisimilitude'. He also noted that the poem was the first of its kind, that its adaptability for the stage was not immediately evident, and that it was in any case too long for performance.[59] In the same year, 1586, the debate over the play began seriously with the publication of Giason Denores' *Discorso*, which initiated an impressive pamphlet war to which Guarini himself contributed and which lasted until 1593. Yet even then the quarrel was not yet over; and in 1600 the question was suddenly raised again as a result of Summo's *Discorsi poetici*, in which the last discourse is a specific attack upon the poem. This renewed criticism was no doubt partly responsible for Guarini's preparation of the 1602 edition, published by Ciotti in Venice, finely illustrated with six plates by Francesco Valesio, and including Guarini's own *annotazioni*.[60] This is significant. The Ciotti edition is of prime textual value; dedicated to Vincenzo Gonzaga, it is in effect a memorial to the 1598 Mantuan performance, and the plates show G. B. Aleotti's designs for a number of scenes including the *Gioco della cieca* – cf. Figure 9. It is also of importance for understanding the musical and choreographic difficulties which were posed by the play, or rather by one scene in it.

It is entirely typical of Vincenzo Gonzaga's extrovert brand of artistic patronage that it was soon after the play's first publication, when it had already become thoroughly controversial, that plans were laid to produce it in Mantua.

During Duke Guglielmo's period, the traditions of court theatre centred on the visits of travelling companies and the often highly praised activities of the Mantuan ghetto. There is some evidence that both these were discouraged during Guglielmo's last years. On the other hand, Vincenzo's taste for the theatre, carefully nurtured by the strong Ferrarese and Florentine traditions of spectacle, produced a noticeable change after 1587. A new theatre was constructed to designs by Viani,[61] and dramatic presentations became a prominent and regular feature of social life at court. The Gelosi troupe returned for the Carnival season of 1589, and during the next few years other companies such as the Accessi and the Uniti became frequent visitors to Mantua.[62] The important aspect of Vincenzo's theatrical tastes is not so much the revival of old traditions as a new enthusiasm for lavish spectacle and the pastoral.[63]

[59] Salviati's corrections, notes and other references to *Il pastor fido* are in BAF Cod. CL.H.276. The annotations alone are published in Pasquazi: *Rinascimento ferrarese*, pp. 251–83, and the whole correspondence is summarised in P. M. Brown: *Lionardo Salviati*, pp. 198–9.
[60] Guarini: *Il pastor fido, tragicommedia pastorale*.
[61] See *Mantova. Le arti*, III, pp. 161–75, and Thieme and Becker: *Allgemeines Lexicon*, XXIV, pp. 321–3.
[62] For further information on the travelling companies and their impact upon Mantuan theatrical life see Lea: *Italian popular comedy*, II, pp. 271ff.
[63] The contrasting theatrical tastes of the two rulers are elaborated in Cavicchi: 'Teatro monteverdiano', pp. 139–42.

Fig. 9 Giovanni Battista Aleotti: Designs for Act III of *Il pastor fido*, Mantua, 1598. Engraving by Francesco Valesio, from the edition printed by Giovanni Battista Ciotti (Venice, 1602)

Vincenzo Gonzaga's interest in *Il pastor fido* dates from 1584, while the play was still unfinished: on 4 April of that year he requested a copy of the manuscript from Guarini in the hope that the play could be produced as part of the festivities celebrating his marriage to Leonora de' Medici. Guarini declined politely, since the fifth act and all the choruses had still not been written;[64] but later in the same year there was an unsuccessful attempt to stage the work at Ferrara, and most authorities agree that the play was staged in some form in Turin in 1585, on the occasion of the marriage of Carlo Emanuele of Savoy and Catalina of Spain.[65] There the matter rested, as far as Vincenzo was concerned, until the last months of 1591, when the ducal secretary Annibale Chieppio again contacted Guarini to inform him of renewed attempts to rehearse *Il pastor fido* – now published – which had begun at the instigation of Agnese Argotta, Marchesa di Grana.

Agnese, the wife of Prospero del Carretto, may have been connected with the Mantuan court as early as 1581, when one of Muzio Manfredi's *Lettere* was addressed to her, and about 1587 she became Vincenzo's mistress. The early 1590s were the period of her greatest influence on court life. Installed at the Palazzo del Te (rather as Isabella Boschetti had been some sixty years earlier), Agnese seems to have shown a considerable interest in the arts, including music. She is the dedicatee of one piece in Giacomo Moro's *Gli encomii musicali* of 1585, where she is described as part of the circle of Barbara Sanseverina, the dedicatee of the volume as a whole.[66] This volume also places her in cultural circles close to the Accademia degli Invaghiti, since the final item is addressed to Giulio Cesare Gonzaga, patron of the academy and dedicatee of Moro's earlier *Canzonette alla napolitana* of 1581; she also seems to have known Bernardo Marliani, sometime Rector of the academy, who included one of his letters to her in his *Lettere*. Documentary evidence shows that at the Palazzo del Te Agnese cultivated a small academy of her own principally devoted to the arts of versification and music. The poetic anthology *Tesoro delle ninfe* is one product of its activities. Another may be Wert's tenth book, which includes many madrigals to texts in the new madrigal style of Tasso and Guarini that also characterises the *Tesoro*, which is dedicated to Agnese and refers to her fondness for both music and poetry. It seems that she was a performer herself, and one of Manfredi's *Cento madrigali* recalls one of her performances that moved the poet to tears.[67]

But Agnese's most ambitious artistic project was the production of *Il pastor fido*. Under her direction arrangements continued throughout November and December 1591 for rehearsing both the play and its accompanying *intermedi*

[64] D'Ancona: *Origini*, II, p. 539. The original of Guarini's reply, Padua 7 April 1584, is in ASM (AG) 1514. [65] D'Ancona: *Origini*, II, p. 536, and V. Rossi: *Battista Guarini*, pp. 85–7.
[66] See Manfredi: *Lettere*, nos. 79 and 107, and G. Moro: *Gli encomii musicali*, p. 2.
[67] See Marliani: *Lettere*, p. 100, *Tesoro delle ninfe*, and Wert: *Il decimo libro de madrigali a cinque voci*, the preface of which is transcribed in MacClintock: *Giaches de Wert*, p. 237. The piece in Manfredi's *Cento madrigali* addressed to her (p. 91) is headed: 'Ella suonava, e cantava una volta, fra l'altre, alcune cose, e sì soavemente, ch'io piansi, ella col proprio fazzoletto in atto piacevolissimo mi asciugi le lagrime.'

on the theme of the harmony of the four elements, and on 19 December
Guarini himself arrived to advise. Nevertheless, there seem to have been
difficulties of production, and it was not until April 1592 that the plans were
taken up again; it is clear from the fresh spate of letters produced by this
revival of interest that the scenery was to be designed by Ippolito Andreasi,
that the performance was to take place in the courtyard of the Palazzo del
Te, and that Aleotti, Alfonso d'Este's principal architect, had been called
upon to take care of constructions and theatrical machines. Again there were
considerable problems, mostly resulting from the intransigence of the actors,
and except for a brief attempt to take up the proposals again in 1593 the
enterprise was abandoned until 1598.[68] On this occasion there were three
performances, the last of which, on 22 November, was given in the presence
of Margherita of Austria, then travelling through Mantua to Spain where
she was to be married.[69]

This is an extraordinary history of delay, and it is clear from the surviving
documents that the problems that bedevilled the 1592 Mantuan performance
stemmed partly from the novelty of Guarini's conception of Act III Scene
ii, incorporating the *Gioco della cieca* (Game of blind man's buff). In this short
scene, with its obvious erotic overtones, four madrigals to be sung and danced
by a chorus of nymphs are interpolated between the speeches of Amarilli,
Mirtillo and Corisca. Difficulties were experienced during rehearsals of the
scene for the projected Mantuan performance of 1592, though the precise
nature of the problem is unclear from the documents. The ducal secretary
Annibale Chieppio wrote to Vincenzo Gonzaga:

The *Balletto della cieca* is giving us difficulty because some of those who have already
rehearsed it before Your Highness have gone now, some are ill, and some have
become so truculent about taking part at all that, after the absence of Isachino
[Massarano, the ballet-master] for a few days, everything had to be begun afresh.
The problem of skilfully introducing it [the *Balletto*] into the tragicomedy has proved
to be even greater. The ballet has four sections besides the exit, and they are all
different. Four madrigals must be sung, and the speeches of Amarilli, Mirtillo and
Corisca inserted.[70]

[68] See D'Ancona: *Origini*, II, pp. 547ff. The Mantuan documentation of the attempts in the early 1590s
to produce the work is in ASM (AG) 2654, 2657, and 2661. One of Guarini's letters to the Marchesa
di Grana about the production, dated 24 April 1592, was published by the poet in his *Lettere*, pp. 38–9.
[69] Margherita arrived on 20 November. Her journey through Italy, including her stop at Mantua and
the performance of *Il pastor fido*, was widely publicised in contemporary Italian, French, and English
pamphlets. See in particular Grillo: *Breve trattato*. The *intermedi* for this performance, for which the music
does not seem to have survived, are given in Neri: 'Gli "intermezzi" del "Pastor fido"', pp. 405ff.
For Viani's involvement see Fleschig: *Die Dekoration*, pp. 30–2. It is now clear from Cavicchi: 'La
scenografia dell'*Aminta*' that the plates of the 1602 Ciotti edition are most probably based upon Aleotti's
designs for the 1598 performance, and it is certainly suggestive that the Ciotti edition is dedicated to
Vincenzo Gonzaga. Aleotti's importance for the 1598 production is further stressed by the documents
in V. Rossi: *Battista Guarini*, pp. 308 and 311, and is implied by Guarini's own remarks on theatrical
machines in his *Lettere*, p. 18.
[70] Letter of Annibale Chieppio, Mantua 23 December 1591, to Duke Vincenzo Gonzaga: see D'Ancona:
Origini, II, pp. 544–6. The original, in ASM (AG) 2654, is given as Appendix II, doc. 76. For Isacchino,
see also above, pp. 41–2.

A further letter from Chieppio to Gonzaga speaks of the difficulties of blending dance and action gracefully, and another note claims that the '*Ballino* [sic]...causes continuous and extreme anguish'.[71] Guarini admitted in a letter of 21 May 1592 that the dance was one of the most troublesome passages in the work,[72] though the notes to the 1602 edition emphasise that the conception had been successfully tried out in other ballets which he had composed for the Ferrarese court.[73] Indeed, it is conceivable that the Mantuan rehearsals of 1592 were preceded by a Ferrarese performance which could thus have been drawn on for experience, though the evidence is inconclusive. Guarini's letters reveal that the play was prepared for the Este court in 1584, and his notes to the 1602 edition state that Luzzaschi composed a setting of the *Gioco*, though this could have been for the 1595 Ferrarese performance.[74] Frustratingly, neither Luzzaschi's music nor the settings of the dance which are known to have been commissioned from Wert and Rovigo for the 1592 Mantuan performance seem to have survived.[75] Consequently, it would appear that the only firmly documented performance of the play before 1592 was the Turin performance of 1585, though since the work had not then been officially published it is difficult to know if the *Gioco* was included in this version. In any event, given the animosity which had characterised relations between the Savoy and Gonzaga courts since the mid-century conflict over the Casale Monferrato question, artistic co-operation – hardly a general characteristic of the north Italian courts – seems a remote possibility.

The point of this is to underline that there may have been no established performing tradition of the play upon which the Mantuan performers of 1592 could rely. Whatever the precise nature of the difficulties which the scene presented, those difficulties could not necessarily have been resolved by reference to performances elsewhere. At the same time, the evidence would suggest a strong Ferrarese element in the 1592 Mantuan preparations. The play was written at Ferrara, a number of Ferrarese participants were involved in the 1592 attempt, and (if D'Ancona's suggestion is correct) Leone de' Sommi, who directed the Mantuan rehearsals, had also been involved in the earlier attempt to stage the play in Ferrara.[76]

Although we cannot be certain what precedents were instructive in staging the *Gioco*, it is possible at least to reach a clearer idea of the precise difficulties

---

[71] D'Ancona: *Origini*, II, pp. 550–2. The original document is in ASM (AG) 2657.

[72] D'Ancona, *Origini*, II, pp. 553–4. The original document is in ASM (AG) 2656.

[73] Guarini: *Il pastor fido, tragicommedia pastorale*, fos. 91–91v. The passage is given as Appendix II, doc. 77.

[74] The 1584 preparations are referred to in Solerti and Lanza: 'Il teatro ferrarese', pp. 148ff. For Luzzaschi's setting of the *Gioco* see Guarini's own remarks in *Il pastor fido, tragicommedia pastorale*, fos. 91–91v (see Appendix II, doc. 77).

[75] Wert and Rovigo are mentioned in the letters published in D'Ancona: *Origini*, II, pp. 542–3.

[76] D'Ancona: *Origini*, II, p. 540. For further on de' Sommi see p. 37 above and the bibliography cited there.

which the Mantuan performers of 1592 experienced. Guarini had started work on the scene by 7 April 1584, when he wrote:

My tragicomedy...is full of novelty and has several large choruses which must be worked out beforehand and rehearsed often on stage. This is particularly true of a game which has been put into the third act. It has been designed as a dance for a chorus of nymphs and is still in the hands of Leone [de' Sommi]. The music is not written yet, much less the words.[77]

The last sentence is crucial, and confirms the author's account in the 1602 edition of the way in which such scenes were constructed. The choreography was planned first, then the music composed, and finally the text added, thus flying in the face of all accepted notions of *poesia per musica*. Guarini pointed out that the text was framed in lines of unequal length to meet the requirements of the music ('necessità delle note');[78] and since the rhythm of the music in turn was dictated by the dance steps, it is clear that the steps must have been grouped in figures of irregular length.

In Gastoldi's *Il quarto libro de madrigali a cinque voci* (Venice, 1602) are four five-voice pieces headed 'Il Gioco de la cieca rapresentato alla Regina di Spagna nel Pastor fido'.[79] There is a strong presumption, though not a certainty, that this was the music used for the 1598 Mantuan performance. In 1598 Gastoldi was *maestro di cappella* at Santa Barbara; and the texts in this 1602 publication – the four danced choruses which occur between the speeches of Amarilli, Mirtillo and Corisca – correspond exactly to the version given in the 1602 Ciotti edition supervised by Guarini. The style of the music conforms to what contemporary theory would have expected in its use of homophony and irregular rhythmic structure; it is thus all the more striking that the compositional priorities generally accepted in Italian secular music of this period were abandoned on this occasion. In place of *poesia per musica* – the doctrine that music should be subservient to text – there is here a total subjugation of words, first to music but above all to choreography. It is equally clear what the extraordinary performance difficulties were. Since the stresses of both music and text were dictated by the steps of the dance, the performers were required to both sing and dance a metrically irregular piece in which the musical rhythms would not necessarily reflect the natural rhythm of the words.

[77] Letter of Giovanni Battista Guarini, Padua 7 April 1584, to Prince Vincenzo Gonzaga: see D'Ancona: *Origini*, ii, pp. 539–40. The original, in ASM (AG) 1514, is given as Appendix II, doc. 78.
[78] Guarini: *Il pastor fido, tragicommedia pastorale*, fos. 91–91v (see Appendix II, doc. 77).
[79] The original function of Gastoldi's music seems to have been first noted in Cavicchi: 'Teatro monteverdiano', pp. 149–50. For the documentation of Gastoldi's career see Tagmann: 'La cappella dei maestri cantori', pp. 380–2. The importance of music in the 1598 Mantuan production is indicated by the *intermedi* (see Neri: 'Gli "intermezzi" del "Pastor fido"') and by the remarks of Bernardino Bertolotti, who stated in his *Terzo libro de madrigali* that he participated in the 1598 production. (Bertolotti was in the Este service from at least 1578 until the dissolution of the court in 1598: see Newcomb: 'The musica segreta', p. 226.)

The artistic difficulties which hindered the Mantuan rehearsals of the *Gioco* are thus clear, but important questions of precedents and influences remain to be resolved. Recent writing has concentrated upon seeing Mantuan theatrical practices of the 1590s as a pale reflection of Ferrarese court theatre, and upon using the 1598 Mantuan performance of the *Gioco* as evidence for the musical aspects of the Ferrarese *balletto della duchessa*, for which no music survives. Apart from the logical problems which this interpretation poses, it imposes an oversimplified view of musical and theatrical influence between the north Italian courts and overstates the importance and novelty of the Ferrarese *balletto* itself. Nevertheless, any evaluation of the stylistic components of the *Gioco* must begin in Ferrara, where Guarini conceived the work.[80]

The already vibrant literary and theatrical traditions of the Ferrarese court received an additional stimulus when, on 27 February 1579, Alfonso II d'Este married Margherita Gonzaga, daughter of the Mantuan duke. It was shortly after her arrival at Ferrara that the *balletto della duchessa*, with elaborate costumes and quite complex choreography, seems to have become a regular feature of court entertainment: surviving documents suggest that it had become firmly established by 1581. Given that it was (as we have seen) partly through Margherita's influence that the second Ferrarese *concerto delle donne* was formed, it is interesting that the participation of women alone remained a consistent feature of the *balletto*. A letter describing the Carnival season of 1583 speaks of a 'dance...prepared by the duchess and eleven other ladies, some dressed in black as gentlemen and some in white as ladies'. This, together with other entertainments, was prepared for the marriage of the Mantuan soprano Laura Peperara; further documents reveal that the text of the ballet was by Guarini.[81]

The *balletto della duchessa* continued to flourish well into the 1590s, and although none of the music that was specifically composed for it seems to have survived, it seems likely that the composers of the Ferrarese court were responsible for providing it. Contemporary accounts mention both Luzzaschi and Fiorino as composers of *balletti*, and Luzzaschi is known to have written at least two such pieces.[82] One of the most elaborate descriptions of a court

---

[80] The documents concerning the Ferrarese *balletto della duchessa* are assembled in Solerti: *Ferrara e la corte estense*, chapter 10, and an additional letter is presented in Torri: 'Nei parentali', pp. 505ff. The major re-interpretation of the *balletto* is Cavicchi: 'Teatro monteverdiano', which uses the documentation surrounding the 1598 performance of *Il pastor fido* as a way of explicating Ferrarese practice for which no music survives. A similar point of view is adopted in Newcomb: 'The musica segreta', where the *balletto* is also related to other aspects of Ferrarese musical culture. It will become apparent from my discussion here that I believe that the interpretations of Cavicchi and Newcomb fundamentally misjudge the innovatory elements in the *balletto* and disregard important developments elsewhere which also influenced theatrical and musical life at Mantua during the 1580s and 1590s.

[81] Solerti: *Ferrara e la corte estense*, p. cxl.

[82] Luzzaschi is also represented by an instrumental dance in one of the manuscripts which originally came from the Gonzaga chapel of Santa Barbara, MS 196/4, consisting of two partbooks believed to have

entertainment at Ferrara during this period mentions both Fiorino and (again) Guarini in the context of the *balletto*. This dates from 1585, a year in which Anna Caterina Gonzaga visited the Este court during the Carnival season:

That evening there was a gathering in the *gran sala*. Twelve dancers, with astounding plumes ordered by the duke himself, performed the *balletti*. It was said to be a most beautiful thing to see; but the violins, harpsichords and organs could be heard only with difficulty. The words, composed by Signor Guarini, were extremely pleasing, and the music, by Fiorino, served them well. The dancing was so well matched to both that it was celestial. I have tried to get hold of the words to send to you, but have been told that they cannot be distributed...[83]

Quite clearly, there are strong similarities between the Ferrarese *balletto* and Guarini's *Gioco*. Both involved carefully rehearsed performances of specially prepared dances of considerable complexity, requiring close collaboration among musician, poet and choreographer. Both contrast sharply with the more conventional types of dancing based on the repetition of commonly understood steps. It seems beyond doubt that the experience of the *balletto* was one of the Ferrarese elements drawn upon for the Mantuan preparations of 1592: for one thing, Ferrarese practice had shaped Guarini's conception of the *Gioco*, and moreover participants from Ferrara (including Guarini himself) brought their direct experience to bear on the Mantuan project. At the same time, the novel aspects of the Ferrarese *balletto* should not be exaggerated. Elaborately prepared and rehearsed dances were not new or peculiar to Ferrara: contemporary dance manuals are full of them, and there are important precedents elsewhere, as will be seen. Neither is the all-female character of the *balletto* without previous example. Even more important traditions are at work, one of which lies beyond the Alps, at the Valois court.

The idea of a lengthy and elaborately choreographed ballet as an integral part of court spectacle lies at the heart of the French *ballet de cour* tradition. It is true that the poets of the Pléiade had occasionally been required to write for royal tournaments, entries, fêtes and masquerades, but it was only with the formation of Baïf's Academy in 1570 that a more organised and integrated approach to court entertainment was possible.[84] The first entertainments which the Academy seems to have influenced were those for the wedding of Henri of Navarre with Marguérite de Valois in 1572, at which

---

been copied before 1600. The surviving parts contain thirty-seven dances, all anonymous except for that on fo. 2, which is headed 'Bertazina [Bertoncina] del Sig[n]or Luzaschi'. See *Conservatorio di musica*, pp. 147–8. Intriguingly, the 1625 inventory of the Este music library preserved in ASMod 1a lists 'Balletti a otto e dodeci del Luzzaco', but these cannot be identified with any surviving music.

[83] Letter of Ambassador Conosciuti, 26 February 1585. Original in ASMod Particolari, Conosciuti. See Newcomb: 'The musica segreta', Appendix V document 39.

[84] See Yates: *The French academies*, chapter 11.

a fête with the theme of the 'Paradise of Love' was given in the Salle de Bourbon. The action, portraying an extremely obvious political allegory, concluded with a highly complex ballet danced by twelve nymphs, which lasted more than an hour (the music has not survived).[85] A similar emphasis upon balletic spectacle was apparent the next year, 1573, when Paris received ambassadors from Poland who had come to offer the crown of their country to Henri, son of Caterina de' Medici. The Poles were treated to a lengthy series of entertainments culminating in Caterina's own special contribution of a ballet, of which a description survives. Jean Dorat's *Magnificentissimi spectaculi*, in Latin verse but including French verses by Ronsard and Amadis Jamyn, describes the ballet with some illustrations. Sixteen nymphs representing the provinces of France entered on a moving rock, from which they descended to dance a long and intricate dance designed by Beaujoyeulx.[86] Although Dorat does not provide anything but the most general clues about the choreography, Brantôme describes the spectacle as 'le plus beau ballet qui fust jamais faict au monde'; and the Polish guests are also on record as being amazed at the novelty of the conception.[87]

The *ballet de cour* tradition can thus be traced back to at least 1572; but the first entertainments of this kind for which words, music, and details of costumes and décor have survived is the *Balet comique de la Royne*.[88] On 18 September 1581 the Duc de Joyeuse was betrothed to Marguérite de Vaudemont, sister of the reigning queen, and the marriage took place on 24 September. Some seventeen entertainments were given during the celebrations, including tournaments in allegorical settings, a water fête, a horse ballet and a firework display. Again the Academy, of which the Duc de Joyeuse was one of the financial backers, was the agency through which the various events were co-ordinated. The *Balet comique* – which, like the ballet for the Polish ambassadors, was planned by Beaujoyeulx, an Italian musician who had come to France from Savoy in 1555 – was given in the Salle de Bourbon on Sunday 15 October. The title of the work, as Beaujoyeulx explains, indicates that it is a musical drama combined with dance, 'comic' only in the sense that it has a happy rather than a tragic ending. Indeed, the balletic elements in the work are more extensive than in any other previous piece in the tradition. In the first act twelve naiads entered to perform a figure in the form of a triangle, followed by twelve further geometrical figures, all

[85] Principal source *Mémoires de l'estat*, pp. 268–9. Discussed in Prunières: *Le ballet de cour*, pp. 70ff, and Yates: *The French academies*, pp. 254ff.

[86] Dorat: *Magnificentissimi spectaculi*, where a moment in the dance is depicted on p. 67. The rock is shown complete with female musicians in Yates: *The Valois tapestries*, pp. 67–72.

[87] Cited in Mérimée and Lacour (eds.): *Pierre de Bourdeille*, x, p. 74. The reaction of the Poles is given in Ruble: *Histoire universelle*, iv, p. 179.

[88] The principal source is Beaujoyeulx: *Balet comique de la Royne*, and the main discussions are Prunières: *Le ballet de cour*, pp. 82–94, Yates: *The French academies*, pp. 236ff, and McGowan: *L'art du ballet de cour*, pp. 42–7.

different. This dance was interrupted by Circe's magic powers but was taken up again at the end of the drama. With Circe thus defeated, this final *grand ballet* proclaimed triumph in a choreographic sequence of unparalleled virtuosity. As Beaujoyeulx's description puts it:

It was composed of fifteen figures arranged in such a way that at the end of each figure all the ladies turned to face the king. When they had appeared before the king's majesty, they danced the *grand ballet* with forty passages or geometric figures. These were all exact and well planned in their shapes, sometimes square, sometimes round, in several diverse fashions; then in triangles accompanied by a small square, and other small figures. These figures were no sooner formed by the naiads, dressed (as we have said) in white, than the four dryads, dressed in green, arrived to change the shape, so that as one ended the other began. At the middle of the ballet a chain was formed, composed of four interlacings, each different from the others, so that to watch them one would say that it was in battle array, so well was order kept, and so cleverly did everybody keep his place and his cadence. The spectators thought that Archimedes could not have understood geometric proportions any better than the princesses and the ladies observed in this ballet.[89]

The allegorical and political significance of these geometrical formations and of the *Balet comique* as a whole has been discussed elsewhere.[90] The main point of interest for the present discussion is the vivid contrast between the highly sophisticated choreographic and balletic techniques required by the *ballet de cour* and those employed in Italian spectacles of the 1570s. The principal difference seems to be that, whereas Italian dance spectacles continued to rely upon set formulas or specially devised choreography of an extremely simple kind, the *ballet de cour* required, at least from 1572, professional choreographers and dancers – a contrast which also throws an interesting light upon the social conventions of the north Italian courts. Whatever may have been the connections between earlier French traditions and the *ballet de cour*, the currents which contributed to the latter are clear. Essentially it was invented by an Italian (Beaujoyeulx) and a Medici (Caterina), and although numerous artists, dancers, musicians and poets contributed to the final result, it was Caterina who, with a highly developed notion of the ballet as a political instrument, was responsible for devising these entertainments. Brantôme confirms that the Queen Mother was responsible for the overall direction of the ballet, which was always the most admired event in a series of entertainments.[91]

The parallels between the French *ballet de cour* and the Ferrarese *balletto della duchessa* are extremely strong and can hardly be coincidental. Both have unusually and essentially long and intricate dances performed to specially composed music and choreography by professionals. There are obvious parallels, too, in the all-female cast of the *Balet comique* and that of the *balletto*,

[89] Original text in Beaujoyeulx: *Balet comique de la Royne*, pp. 55–6.
[90] Yates: *The French academies*, pp. 248ff.
[91] Mérimée and Lacour (eds.): *Pierre de Bourdeille*, x, p. 76.

and in the roles of Caterina de' Medici and Margherita Gonzaga – both responsible for training the ladies of their court to perform elaborate ballets in settings of their own devising.

Given the strong cultural connections between the French and Ferrarese courts at this period, these parallels are hardly surprising. It may be significant that Ferrarese interest in elaborate danced spectacles in the French manner can be dated from the year after the Polish entertainments in Paris. In July 1574, Henri III arrived in Ferrara in the course of his return journey from Kraków, where he had been crowned King of Poland. On the thirtieth of the month there was an elaborate *ballo* involving eight ladies and *intramezzi di musica*.[92] The surviving documentation suggests that here, some six years before Margherita Gonzaga's arrival at the Este court, the choreographic practices and female personnel of the *balletto della duchessa* are presaged. Again, it may be noteworthy that the 1574 Ferrarese *ballo* was arranged in connection with the same set of political manoeuvres which the Polish festivities in Paris had subserved.

It is clear that the rather more progressive atmosphere of the Este court was one which appealed considerably to Vincenzo Gonzaga during the 1580s. Consequently, the important Mantuan production of *Il pastor fido* in 1598 is not only symbolic of the new interest in advanced theatrical techniques that is characteristic of the Mantuan court of the 1590s and prophetic of the lavish spectacles of the first decade of the seventeenth century: it also represents the fruits of Ferrarese experimentation as conveyed by the participation of Guarini himself, and others from Ferrara, in Mantuan attempts to produce the work. It is also true that there was some scepticism over whether the complexities of co-ordinating choreography, texts and music could be conquered, and as late as the 1602 Ciotti edition Guarini was still obliged to emphasise that his conception had actually been put into practice. No doubt there were still doubts about whether *Il pastor fido* should be staged at all; it will be remembered that Salviati (though not primarily concerned with the *Gioco*) had voiced concern about the suitability of the work for the stage in his critique of 1586.

Yet, notwithstanding the importance of Ferrarese example and experience, the most direct influence upon the rejuvenation of Mantuan theatrical life during the 1590s was a Florentine one. If connections between the Valois and the Este were strong, those between the Valois and the Medici were even stronger, and it was into the Medici house that Vincenzo Gonzaga had married in 1584. In general terms, the brilliance of Mantuan musical and theatrical life during Vincenzo's period owed a good deal to Florentine developments and even to Florentine personnel, the most notable of whom was Francesco Rasi. More to the point, the French *ballet de cour* tradition was

---

[92] De Nolhac and Solerti: *Il viaggio in Italia di Enrico III*, pp. 176–7 and 258–60.

in part a Florentine creation, nurtured with the humanistic ideals of Baïf's Academy but principally evolved (by Beaujoyeulx) under the direct control of a Medici. Moreover, it was in Florence, the home of the most spectacular Italian court entertainments of the sixteenth century, that the *ballet de cour* itself asserted its influence upon the Italian tradition of dance spectacle in a most startling way.

The remarkable series of Medici *feste* inaugurated by those arranged to celebrate Cosimo I's marriage to Eleonora of Toledo, and thereafter punctuating Medici history at strategic points, are separated in time, but connected in political and dynastic purpose and often in their use of imagery and symbolism. A high point in the sequence was the 1589 arrangements celebrating the marriage of the granddaughter of Caterina de' Medici to Ferdinando, Grand Duke of Tuscany. The centrepiece of the occasion was the performance of Bargagli's *La Pellegrina*, with six *intermedi*, by the Intronati of Siena in the theatre in the Uffizi. As we have seen, these six *intermedi*, the fruits of a collaboration between Buontalenti, Cavalieri, and Bardi, involved a number of Mantuan performers and acted almost as a showcase for Vincenzo's musical establishment.[93]

The subject of the *intermedi* is music, or rather classical myths and neo-Platonic concepts of music, illustrated in allegories and through symbolic figures. Three of the *intermedi* deal with the supreme harmony of the cosmos; the remaining three represent the power of human harmony. Because of the complicated and detailed series of classical allusions and references upon which Bardi had constructed a vast edifice of musical and theatrical effects, it would seem that the thread of the argument could only be understood by classical philologists. Musically, the *intermedi* for *La Pellegrina* display a curious mixture of styles representing traditional theatre music as well as experimental elements – though which aspects are traditional and which not has been the subject of some curious judgements. Surely the most startling moment occurs not in the monodic or 'pseudo-monodic' songs but, with a degree of calculation that must have seemed fashionably amusing, at the very end of the work. After the comedy proper had finished, the heavens opened to show twenty pagan gods. Seven clouds appeared, five of which came down to earth while two remained above. The central cloud held Apollo, Bacchus, Harmony and Rhythm, while on another, close to it but lower, stood the three Graces. The Muses were scattered over the remaining clouds. As these five slowly descended, three madrigals were sung, the first by Apollo and his group, the second by the three Graces and three of the Muses, and the third by the six remaining Muses. Twenty pairs of mortals in pastoral dress now appeared, apparently enticed by the sound. When the clouds finally touched the earth, the gods descended and, taking the mortals by the hand, taught them to dance.[94]

[93] See pp. 128–32 above, and the bibliography cited there.   [94] [Rossi]: *Descrizione*, pp. 6off.

This scene was borrowed, like the other *intermedi*, from Plato. Specifically, it is modelled on a passage in the second book of Plato's *Laws* which treats the gods' gift of music and dance to the mortals:

But the gods, in their compassion for the hardships incident to our human lot, have appointed the cycle of their festivals to provide relief from this fatigue, besides giving us the Muses, their leader Apollo, and Dionysus to share these festivals with us and keep them right... Now animals at large have no perception of the order or disorder in these motions, no sense of what we call rhythm or melody. But in our own case, the gods of whom we spoke as given us for companions in our revels have likewise given us the power to perceive and enjoy rhythm and melody. Through this sense they stir us to movements and become our choir-leaders. They string us together on a thread of song and dance, and have named our 'choirs' so after the delight [*chara*] they naturally afford.[95]

This subject matter clearly suited the idea of a finale in a number of ways. It introduced a danced *intermedio* which, since Poliziano's *Orfeo*, had become a traditional final item. Moreover, the Platonic source emphasises rhythm, the variety of which is a conspicuous part of Cavalieri's music. Indeed, the result presents a number of novel and even revolutionary aspects. The sheer size of the conception is unparalleled in contemporary Italian spectacles. In addition, by devising an ingenious variety of rhythmic variations on one set of harmonic and melodic materials, Cavalieri had essentially opened the way for more complex and longer balletic scenes. By operating all the various permutations and variations the material could become self-perpetuating, and it was the variation structure of the piece which seems to have ensured its success as a model or fund of melodic and harmonic material for an impressive series of instrumental and vocal pieces throughout the seventeenth century.[96] Giovanni Battista Doni, writing towards the middle of the seventeenth century about this type of composition, emphasised that to be successful such pieces needed to be worked out by someone talented in the arts of both choreography and musical composition:

The *ballo* should be organised by a knowledgeable person, skilled in the one profession and in the other, as was that Signor Emilio del Cavaliere, inventor of that fine *ballo* and of the same air [*aria*] called the *Granduca*; he was not only an extremely expert musician but also a most graceful dancer.[97]

It is difficult to overestimate the novelty of this compositional process and its significance for balletic scenes of the early seventeenth century. It was remarkable that, at a time when theorists and composers were in general still attached to the idea of *poesia per musica*, the words should become the final addition to a structure which had already been fashioned by the needs of

[95] A. E. Taylor (trans.): *The laws of Plato* (London, 1934), p. 30.
[96] The influence of the piece is traced in Kirkendale: *L'Aria di Fiorenza*. To the list of sources given there should be added those in R. Hudson's review of the book, along with Florence, Biblioteca Nazionale Centrale MSS Magl. VIII.1222bis, fo. 5v, and Magl. VII.894, fo. 30. The last two are not catalogued in Becherini: *Catalogo dei manoscritti musicali*.   [97] G. B. Doni: *Lyra Barberina*, II, p. 95.

choreography and spectacle. It has become clear that this was the procedure followed for Guarini's *Gioco della cieca* in Mantua in 1592 and again (more successfully) in 1598; similarly, Cavalieri's *Ballo* is headed with the legend 'La Musica de questo ballo, & il ballo stesso fù del Sig. Laura Lucchesini de' Guidiccioni gentildonna principalissima della città di Lucca ornata di rarissime qualità e virtù.'[98] This in itself is surprising, since Rinuccini's text in Rossi's *Descrizione* is metrically quite regular, while Laura's text as given in the printed music is as irregular as Guarini's in the *Gioco*.[99] There would seem to have been some conflict between various members of the Accademia della Crusca responsible for the *intermedi* for *La Pellegrina* – between Bardi and Rossi on the one hand (both old-established members) and the newcomer Cavalieri on the other – and quite apart from questions of personality and temperament, it may have been the experimentalism of Cavalieri's ideas which caused his colleagues to shy away.[100] D. P. Walker's explanation of the discrepancy seems the most logical: Rossi's *Descrizione* represents the original intentions, the published music the final version.[101] Nevertheless, that final version still presented, in the absence of any valid reason for the sometimes severe conflicts between textual stress and musical accentuation, a more problematic aspect, intensified since the *ballo* was apparently the product of Florentine musical humanism at a point of high development. It emerges from a comparison with Gastoldi's music for the *Gioco* that in all probability Cavalieri's first task was to devise the elaborate choreography which, significantly, is set out in so much detail in Malvezzi's edition of the music,[102] and no doubt the fact that Cavalieri's conception clearly contravened humanistic principles was an additional reason why Bardi and Rossi should seek to exclude him from the arrangements.

If the significance of the Cavalieri–Gastoldi model for the seventeenth century can be readily appreciated, its origins remain obscure. As has already been suggested, the influence of the *ballet de cour* upon Italian ballets of the 1580s was probably considerable, and it is precisely the contrasting sections in different metres, reflecting contrasts in the choreography, which distinguish the *Balet comique de la Royne* from its Florentine forebears. There is a crucial difference between the *ballet de cour* and the balletic compositions of Cavalieri and Gastoldi, or Luzzaschi's lost setting of the *Gioco*: the Italian examples were texted, and it was the problems of co-ordinating song and dance that perplexed the Mantuan would-be performers of 1592. Whether these

---

[98] [Malvezzi]: *Nono parte*, p. 19.

[99] Similarly, of the two stanzas beginning 'Alle dure fatiche' leading up to the *ballo* in Rossi's account, the first is omitted. The second was composed as the 'pseudo-monody' 'Godi turba mortal' by Cavalieri but was not printed as such in Malvezzi's edition of the music: see Walker (ed.): *Les fêtes du mariage*, pp. lii–liii and 120–1.

[100] Pirrotta: 'Temperaments and tendencies', p. 169. See also the evidence in Rolandi: 'Emilio de' Cavalieri', pp. 26ff, and, on the experimentalism of the *Ballo*, Solerti: 'Laura Guidiccioni', pp. 797ff.

[101] Walker (ed.): *Les fêtes du mariage*, p. xxix.

[102] [Malvezzi]: *Nono parte*, sig. KK ff.

difficulties were first solved in Ferrara must remain an open question. Given the strong links between the French and Medici courts, and the brilliance of the arts of spectacle at the latter, it seems likely that it was at Florence rather than Ferrara that the complexities of choral balletic scenes were resolved. Moreover, since the evidence for a Ferrarese performance of *Il pastor fido* is slim, and since Luzzaschi's setting of the *Gioco* might well have been for either of the suggested dates (1586 or 1595), Ferrarese priority is hardly proven. Again, if the 1595 Ferrarese performance did take place, and if it was to this that Guarini referred in the 1602 edition, Luzzaschi may have been indebted to Cavalieri not only for the *Ballo del Granduca* but also for his setting of the *pastorella Il gioco della cieca* which is known to have been adapted by Laura Guidiccioni from *Il pastor fido*, performed before Cardinal Montalto on 29 October 1595 in the Hall of Statues in the Palazzo Pitti, and repeated there on 5 January 1599. Although the music is not extant, contemporary observations suggest that this was a large-scale balletic spectacle on the scale of the 1589 *ballo*, and it is possible that Cavalieri's approach to Guarini's scene also influenced the Mantuan performers of three years later. What is inevitable is that while the 1598 Mantuan performance was indebted to Ferrarese experience, and to personnel who may have been unemployed after the transfer of Ferrara to Papal control earlier in the year, Gastoldi's setting of the *Gioco* undoubtedly reflects Cavalieri's achievements. This in itself is symbolic of the shifting relative importance of Ferrara and Florence for Mantuan music and theatre during the 1590s; and in this, as in a number of other respects, the prophecies of 1598 were fulfilled in the events of 1607 and 1608.

Throughout the sixteenth century the question of precedence had remained a constant feature of North Italian politics,[103] and after Cosimo I's re-establishment of the Medici as rulers of Tuscany (leaving aside the unhappy tenure of Alessandro de' Medici), the rivalry between the Mantuan, Ferrarese, and Florentine courts was particularly strong. That sense of competition, invading every phase of political relationships, was further intensified after the Medici were raised to the status of grand dukes by Pius V in 1569, and reached a peak in the decades before Ferrara passed to Papal control in 1598. In one sense, the rivalry over new cultural fashions which is such a feature of the dealings amongst these three courts, so closely related to each other through common historical backgrounds and intermarriage, is merely a reflection of a broader issue. Neither can it be accidental that artistic developments such as the *concerti delle donne* or the cultivation of new forms of balletic spectacle agree so well with another set of contemporary ideas, derived from theories of princely decorum. Magnificence, liberality

[103] See Gribaudi: 'Questioni di precedenza'.

and erudition were all considered regal virtues, and that belief is well expressed through lavish spectacles and the support of a *musica secreta* (in social terms a variation on the theme of *musica reservata*). There is no better example of this structural component at work in contemporary music and theatre than the 1589 Florentine *intermedi* for *La Pellegrina*, spectacles of great elaboration based on classical myths, spectacles which capitalise upon the theme of the power of music (well established within the rhetoric of political propaganda as the appropriate symbol of a government consonant, harmonious, well tempered, balanced in the relationship of its parts), to celebrate a dynastic marriage. And whatever the genuine artistic tastes of individual rulers, these same values are no less expressed through the formation of the Mantuan *concerto delle donne*, and through Vincenzo Gonzaga's patronage of Guarini's pastoral and the complexities of the *Gioco della cieca*. Important too in these contexts is contemporary admiration for 'wonder' as an experience, something obviously catered for in the elaborate costumes, lighting, choreography and scenic effects of the new arts of spectacle. 'Wonder' was also a necessary ingredient of music which had to stupefy the listeners, a requirement which, if contemporary reports can be relied on at all, was repeatedly satisfied by the concerted virtuosity of the *concerto delle donne*. Competition was intense between the courts to secure the most agile voices and the most able choreographers, and to construct the most elaborate theatrical machines, and in this sense the new styles of music and spectacle were merely part of a more serious game. Musicians, so frequently the subjects of history, must be carefully distinguished from its masters.

Appendix I. Archival sources

Two large groups of unpublished material that have been consulted are preserved in the Biblioteca Bertoliana in Vicenza and the Archivio Diocesano in Mantua, and in the absence of published inventories of these collections some idea of the scope and possibilities of these documents is given here. For the Archivio di Stato in Mantua, see Luzio and Torelli: *L'Archivio Gonzaga*.

(i) VICENZA, BIBLIOTECA COMUNALE BERTOLIANA – BBV

Libri dell'Accademia Olimpica

The documents of the Accademia Olimpica have been used only in passing in the present study; but in view of the confusing nature of the documents and the misleading way in which they have been used in the past, it might be worth while to offer a clarification. Two separate sets of contemporary minutes of the meetings of the Accademia's council have survived, though neither seems to have been used before at least by musicologists or theatre historians. These record only certain kinds of information, say little about social or educational activities at the Accademia, and are often imprecise. They carry the shelf-marks MSS Accademia Olimpica o.9.2.4.D and o.9.2.4.E.

In addition, any study of the Accademia's business must make use of the Ziggiotti manuscripts in the Biblioteca Bertoliana. Ziggiotti, a local antiquary of the eighteenth century, had at his disposal many documents which are no longer available. The most important item, Ziggiotti MS 2916, is substantially based upon the two minute books mentioned above. Nevertheless, although Ziggiotti's manuscripts are valuable records of apparently irrecoverable sources, they are not simple transcriptions but often a collation or précis of various documents. They are often impressionistic and should be used with caution.

Most historians, including Schrade and Mantese, have used Ziggiotti MS 2916 almost exclusively. But MS 2916 cannot be interpreted without two further sources, MSS Accademia Olimpica o.9.2.11 (M) and o.9.2.13 (O), both drafts for Ziggiotti MS 2916 but often substantially different. Two further documents are also of fundamental importance: Venice, Biblioteca Correr Cod. Cic. 3251/IV and Milan, Biblioteca Ambrosiana Cod. R.123 supp. The latter is particularly important for the inaugural production of the theatre of the Accademia, Giustiniani's vernacular version of Sophocles' *Oedipus Rex*.

163

(ii) MANTUA, ARCHIVIO STORICO DIOCESANO

The Archivio Storico Diocesano di Mantova contains a wide range of material relating to the economic, political, artistic, religious, and social life of the Diocese of Mantua, beginning in A.D. 945 and extending up to the present day. The documents are arranged in five principal *fondi*, in addition to which the archive houses rare items from suppressed monastic institutions in the diocese, including illuminated chant manuscripts from San Benedetto Po and incunabula from Sermide, as well as the parochial archives of Casalmoro, Roverbella, Ostiano, Cereta, and Pozzolo. The following summary list includes all the sixteenth-century material in the five major collections, whether it has been cited or used in the present study or not.

Archivio della Mensa Vescovile – ASDM (MV)

Parchments, notarial papers relating to feudal rights (*registri*), papers concerning the economic affairs of the bishopric (*registri*), receipts (*filze di fatture*), papers relating to the legal dealings (*cause feudali*) of the bishopric (*registri* and *filze*), and *licenze* (*registri* and *filze*).

Archivio della Curia Vescovile – ASDM (CV)

Parchments, papers and reports relating to pastoral visits, pastoral letters, bishops' correspondence, material concerning Diocesan Synods, ordinations, the clergy, monasteries, trials, benefices, marriages, worship, administrative documents (*licenze amministrative*), and inventories. A further section contains miscellaneous papers.

Archivio del Capitolo della Cattedrale – ASDM (Cap.)

Parchments, account books (*registri*; income and expenditure of the chapter), receipts (*filze di fatture*), legal documents (*filze*), administrative papers, documents relating to confraternities (*filze* and *registri*), papers concerning canonries and chaplaincies in the cathedral chapter, capitular papers (*atti capitolare*), and a series of chant manuscripts and liturgical books. There is also a series of miscellaneous papers, a manuscript of polyphonic music dated 1616, and the capitular library.

Archivio della Basilica di Sant'Andrea – ASDM (SA)

Parchments, notarial papers (*registri*), and collections of records of attestation, trials, and the affairs of the *primicerii*. There is also a small collection of chant manuscripts and liturgical books, and some sacristy accounts. Much of the archive was pillaged and set on fire by the occupying Austrian forces in 1848, when the basilica was used as a garrison.

Archivio della Basilica di Santa Barbara – ASDM (SB)

Parchments, notarial records (*registri*), receipts (*filze di fatture*), notarial papers relating to San Benedetto Po (*registri*), trials (*filze* and *libri*), ordinations and the clergy, and the proceedings of the chapter (*atti capitolare*). The principal part of the music collection is now in Milan, but there remain a collection of chant manuscripts and a library which includes liturgical books.

The material is subdivided as follows:

(1) Miscellanea secoli XVI–XVIII (*olim* Mandati di pagamento – Ricevute. Spese Capitolari di Sagristano 1740 e 1756). Contains a single document of September 1595, and payment receipts for the period 17 March 1573 – 14 December 1610.

(2) Filcia LXXVII. Mandati di spesa del 1579 et 1580. Covers the period 22 September 1579 – 10 July 1585.

(3) Filza 1600–1601. Contains *provisione* for December 1572 – October 1574, and *distributioni* for July 1594 – January 1630.

(4) Filza delli anni 1690–1700. *Sponte* and *provisione* for the period January 1579 – May 1588.

(5) Filza degli anni 1690 e 1760. Canonico Steffani Camerl. Various documents.

(6) Filza XXIX Prestanze. Payment receipts 19 August 1595 – June 1612.

(7) Cerimoniale.

(8) Atti abbaziali.

(9) Vestizioni e ordinazioni di chierici Fellini canonici et notarii ab anno 1631 ad 1634 nec non abbadini caerimoniarii et notarii usque ad annum 1650.

(10) Carte da consultarsi. Inventari di sagrestia.

(11) Atti Capitolari 1575–1793.

(12) Decreti di nomine presentazioni e rinuncia.

(13) Filza 1656. Signor Canonico Massaro Mollini.

(14) Diario dal 1572 al 1602 et altri.

(15) Constitutiones.

(16) Cronaca di un ecclesiastico di Santa Barbara 1569–1601.

(17) Ricevute di amministrazione 1596–1637.

(18) Spese per la fabbrica della chiesa di Santa Barbara 1569–1572.

(19) Filza XXI per la fabbrica della Canonica e nota delle spese occorse 1584–1592.

Appendix II. Documentation

Several principles have guided the selection of documents for inclusion in this appendix. In some cases they have been chosen because they seem to be particularly good examples of a class of material which has been drawn upon extensively, in others because they are untypically informative. In general, documents which are already published in reliable transcriptions have been avoided, but in a small number of cases where the transcriptions are almost as difficult to consult as the originals I have presented my own versions: this is the case with the letters of Lodovico Agostini. And in some cases it seemed best to provide fresh transcriptions of documents published elsewhere with readings substantially different from my own.

Except in titles, forms of address, and some standard formulaic expressions, abbreviations have been realised, and capitalisation, punctuation and accents regularised. Original spellings have been retained.

The unit of currency most frequently cited is the *scudo*, or more properly *scudo di moneta*, which was subdivided into 100 *baiocchi*. Occasionally the documents mention the gold *scudo*, the *scudo d'oro in oro*, which was worth 105 *baiocchi*, and some payments are quoted in *lire* which broke down into 20 *soldi* or 240 *denari*. The exchange rate between the *scudo* and the *lira* varied, but for much of the second half of the sixteenth century the value of the *scudo* moved between 75 and 80 *soldi*.

The Mantuan year began, throughout most of this period, on Christmas Day; original dates have been retained throughout.

CONTENTS OF APPENDIX II

63 ASM (AG) 403. Rollo della famiglia di S.A. per la paga del mese d'Agosto 1595, fo. iv

64 ASM (AG) 395. Rollo de' salariati del Prencipe. . . intitolata affari camerale, fos. 8v–9

65 ASM (AG) 395. [Rollo de' salariati], fos. 156v, 159v

66–67 BBV. Atti ordinarii et straordinarii dell'accademia
    66. libro D
    67. libro E

68 ASF (AM) 768, fo. 640. Letter of Alessandro Striggio, Mantua 17 August 1584, to Grand Duke Francesco de' Medici

69 ASM (AG) 2952 lib. 381, fos. 9–9v. *copialettera* of Teodoro San Giorgio, Bologna 2 March 1581, to Federico Pendaso

70 ASM (AG) 1161. Letter of Cardinal Gabriele Paleotti, Bologna 10 March 1581, to the Duke of Parma

71 ASM (AG) 1161. Letter of Cardinal Cesi, Bologna 11 March 1581, to Duke Guglielmo Gonzaga

72 ASM (AG) 1161. Letter of Federico Pendaso, Bologna 27 March 1581, to Aurelio Pomponazzi

73 ASM (AG) 2213. Minute della cancelleria. Minute from Teodoro San Giorgio, Montiggiana 11 July 1582, to Pirro Malvezzi

74 ASM (AG) 2955 lib. 391. *copialettera* of Prince Vincenzo Gonzaga, Poggio 6 November 1584, to Giaches de Wert

75 ASM (AG) Raccolta d'autografi 10. Letter of Giaches de Wert, Mantua 15 November 1584, to Prince Vincenzo Gonzaga

76 ASM (AG) 2654. Letter of Annibale Chieppio, Mantua 23 December 1591, to Duke Vincenzo Gonzaga

77 Giovanni Battista Guarini: *Il pastor fido, tragicommedia pastorale*, fos. 91–91v

78 ASM (AG) 1514. Letter of Giovanni Battista Guarini, Padua 7 April 1584, to Prince Vincenzo Gonzaga

1 ASM (AG) 2993 lib. 13, fo. 38v. *Copialettera* of Marchesa Isabella d'Este, Ferrara 7 February 1502, to Marchese Francesco Gonzaga

La giornata di sabato passò in questa freddura: la sposa non si vide quello dì, per haverlo speso tutto in laves ri la testa et scrivere: la sera privatamente secundo m'è dicto apontò li privilegij de la liberatione dil prebendo al Signor Duca mio padre. La Duchessa di Urbino et mi accompagnate da li signori miei fratelli, et quasi tutta la corte andassimo a solazo per la terra et retornate a casa vene lo ambasciatore francese quale se havea invitato a cena cum noi. A tavola eravamo lo dicto Ambasciatore, la Duchessa de Urbino, Don Ferrante e Don Julio. Lo Signor Hercolano da Cosenza, cum Madama Laura, mi et le mie donzelle maritate: inframezate da alcuni francesi et spagnoli: quali seranno nominati per la signora. Doppo cena facessimo il ballo dil capello: finito che fu, per tante preghiere et croci mi furono facte, fui necessitata far li mei atti nel cantar in lo lauto et cossì finissimo la giornata alle cinque hore di nocte. Domenica mattina che fu heri se cantò una messa solenne per il Vescovo di Carinda in Vescovato: dove intervenero solamente don Alphonso, lo Ambasciatore francese et parte de la corte: ma populo assai. Finita la messa uno cubiculario dil Papa nominato messer Leandro apresentò una bolla serrata a Don Alphonso: la quale fu aperta et lecta publicamente. La sententia è questa: che essendo consueto da li summi pontifici benedire ogni anno la nocte di Natale una spata et capello et donarla a qualche principe christiano benemerito di la ghiesia, havea electo questo anno la nobiltà sua si per dignità di la casa como per la prestantia di la persona sua: la spata si dava per diffensione di la fede Christiana, il capello per diffensione di la persona sua. La spata è de la sorte che è quella che si porta inanti a la V. Ex., el capello è de veluto berettino cum uno razo in cima di perle minute: uno friso intorno de oro tirato incrosato et pendente gioso in forma di stola fodrato de Armeline cum le codette pendente. Lecta la bolla andò ad ingenochiarsi allo altare et lo episcopo sedente disse alcune oratione: poi gli puose il capello in testa e la spata in mano: stato cussì uno pochette ge le levo di mano et testa, et lui levatossi in pede chiamò messer Julio Faxono et li dette la spata in mano in cima di la quale era il capello, et a sono di trombe uscite di chiesa. Doppo desnare andassimo la Duchessa di Urbino, li fratelli et mi a levare la sposa di camera dove, mentre se fermassimo, retornavi in la sala grande dove erano adunate le zentildonne: si ballò per spatio de due hore e la sposa danzò cum una sua donzella alcune basse francese molto galantemente. Alle XXIII et meza andassimo al fastidioso spectaculo de la comedia dil soldato la quale se bene è arguta, ingegnosa et piacevole molto, non di meno per la longheza de li versi, et strepito de le persone non delectò ale orechie como havia facto a casa nostra. Li intramezi furono tre moresche: In la prima uscì Amore il quale passegiò per la scena saetando, et recitò alcuni versi. Poi uscirono duodeci homini coperti di stagnolo tagliato et carichi de candelotti aciesi cum spechietti. In testa uno ballono forato, et cossì in mane pur charichi di candelotti che non fu brutto spectaculo. La secunda fu de Bechi: quali scornegiando andavano saltando e dreto gli era il capraro. La tertia fu de fanti in zuppone de brocato d'oro et de argento, cum calce tutti ad una livrea bianche et rosse et berette de veluto negro in testa cum penne bianche, capigliata postizza cum dardi in mano et pugnaletti al fianco: quali cum li dardi prima, poi cum li pugnaletti andavano scherzando, et batendo il tempo. Lo ultimo atto finì senza moresca alle cinque hore di nocte. Questi combattenti per non essere accordio dil cavallo non combatteranno hogi: perhochè il bolognese voria potere ferire il cavallo, et Vesino non voria: il Signor mio Patre va tramando la pace: non scio mo' quello seguirà: nè anche combatteranno Paulo et Bartolomeo: per non essere fino qui comparso homo di loro. Il Cardinale di libretto de Franza giunse heri per andare a Roma: non intendo la causa: nè altro mi resta se non che augurandomi appresso V. Exc. la baso insieme col puttino.

Ferrariae, VII Februarij 1502

Post Scriptum – Questa mattina se è concluso che Vesino e il nemico suo abiano ad combatere et possano amazare cavalli. Cussì ale XX hore se conduranno in campo.

2   ASM (AG) 2993 lib. 13, fo. 40v. *Copialettera* of Marchesa Isabella d'Este,
Ferrara 8 February 1502, to Marchese Francesco Gonzaga

Heri sera finito il duello andassimo alla representazione de la comedia Asinaria: la
quale veramente fu bella et delectevole: sì per non essere stata troppo longa, como
per essere state meglio recitata de le altre et cum mancho strepito. Li intramezi furono
tre: al secundo atto uscirono deci homini salvatici: quali corseno et saltorono uno
pezo spaventosamente per la scena, poi sentito sonare il corno, dubitando de cani
et caciatori se imboscorono: et stando in aguaito videro uscire conioli a li quali
seguirno cum bastoni amazandoli et pigliandoli: sentito un altra volta il corno si
ascosero et visti uscire doppe caprioli et camozi: uscitero anche loro caciandoli cum
li bastoni et pigliandoli. Al tertio sono dil corno retornorono in la selva per la uscita
de una panthera et uno leone: li seguitorono et assaltandoli cum li bastoni: et
defendendossi molto gagliardamente li animali: finalmente restarono presi che fu
bello spectaculo.

Ligati li animali plaudendo et saltando se redussero da uno capo de la scena tutti
in uno trapello et fatto uno cerchio quatro di loro congiunsero li brazi loro insieme
sopra li quali montrono altri quatro cum li brazi medesimamente coniuncti et cussì
a sono de fistule andavano ballando: li altri che non erano coniuncti saltandoli
appresso li segregorono: questi salvatici haveano sonaglij quali ballando alcuna volta
sonavano et alcuna volta non se senteano secundo la mutatione dil sono et tempo.
Al tertio atto uscì la musica dil Tromboncino, Paulo, Pozino et compagni: cum la
quale si fece magior honore ai Mantuani che a' Ferraresi. Al quarto atto a sono di
tamburino uscirono dodici contadini quali representarono tutta la agricultura: prima
uscirono cum le zappe zapando la terra: deposte le zappe uscirono cum cesti pieni
di oro pagliolo tagliato minute et andorono seminando: retornorono cum le messore
a mettere la biava: cum le verghe la batterono e cum le pale andorono a palando.
Dreto li quali uscirono femine contadine cum botazi pane et lavezi per darli da
solvere cum le pive inanti: li contadini deposte le pale uscirono ballando in camisa
et preseno le femine: cum le quale uscendo di scena finirono la morescha et nanti
la quatro hore di nocte fu compita la comedia. Heri sera per fretta di exspedire il
cavallo cum la victoria di Vesino se omise scrivere como lo inimico suo, nel primo
corso de la lanza, si lassò cadere inadvertentemente il stocho nudo che l'havea ne
la mano de la briglia e come che Vesino tra li altri serventi fu prestato gran favore
per il Signor Don Ferrante, Signor Hercolano da Cosenza, conte Lodovico de la
Mirandola e conte Albertino Boschetto per respecto de la Ex. V. e lo conte
Lodovico, lo menò tutta quella sera a brazo; et detegli cena. Grande honore ha
aquistato Vesino: ma magior la Exc. V. attribuendosi la valorosità sua de essere
allevo di quella. El Signor mio Padre non ha anchora declarato il caso suo, ma per
questo si può comprendere non intende già dargli presone ma fargli una patente per
la quale se manifesta che Vesino ha havuto la victoria: havendo conducto lo inimico
a termine che non essendo spartito facilmente lo faceva presone et che non possi mai
più combattere cum lui; Vesino iusta de haverlo presone, o che gli paghi tutte le spese.
Io non li mancho de ogni favore et lo Signor Hercolano de Cosenza qual se intromette
in questo fa lo officio di vero partesano de la Exc. V. ma segni ciò che voglia, tutto
il mondo ha dato la sententia in favore di Vesino. De la risolutione V.S. serà advisata:

el cavallo del bolognese è morto et lo pagharà per centocinquanta ducati: quello di Vesino non fu tocho nè ha male alcuno: in bona gratia de V. Exc. ne recomando, non si scordando de dare infiniti basi al mio puttino per mio amore.
Ferrarie VIII Februarii 1502

3   ASM (AG) 2993 lib. 13, fo. 42. *Copialettera* of Marchesa Isabella d'Este, Ferrara 9 February 1502, to Marchese Francesco Gonzaga

Heri doppo desnare li Ambasciatori andorono alla camera de la sposa et gli fecero li presenti: ma prima lo Ill.mo S. mio patre l'havea apresentata: molto più honorevolmente havendoli consignato quasi tutto il resto de le zoglie sue che sonno molto belle et di gran pretio: li Venetiani gli apresentorno li manti di veluto cremesino foderati di panze: il fiorentino una peza di panno d'oro grizo alto et basso de trentacinque braza molto bello. Li senesi dui vasi di arzento: li luchesi una bacilla et lo bronzo: se reducissimo poi in sala: dove se ballò fino alle xxiiij hore. Andassimo alla comedia de la Cassina: la quale se principiò circa una hora di notte: et prima uscì la musica dil Tromboncino cantando una barzelletta in laude de li sposi. La comedia fu lasciva et dishonesta quanto si possa dire. Li intramezi furono questi: al primo atto uscì una femina alla francese a sono di tamburino; dreto la quale uscirno dece giovini vestiti de zendale alla divisa di Don Alphonso: cioè biancha et rossa cum sesti in mane ne li quali era descripto: Amore non vole; ballando questoro la donna gli andava togliendo di mano li sesti et gettandoli via: li giovini sdegnati partirono de scena: retornorono poi cum dardi in mane cum li quali ferendo la femina la lassarono quasi tramortita: ma Amore sopragionse, et saettando li giovini li fece cadere in terra et liberà la donna.

Levati et partiti questoro, uscì un altra musica: ne la quale erano tre barberi mantovani che cantorono una frottola di speranza. Al secundo atto uscirono sei homini salvatici li quali andorono in capo della scena a tirare in mezo una balla grande ne la quale erano le quatro virtù serrate dentro. Al sono de uno corno se aperse la balla et queste virtù cantorono certe canzone ~~alla spagnola perchè erano due donne et dui homini che stanno cum dona Lucretia quali cantono molto bene.~~ Al tertio atto venne la musica de le viole a sei; fra quali era el sig.re Don Alphonso et nota la Ex. V. che quasi in tutte le moresche S.S. intervenne insieme cum Don Julio.

Al quarto atto uscirono dodici armati alla thodischa cum peoti, allabarda, cortella, et uno penachio in testa quali cum ciascuna de esse arme fecero la morescha. All'ultimo atto uscirono dodici cum una torza longa in mano accesa da ogni capo: cum le quale morescando fecero bello spectaculo et cossì alle sei hore di notte fu finita et ognuno secundo usanza andò a cena a casa sua.

Fra hogi et dimane partiranno tutti li ambasciatore, excepto li donne romane et tutti quelli che da Roma venero cum la sposa: havendoli scripto il Papa che se firmano quì finchè haveranno altro: perchè forsi le fa a expectare quà la moglie dil duca Valentino che quanto piacia questa festa al S. mio padre la Exc. V. lo può considerare; alla bona gratia de la quale sempra me ricomando.

4 ASM (AG) 1454. Letter of Ambassador Giovanni Battista Malatesta, Venice 14 June 1520, to Marchese Federico Gonzaga

Son statto a ritrovare el M^{ro} de quel instrumento qual non è puro organo anzi sona organo, clavicimballo, flauti et cornamuse: et è in forma d'un clavacimballo. Le cornemuse non vi sonno anchora per essere statto el M^{ro} amallatto, ma in termini de xx giorni dice che 'l sera fornitto. Havendollo instatto dil precio, mi ha risposto che se teneria a carico far mercato cum V. Exma che lo fornirà et lo porterà a Mantua. Et starà al quanto piacera a V. Exma...
(See also Federico's letter to Malatesta, Mantua 10 June 1520, in ASM (AG) 2963 lib. 11: '...Quando eramo a Venezia tu ne parlasti d'un certo organo picolo, quale voremo che vadi a vedere...')

5 ASM (AG) 1803. Letter of Giulia Gonzaga, Casalmaggiore 13 October 1520, to Marchese Federico Gonzaga

Intendendo io che V. Exma S. ha molto a piacere et si dilecta di cose di musica et maxime cose nuove; desiderosa farli cosa grata, gli mando qui alligato un motetto quale ha composto Mr Sebastiano Festa, servitore del R^{mo} Mons^{re} de Mondovi mio zio hon^{mo}, el quale motetto anchore non è in mano di persona, reprometendomi che 'l deba piacere asai a V.S. Illma in gratia de la quale basandoli le mani humilmente mi racomando et foelicissime valeat.

6 ASM (AG) 1803. Letter of Giulia Gonzaga, Casalmaggiore 2 January 1521, to Marchese Federico Gonzaga

Havendo havuto accepto l'altro motetto qual mandai ad V. Illma S., mi son sforciata farne mettere un altro insieme, per far piacere ad quella: la quale si dignarà acceptare con quel buon cuore le è mandato, ch'io non ho altro piacere che di far piacere ad V.S. Illma...

7 ASM (AG) 2500. Letter of Gerolamo Arcario, Mantua 22 November 1521, to Marchese Federico Gonzaga

Questa mattina ho fatto cantar in canto figurato con li organi una solenne messa a Nostra Donna in S. Petro, a la quale è stato senza altro invito la Illma et Exma Madama vostra madre, li fratelli de Ex^{tia}, la Illma Madama Laura, tutti con le corti sue, et una innumerabile moltitudine di signori zentilhomini, zentildonne, et altre persone. Ho fatto ancor celebrar misse in altri logi et precipue al precioso sangue de Cristo, facendo far oratione per V. Ex^{tia} se farà anchora...questa matina dopo cantata la Messa, le giese et la torre cominciorno a martillare di festa.

8 ASDM (MV) Sezione III – Buste. Serie "Carteggio inerente ad affari dell'episcopato". Busta 7 – Carteggio 1482–1620, fasc. II, fo. 11. Letter of Cardinal Ercole Gonzaga, Rome 30 March 1535, to Francesco Andreasio

Havendomi scritto M^ro Giachetto essergli capitato uno tenorista buono per la chiesa, quale vorria provisione di dui scudi et mezzo il mese appresso quello che gli è dato par l'ufficiare d'essa chiesa, voglio che voi gli assigniate la detta provisione a conto mio et oltra di questo che al contr'alto sia cresciuta la sua d'uno scudo più il mese. Il che per la presente vi commetto debbiate esseguire, nonostante altro in contrario; state sano...

9   ASDM (MV) Sezione III – Buste. Serie "Carteggio inerente ad affari dell'episcopato". Busta 7 – Carteggio 1482–1620, fasc. ii, fo. 20. Letter of Cardinal Ercole Gonzaga, Rome 3 May 1535, to Francesco Andreasio

Per la presente vi commetto che ad uno figliuolo del Capitano Staffirino, quale per la buona relatione fattami di lui da M^ro Giachetto, ad instanza dello Illmo Sig. Duca mio fratello et Signore, ho accettato nel numero delli chierici eletti, debbiate dare quella medesima provisione che date à gli altri, et consignarlo da parte mia alli mastri di grammatica et canto fermo, che così gli habbiano da insegnare come a qual altro si voglia che habbiano nelle mani. State sano...

10   ASDM (MV) Sezione III – Buste. Serie "Carteggio inerente ad affari dell'episcopato". Busta 7 – Carteggio 1482–1620, fasc. ii, fo. 22. Letter of Cardinal Ercole Gonzaga, Rome 2 June 1535, to Francesco Andreasio

Accioche 'l Prete da Bassano cantor nella mia chiesa non habbia da diffidarse di quello trattenimento che gli è stato promisso, oltra la provisione ch'io gli faccio pagare, come sapete, voglio che di mese in mese et così vi commetto gli rispondiate voi à conto mio la portione del guadagno che gli è stato assignato sopra la capellania quale ha da ufficiare, et che dall'essator mio del vescovato facciate poi riscotere li denari, et vi li rimborsiate, si ch'egli non ne senta altro fastidio, et appresso chiedendomisi per lui il pagamento alla rata d'un mese prima che 'l servigio suo cominciasse, con allegare d'essere stato tenuto quel tempo suspeso et senza risolutione, vi dico che mi contento sia compiacciuto, et così essequirete. State sano...

11   ASDM (MV) Sezione III – Buste. Serie "Carteggio inerente ad affari dell'episcopato". Busta 7 – Carteggio 1482–1620, fasc. ii, fo. 71. Letter of Cardinal Ercole Gonzaga, Rome 10 December 1535, to Francesco Andreasio

Ogni volta che a M^ro Giachetto mio maestro di capella accascarà bisogno alcuno di fare notare o spendere in cosa che appertenga alla musica, via commetto per virtù di questa mia et voglio che gli provediate di quelli denari ch'egli vi ricercarà senza aspettare da me commissione più particolare di questa. La quale intendo che serva adesso perchè gli habbiate a dare il modo di farmi notare uno libro di motetti, et nell'avenire fin a tanto che da me vi sarà commesso altro in contrario. State sano...

12 ASDM (MV) Sezione III – Buste. Serie "Carteggio inerente ad affari dell'episcopato". Busta 7 – Carteggio 1482–1620, fasc. II, fo. 163. Letter of Cardinal Ercole Gonzaga, Rome 7 October 1536, to Francesco Andreasio

Sarete insieme con M^{ro} Borgondio... Et perchè intendemo che vacano forsi tre luoghi nelli nostri chierici, volemo sia posto in uno il figliuolo di Don Simone, et che per Maestro Giachetto, et Don Giovanni loro precettori ne siano proposti dui di quelli che loro parranno meglio disposti alla musica et alle lettere, fra' quali si connumeri uno de' slanzapani, pure che sia chierico raccomandatoci da Mons^{re} l'Arcivescovo perchè poi vi commetteremo che siano admessi.

13 ASM (AG) 1919, fo. 306. Letter of Adriano Willaert, Venice 23 February 1549, to Cardinal Ercole Gonzaga – see Figure 10

Ho veduto le lettere de V.S. R^{ma} con quella reverentia che a me si conviene, et inteso il suo voler circa li contrabassi ne ricercai duoi de' nostri che sonno al servitio di questa Illma S^{ria} [Venice] quali a me parve fossero sofficienti al proposito suo, et quelli ritrovai prontissimi anzi desiderosissimi di far cosa grata a V.S. R^{ma}, giudico ancho che per essere buon compagni saranno de non poca sua soddisfatione. Et V.S. R^{ma} potra accomodarsi...

(See also ASM (AG) 1919, fo. 320. Letter of Adriano Willaert, Venice 11 October 1549, to Cardinal Ercole Gonzaga: 'Ho ricevuto una altra di V.S. Illma, la quale fu necessaria per lo aviso del contralto...mando li adunque tutte tre insieme...')

14 ASDM (MV) Sezione III – Buste. Serie "Entrate e uscite". Busta 18 "Spese Camere" 1528–1558, fasc. II 1535–1538, fos. 139, 169v

fo. 139 [16 February 1538]
    ...undecj ghirlande de ledria per li musici che sonorno al pasto   L– s3
fo. 169v [13 April 1538]
    ...Adi 13 Marzo 1538 per aver ligato duj quinternj de carta terzarola rigata per otto libri, cioè quatro per le Elementatione et quatro per li innj avuti M^{ro} Iachetto...   L2 s8

15 ASDM (MV) Sezione III – Buste. Serie "Entrate e uscite". Busta 18 "Spese Camere" 1528–1558 fasc. II 1535–1538, fo. 22

fo. 22 [2 May 1537]
    ...Adi ii Maggio 1537 libri dieci e soldi dieci datti alli Trombetti dal S. Duca nostro che Sua S. R^{ma} gli dona   L10 s10
    E più adì istesso alli piffari del predicto Signore libri quindeci e soldi quindeci donati ut supra   L15 s15
    A più ad un altra muda de piffari forastieri un scudo d'oro donato ut supra   L5 s7
    E più alli Tamburini della guardia del predicto signore libri cinque et soldi cinque donati ut supra...   L5 s5

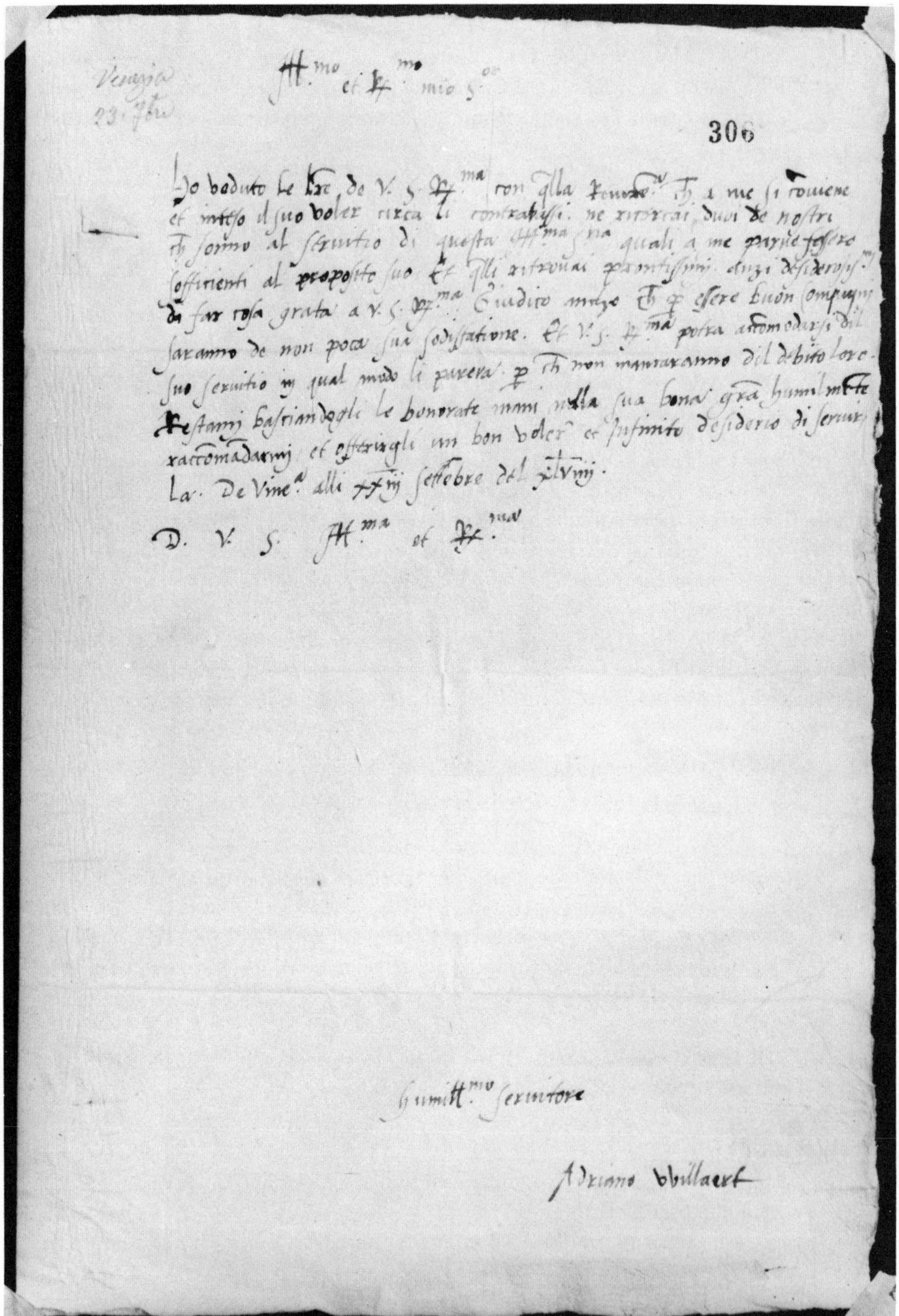

Fig. 10 Letter of Adriano Willaert, Venice 23 February 1549, to Cardinal Ercole Gonzaga (Appendix II, doc. 13) (photo: Giovetti, Mantua)

16   ASDM (MV) Sezione III – Buste. Serie "Entrate e uscite". Busta 18 "Spese
Camere" 1528–1558, fasc. III 1546–1547, fos. 284, 331–331v, 378, 390

fo. 284   [n.d.]
           M^{ro} Giovanni dalli Violoni de' haver dalla corte del R^{mo} Cardinale
           di Mantova Lire nove Soldi dieci per il pretio de donzene dieci de
           corde da violoni, tolte in più volte per li violoni de S.S. R^{ma} come
           apparare nel libro della fattoria.   L9 s10

fos. 331–331v [March 1547]
           ...Adi 21 per i 31 fogli terzaroli rigati per far cinque libri da cantare
           have Mr Prelauro...   L4 s18
           [March 1547]
           ...Adi 23 ditto per haver posto le coperte a cinque volumi in foglio
           con le sue stringe quali fu spanto inchiostro...   L2 s10
           [31 March 1547]
           ...E più de' dar per un altro quinterno de carta terzarola rigata have
           Don Paulo Campora...   l– s10
           [April 1547]
           ...E adì 6 Aprile per 20 fogli di carta terzarola per agiongere alli
           5 libri fatti have Mr Prelauro...   l– s15
           [April 1547]
           E adi 8 ditto per haver ligato cinque libri de carta terzarola per
           cantare ligati alla romana have Mr Prelauro...   L3 so

fo. 378   1 October 1547
           ...M^{ro} Gio. Cremonese de havere dalla corte dell'Illmo et R^{mo}
           Signore Cardinale di Mantova Lire diecinuove per il pretio de
           dozzine venti di corde de viole a soldi diecinuove la dozzina, tolte
           in più volte per bisogno delle viole di S.S. R^{ma} et Illma come appare
           al libro della fattoria...   L19 s–

fo. 390   19 August 1547
           ...Maistre Bassino marangone...per la manifattura di doi casse da
           violon et più per dodeci picche da combattere alla sbara...

17   ASDM (MV) Sezione III – Registri. Serie "Entrate e uscite". Registro 54
     "Libro Marte – Spese di Casa del Cardinale Ercole Gonzaga 1542", fos. 5v–6,
     6v–7, 72v–73, 128v–129

1542
fos. 5v–6   M^{ro} Bernardino Leale musico
fos. 6v–7   M^{ro} Jachetto musico
fos. 72v–73   Juilio brusco cherico in San Pietro
fos. 128v–129   Pre Vincentio d'Asso cantor M^r Zo di Monte Cantor Francese

18   ASDM (MV) Sezione III – Registri. Serie "Entrate e uscite". Registro 59
     "Libro Pico – Entrata dell'Episcopato e delle Abbazie di Acquanegra e
     Felonica 1557", fos. 26v–27

1557
fos. 26v–27   M^{ro} Zovan Battista Fachetto

19   ASDM (MV) Sezione III – Registri. Serie "Entrate e uscite". Registro 53 "Libro Cigno – Entrate e uscite del Cardinale Ercole Gonzaga e delle amministrazioni a lui affidate 1528", fos. 31v–32

1528
fos. 31v–32   Francesco cantore

20   ASDM (MV) Sezione III – Buste. Serie "Entrate e uscite". Busta 20 "Spese diverse" 1537–1561, fos. 387, 393, 422v, 474, 519

fo. 387 [28 March 1561]
    ...a M^{ro} Zoan organista de' aver dalla corte di Monsig. Sig. Illus^{mo} R^{mo} Cardinale di Mantova libri due soldi dieci per aver conzio il chiclavichordo [*sic*]...   L2 s10
fo. 393...M^{ro} Zoann deve aver dalla corte di M. Illmo R^{mo} Cardinale di Mantova lire quattro soldi due pel precio di uno archettino novo per donzene de corde per li viole...   L4 s2
fo. 422v..Al primo di Aprile...più pagati 4 cavallj allj cantorj da Trento a Torbole, piu alli cantorj da spender nel viaggio...
fo. 474 M^{ro} Zoan Jacomo Trombettino de haver da Monsr Illmo et R^{mo} di Mantoa. Lire duj per tante corde de liutto, datte a me, Gio. maria di rossi, per servitio de S.S. Illma et R^{ma} adi 20 Luio 1561...   L2 s–
fo. 519 [1561]
    ...de' dar li infrascritti dinari a mi M^{ro} Giovane dalle Viole per tanta roba quale gli ho datto per bisogna delle viole et liuti...
fo. 519 [1561]
    ...Prima adi 20 di Maggio per tre donzene de corde consegnate a Mr Jer^{mo} de Veschova quale li ha mandate a Trento a Mr Zovanmaria bressano...
                                                                                          L2 s14
fo. 519...A di primo Agosto 1561 per altre trei donzene de corde consegnate a M^{ro} Jer^{mo} de Veschova quale li ha mandata a Trento a M^{ro} Zoanmaria Bressano
    ...   L2 s14
    [etc.]

21   ASDM (AG) Registro dei decreti, 40. Registrum decretorum de anno 1532 ad 1538, fos. 21–21v

Pro Jacobo Collebaudi Civilitas: Cum Jacobus Collebaudi de Vitré Gallus Rhedonensis diocesis cognomento Jachettus cantor artis musicae peritissimus hac in civitate nostra Mantua vitam ducere constituerit cupiatque ad iura civitatis admitti et civium nostrorum numero adscribi ipsius votis annuendum duximus...et alio bene deliberato ipsum Jacobum, eiusque filios, nepotes, pronepotes, et descendentes utriusque sexus in infinitum facimus constituimus et creamus cives nostros Mantuanos eosque omnes civitate hac nostra donamus...

22   Gregorio Comanini: *Oratione … nella morte del Serenissimo Signor Duca Guglielmo…*, p. 37

…Ma nella Musica, della quale prendeva maraviglioso diletto, si come il sapere, così non gli mancò già il volere: percioche nell'hore, ch'egli si sottraeva alle cure, e studi più gravi per allentare alquanto l'arco dell'animo, impiegandosi ne' componimenti armonici formò così dolci, e dotte melodie, particolarmente di quelle, con cui si cantano le divine lode; ch'ad udirle s'infiammano nell'amor di Dio i più freddi, & agghiacciati cori de gli huomini. Non è poi maraviglia, s'egli era il Mecenate de' Musici, e gli honorava e pregiava molto: imitando il magno Alessandro, che ad Aristonico fè drizzare una statua di bronzo con una lancia in uno mano, & con una cetera nell' altra, per honorare in lui così la virtù della musica, come il valore della militia…

23   ASM (AG) 1112. Letter of Stefano Rossetto, Florence 20 December 1566, to Duke Guglielmo Gonzaga

…io sonno qua nel servitio dell'Illmo et R^{mo} de Medici, la Illma et Exma S^{ra} Donna Isabella m'ha fatto favore comandarme che volessi farle in musica il presente lamento d'Olimpia, e perchè pare che sie reuscitto per quanto sie puoco sapere di questa perfettione in assai contento dell'Ecc^{ze} loro Ill^{me}, et anco d'alcuni virtuosi, io mi son risoluto di volerlo presentare all'Ecc^{za} V. Illma, perch'io son certo che si degnerà sentirlo et pigliarsene talvolta (se da tanto fussi) un può de diporto per passar la noia. Et sapend'io come per publica fama è per il mondo, che la Ecc^{za} V. è eccellentissima e di rarrisimo juditio senza parangone ho puo che [*sic*] d'ogni sorte virtù, a particolarmente mi ricordo aver inteso dire ch'ella si piglia anco piacere particulare de intender il buono e bello che contengono l'opere di tal persone, la suplico humilmente a volermi far tanta gratia, tanto favore, degnarsi farmi sapere, che le parrà di questa mia operetta, se non per quanto merita la Ecc^{za} V. sentir cose rare al mondo, almeno per quanto si mostrarà degnarsi ad uno humilissimo servitore, e particularmente a lei voglio essere schiavo perpetuo…

24   ASM (AG) 1112. Letter of Alessandro Striggio, Florence 21 August 1561, to Duke Guglielmo Gonzaga

…Essendo io stato servitore et vassallo di V^{ra} Ecc^{tia} Illustrissima mi avrebbe parso di manchare molto al debito mio et a l'obligo ch'io le tengo se in questo suo felicissimo maritaggio non mi havessi ralegrato non solamente col core, ma ancora con gli effetti esteriori et ancora ch'io sia l'ultimo a rallegrarmi con Vostra Ecc^{tia} havro almeno questo di più de gli altri che la tardanza di questo uffitio le farà venir la mia allegrezza in qualche consideratione, dove prima forse sarebbe oscurata da quella di molti e di maggior momento ch'io non sono, e per che al presente mi trovo haver fatto una musica a quaranta voci sopra a alcune parole fatte in lode di Vostra Ecc^{tia} Illma et del suo felicissimo matrimonio, et essendo reuscita al giudicio de molti signori et vertuosi per cosa degna di lei, essendo cosa non mai più sentita in si gran numero. Ancora ch'io sia sicuro che al valor et grandezza di Vostra Ecc^{tia} merita cose di maggior suggietto pur considerando a la molta benignità di quella mi son risoluto di venerli con questa mia in anzi a farli riverenza con racordarli ch'io li sono servitore humilissimo cosi per natura come per obligo, sperando che l'habbia aver per acetto il buon animo mio, qual sempre imobile versa Vostra Ecc^tia Illma. Le mando adunque apresso alla musica le parole in questa medema lettera accio la vegga che ne le medema parole vi intraviene 40 persone et questa riuscirebbe o in una mascherata o in una fine di comedia o come più li sara agrado...

25   ASM (AG) 1254. Letter of Don Lodovico Agostini, Ferrara 9 February 1575, to Duke Guglielmo Gonzaga

...E' gran pezzo, ch'io desiderava fare riverenza a V. Altezza, né mai ho havuto cosa degna di lei, con la quale habbia potuto pigliare il soggetto. Hora humilmente vengo ad offerirli queste poche notte, et insieme l'alma mia, la qual supplico con ogni affetto di core concerdermi gratia d'accettarle con lieto ciglio, benché d'un tanto signore non siano degne, et me pur suo fidelissimo, et devotissimo servidore, il che facendo mi darà ardire di studiare con più ardente desio, che Nostro Sig^re Iddio l'essalti, conservi, et concedi il fine de suoi alti desiri, et le bascio le serenissime mani con quella maggiore riverenza, e devotione ch'io so, et posso...

26   ASM (AG) 1254. Letter of Don Lodovico Agostini, Ferrara 15 April 1578, to Duke Guglielmo Gonzaga

Il ritorno di M. Giulio Cesare mi dà occasione felice di fare riverenza a V.A. Ser^ma, et anco di supplicandola con ogni humiltà à concerdermi gratia d'accettare con lieto ciglio queste mie poche fatiche, le quali saranno testimonio in parte del debito, che ho con V.A. Ser^ma...

27   ASM (AG) 1255. Letter of Don Lodovico Agostino, Ferrara 27 December 1580, to Duke Guglielmo Gonzaga

...Con l'occasione di M. Abraamo, et del R. Cavaliere, che envio all'Altezza vostra Ser^ma per capellano et contralto me l'inchino à terra con la maggiore humiltà, che m'é concessa, et appresso l'appresento questi madregali, supplicando V.A.S. à perdonarmi, se non sono quali e il mio debito, et così con ogni sommissione le baciarò 'l genocchio...

28   ASM (AG) 1255. Letter of Don Lodovico Agostini, Ferrara 27 May 1581, to Duke Guglielmo Gonzaga

...Perché Ser^mo Sig^r mi trovo haver fatto di fresco à divotione di V.A.S. questo Epigramma, perciò con la maggiore riverenza, et humiltà che posso il porgo: et sì come sempre V.A.S. ha visto le cose mie (per immensa et infinita sua gratia) con buona mente; così hora supp^co l'Altezza V^ra Ser^ma à concedermi gratia di vedere altresì questo, che mi renderà felicissimo...

29   ASM (AG) 1256. Letter of Don Lodovico Agostini, Ferrara 20 November 1582, to Duke Guglielmo Gonzaga

...Trovomi una opera hor hora uscita dalla stampa, la quale quanto più humilemente posso con ogni affetto di core l'offerisco à V.A.S. supplicandola per gratia singolare à restare servita, ch'io le sia sempre servidore devotiss°, alla quale genuflesso baccio il felicissimo genocchio...

30   ASM (AG) 1256. Letter of Don Lodovico Agostini, Ferrara 4 December 1582, to Duke Guglielmo Gonzaga

...Con l'occasione di questa nuova operetta m'appresenterò genuflesso à V.A.S. offerendogliela, e supp^la à concedermi gratia singolare d'accettarla con lieto ciglio, benchè sia di poco valore, et uscita per altra mano che di mia: che se V.A.S. me lo concederà, renderami sopra li felici suoi ser^vi felicissimo...

31   ASM (AG) 1256. Letter of Don Lodovico Agostini, Ferrara 5 January 1583, to Duke Guglielmo Gonzaga

...Trovomi haver partorito di fresco questo madregale, per il che con quella più humile riverenza, che posso, genuflesso à V.A.S. l'offerisco, supp^la à restare servita più dell'affetto del animo mio, che d'esso, quale sarà sempre pronto per ubidirla...

32   ASM (AG) 1256. Letter of Don Lodovico Agostini, Ferrara 5 February 1583, to Duke Guglielmo Gonzaga

...Questo è un'ECHO Ser^mo Prencipe, le rime del quale sono (se m'è lecito il dire) del Divino Sig^r Tasso, quale genuflesso offerisco à V.A.S. con quel più puro affetto, che posso, e debbe: Restando servita, ch'io le sia quel vero humile, e fedel servitore, che sempre ho desiderato di esserle, e desidero più, che si sia da me altra cosa bramata.

33   ASM (AG) 1256. Letter of Don Lodovico Agostini, Ferrara 14 April 1583, to Duke Guglielmo Gonzaga

...il Mag^co Mr Antonio [?Rizzi] ritorna tutto satolo della musica di queste Ill^me Sig^re, il quale dirà à V.A.S. i favori, che le hanno fatto questi Ser^mi Prencipi. Io per non mancare in tutto all'infinito debito, che tengo à V.A.S. genuflesso con questa le bacio il sempre felicissimo genocchio, supp^la à concedermi gratia di vedere con l'occhio della sua immensa benignità questi dua madrigali, che ne sentirò felicità perpetua...

34   ASM (AG) 1256. Letter of Don Lodovico Agostini, Ferrara 23 July 1583,
to Duke Guglielmo Gonzaga

...Poiché V.A.S. m'hà fatto gratia, che'l Sig^r Ercole Ricciardo m'habbia datto i
libri delli suoi (non mai à bastanza lodati) madregali, non so con qual più debito
mio di riverenza interiore, et esteriore laudare, et riferire gratie immortali à V.A.S.
di cotanta benignità, et buona gratia sua, perché quanto più proporei dire, men
potrei. Godrò dunque questa sua felicissima musica, come cosa à me più cara, et
grata di tutte le altre. Scrissi alle Casette questo sesto [i.e. for six voices] e sua Altezza
l'udì. Ancora questi dua Ottavi alla Villa, mentre che S.A.S. era alle Casette poco
fà: Così hora V.A.S. mi concederà supp^{co} gratia vederli con quella buona mente,
che sempre hà concesso alle cose mie per sua grandezza tanto, e non perché
vaglino...

35   ASM (AG) 1256. Letter of Don Lodovico Agostini, Ferrara 30 July 1583, to
Duke Guglielmo Gonzaga

...Ancor che la Sig^{ra} Lucretia Ricciarda, per adempir quel tanto di che V.A.S.
l'havea fatto ricercare, havesse mandato molti giorni sono ser^{ri} per trovarmi à casa
non poterno cio conseguire, per esser io forse fuori della città in questi istanti, che
di me cercorno, senza però lasciare à i miei embasciata alcuna, finalmente detta Sig^{ra}
veduta la lettera di V.A.S. per la quale la ringratiava del veluto presentatomi, di
nuovo mandò suoi ser^{ri} tanto, che mi trovorno hier sera porgendomelo in dono à
nome della magnanimità di quella, la quale tanto più risplende quanto è minore
il merito in me, che tanto estremamente le sono ubligato; Lo goderò per l'amore,
et ad honore di lei. Ho cantati con assai buona compagnia i madrigali di quella,
che di gran lunga hanno avanzato la grandissima speranza, che di quelli si haveva,
tal che hanno colmati di meraviglia, chi gli hà cantati, et uditi, et non solo
d'ammiratione, ma d'imitatione ancora sono stati reputati degni...

36   ASM (AG) 1256. Letter of Don Lodovico Agostini, Ferrara 15 October 1583,
to Duke Guglielmo Gonzaga

...Hieri mattina fummi dato à nome di V.A.S. i libri delli mottetti dell'A.V.S. i
quali legai, e la sera gli presentai al Ser^{mo} Sig^r Duca [Alfonso II d'Este] in presenza
del Sig^r Giaches [de Wert]. L'Alt^a S.S. gli accettò lietamente et ne fece cantare
benché fosse l'hora tarda, et se ne compiacque assai. Poi comandò, che fossero portati
alle Casette, che là gli udirebbe tutti. Io cantando udì tanta arte, et inventioni che
non so, se ardirò più di pigliare penna per mottetti, perche confesso ne' miei studi
passati, non havere posto quella cura, che dovevo. Hora, Ser^{mo} Sig^r sono tanti, sì
alti, et infiniti, i favori, che V.A.S. mi fà tutto di, che non ho spirito tanto, che possa
riferir bene quelle più gratie immortali che dovrei, e vorrei, perciò l'A.V.S. mi
conceda perdono ove manco, et resti servita sapere, che le hò dedicato l'anima mia,
per sì servirla, et ubidirla quanto V.A.S. comanderà...

37   ASM (AG) 1257. Letter of Don Lodovico Agostini, Ferrara 4 December 1584, to Duke Guglielmo Gonzaga

...Nel ritorno di Milano ho trovato molte cose nuove di S.A.S. da porsi a libro, però in parte ho sodisfatto; et poi che queste Ser^me Altezze sono a Marina, mi è venuto scritto l'annesso sonetto in musica, il qual offerisco a V.A.S. per tributo, con supplicarla a non isdegnarlo, ma per sua grandezza favorirlo, come sempre ha fatto, i miei parti, benché di poco spirto fossero, et con esso lui genuflesso le baciarò il real genocchio, augurandole dal sommo fattore vera et perpetua felicità...

38   ASM (AG) 1257. Letter of Don Lodovico Agostini, Ferrara 19 January 1585, to Duke Guglielmo Gonzaga

...Con l'occasione del Sr Dottor Regale, che se ne ritorna costì, humilissimamente farò riverenza a V.A.S. et per arra di debito sarà con questa uno mottetto hor hora finito, et desidero supp^re l'A.V.S. quanto più posso mi conservi nella sua gratia, con la quale viverò sempre felicissimo...

39   ASM (AG) 1257. Letter of Don Lodovico Agostini, Ferrara 29 March 1586, to Duke Guglielmo Gonzaga

...Quando mi trovai costì [in Mantua], emparai, che V.A.S. faceva la carità à dodeci poveri il Giovedì Santo, col lavarle i piedi, io perciò ho accompagnato l'Evangelo con queste poche note, né per altro, che per a lei farne dono, a profunda riverenza, et raccordarlemi devotissimo, et fedelissimo ser^re, alla quale genuflesso bacio le reali mani...

40   ASM (AG) 1257. Letter of Don Lodovico Agostini, Ferrara 22 April 1586, to Duke Guglielmo Gonzaga

...La lettera di V.A.S. che degnò concedermi all'Illmo et R^mo Cardinale Canano à favore del sig^r Stefano Augustini, e compagni empetrò gratia della loro liberatione, né altro si potea sperare; però egli come ubbligatissimo servidore di V.A.S. con questa sua le fà humilissima riverenza...

41   ASM (AG) 3294. Notta di tutta la spesa ordinaria che si fa in un anno nella chiesa di S. Barbara [1588]

Monsr R^mo Abbate lire 500 danno	3000 - 00 - 0
Dignitadi n° 6 a lire 150 per uno danno	5400 - 00 - 0
Canonici n° 12 a lire 85 per uno danno	6120 - 00 - 0
Mansionarii et ceremoniarii n° 6 a lire 76 per uno danno	2736 - 00 - 0
Capellani n° 6 a lire 70 per uno danno	2520 - 00 - 0
Diaconi et subdiaconi n° 4 a lire 24 per uno danno	576 - 00 - 0

Mastro de Chierici, et sacristano a lire 90	
per anno danno	2520 - 00 - 0
Mastro de Canto fermo, et salario del massaro	
a lire 18 per uno	216 - 00 - 0
Cantori in tutto lire 180 danno	1080 - 00 - 0
Campanaro lire 30 danno	180 - 00 - 0
Capellano di S. Anna di Luzara lire 12	72 - 00 - 0
Sr Soardo guidice	
Sr Chiappone avvocato lire 12 danno	72 - 00 - 0
Sr Cardo procuratore lire 10 - 4 - 16 in tutto	64 - 16 - 0
Mr Alberto Coverchino lire 6 danno	36 - 00 - 0
Vestiario de' chierici n° 24 lire 150 danno	900 - 00 - 0
Fatti di case a' Reverendi n° 8 a lire 15 per	
uno danno	720 - 00 - 0
Per fare stampar il calendario lire 6 danno	36 - 00 - 0
Per far batter le tapezzarie una volta l'anno,	
i tapeti due volte, spazzar le telarine della	
chiesa et cubbe due volte, et stoppar le	
fissure delle finestre delle cubbe a tutto 6	
[lire] per volta	36 - 00 - 0
[etc.]	

42   Ippolito Donesmondi: *Dell'istoria ecclesiastica di Mantova*, II, pp. 211–16

E' pertanto la sodetta Chiesa fabricata allato al Castello, & hà una sol nave, con tre Capelle da ogni lato, serrate da cancelli di ferro, delle quali quella di mezo è più grande dell'altre due, con le loro icone fatte per mano d'eccellentissimi pittori. La Capella maggiore, che è posta in faccia, si alza dal pavimento della Chiesa alcuni gradi, & vi s'ascende nel mezzo con una scalinata di marmo ritonda, essendo pure anch'essa chiusa da un serraglio di ferro, ornato di vasi d'ottone, lavorati con bella proportione. L'Altar grande è posto nel mezo di quella, sotto una cupola alta, havendo di dietro, in figura di mezo tondo, spacio competente per il coro de' Sacerdoti. Sotto la Capella maggiore vi è un santuario (ch'anticamente chiamavasi confessionale) destinato per le sacre reliquie, sostenuto da colonne di marmo, con un'Altare dedicato alla Beata Vergine; e più à dentro, un tempietto con l'altare della Santissima Croce. Nella facciata della Chiesa evvi un portico, sopra'l quale è un'altro coro, che risguarda nella Chiesa, nel quale stanno i musici à cantare le feste solenni. Nel mezo della nave della Chiesa, frà le due Capelle grandi s'innalza un'altra cupola simile à quella, ch'è sopra l'Altar maggiore, da tutte due le quali, c'hanno dodeci grandi finestre per ciascuna, piglia il lume essa Chiesa. Sopra le capelle picciole vi sono corridori, & camere per vedere in Chiesa, in uno de quali spatij è situato l'organo. Dal lato sinistro della Chiesa v'è la sacrestia ben fornita, & assai commoda, & spaciosa: & presso quello è fondato il campanile fatto di pietre cotte, alla moderna, colle scale piane à lumaca, di simil materia, & la cupola ornata di marmi, & coperta di piombo: à cui sotto stanno grosse campane, e di buon tuono, che si suonano regolatamente secondo le diverse solennità. L'Abbate, che tiene il primo luogo, &

le sei Dignità, hanno l'uso della mitra, e celebrano con gli habiti Pontificali, e come Protonotari Apostolici, insieme coi Canonici, portano in Chiesa il rocchetto, sopra'l quale porta l'Abbate la mozzetta, eccetto quando è Capella, e non celebra, che và in cappa. Le dignità portano il mantelletto sopra il rocchetto, e sopra questo portano i sei primi Canonici le cotte con le maniche aperte, e gli altri sei le cotte, che si piegano sopra le spalle. Tutti essi Canonici portano le muzze ornate de' dossi: E quando si fà capella solenne, usano sotto il rochetto, l'habito di color morello. Ha inoltre questa Chiesa il suo Breviario, Diurno, e Messale particolari, approvati dall'Apostolica Sede per opra di Monsignor Federico Catani: assendosi il Serenissimo Guglielmo nel comporli, & ordinarli, servito del giudicio, & sapere di molti dotti, & valenti Teologi (oltre l'essere anch'egli versatissimo nella scrittura Sacra, & ne' Dottori,) e specialmente del Padre Ottaviano di Mantova Franciscano già detto, havendo prima dal dottissimo Pietro Galesini fatta descrivere la vita di Santa Barbara con ogni diligenza; & essendosi servito dell'opra di Marc'Antoni Mureti nel comporre gli inni del Breviario, che poi (oltre il Diurno, & Messale) fece stampare in Venetia, & ristampare in Mantova in bellissima forma, & carattere, l'anno M D LXXXV. Et accioche possano i beneficiati di quella più assiduamente attendere al coro, sono essenti dalle processioni ordinarie della Città; e quando pure in occasione di Giubileo, overo per qualche altra gravissima cagione vi vanno, precedono à tutte l'altre Chiese collegiate della Città, quantunque siano antiche, eccetto alla Catedrale, quando però vi si trova presente il Capitolo. Ordinatamente fanno gli ufficij tutti i predetti beneficiati in sei settimane compartiti, ma nelle solennità più principali fà l'ufficio l'Abbate in pontificale, adoperando una mitra pretiosa gioiellata, il pastorale d'argento indorato, la croce pettorale gioiellata, & il chiappone del piuviale con gioie; i paramenti con riccami di perle, & il Calice d'oro con gioie, e la patena similmente d'oro; assistendogli le sei Dignità con le mitre, & i dodici Canonici apparati: E s'apparecchiano due credenze con vasi d'argento indorati. Ma quando celebra una delle dignità, se n'apperecchia una sola, pur con vasi d'argento, adoperando il Sacerdote il Calice con la patena d'oro, si come i Canonici gli adoprano d'argento indorati. Nelle feste di Capella s'appara la parte superiore del Coro d'arazzi finissimi di seta, con l'istorie intessute de gli atti Apostolici: e l'inferiore di velluti, con fregi grandi di broccato: Eccetto nelle Domeniche d'Avvento, e di Quaresima, che s'adoprano tapezzarie di lana. D'intorno all'Altare si cuopre il pavimento con tapeti grandi; ma quando celebra l'Abbate, il tutto à coperto di finissimi tapeti di vari colori, e 'l seggio d'esso Abbate di damasco del colore conveniente. Ne i doppi maggiori sopra l'Altare stà un tabernacolo grande d'argento indorato, con una croce sopra gioiellata, c'hà dentro del legno della Santissima Croce, e sei candellieri d'argento anch'essi indorati, con quattro grandi reliquiarij framezzati: oltre i quali vi sono anche dodeci bracci intieri d'argento, & due grandi teste, co'l busto d'argento similmente, l'una di San Silvestro primo Papa, & l'altra di Sant'Adriano martire. Alle quali cose vi ha aggiunto il Serenissimo Duca Vincenzo per maggior ornamento, & divotione, venti teste d'argento, con altri reliquiarij ricchissimi d'argento, & oro, & di christallo di montagna in varie guise lavorato. Le tovaglie poi si pongono ne gli stessi doppi maggiori fregiate d'oro, de i colori convenienti: E nell'altre solennità s'adoprano lavorate di seta. Ne i doppi minori, la Croce, & li sei candellieri s'adoprano d'argento schietto, E perche non solo immantinente che fù finita la Chiesa donò il Serenissimo Duca alla Sacristia di quella, paramenti pretiosi, che passavano il valore di sei mila scudi; ma anco successivamente fino alla morte gliene donò sempre, & in buon numero; quindi è, che quei, che s'adoprano ne' doppi maggiori sono di broccato d'oro, e ne' doppi minori di brocatello: ne i semimaggiori di veluto, ò damasco, con fregio d'oro, e ne i semiminori di raso, di Zambelloto con fregio di raso, de i colori competenti: e questi per la moltitudine loro si variano quasi sempre per il cerchio dell'anno. E cosi gli altari ne i doppi maggiori, & altre feste tutti s'apparano uniformemente secondo le solennità correnti, e conforme alle pianete, ch'in cotali giorni s'adoprano. E' questo sacro tempio, oltre le pretiose reliquie, che l'adornano (come più in particolare nel sequente libro dirassi) ricco anche di celestiali tesori d'indulgenze, sì che ogno mercordì visitandosi l'altare della Santissima Croce à basso nel Santuario, si guadagnano cent'anni d'Indulgenza, & altrettanti anni, e tante quarantene conseguisce chiunque si trova presente alla solenne benedittione, che l'Abbate, overo l'altre dignità danno. Et chi confessato, ò almen contrito interviene alli mattutini, le notti di Natale, di Pasca, e di Santa Barbara, ottiene Indulgenza plenaria in forma di Giubileo, come anco ogni Sacerdote che in giorni tali celebra messa in essa Chiesa. Finalmente nella quattro Domeniche dell'Avvento, visitandosi i sette altari, che sono nel corpo di quella, si guadagnano l'Indulgenze della sette principali Chiese di Roma. Può in oltre l'Abbate, & in sua assenza le dignità rispettivamente, assolvere i preti d'essa Chiesa in articolo di morte, da tutti i lor peccati in forma di Giubileo.

43   ASDM (SB) Constitutiones Capituli Sanctae Barbarae Mantuae (1568) [extracts]

De Praefecto chori Tit. iiij. Cap. i

Alius Musicorum modorum peritus praeerit Choro, qui, ut omnia ad Chori tonum rite, et apte cantentur, prout tempus, et festi dies requisiverunt operam det.

Caput ij

Mansionarios instruat, ut cantanda praeparent praevideantque singula, ne in Choro haerreant aut errent, labantesque levi voce sublevet.

Caput iij

Doceatque unumquemque extra Chorum, quemadmodum iuxta tonorum rationem ac varietatem Psalmi, Antiphonae, Hymni, reliquaque omnia quae cantantur, intonanda sint curetque, ut omnia eodem vocis modo, cantentur.

Caput iiij

Quod super omnia est, praeauscultet singulos aliquid pro hebdomade officio ad altare, vel in Choro cantaturos, ut qui Missam cantando est celebraturus, Orationes, Praefationem, Pater Noster, et Ite missa est, vel Benedicamus Domino congrua, ac decenti voce id faciat quod et in eis, quae ad hebdomadarios in Choro, aut ad altare cantandis pertinent, ab eo observandum est.

De Cantorum Magistro Tit. xlv. Cap. i.

Cantorum Magister in duplicibus festis maioribus, ad Matutinum, Vesperas utrasque Tertiam, ad Missam, et Completorium utrunque. In festis autem Sanctae Barbarae, Nativitatis, et Resurrectionis domini, et Pentecostes ad omnes horas. In duplicibus minoribus ad utrasque Vesperas, Tertiam, Missam, et utrunque Completorium. In semiduplicibus vero maioribus, et Dominicis ad utrasque Vesperas pro Hymno, et Magnificat, atque in semiduplicibus minoribus ad Missam cantum, ac in Sabbatis ad Completorium pro Anna Beatae Mariae. In Dominicisque Adventus, Septuagesimae, Sexagesimae, Quinquagesimae, et Quadragesimae, ad nonum Responsorium ad Missam quoque feriales in vigilijs, et diebus ieiuniorum, ad officiumque Mortuorum, et Missas eorum quando officium huiusmodi, et duplex maius cum Cantoribus venire est solitus, tamen quia id est arbitrij Illustrissimi et Excellentissimi Ducis nihil oneris ei ab ecclesia nostra imponitur, nisi ut modeste se se cum Cantoribus gerat, devoteque cantet, faciatque ut cantores cantent ad Omnipotentis Dei laudem, unde mentes circumstantium in Deum excitentur.

De Organorum Magistro Tit. xlvi. Cap. i.

Magister Organorum in festis Sanctae Barbarae, Nativitatis, et Resurectionis Domini, et Pentecostes ad omnes horas. In duplicibus maioribus et minoribus ad omnes horas praeter Nonam. In semiduplicibus minoribus ad Missam. In semimaioribus ad verasque vesperas exceptis Sabbatis Dominicis Adventus, a Septuagesima usque ad Pascha nisi hoc tempus festa cadat Organa pulset, ita ut audientes delectentur animum in Deum intendentes. Caveat vero ne modos amatorios aut saltatorios his sonet, ne quae laudandum inventa sunt in usum obscanum cedant.

De Socijs Praefecti Chori Tit. xi. Caput i.

Alij duo in modis omnibus Musicis versati dentur socij Praefecto Chori, ut per hebdomadas alter alteri inofficio succedat. Praevideant singuli, quae cantanda fuerint. Praefectum Musices anteque Chorum ingrediat ac admoneat, ut omnia eius officio necessaria praesto sint, satagatque ut re qui scriptum fuerit adimpleatur. Moneant Mansionarios, ut diligenter omnia cantanda praevideant. Doceant imperitos modorum sacerdotes, qua voce, Orationes, Praefationes, Pater Noster ac lectiones reliquaque omnia cantanda sint. Operamque dent, ut Diaconi, Subdiaconi, Clericique omnes cantum discant, peritique modorum musicorum fiant.

De Mansionarijs Tit. xvi. Caput. i.

Quattuor sunt Cantores, quos Mansionarios appellanus, qui modos saltem Gregorianos id est cantum (quod vulgo dicunt) firmum; humanarum literarum ad Rubricas, caeteraque, quae ad ipsorum officium pertinent, discutienda, non imperiti, percalleant. Ad hos enim spectat intonare, Psalmos, Antiphonas, Hymnos ad omnes horas, et ad Matutinum, praeter haec, Responsoria post lectiones; Antiphonasque post Psalmos quotiescunque Organa non pulsantur in festis duplicibus maioribus, aut minoribus.

44   ASM (AG) 2578. Letter of Don Antonio Ceruti, Mantua 3 February 1567, to a ducal official

...Nel primo di questo mese, alle 17 hore, con felice et prospero vento, partì per Venecia la barca d'amore per la cui partita la nostra città è rimasta vidua. L'ordine di questa andata è in questo modo: nella barca regia vi sono le S^{re} Hortesia, Fulvia, Ottavia, col Sr Borgoforte condotore di quelle, il Scalco, et il Megliareto, et per compagnia vi è andata la vicaria di Poletto, vi è la musica, Mes^r Jaches, Mes^r Gio. Maria, D^n Hercole, Semideo, et altri musici, dove in quella barca non si sente altro che angelica harmonia...

45   ASM (AG) 2576. Letter of Guglielmo [Testore] cantore, Mantua 7 August 1566, to Duke Guglielmo Gonzaga

...Dopio baciato le mani di V.S. le fo' intendere come qui son capitati due cantori del R^{mo} di Ferrara, non so in che modo intertenergli; supp^{co} V.S. che la se degni farlo sapere a sua Ecc^a et se gli piacerà commettere che se gli sia data la spesa, o vero ch'eglino venghino a basciar le mani di Sua Ecc^a; V.S. mi farà sommo piacere quanto più presto del tutto farmene avisato, et con questo resto baciando le mani di V.S....

46   ASM (AG) 2579. Letter of Giulio Aliprandi, Mantua 11 February 1568

...Hieri l'altro di sera S. Ecc^{za} cenò col Sr Andrea [Gonzaga] Illmo et la andarono a ritrovarla de commis^{ne} sua con un concerto di musica a otto, nel quale tra gli altri erano il M^{ro} di Capella di S. Pietro, Mes^r Giaches, Mes^r Valeriano Cattaneo, Mes^r Agostino Bonvicino, et io, et de là usciti con certi manti si partirono et andarono a casa delli S^{ri} Aldigatti...

47   ASM (AG) 2573. Letter of Giovanni Battista Bertani, Mantua 19 July 1565

...Mes^r Giarolamo di Urbino et M^{ro} Gratiadio organaro me hanno fato instantia che li fatia far la bulletta ispedita del suo credito per haver fatto lo organo per la chiesa di Sta Barbara, al quale ancor vi manca alchune canne ad essere condotto ad perfettione, sì come mi certifica il sudetto Mr Giarolamo per le quali M^{ro} Gratiadio volendo andare a casa alla sua patria, si contenta lasciar in mano del Migliareto ducati 50, sino al Settembre...

48   ASM (AG) 2573. Letter of Girolamo d'Urbino [Cavazzoni], Mantua 3 July 1565

...Mr Graciadio ha fornito l'organo di tutto ponto, con gli 12 registri...l'organo è riuscito tanto buono che io non saprei dimandar meglio...per questo del che ne ringracio Iddio che mi sia riuscito bene. In quel che e statto mio caricho, in vivo l'organo sera sempri estimato raferimento di 600 ducati...

49   ASM (AG) 2573. Letter of Girolamo d'Urbino [Cavazzoni], Mantua 17
October 1565

...che haverei molto a caro che V^ra Ecc^za mi facessi comprare meza dozina di
cucchiari d'argento perche ho le forzine et gli cortillj però mi manchano i cucchiari.
Io ho volutto altre volte agravar V^ra Ecc^za di simil cosa, pur non ho preso il costo;
credo che non passeva sei ducati in circa...

50   ASM (AG) 2950 lib. 370, fo. 107. *Copialettera* of Duke Guglielmo Gonzaga,
Mantua 27 May 1570, to Cavaliere Capilupi

...Manda anco S. Ecc^za Francheschino, acciò habbia da star con lei, tenendo per
fermo, che lo vedrà voluntieri, et per rispetto suo l'havrà caro, et nanti che essa sia
andata a Gonzaga nel volersi partir, che cenava io [*sic*], mi fece dir per il Sr Fermo,
che lo volessi mandar con questa occasione, et lo accompagnassi con una mia a V.S.,
con farli sapere che ogni cortesia che usarà a questo giovane le sarà accetta, et so
anco che serà caro a S. Ecc^a che V.S. parli con M. Claudio, et con altri di quelli
eccellenti organisti, et faccia la riuscita, che S. Ecc. desidera solicitandolo a studiare
et ad affaticarsi per quel tempo...

51   ASM (AG) 1501. Letter of Claudio di Correggio [Merulo], Venice 17 June
1569, to Duke Guglielmo Gonzaga

...l'istrumento è ecc^mo et io per me non ho udito fin'hora la più bella fantasia...
anco, che habbia uno appresso, che continuamente gli sia atorno per la moltitudine
de' registri che vi son dentro...

52   ASM (AG) 1502. Letter of Cavaliere Capilupi, Venice 3 June 1570, to the
Castellano of Mantua

Francheschino organista è giunto a salvamento...l'ho poi condotto meco in gondola
a Grasco [Gratz] per Vinegia, et rimane stupido...Finché non sia partito il dottore
non potrò essere con Mr Claudio organista di S. Marco ma subito io lo farò, et non
mancarò di sollecitare Franceschino ad imparare...

53   ASM (AG) 2573. Letter of Don Giulio Bruschi, Mantua 15 June 1565, to
Duke Guglielmo Gonzaga

Il Cardinale di Augusta ha licenciato la sua capella et per passaggio son capitati
qui per le magior parte i suoi cantori delli quali, havendone io spia li feci invitare
a desinare hieri mattina e a cantare la messa, eran i tre castrati fra quali elessi il
migliore, et col mezzo di Mr Sales...il quale spinto da mie parole si è adoperato
benissimo in vero per mezano, essendo il castrato anch'egli Spagnuolo di anni in 28
prete da missa et per quanto intendo è di buona vita e molto quieto e mostra di
compiacersi del servizzio di V^a Ecc^za...quanto alla statura egli è un poco più alto
di Mes^r Jacomo, quanto alla voce è acuta e chiara, un alto e ha buon contraponto

di modo che mi pare che V. Ecc. haverà acquistato assai, delli altri duoi ho havuta informatione che il picciolo non era castrato et il picciolo non era per noi. Questa matina ho fatto ricercare il basso per delli istessi cantori, il quale mi ha fatto rispondere che non potrebbe star saldo alla fatica, et io poco non me son curato, sì per questa risolutione quanto anche per avere inteso la voce non essere molto grande e più tosto da camera che da capella...

54   ASM (AG) 907. Letter of Francesco Fullonica, Rome 12 August 1570, to Aurelio Zibramonte

...addoperarmi per servitio del Sr Duca Ecc^{mo}, Nostro S^{re} in materia de trovargli cantori da coro, hor subito havuta questa sua, non ho mancato far pratica con amici et in queste chiese, ove so si fa capella, per trovar huomo a proposito per Sua Ecc^{za} con quelle qualità che la mi ricerca, infatti uno mi è cappitato, ch'è buonissimo, et sufficiente savio per la parte del tenore con voce gagliarda et piena, bellissimo cantante et di buon contrapunto ma per quanto mi referisce un mio amico, che tutto e suo, non uscirà di Roma se non ben paggato, vivendoseni qui a speranza de entrare in cappella del Papa, come prima vi fosse il luoco, standosene adesso anco con buon intratenimento con un abbate Napolotano; a quello mio amico ho detto, di che maniera sono trattati cantori da S. Ecc^{za}...questa professione di musica al presente in Roma è tanto al basso, che non ci cappitano huomini come solea, s'il Cardinale di Ferrara et quel di Trento [non] accappitassero questa sorte d'huomini, la musica correrìa tutt'il giorno alla staffa, dietro a cocchi, et a nulle, li quali Cardinali tutti due sonno fuori di Roma, et hanno de buoni huomini in tal professione...

55   ASM (AG) 2950 lib. 368a, fo. 15. *Copialettera* of Duke Guglielmo Gonzaga, Casale 14 July 1565, to Ambassador Negri

...Havendo noi veduto quanto ci havete scritto nel particolare de castrati, che noi desideriamo per la musica nostra, vi diciamo che ne habbiamo tre a' quali diamo di provisione tre ducati al mese et le spese, vero è che un di loro per essere molto tempo che sta al nostro servizio et per essersi portato bene ha havuto una volta in dono da noi cento scudi...

56   ASM (AG) 941. Letter of Scipione Gonzaga, Patriarch of Jerusalem, Rome Holy Saturday 1586, to Federico Cattaneo

...Egli à voce piena, canta contr'alto, e così canta in cappella di N. S^r, in camera, e in oratori canta soprano, e va alto assai. Canta con molti passaggi per ordine e porta la voce con buona gratia secondo l'uso però di quà, che tieneva poco del Napolitano, il quale non so come convenga con quello di Lombardia. Ma assai è, che il giovane, per quanto intendo da altri virtuosi suoi domestici, è di buona natura, e si accommoda facilmente alla voluntà e il gusto de' padroni. M. Gio: Battista poi canta come scrissi un suo tenore assai ordinariamente. La voce sua è più tosto gagliarda che soave, e in somma non ha nel cantare alcuna eccellenza, canta però sicuro, e fa contrapunto à mente. Compone qualche cosa ma anche in questo non passa certa mediocrità. Ho fatto grande opera per haver alcune sue compositioni ma non mi è successo di poter haver se non un solo madrigale il quale sarà qui allegato, e questo ancora ho havuto così tardi questa mattina medesima che non è stato possibile il farlo copiare à tempo. Se potrò havere alcuna altra cosa del suo, e particolaramente una messa, che intendo lui haver fatto, la manderò con le predette ò quanto prima potrò. Ma non bisogna aspettar gran cose da lui, perché in somma la sua propria professione è di sonare, e non di cantare ò comporre...

57   ASM (AG) 941. Letter of Scipione Gonzaga, Patriarch of Jerusalem, Rome 19 April 1586, to Federico Cattaneo

...Ho preso informatione di tutti i musici che teneva Madama d'Austria, et trovo, che oltre il M^{ro} di Cappella, il quale era chiamato M. Verius Vallone, ella haveva quattro soprani, tre putti e un castrato. Il castrato è quello del quale scrive Monsr Capilupi, che ha un canonicato nell'Aquila et perchè sta bene verisimile cosa è ch'egli non partirebbe di là senza molto gagliardo partito. Ài tre putti Madama ha lasciato danari, e commodità perche se ne tornino in Fiandra, dove furono presi e cosi hanno già fatto. Appresso à questi haveva tre contralti, l'uno Spagnuolo e, come intendo, non molto buono, il quale se n'è ito à Napoli. Gli altri due Fiaminghi, i quali anch'essi già se ne sono tornati alla patria. I tenori erano medesimamente tre: due pur Fiamminghi, che sono partiti et un'Italiano, chiamato Gio: Paolo di Urbino, e questo è quello che per esservi stato altre volte, à stato di nuovo accettato qui in San Luigi, ma, per quanto mi vien detto, non senza qualche difficoltà, non essendo cosa molto rara. Finalmente i bassi erano due, l'uno trombone, del quale non so che sia avvenuto, l'altro, chiamato Ugo, è quello che si è accomodato nella cappella di S. Giovanni Laterano. Ma intendo non esser huomo di farvi gran fondamento sopra, per haver una vena rotta nel petto...

58   ASM (AG) 943. Letter of Camillo Capilupi, Rome 8 February 1586, to Federico Cattaneo

...Domandai informatione dell'uno et dell'altro à M^{ro} Gio: Maria Nanino il quale di Gio: Battista mi disse che era il migliore che sonasse quello strumento che fosse in Roma, et che di clavicordo et d'arpa mi pare che dicesse era bonissimo et che era huomo di più di 30 anni. Di Gio: Luca [Conforto] mi disse che era ottimo per camera et per capella et che pensava certo che sodisfarebbe à S.A....

59   ASM (AG) 943. Letter of Camillo Capilupi, Rome 22 March 1586, to Federico Cattaneo

...M. Gio: Battista...nella musica è più che mediocre; canta di testa et fa contrapunti (et come si dice di gorga che pare un rosignolo benchè alcuni vogliono che la voce potesse esser più delicata, ma in camera riesce eccellente et più dolce) et in camera il falsetto il miglior che sia in Roma, et contralto in capella, canta in tutti li strumenti, et suol cantar di capriccio et di suo capo, et in somma per quello ch'io intendo da Mr Don Pauolo [Faccone], et dal Nanino; et Mons. Illmo Patriarca Gonzaga dice ch'intende il medesimo egli è de' migliore suggetti che sia in Roma della sua professione et congiunte con Gio: Battista S.A. potrebbe dire d'haver una musica da far sentire ad ogni Prencipe...

60 ASL, Orsucci MS 48. Vincenzo Giustiniani: 'Discorso sopra la musica', fos. 116v–117v

...Ma sì come le Villanelle acquistarono maggior perfettione per lo più artificioso componimento, così anche ciascun autore, a fine che le sue composizioni riuscissero di gusto in generale, procurò d'avanzarsi nel modo di comporre a più voci, e particolarmente Giacches Wert in Mantova, il Luzzasco in Ferrara. Quali erano sopraintendenti di tutte le musiche di quei Duchi, che se ne dilettavano sommamente, massime in fare che molte dame e signore principali apparassero di sonare e cantare per eccellenza; a segno tale che dimoravano tavolta i giorni intieri in alcuni camerini nobilmente ornati di quadri e fabricati a questo solo effetto, et era gran competenza fra quelle dame di Mantova et di Ferrara, che facevano a gara, non solo quanto al metallo et alla disposizione delle voci, ma nell'ornamento di esquisiti passaggi tirati in opportuna congiuntura e non soverchi (nel che soleva peccare Gio. Luca falsetto di Roma, che servì anche in Ferrara), e di più col moderare e crescer la voce forte o piano, assottigliandola o ingrossandola, che secondo che veniva a' tagli, hora con strascinarla hora smezzarla, con l'accompagnamento d'un soave interrotto sospiro, hora tirando passaggi lunghi, seguiti bene, spiccati, hora a gruppi, hora a salti, hora con trilli lunghi, hora con brevi, at hor con passaggi soavi e cantati piano, dalli quali tal volta all'improvviso si sentiva echi rispondere, e principalmente con azione del viso, e dei sguardi e de' gesti che accompagnavano appropriatamente la musica e li concetti, e sopratutto senza moto della persona e della bocca e delle mani sconcioso, che non fusse indirizzato al fine per il quale si cantava, e con far spiccar bene le parole in guisa tale che si sentisse anche l'ultima sillaba di ciaschuna parola, la quale dalli passaggi et altri ornamenti non fusse interrotta o soppressa, e con molti altri particolari artificij et osservationi che saranno a notitia di persone più esperimentate di me...

61 ASM (AG) 3146, fos. 47–53. Nota delli salariati dell'Altezza Sua [extracts][1]

fo. 47		
M. Antonio de Grossi trombetta		3 - 10 - 0
Abraam dall'Arpa		16 - 4 - 0
M. Antonio Riccio musico		13 - 19 - 0

[1] Regrettably, few account books listing court musicians from the second half of the sixteenth century have survived, other than the Santa Barbara papers in ASDM (SB). One, in ASM (AG) 3146, is noted on p. 109; the remainder known to me are excerpted here as docs. 61–65. Although only doc. 63 carries a contemporary date, the other lists can be tentatively assigned to circumscribed periods. Doc. 61 must date from no earlier than 1590, when Francesco Rovigo returned to Mantua after serving Duke Wilhelm V of Bavaria in Graz, and no later than 1596, when Giaches de Wert died. From about the same period is doc. 62: it includes Wert, and also Claudio Monteverdi who arrived at court in 1589–90. Since this list also records Paolo Masenelli's name it most probably dates from before 1592; after that his name is not found in Mantuan documents, and certainly by 1596, according to the dedication of his second book of five-voice motets, he had returned to his native Verona as organist at the cathedral. The title and the date '1591' on the cover of doc. 64 are written in a much later hand; the document

fo. 47v	M. Agostino Seraffino musico	13 - 19 - 0
fo. 48	M. Bartolomeo Volta sonatore	155 - 0 - 0
	Sr Camillo Gattico sonatore	155 - 0 - 0
fo. 48v	Don Camillo Sassola musico	13 - 19 - 0
fo. 49	Dario Zuega musico	13 - 19 - 0
fo. 49v	Don Francesco Guavazzo musico	13 - 19 - 0
	M. Francesco Rovigo musico	19 - 7 - 0
	M. Filippo Maria Parabovi musicho	13 - 19 - 0
	M. Filippo Angeloni musico	13 - 19 - 0
fo. 50	M. Giorgio del Carretto sonatore	155 - 0 - 0
fo. 50v	M. Jaches Vuart cioè Mastro di Capella	45 - 0 - 0
fo. 51	M. Margarino Dupré cantore	13 - 19 - 0
fo. 51v	M. Marco strada sonatore	155 - 0 - 0
fo. 52	M. Ruggiero Roverso organista	13 - 19 - 0
fo. 52v	M. Zoanni Crocero cantore	13 - 19 - 0
fo. 53	Don Zoanni Bartioli cantore e capellano	13 - 19 - 0

62   ASM (AG) 3146, fo. 64. Provisioni che si pagano ogni mese [extract]

fo. 64	Sr Giaches Wert	84 - 6 - 3
	M. Benedetto Pallavicino	39 - 3 - 0
	M. Giovanni Battista Marinone	53 - 12 - 9
	M. Andrea Cozzoli	62 - 18 - 9
	M. Paulo Masenelli	66 - 5 - 0
	Padre Serafino Terzi	15 - 0 - 0
	M. Giulio Cesare Perla	13 - 19 - 0
	Don Bassano Casola	18 - 12 - 0
	M. Annibal Pelizzari	91 - 13 - 4
	M. Claudio Monteverdi	75 - 0 - 0
	M. Felippo Angelone	34 - 10 - 0
	Don Giuseppe Clerici	39 - 18 - 6
	Don Giovanni Barthioli	49 - 4 - 1
	Don Camillo Sassola	39 - 18 - 6
	Don Federico Bottazzino	52 - 3 - 4
	Don Federico Follino	82 - 3 - 4
	M. Bartholomeo Pellizzari	45 - 16 - 8
	M. Francesco Rovigo	38 - 15 - 0
	Europa di Rossi	13 - 19 - 0
	Salamone di Rossi	13 - 19 - 0
	Isachino della Praefeta	35 - 6 - 9
	M. Giordano Floriano	25 - 4 - 0
	Mª Isabetta di Pellizzari	25 - 4 - 0

itself must date from the early years of the seventeenth century, not only because of the presence in it of Francesco Rasi, who did not enter Gonzaga service until 1598, but also because of the membership of the ducal family listed on its early folios. (I am grateful to Susan Parisi for help with this document.) Doc. 65 dates from between 1586, when Striggio returned to Mantua, and 1592, when he died.

Sr Giulio Cesare Petrozani	61 - 5 - 0
Mª Lucia di Pellizari	46 - 19 - 4
Sr Ottavio Wert	9 - 5 - 9

63   ASM (AG) 403. Rollo della famiglia di S.A. per la paga del mese d'Agosto 1595,[2] fo. 1v

fo. 1v	Sr Claudio Montiverde	L6. 5.
	Padre M^{ro} Theodoro Bacchino	L8. 2.
	Padre Seraffino Basso	L5. 0.
	Padre Valerio da Ferrara capellano	L4. 0.
	M. Giovanni Battista Marinone	L2. 1.

64   ASM (AG) 395. Rollo de' salariati del Prencipe che si è trovato nella filza dell'anno 1591, intitolata affari camerale,[3] fos. 8v–9

fos. 8v–9	Signora Lucia Pellizari	35 - 17 - 2
	Signora Isabetta Pellizari	35 - 17 - 2
	Signora Lucretia Urbana	120 - 0 - 0
	Signora Caterina Romana	
	M. Giovanni Battista Marinone	13 - 19 - 0
	M. Don Bassano Casuola	52 - 4 - 0
	M. Annibale Pellizzari	35 - 17 - 2
	M. Don Eleuterio Buosio	50 - 0 - 0
	M. Pandolfo del Grande	50 - 0 - 0
	Sig. Henrico Vilardi Romano	50 - 0 - 0
	Sig. Francesco Rasio	84 - 0 - 0

65   ASM (AG) 395. [Rollo de' salariati], fos. 156v, 159v[4]

fo. 156v	Cantori	
	Sr Jaches M^{ro} di Capella	L45 - 0 - 0
	Mr Benedetto Pallavicino	L18 - 12 - 0
	Mr Gio. Batta. Marinoni	L13 - 19 - 0
	Mr Andrea Cochiola	L23 - 5 - 0
	Mr Pauolo Masenello	L30 - 0 - 0
	Mr Filippo Angelloni	L13 - 19 - 0
	Mr Benato Renato	L30 - 0 - 0
	Mr Don Bassano da Lodi	L18 - 12 - 0
	Mr Don Matteo Foverto	L13 - 19 - 0
	Mr Antonio di Pelizzari	L175 - 0 - 0

[2] A similar list in ASM (AG) 403 for September 1595 includes these five names and notes 'di quelli die sono con S.A. nel campo di Ungaria' (i.e. part of Vincenzo Gonzaga's first campaign against the Turks).

[3] On the dating of this document see p. 192, note 1.

[4] On the dating of this document see p. 192, note 1.

Mr Paolo Pigino da Bologna   L36 - 0 - 0
Mr Francesco Gratia   L23 - 5 - 0

fo. 159v   Extraordinarij
         Sr Alessandro Streggi   L129 - 0 - 0
         Mr Salamone di Rossi hebreo   L13 - 19 - 0
         Madama Europa sua sorella   L13 - 19 - 0

66   BBV. Atti ordinarii et straordinarii dell'accademia, libro D

7 Gennaio 1582. Essendo ridotto questa mattina li Clarissimi Signori Rettori della Città et li Magnifici Signori Deputati con tutta la Nobiltà di Vicenza nella Chiesa di S. Michele ad udire la Messa solennemente celebrata per la entrata del Magn. Sig. Giulio Pogliana novo Prencipe dell'Accademia nostra Olimpica insieme con tutti gli Accademici per dar principio con felici auspici al suo Magistrato, e stata la detta Messa celebrata con somma soddisfazione, anzi stupore di tutti per causa della musiche in esse udite. Le quali per di più et le più eccellenti sono state fatte dal Messer Antonio nostro Bidello et Musico e da due sue sorelle, perchè par cosa ragionevole, riconoscendo le virtù delle dette due putte sorelle del detto messer Antonio potersi valere di esse per la musica nelli bisogni con salario di ducati xx per una all'anno con conditione che messer Antonio insieme con alle siano obbligati far musica due volte alla settimana per ordinario et de più ogni volta ve ne sarà bisogno et ocasione...

67   BBV. Atti ordinarii et straordinarii dell'accademia, libro E

Il Ser^{mo} Sig^r Guglielmo Gonzaga Duca di Mantoa essendo allogiato di passaggio in Vicenza, volse vedere il Teatro Olimpico; et il giorno seguente, che fù il vig^{mo} secondo d'Agosto M.D.LXXXij venuto all'Accademia udì nel Teatro una breve, ma ornatissima, et facondissima oratione fattagli dal mag^{co} M. Antonio Maria Angiolello Academico alla quale processero, et seguirono diversi concerti di Musica et furono recitati diversi componimenti di Poesia da Mr Gio Battista Magenta Acad^{co}, così in lingua culta, come nella rustica Vicentina. Et Sua Altezza mostrando quanto sodisfacimento n'havesse havuto, creo publicamente nel teatro l'Angiolello suo cavalliero postagli di sua mano una collana d'oro di cento scudi al collo, et fece far doni al Maganza et a' Musici dell'Accademia...

68   ASF (AM) 768, fo. 640. Letter of Alessandro Striggio, Mantua 17 August 1584, to Grand Duke Francesco de' Medici

...Io ritornai da Ferrara sei giorni fa et subito giunto in Mantova. Io mi missi a comporre il Madrigale che vostra Al. Ser^{ma} mi mandò conforme a quanto mi comanda et secondo l'ordine et instrutiona di Mr Giulio [Caccini] la quale è conforme alle musiche di Ferrara. Così con questa Io lo mando a Vostra Altezza Serenissima l'altro madrigaletto...Son stato da 20 giorni in Ferrara con molto mio gusto e satisfatione, sentendo ogni giorno qual concerto tanto vario et unico per tre hore continue di quelle sig^{re} Dame, anzi angeli del paradiso; et Sandrino è stato molto accarezzato e favorito, et il giorno che partimo sua Altezza gli fece donare una colana di 100 ducati. Né sendo questa per altro, con ogni debita reverenza et humiltà le bacio le ser^{mi} mani e prego il Sr Dio per ogni sua maggior felicità. Di Mantoa il dì 17 d'Agosto 1584...

69   ASM (AG) 2952 lib. 381, fos. 9–9v. *Copialettera* of Teodoro San Giorgio, Bologna 2 March 1581, to Federico Pendaso

È stato riferito al mio Ser^{mo} da Don Annibale Capello, altre volte capellano dell'Al.S. et hora dell'Ill S. Card. [Luigi] d'Este ch'essendo egli stato a questi giorni passati in questa città [Bologna], ha udito cantare, et sonare di molti stromenti, una giovane da marito nata nobilmente, et d'ottimi costumi, nipote di Mons. Bovio celebrandola per cosa quasi che miracolosa; il che ha acceso l'animo dell'Al.S. di desiderio di haverla per damigella della Sua S^{ra} Prencipessa sua nuora che si diletta molto di musica...

70   ASM (AG) 1161. Letter of Cardinal Gabriele Paleotti, Bologna 10 March 1581, to the Duke of Parma

Ha mandato qua il Sr Duca di Mantova persone sue per informarsi bene delle qualità della giovene, di che ancora m'ha scritto V. Ecc^{za} Illma talmente che si è contentato Monsr Bovio di lasciarli e vedere et ascoltare anco la giovene nelle cose di musica, et si è risoluto di voler prima intendere se il Sr Duca persisterà nel medesimo pensiero dopo ch'haurà havuta la relatione da i suoi: et crederò io che quando le SS. VV. Ill. Ill^{me} desiderino che la cosa vada inanzi, che Monsr suo zio non mancarà di servirle...

(See also Paleotti's letter of the same date to Duke Guglielmo Gonzaga, also in ASM (AG) 1161.)

71   ASM (AG) 1161. Letter of Cardinal Cesi, Bologna 11 March 1581, to Duke Guglielmo Gonzaga

Havendo visto quello che mi scrive V. Alt^a per la sua delli iij del presente et inteso quanto mi ha esposto il mandato da lei, che me l'ha resa, ho mandato a chiamare il Primicerio Bovio, zio della giovane, che desidera V. Alt^a al servitio della S^{ra} Principessa sua nuora...

(See also Cardinal Paleotti's letter of the same date to the Duke of Parma, also in ASM (AG) 1161.)

72   ASM (AG) 1161. Letter of Federico Pendaso, Bologna 27 March 1581, to Aurelio Pompanazzi

La figliola al presente è nelle monache di S. Lorenzo dove nelli ufficij di questa settimana è concorso molto popolo per udirla a cantare et sonare. Mons. Bovio, raggionnando meco li giorni passati mi disse, che se bene si riputava a grandissima gratia che S.A. Ser^{ma} si fosse degnata di chiedere questa figliola a servizzio tanto principale et honorato...

(See also Pendaso's two letters of 21 March 1581 to Pompanazzi, also in ASM (AG) 1161.)

73   ASM (AG) 2213. Minute della cancelleria. Minute from Teodoro San Giorgio, Montiggiana 11 July 1582, to Pirro Malvezzi

Desidera sommamente il S^r mio Ser^{mo} d'havere al suo servitio un figliuolo di M^{ro} Leonardo Maria dal Leuto il quale l'Al. S. è informata che sona benissimo, perciò confidando molto nell'amorevolezza di V.S. Illma m'ha comandato ch'io la preghi colla presente in nome dell'Alt^a sua a volere interponere l'autorità sua perchè questo figliuolo venga a servirla, assicurandola che sarà trattato benissimo, et che l'Al. S. non mancherà fra l'altre cose di aiutarlo acciò ch'egli impari et gionga alla perfetione della sua professione della musica... M^{ro} Filippo Maria Perabovi cantore dell'Alt^a S., il quale viene da lei mandato per questo effetto. Havendo l'Al. S. musichi eccellentissimi che già hanno tirato avanti degli altri, com'è stato M^{ro} Francesco [Rovigo] ch'è riuscito tanto raro nel sonare dell'organo; et se forse il padre di questo giovine si sgomentasse dal sapere che quelli che sonavano di trombone partirono de qui perché erano poco adoperati et che la Mezovillana se ne sia partita parimente, si può risponderle che quelli facevano una musica strepitosa che non diletta per l'ordinario a S. Alt^a et essendo in molti non tornava commodo il menarli intorno, come sarà di questo giovine che può sonar lui solo, et quanto alla Mezovillana non si crede che si possi lamentare che non sia stata ben trattata, et s'ella è partita è stato perchè la Ser^{ma} S^{ra} Prencipessa per servitio della quale fu presa, non s'è dilettata della musica come si credeva...

74   ASM (AG) 2955 lib. 391. *Copialettera* of Prince Vincenzo Gonzaga, Poggio 6 November 1584, to Giaches de Wert

Musico mio carissimo. Mi farete servitio gratissimo mandandomi quanto prima una copia della musica fatta da voi sopra le stanze del Tasso che cominciano Qual musico gentil ch'al canto snodi et amo qualche altro madrigale novo de' vostri se ne havete, et quanto maggior sarà il numero delle compositioni vostre che m'inviarete, più ve ne resterò obligato per mostrarmevi grato in qual si voglia nostre occasione. Intanto conservatevi sano...

75   ASM (AG) Raccolta d'autografi 10. Letter of Giaches de Wert, Mantua 15 November 1584, to Prince Vincenzo Gonzaga – see Figure 11

Mando a V.S. le stanze del Tasso con alcune altre compositioni mie come s'è degnata comandarmi et poi chè mi favoriscie tanto in volerse servire delle opere mie, non mancarò di mandarne a V.A. non essendo cosa in questo mondo ch'io non facessi per lei; che la voglio non solo reverire et servire ma adorare per l'Idolo mio che così son obligato per li molti favori ricevuti da l'Altezza nostra alla quale con ogni reverenza basio le Ser^{me} mani...

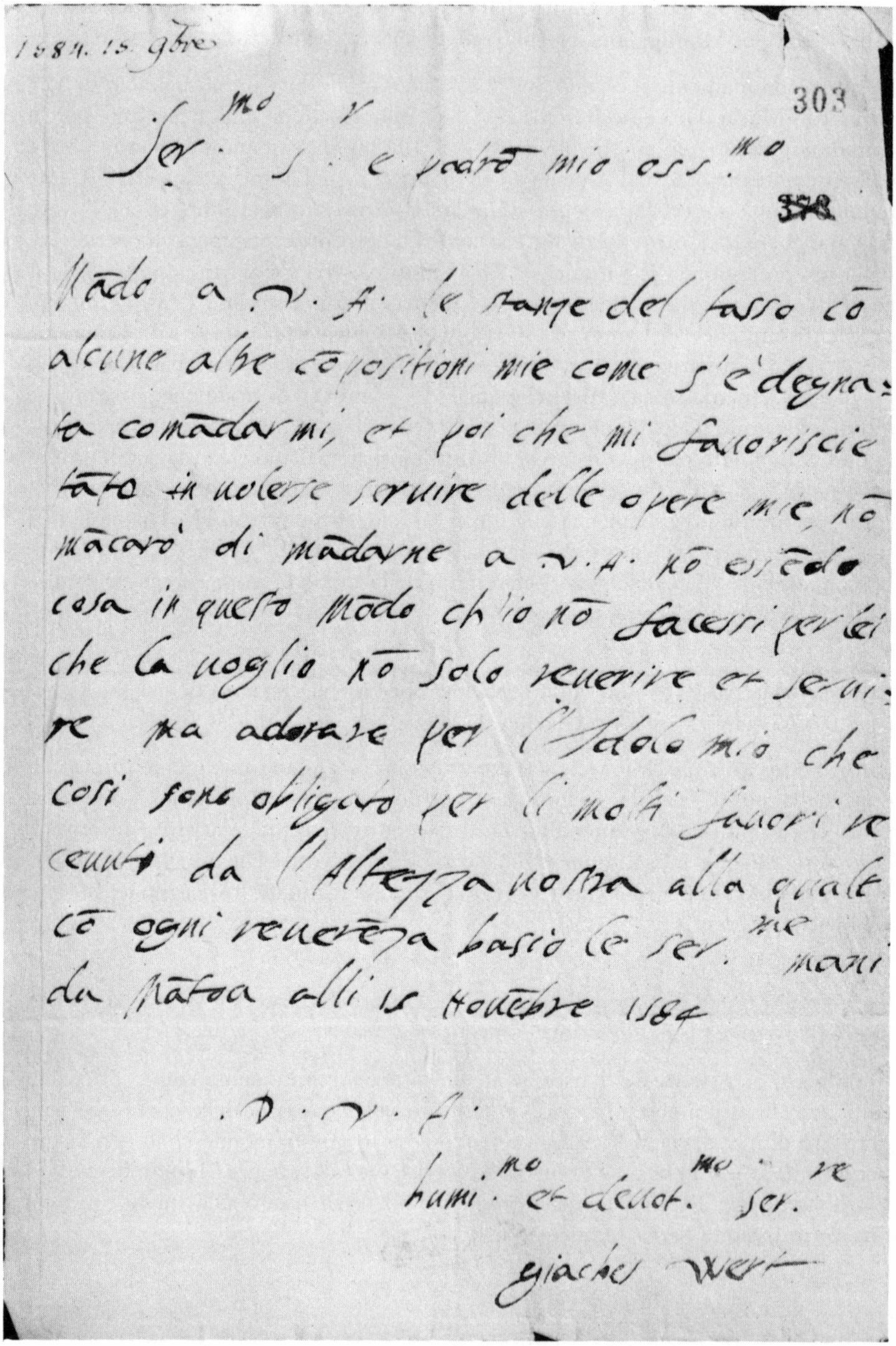

1584. 15 9bre

303

378

Ser.mo S.r e padre mio oss.mo

Mãdo a V. A. le stanze del tasso cõ
alcune altre cõpositioni mie come s'è degna=
ta comãdarmi, et poi che mi favorisce
tãto in volerse servire delle opere mie, nõ
mãcarò di mãdarne a V. A. nõ essẽdo
cosa in questo modo ch'io nõ facessi per lei
che la voglio nõ solo reverire et servi=
re ma adorare per l'Idolo mio che
così sono obligato per li molti favori re=
ceuti da l'Altezza vostra alla quale
cõ ogni reverẽza basio le ser.me mani
da Mãtoa alli 15 Novebre 1584

D. V. A.

humi.mo et devot.mo ser.re

giaches Wert

Fig. 11 Letter of Giaches de Wert, Mantua 15 November 1584, to Prince Vincenzo Gonzaga (Appendix II, doc. 75) (photo: Giovetti, Mantua)

76   ASM (AG) 2654. Letter of Annibale Chieppio, Mantua 23 December 1591, to Duke Vincenzo Gonzaga

Gionse giovedi il Sr Cav. Guarino, et fatti congregare la sera questi giovani che essercitano la sua Tragicomedia, gliela feci sentire poco meno che tutta intiera, onde restò egli in pensiero che se ne potesse sperare qualche buona riuscita, eccettuate le parti di Titiro et di Uranio, che tengono il Cipada et il Spigo, delle quali dubito assai, mancando in essi le qualità naturali et principali della presenza et della voce, che con l'arte non possono ristorarsi, et perciò si procurano soggetti per mutarli in meglio, et sodisfarlo se si potrà. Dell'Amarillide non si è fatta anchora deliberatione certa, per l'incredibile scarsezza di giovani a proposito, rispetto alla bellezza, affetto et leggiadria di quella parte: ma in ogni caso si scieglierà tosto, de' tre che l'hanno imparata, il meno difettoso degli altri. Il Balletto della Cieca ci da che fare, perchè di quelli che lo provarono già, come intendo, alla presenza di V.A., alcuni mancano, alcuni sono infermi, et alcuni si sono resi per un pezzo cosi ostinati in non volervi intervenire, che dopo l'assenza d'Isachino di parecchi giorni, è convenuto tornar da capo, e la difficoltà s'è ritrovata maggiore, nell'interdurlo con garbo nella Tragicomedia, in quattro parti oltre l'uscita et tutte varie, si come sono quattro i madrigali che si dovrebbono cantare con inserirvi dentro i ragionamenti di Amarillide, di Mirtillo et di Corisca, che con molto difficile rappresentatione intervengono nella med^{ma} scena...

77   Giovanni Battista Guarini: *Il pastor fido, tragicommedia pastorale*, fos. 91–91v

L'ordine, & fine di questo giuoco è tale, che la ciecca, ciò è quella, che ha bendati gli occhi, vien per cosa da tutte l'altre, la quali sono sbendate; & ella fà pruova di prender alcuna di loro; & prendendola, quella presa è ubbligata à bendarsi gli occhi, ed esser la cieca anch'ella: Il che tutto si manifesta nel progresso del giuoco stesso, il quale si bene rappresentato, che chiunque non l'havesse mai veduto, quinci l'imparebbe. Ma bisogna avvertire, che tutti i moti, che sogliono esser in cotal giuoco inordinati, & casuali, in questo della Scena sono studiati con numero, & armonia: in modo che non è meno ballo, che giuoco. Il quale imita il costume antico de' greci, & anche i Latini; si come chiaramente dimostra Luciano in quel suo bellissimo trattato del'arte saltatoria, con la quale i professori loro saltando, & gesticolando facevano miracoli nell'esprimere qual si voglia grande, & malagevole impresa, ed attione humana si vivamente, che non v'era niuno degli spettatori, che non intendesse quella muta favella, & di moti, & di gesti di colui, che saltava. Nel che bisogna sapere, che questo Choro non cantava: ma si moveva, come color, che ballano secondo le leggi, e'l tempo di quel suono, che faceva la musica invisibile dietro al palco: imitando pur anche in cio l'uso antico descritto dal medesimo Luciano, il qual dice, che anticamente, ciò è molto prima die tempi suoi, i saltatori in un medesimo tempo cantavano, & saltavano. Ma percioche era troppa fatica, & male potevano far l'uno, & l'altro, ordinarono i sonatori, ò cantatori, come hoggi si fà ne' balli, che fossero separati da i saltatori; i quali alle regole di quel canto, saltavano. Ne mi par di tacere il modo, con che il poeta nostro compose le parole di questo ballo, che fù così. Prima fece compore il ballo à un perito di tale esercitio;

divisandogli il modo dell'imitare i moti, e i gesti, che si sogliono fare nel giuoco della cieca molto ordinario. Fatto il ballo fù messo in musica dà Luzzasco eccellentissimo musico de' nostri tempi. Indi sotto le note di quella musica, il poeta fe le parole, il che cagionò la diversità de i versi, hora di cinque sillabe, hora di sette, hora di otto, hora di undeci, secondo che gli conveniva servire alla necessità delle note. Cosa, che pareva impossibile: & se egli non l'havesse fata, molte altre volte con tanta maggiore difficoltà, quant'egli negl'altri balli non era padrone dell'inventione, come fù in questa, non si sarebbe forse creduto. Percioche in detti balli non haveva una sola fatica di metter le parole sotto le note; ma di trovar da i movimenti del ballo inventione, che gli quadrasse, & havesse viso di favola; ciò è principio, mezzo, & fine: traendola dalla confusa, causale, & inconsiderata maniera del maestro del ballo, si come si può vedere nelle parole di detti balli, fatte da lui nella Città di Ferrara per ubbidire all'hora à quel Duca suo signor naturale. . .

78   ASM (AG) 1514. Letter of Giovanni Battista Guarini, Padua 7 April 1584, to Prince Vincenzo Gonzaga

V.A. favorisce troppo le cose mie, et dico troppo, et perchè la mia fortuna non vuole ch'io possa goder del favore ch'ella mi fa. Scrissi già un'altra volta, pur in risposta d'una sua lett^a della med^{ma} instanza, che la mia Tragicomedia Pastorale per mia somma disgratia non poteva esser all'ordine a pena per tutto questo anno, se ben il desiderio mio sarebbe stato di finirla quanto prima, per poterne servire l'A.V., la quale saprà che dopo ch'io son qui, non ci ho potuto mai metter mano, et manca ancora tutto il quinto atto e tutti i chori, e io son di cosi fatta natura nel poetare, che s'io non ho tutto il cervello ben riposato, non posso far verso che mi compiaccia massimamente in poema cominciato da me con molto sottile et esquisito gusto, intanto che ho pensato tre anni a farne li quattro atti che son in essere, et in essi ancora mancano alcune cose di qualche importanza. Ma tutto che l'opera fosse compitissima, credami certo l'A.V. che non si metterebbe all'ordine in tre mesi: et questo perchè, oltre l'esser di molte et lunghe parti dal primo atto infuori, et tutta piena di novità et di grandissimi movimenti, i quali vogliono essere concertati, et con lungo studio provati e riprovati in scena, et massimamente un giuoco, che va nel terzo atto ridotto in forma di ballo, fatto da un choro di Ninfe, et questo è ancora nelle mani di Leone nè la musica è fatta, et tanto men le parole. . .

Appendix III. The Santa Barbara Library

Most of the music collection from Santa Barbara is now in Milan and has been described in a detailed published catalogue.[1] It seems almost certain, as is suggested at a number of places in this study, that the Milan collection contains the repertory for successive Gonzaga chapels beginning with Marchese Francesco's foundation, and the following list of printed polyphony from the collection shows quite distinct shifts of taste which mirror the main stages of the chapel's development. Regrettably, it has not been possible to examine the manuscripts in the collection and include them in the list because of the unhelpful attitude of the former director of the library at an early stage, and the closure of the library due to severe administrative problems at a later one. Payments for copying, re-copying, and binding some of the Santa Barbara manuscripts survive in Mantua,[2] and it should be possible to date some sources quite exactly by examining their physical structure and contents in the light of the documents, though it is doubtful whether addition of the manuscripts to the present list would greatly alter the impression conveyed by the printed polyphony alone. In addition to those at Milan, manuscripts at Casale, Mantua, and Udine are associated with Santa Barbara in that they were copied by the Basilica's principal scribe at the end of the sixteenth century and during the first decades of the seventeenth, Francesco Sforza.[3] The Casale manuscript, copied in 1594, was compiled for presentation to the Bishop of Casale Monferrato, and the Mantuan source, dated 1616, was prepared as a gift for Francesco Gonzaga, Bishop of Mantua, whose patronage of the arts during his episcopacy almost rivalled the example of Cardinal Ercole Gonzaga. Cesare Gonzaga, another member of the Guastallan branch of the family whose strong tradition of musical and literary interests is described briefly elsewhere, was the recipient of the Udine manuscript, written in

---

[1] See *Conservatorio di musica*, which must be used in the light of Oscar Mischiati's review of the book. Mischiati also provides a useful table cross-referencing the old Santa Barbara shelf-marks to the new catalogue numbers.

[2] ASDM (SB) Filcia LXXVII. Mandati di spesa del 1579 et 1580, and Miscellanea secoli XVI–XVIII, both including payments for paper, copying, and binding. Compositions are often named, composers specified, and the quantity of paper specified. The name most frequently mentioned in the period before Francesco Sforza's activity is that of Giuseppe Vicentini, concerning whom see also p. 104 above.

[3] See MacClintock: 'New sources of Mantuan music', Crawford: 'The Francesco Sforza manuscript', and *Conservatorio di musica*, pp. xxx–xxxiii. MacClintock's view that Sforza can be identified with the Marchese di Varzi (1562–1624) is queried by Crawford. It can also be discounted since Sforza's ecclesiastical career, which patently establishes him as a different person, can be constructed from material in ASDM (SB). See, for example, the documents cited in note 2 above and, in the same archive, Fortunato Bresciani: 'Stato del clero e necrologia del R° Capitolo Palatino di S. Barbara dalla sua fondazione', a MS dated 1901.

1622.[4] All three sources emphasise once again the strength of the familial system in artistic matters.

In addition to the polyphonic codex copied by Sforza, a small group of printed liturgical books from Santa Barbara also survives in Mantua. This collection has not been described in print, and some of the books are not recorded elsewhere.[5] Those published before 1600 are noted here, and assuming these to reflect contemporary practice it would seem that on some liturgical occasions the Roman rite was practised at the Basilica. The chant repertory of the Santa Barbara rite itself survives in a numbered series of codices in Mantua, and the contents of each manuscript are described in summary form in section (iii) of the appendix. Some of these sources were undoubtedly copied after 1600, but since they transmit a fixed rite they are included to provide a more complete account of the Santa Barbara liturgy. In addition to the numbered volumes there are some unnumbered choirbooks; these generally duplicate chants from the numbered books, but it is worth noting that they include a Processional and chants for the Office for the Dead. Apart from these large volumes in choirbook format, there are also four small-format volumes containing chant, all written and then finely decorated in coloured inks by Sforza or by a scribe close to him. These, listed in section (iv), were presumably for use by the officiating clergy. (In listing these chant books I have indicated the liturgical category where necessary, thus: [M] for Missal and [B] for Breviary.)

(i)

Josquin des Pres: *Liber primus missarum* (Venice, Petrucci 1502)
Obrecht, Jacob: *Misse obrecht* (Venice, Petrucci 1503)
Brumel, Antoine: *Missae* (Venice, Petrucci 1503)
La Rue, Pierre de: *Misse* (Venice, Petrucci 1503)
Orto, Marbriano de: *Misse* (Venice, Petrucci 1505)
Moteti libro quarto (Petrucci 1505)
Josquin des Pres: *Missarum...liber secundus* (Venice, Petrucci 1505)
Isaac, Heinrich: *Misse* (Venice, Petrucci 1506)
Weerbecke, Gaspar van: *Misse* (Venice, Petrucci 1507)
Missarum diversorum auctorum liber primus (Venice, Petrucci 1508)
Liber primus...motetos complectitur (Paris, Attaignant 1534)
Liber secundus...motetos (Paris, Attaignant 1534)
Liber tertius...motetos (Paris, Attaignant 1534)
Liber quartus...modulos (Paris, Attaignant 1534)
Liber sextus...magnificat continet (Paris, Attaignant 1534)
Liber septimus...modulos (Paris, Attaignant 1534)
Liber octavus...motetos (Paris, Attaignant 1534)
Liber nonus...daviticos musicales psalmos (Paris, attaignant 1535)
Liber decimus...passiones (Paris, Attaignant 1535)
Liber undecimus...modulos (Paris, Attaignant 1535)
Liber duodecimus...ad virginem christiparam salutationes (Paris, Attaignant 1535)
Tomus primus psalmorum selectorum (Nuremburg, Petreius 1538)

[4] For both Bishop Francesco Gonzaga, and the traditions of patronage practised by members of the Guastallan branch of the Gonzaga, see pp. 59 and 34ff respectively.
[5] For other recorded copies of various editions of the Santa Barbara Breviary see Bohatta: *Bibliographie*, nos. 2404–6.

Tomus secundus psalmorum selectorum (Nuremburg, Petreius 1538)

Ruffo, Vincenzo: *Il primo libro de motetti* (Milan, Castiglione 1542) – two copies

Jachet da Mantoa: *Motecta...liber primus* (Venice, Scotto 1544)

Morales, Cristóbal de: *Missarum liber primus* (Rome, Dorico 1544)

Concentus octo, sex, quinque & quatuor vocum (Augsburg, Ulhard 1545)

Cantiones, septem, sex et quinque vocum (Augsburg, Kriesstein 1545)

Selectissimae symphoniae (Nuremburg, Montanus and Neuber)

Othmayr, Kaspar: *Epitaphium D. Martini Lutheri* (Nuremburg, Montanus and Neuber 1546)

Quinque missarum (Venice, Gardane 1547)

Bartholomeus, Conte: *Motetta quinque vocibus* (Venice, Gardane 1547)

Primo libro de motetti a cinque voci (Venice, Scotto 1549)

Excellentissimorum autorum diverse modulationes (Venice, Scotto 1549)

Gombert, Nicolas: *Liber secundus cum quinque vocibus* (Venice, Gardane 1552)

Carli, Girolamo: *Motetti del laberinto* (Venice, Scotto 1554)

Jachet da Mantoa: *Il primo libro de le messe* (Venice, Scotto 1554)

Phinot, Dominique: *Liber secundus mutetarum* (Venice, Gardane 1555)

Canticum Beatae Mariae Virginis (Paris, Le Roy and Ballard 1557)

Contino, Giovanni: *Modulationum [5vv.]...liber primus* (Venice, Scotto 1560)

Contino, Giovanni: *Modulationum...liber secundus* (Venice, Scotto 1560)

Contino, Giovanni: *Modulationum [6vv.]...liber primus* (Venice, Scotto 1560)

Kerle, Jacob: *Hymni totius anni* (Rome, Barrè 1560)

Jachet da Mantoa: *Messe del fiore...libro primo* (Venice, Scotto 1561) – two copies

Jachet de Mantoa: *Messe del fiore...libro secondo* (Venice, Scotto 1561)

Magnificat omnitonum cum quatuor vocibus (Venice, Gardane 1562)

Rinaldo da Montagnana: *Il primo libro di motetti* (Venice, Gardane 1563)

Gabrieli, Andrea: *Sacrae cantiones* (Venice, Gardane 1565)

Jachet da Mantoa: *Motetti...libro primo* (Venice, Scotto 1565)

Jachet da Mantoa: *Motetti...libro secondo* (Venice, Scotto 1565)

Ortiz, Diego: *Liber primus himnos, magnificas* [etc.] (Venice, Gardane 1565)

Jachet da Mantoa: *Himni vesperorum totius anni* (Venice, Scotto 1566)

Palestrina, Giovanni Pierluigi da: *Missarum liber secundus* (Rome, Dorico 1567)

Novi thesauri musici liber primus (Venice, Gardane 1568)

Portinaro, Francesco: *Il secondo libro de motteti* (Venice, Gardane 1568)

Isnardi, Paolo: *Psalmi omnes ad vesperas per totum annum* (Venice, Gardane 1569)

Lasso, Orlando di: *Sacrae cantiones...liber primus* (Venice, Gardane 1569)

Lasso, Orlando di: *Sacrae cantiones...liber tertius* (Venice, Gardane 1569)

Lasso, Orlando di: *Sacrae cantiones...liber quartus* (Venice, Gardane 1569)

Lasso, Orlando di: *Sacrae cantiones...liber quintus* (Venice, Gardane 1569)

Monte, Philippe de: *Il secondo libro delli madrigali a sei voci* (Venice, Scotto 1569)

Palestrina, Giovanni Pierluigi da: *Missarum liber tertius* (Rome, Dorico 1570)

Contino, Giovanni: *Magnificat...liber primus* (Ferrara, Rubeo 1571)

Lasso, Orlando di: *Sacrae cantiones...liber secundus* (Venice, Gardane 1566 (c.b.); 1572 (a.t.q.))

Palestrina, Giovanni Pierluigi da: *Missarum liber primus* (Rome, Dorico 1572)

Palestrina, Giovanni Pierluigi da: *Motettorum...liber secundus* (Venice, Scotto 1572) – two copies

Contino, Giovanni: *Missae cum quinque vocibus liber primus* (Milan, Pontio 1572 (c.); 1573 (A.T.B.Q.))

Morales, Cristóbal de: *Magnificat...cum quatuor vocibus* (Venice, Gardane 1575)

Palestrina, Giovanni Pierluigi da: *Motettorum...liber tertius* (Venice, Scotto 1575)

Merulo, Claudio: *Liber secundus sacrarum cantionum* (Venice, Gardane 1578)

Cavaccio, Giovanni: *Missae* (Venice, Gardane 1580)

Victoria, Tomás Luis de: *Hymni totius anni* (Rome, Basa 1581)

Victoria, Tomás Luis de: *Cantica Beatae Virginis* (Rome, Basa 1581)

Wert, Giaches de: *Il secondo libro de motetti* (Venice, Scotto 1581)

Wert, Giaches de: *Modulationum...liber primus* (Venice, Scotto 1581)

Asola, Giovanni Matteo: *Psalmodia ad vespertinas* (Venice, Scotto 1582)

[Gonzaga, Guglielmo]: *Sacrae cantiones quinque vocum* (Venice, Gardane 1583)

Victoria, Tomás Luis de: *Motecta festorum totius anni* (Rome, Basa 1585)

Asola, Giovanni Matteo: *Missae...primo libro* (Venice, Vincenti and Amadino 1586)

Asola, Giovanni Matteo: *Secundus liber...missae* (Venice, Vincenti and Amadino 1586)

Cavaccio, Giovanni: *Litanie...a doi chori* (Venice, Gardane 1587)

Baccusi, Ippolito: *Il primo libro delle messe* (Venice, Gardane 1588)

Baccusi, Ippolito: *Missarum...liber secundus* (Venice, Vincenti and Amadino 1585 (c.a.t.b.q.); 1588 (s.))

Bacchini, Giovanni Maria: *Missarum...liber primus* (Venice, Amadino 1589)

Baccusi, Ippolito: *Missarum...liber tertius* (Venice, Amadino 1589)

Ingegneri, Marco Antonio: *Liber sacrarum cantionum* (Venice, Gardane 1589)

Palestrina, Giovanni Pierluigi da: *Missarum...liber primus* (Venice, Vincenti 1590)

Ingegneri, Marco Antonio: *Sacrae cantiones...liber primus* (Venice, Gardane 1591)

Palestrina, Giovanni Pierluigi da: *Magnificat octo tonum* (Venice, Gardane 1591)

Palestrina, Giovanni Pierluigi da: *Missarum...liber quintus* (Venice, Scotto 1591)

Psalmodia vespertina...quinque vocibus (Venice, Amadino 1592)

Massaino, Tiburzio: *Sacri modulorum concentus* (Venice, Gardane 1592)

Asola, Giovanni Matteo: *Vespertina psalmodia...sex vocibus* (Venice, Amadino 1593)

Baccusi, Ippolito: *Missarum...liber quartus* (Venice, Gardane 1593)

Gastoldi, Giovanni Giacomo: *Vespertina psalmodia* (Venice, Amadino 1593)

Alberti, Innocenzo: *Motteti à sei voci...libro secondo* (Ferrara, Baldini 1594)

Croce, Giovanni: *Motetti a otto voci* (Venice, Vincenti 1594)

Palestrina, Giovanni Pierluigi da: *Missarum...liber tertius* (Venice, Gardane 1594)

Palestrina, Giovanni Pierluigi da: *Missae...liber septimus* (Rome, Coattino 1594)

Palestrina, Giovanni Pierluigi da: *Offertoria totius anni...pars prima* (Venice, Gardane 1594)

Cortellini, Camillo: *Salmi a sei voci* (Venice, Vincenti 1595)

Baccusi, Ippolito: *Missae...octo vocibus* (Venice, Amadino 1596)

Palestrina, Giovanni Pierluigi da: *Missarum...liber sextus* (Venice, Gardane 1596)

Palestrina, Giovanni Pierluigi da: *Offertoria totius anni...pars secuna* (Venice, Gardane 1596)

Baccusi, Ippolito: *Psalmi...cum duobus magnificat...octo vocibus* (Venice, Amadino 1597)

Gastoldi, Giovanni Giacomo: *Magnificat per omnes tonos* (Venice, Amadino 1597)

Gastoldi, Giovanni Giacomo: *Completorium...quaternis vocibus liber secundus* (Venice, Amadino 1597)

Massaino, Tiburzio: *Tertius liber missarum* (Venice, Amadino 1598)

Palestrina, Giovanni Pierluigi da: *Missarum...liber secundus* (Venice, Gardane 1598)

Rogier, Philippe: *Missae* (Madrid, Royal Printing House 1598)

Palestrina, Giovanni Pierluigi da: *Missarum liber octavus* (Venice, Scotto 1599)

Palestrina, Giovanni Pierluigi da: *Missarum...liber nonus* (Venice, Scotto 1599)

Croce, Giovanni: *Messe a otto voci* (Venice, Vincenti 1600)

Gastoldi, Giovanni Giacomo: *Messe a cinque et a otto...libro primo* (Venice, Amadino 1600)

Gastoldi, Giovanni Giacomo: *Vespertina psalmodia...editio secunda* (Venice, Amadino 1600)

Lappi, Pietro: *Vespertina psalmodia...octonis vocibus* (Venice, Gardane 1600)

Massaino, Tiburzio: *Missarum octonis vocibus liber primus* (Venice, Amadino 1600)

Palestrina, Giovanni Pierluigi da: *Missarum...liber decimus* (Venice, Scotto 1600)

Viadana, Lodovico: *Officium defunctorum* (Venice, Vincenti 1600)

Gastoldi, Giovanni Giacomo: *Tutti li salmi...a otto voci* (Venice, Amadino 1601)

Palestrina, Giovanni Pierluigi da: *Missae quattuor octonis vocibus* (Venice, Amadino 1601)

Palestrina, Giovanni Pierluigi da: *Motectorum...liber quartus* (Venice, Gardane 1601)

Lappi, Pietro: *Missarum octonis vocibus liber primus* (Venice, Gardane 1601, except for B.c. dated 1602)

Baccusi, Ippolito: *Psalmi...quinque vocibus* (Venice, Amadino 1602)

Gastoldi, Giovanni Giacomo: *[Missae]* (Venice, Amadino 1602) – two copies

Gastoldi, Giovanni Giacomo: *Vespertina omnium solemnitatem psalmodia* (Venice, Amadino 1602)

Pallavicino, Benedetto: *Liber primus missarum* (Venice, Amadino 1603)

Vecchi, Orfeo: *Magnificat...liber primus* (Milan, Tradate 1603)

De Lorenzi, Lorenzo: *Sacrae cantiones...liber primus* (Venice, Amadino 1604)

Lasso, Orlando di: *Magnum opus musicum* (Munich, Hienrich 1604)

Serra, Michelangelo: *Missae...liber primus* (Venice, Vincenti 1604)

Croce, Giovanni: *Motetti a otto voci...libro secondo* (Venice, Vincenti 1605)

Pallavicino, Benedetto: *Sacrae dei laudes* (Venice, Amadino 1605)

Agazzari, Agostino: *Sacrae cantiones...liber quartus* (Venice, Amadino 1606)

Massaino, Tiburzio: *Sacrae modulorum* (Venice, Gardane 1606)

Viadana, Lodovico: *Completorium...liber secundus* (Venice, Vincenti 1606)

Cortellini, Camillo: *Magnificat a sei voci* (Venice, Vincenti 1607)

Gastoldi, Giovanni Giacomo: *Messe et motetti a otto voci...libro primo* (Venice, Amadino 1607)

Gastoldi, Giovanni Giacomo: *Salmi intieri...libro secondo* (Venice, Amadino 1607)

Lappi, Pietro: *La terza...a otto voci* (Venice, Raverii 1607)

Lappi, Pietro: *Missarum...liber secundus* (Venice, Raverii 1608)

(ii)

BREVIARII / S. BARBARAE / GREGORII XIII. PONT. MAX. / Auctoritate approbati. / Pars Prima. (Secunda) / A Prima Domenica Aduentus vsque ad Festum

Sanctissimae Trinitatis. (A Festo Sanctissimae Trinitatis, vsque ad / Primam Domenicam Aduentus.) / [Device] / VENETIIS, APVD IVNTAS. / M D LXXXIII.
Volume ɪ: [xvi] + 276 fos.
Volume ɪɪ: [xv] + 255 fos.

BREVIARII / S. BARBARAE / GREGORII XIII. PONT. MAX. / Auctoritate approbati. / PARS PRIMA. (SECVNDA) / A prima Domenica Adventus vsque ad Festum / Sanctissimae Trinitatis. (A Festo Sanctissimae Trinitatis vsque ad primam / Domenicam Aduentus.) / [Gonzaga arms] / MANTVAE, M D LXXXV. / Ex Officina Francisci Osanae.
Volume ɪ: [xii] + 288 fos.
Volume ɪɪ: [xii] + 239 + i fos.

BREVIARII / S. BARBARAE / GREGORII XIII. PONT. MAX. / Auctoritate approbati. / Pars Prima. (Secunda.) / A prima Domenica Aduentus vsque ad Festum / Sanctissimae Trinitatis. (A Festo Sanctissimae Trinitatis vsque ad primam / Domenicam Aduentus.) / [Device] / VENETIIS, M D LXXXIII. / Apud Dominicum Nicolinum.
Volume ɪ: [xii] + 228 fos.
Volume ɪɪ: [xii] + 190 fos.

MISSALE / S. BARBARAE / GREGORII XIII. PONT. MAX. / AVCTORI-TATE APPROBATVM. / [Device] / VENETIIS, / Apud Ioan Antonium Rampazzetum. / M D LXXXIII.

MARTYROLOGIVM / ROMANVM / AD NOVAM KALENDARII RAT-IONEM, / Et Ecclesiasticae historiae veritatem restitutum. / GREGORII XIII. PONT. MAX / IVSSV EDITVM. / ACCESSERVNT NOTATIONES / Atque Tractatio de Martyrologio Romano. / AVCTORE CAESARE BARONIO SORANO / Congregationis Oratorij Presbytero. / [Papal arms] / CVM PRIVI-LEGIO, ET PERMISSV SVPERIORVM. / ROMAE / Ex Typographia Dominici Basae. M D LXXXVI.

VERBA EVANGELISTAE. / CANTVS ECCLESIASTICVS / PASSIONIS DOMINI NOSTRI / IESV CHRISTI, / Secundum Matthaeum, Marcum, Lucam, / & Ioannem. / IVXTA RITVM CAPELLAE. S. D. N. PAPAE, / ac Sacrosanctae Basilicae Vaticanae. / A IOANNE GVIDETTO BONONIENSI, / eiusdem Basilicae Clerico Beneficiato in tres Libros diuisus, / & diligenti adhibita castigatione, pro aliarum Ecclesiarum commoditate Typis datus. / LIBER PRIMVS. / [Device] / SVPERIORVM PERMISSV. / ROMAE / Apud Alexandrum Gardanum. 1586.

ORDO / DIVINORVM OFFICIORVM, CVM MOBILIBVS FESTIS. / QVATVOR TEMPORVM IEIVNIIS, SINGVLISQ. NVPTIARVM TEM-PORIBVS, AC LVNAE CVRSV. / Ad usum Ecclesiae Sanctae Barbarae, pro Anno Domini. M. D. X. CI.

[This last is in ASM (AG) 3296, which also preserves a calendar for 1590; a copy of the calendar for 1570 is in ASM (AG) 3295]

PONTIFICALE / ROMANVM / CLEMENTIS VIII. / PONT. MAX. / IVSSV / RESTITVTVM / ATQVE EDITVM / ROMAE, M D. XCV.
Colophon: ROMAE / Apud Iacobum Lunam. Impensis Leonardi Parasoli, / & Sociorum. M D XCV. / [Device] / EX AVCTORITATE SVPERIORVM.

(iii)

1. Kyriale ad usum ecclesie Sancte Barbare. 54 fos.
2. Proprium de tempore a Pascha usque ad Adventum. 123 fos. [M]
3. [Ad Missam ab Adventu ad Quadragesimam]. 100 fos.
4. Proprium Sanctorum...Ad Missam. 124 fos., of which four are much later additions
5. Commune Sanctorum. 112 fos., including three with later additions [M]
6. Commune quadragesime...Ad Missam. 115 fos. [M]
7. [Votive masses]. 84 fos. [M]
8. Hymnarium. 122 fos. [B]
9. [Antiphons, Hymns, Responses, Proprium Sanctorum, from December to June]. 94 fos. [B]
10. Antiphone et Hymni. 132 fos. [B]
11. [Antiphons, Hymns and Responses, Proprium Sanctorum from June to August]. 89 fos. [B]
12. Antiphonarium de tempore. A Dominica Septuagesima usque ad festum Resurrectionis Domini. 89 fos. Written by Giuseppe Vicentini and decorated by Francesco Sforza; dated 1617 [B]
13. [Antiphons, Hymns, and Responses. Proprium Sanctorum from September to November]. 86 fos. [B]
14. Antiphonarium de tempore [ab Adventu ad Dominicam sextam post Epiphaniam]. 136 fos., including one between fos. 68 and 69 written and dated 1888 [B]
15. Commune Sanctorum. [Hymns, antiphons, psalms and responses]. 94 fos. [B]
16. Sequentes Missae Feriales...de Feria ab Octava Epiphaniae usque ad Septuagesimam et ab Octava Pentecoste usque ad Adventum Domini. 55 fos. [M]
17. Ordo Psalterii: Dominica, feria secunda et tertia. 107 fos. [B]
18. [Ordo Psalterii. In Dominicis prima, tertia, sexta, nona, et vesperae; In feriis, vesperae]. 102 fos. [B]
19. [Ordo Psalterii. Feria quarta, quinta, sexta, et Sabbato.] 141 fos. [B]
20. [Ordo Psalterii. In Dominicis]. 87 fos. [B]
21. Officium Defunctorum [Hymns, antiphons, psalms, and responses]. 84 fos. [B]
[22]. [Office for Matins, Lauds and Vespers for Holy Thursday, Good Friday, and Holy Saturday]. 88 fos. [B]
[23]. [Antiphons, Hymns and Litanies for parts of Holy Week, Saints' Days, the Purification of the Virgin, and the Installation of the Abbot of Santa Barbara]. 34 fos. [M]
[24]. [Antiphons, Hymns and Litanies for parts of Holy Week, Saints' Days, the Purification of the Virgin, and the Installation of the Abbot of Santa Barbara]. 36 fos. [M]

(iv)

[i]. [Parts of the Ordinary of the Mass]. Signed and dated 1621 by Francesco Sforza. 25 fos. [M]

[ii]. [Liturgy for the Mass of Santa Barbara]. Signed and dated 1601 by Francesco Sforza. 9 fos. [M]

[iii]. [Chants for Easter, the feast of Santa Barbara, Christmas, and Pentecost]. Partly nineteenth century, and partly the work of Francesco Sforza, who dated one folio 1626. 4 fos. [M]

[iv]. [Part of the liturgy for Ash Wednesday, Psalm Sunday, and Good Friday]. Written and decorated in the style of Francesco Sforza. 20 fos. [M]

Bibliography

WORKS PRINTED BEFORE 1700

Agostini L.: *Canones, et echo sex vocibus...eiusdem dialogi, liber primus* (Venice, 1572)
L'echo, et enigmi musicali a sei voci...libro secondo (Venice, 1581)
Le lagrime del peccatore a sei voci...libro quarto. Opera XII (Venice, 1586)
Madrigali del R. Monsig. Don Lodovico Agostini Proto: Apostolico, Capellano, et Musico del Serenissimo, & Invitiss. Sig. Duca di Ferrara. Libro terzo a sei voci (Ferrara, 1582)
Il nuovo echo a cinque voci del R^{do} Mons^{or} Don Lodovico Agostini Ferrarese, Protonotario Apostolico, Capellano, & Musico del Sereniss. & Invitissimo Signor Duca di Ferrara. Libro terzo. Opera decima (Ferrara, 1583)
Allacci, L.: *Drammaturgia...divisa in sette indici* (Rome, 1666)
Andreasi, A.: *Constitutiones in diocesano synodo promulgatae anno domini MDLXXXV* (Mantua, 1586)
Aretino, P.: *Il marescalco* (Venice, 1536)
Ariosto, L.: *Orlando furioso* (Ferrara, 1516)
[Arrivabene, A.]: *I grandi apparati, le giostre, l'imprese, e i trionfi, fatti nella città di Mantova, nelle nozze dell'Illustrissimo & Eccellentissimo Signor Duca di Mantova* (Mantua, 1561)
Arrivabene, L.: *Vita del serenissimo Signor Guglielmo Gonzaga Duca di Mantoa, et di Monferrato* (Mantua, 1588)
Baccusi, H.: *Il primo libro de madrigali a cinque & a sei voci, con doi a sette & otto* (Venice, 1570)
Il quarto libro de madrigali a sei voci (Venice, 1587)
Missarum cum quinque, sex, & octo vocibus liber secundus (Venice, 1586/1588)
Baldini, V. (pub.): *Il lauro secco. Libro primo di madrigali a cinque voci di diversi autori* (Ferrara, 1582)
Il lauro verde. Madrigali a sei voci di diversi autori (Ferrara, 1583)
Beaujoyeulx, B.: *Balet comique de la Royne, faict aux nopces de Monsieur le Duc de Ioyeuse & madamoyselle de Vaudemont sa soeur* (Paris, 1582)
Belli, G.: *I furti amorosi a sei voci* (Venice, 1587)
I furti...Il secondo libro de madrigali a sei voci (Venice, 1584)
Bertolotti, B.: *Il terzo libro de madrigali a cinque voci* (Venice, 1609)
Borromeo, C.: *Instructionum fabricae et supellectilis ecclesiasticae libri duo* (Milan, 1577)
Boyleau, S.: *Madriali, a IIII, V, VI, VII, et VIII voci* (Milan, 1564)
Bozi, P. (ed.): *Novelli ardori. Primo libro de madrigali a quatro voci, di diversi eccell. auttori* (Venice, 1587)

Caccini, O.: *Madrigali et canzonette a cinque voci* (Venice, 1585)

Cantino, P.: *Il primo libro de madrigali a cinque voci* (Venice, 1585)

Carli, G.: *Il primo libro de madrigali a cinque voci* (Venice, 1567)

[Castellani, G.]: *Componimenti volgari et latini di diversi et eccellenti autori, in morte di Monsignore Hercole Gonzaga, Cardinal di Mantova, con la vita del medesimo...* (Mantua, 1564)

Cavallino, S.: *Raccolta di tutte le solennissime feste nel sponsalitio della Serenissima Gran Duchessa di Toscana fatte in Fiorenza il mese di Maggio 1589* (Rome, 1589)

Cervio, V.: *Il trinciante...ampliato et ridotto a perfettione dal Cavallier Reale Fusoritto da Narni* (Venice, 1581)

Chamaterò, H.: *Il quarto libro delli madrigali a cinque voci* (Venice, 1569)

Clerico, P.: *Li madrigali a cinque voci libro primo* (Venice, 1562)
Li madrigali a cinque voci libro secondo (Venice, 1562)

Coma, A.: *Il terzo libro de madrigali a cinque voci* (Venice, 1585)
Il quarto libro de madrigali a cinque voci (Venice, 1587)

Comanini, G.: *Oratione...nella morte del Serenissimo Signor Duca Guglielmo...* (Mantua, 1587)

Componimenti volgari et latini di diversi nella coronatione del Serenissimo Sig. Vincenzo Gonzaga Duca di Mantova (Mantua, 1587)

Cortellini, C.: *Il primo libro de' madrigali a cinque voci* (Ferrara, 1582)

Donesmondi, I.: *Cronologia d'alcune cose più notabili di Mantova* (Mantua, 1616)
Dell'istoria ecclesiastica di Mantova, vol. II (Mantua, 1616)

Dorat, J.: *Magnificentissimi spectaculi...descriptio* (Paris, 1573)

Equicola, M.: *Chronica di Mantua* (?1521)

Faa, O.: *Il primo libro di madrigali a cinque voci* (Venice, 1569)

Fabriano, G. da: *Dialogo degli errori de' pittori circa l'historia* (Camerino, 1564)

Faroni, M.: *Le due fulvie* (Venice, 1602)

Folcheri, A.: *Vita della Serenissima Eleonora...Duchessa di Mantova* (Mantua, 1598)

Follino, F.: *Compendio delle sontuose feste fatte l'anno 1608...nella città di Mantova, per le...nozze...principe D. F. Gonzaga con...Margherita di Savoia* (Mantua, 1608)
Descrittione dell'infirmità, morte et funerali del Sig....Guglielmo Gonzaga III. Duca di Mantova (Mantua, 1587)

Gabrieli, A.: *Chori in musica composti da M. Andrea Gabrieli sopra li chori della tragedia di Edippo Tiranno. Recitati in Vicenza l'anno M.D.LXXXV. Con solennissimo apparato et nouamente dati alle stampe* (Venice, 1588)

Gardane, A. (ed.): *Villotte mantovane a quattro voci* (Venice, 1583)

Gastoldi, G.: *Balletti a cinque voci con li suoi versi per cantare, sonare & ballare; con una mascherata de cacciatori a sei voci, & un concerto de pastori a otto* (Venice, 1591)
Il quarto libro de madrigali a cinque voci (Venice, 1602)

Gonzaga, E.: *Breve ricordo...delle cose spettanti alla vita de chierici, al governo delle chiese, & alla cura delle anime di questo suo vescovato di Mantova* (Mantua, 1561)
Costitutioni per il clero (Mantua, 1561)
Costitutioni per la chiesa cathedrale di Mantova (Mantua, 1558)

Gonzaga, F.: *Constitutiones et decreta facta in diocesana synodo habita Mantuae anno domini MDXCIIII* (Mantua, 1594)

[Gonzaga, G.]: *Madrigali a cinque voci* (Venice, 1583)

Sacrae cantiones quinque vocum in festis duplicibus maioribus ecclesiae Sanctae Barbarae (Venice, 1583)

Grillo, A.: *Rime* (Venice, 1599)

Grillo, G. B.: *Breve trattato di quanto successe alla maestà della regina D. Margarita d'Austria N.S. della città di Trento...sino alla città di Genova...con le particolarità del sponsalitio* (Naples, 1604)

Guarini, A.: *Varie compositioni raccolte in diverse materie* (Ferrara, 1611)

Guarini, G. B.: *Lettere* (Venice, 1593)

  Il pastor fido, tragicommedia pastorale (Venice, 1602)

Hoste da Reggio: *Primo libro de madrigali a quatro voci* (Venice, 1547)

Invito fatto a tutti li onoratiss. principi della christianità (n.p., 1571)

Isnardi, P.: *Il primo libro de madrigali a cinque voci* (Venice, 1568)

Le Roy, L.: *De l'excellence du gouvernement royal avec exhortation aux François de perseverer en iceluy* (Paris, 1575)

Lomazzo, G. P.: *Rime* (Milan, 1587)

  Trattato dell'arte de la pittura (Milan, 1584)

Luzzaschi, L.: *Madrigali di Luzzascho Luzzaschi per cantare, et sonare a uno, e doi, e tre soprani, fatti per la musica del gia Ser^{mo} Duca Alfonso d'Este* (Rome, 1601). (See also Bibliography: Works printed after 1700, Cavicchi (ed.): *Luzzasco Luzzaschi*)

Magiello, D.: *Il primo libro di madrigali a cinque voci* (Venice, 1567)

[Malvezzi, C.]: *Nono parte. Intermedii et concerti fatti per la commedia rappresentata in Firenze nelle nozze del Serenissimo Don Ferdinando Medici, e Madama Christina di Lorena, Gran Duchi di Toscana* (Venice, 1591)

Manfredi, M.: *Cento madrigali* (Mantua, 1587)

  Lettere brevissime...a chiunque habbia dilettatione, o bisogno di brievemente e puramente scriverne (Venice, 1606)

Marenzio, L.: *Motecta festorum totius anni, cum communi sanctorum quaternis vocibus...liber primus* (Venice, 1585)

  L'ottavo libro de madrigali a cinque voci (Venice, 1598)

  Il primo libro de madrigali a sei voci (Venice, 1581)

Marliani, B.: *Lettere* (Venice, 1601)

Merulo, C.: *Canzoni d'intavolatura d'organo di Claudio Merulo da Correggio a quattro voci fatte alla francese...al Serenissimo Prencipe di Parma et Piacenza il Signor Ranuccio Farnese* (Venice, 1592)

Milleville, A.: *Madrigali d'Alessandro Milleville organista dell'Altezza sereniss. di Ferrara. Libro secondo a cinque voci* (Ferrara, 1584)

Monteverdi, C.: *Il terzo libro de madrigali a cinque voci* (Venice, 1592)

Mori, A. de': *Giuoco piacevole* (Mantua, 1575)

Moro, G.: *Gli encomii musicali del Moro a quattro et a cinque voci* (Venice, 1585)

Muret, M. A.: *Hymnorum sacrorum liber, iussu Serenissimi Guglielmi, Ducis Mantuae, &c. conscriptus. Eiusdem alia quaedam Poematia* (Venice, 1586)

Musica de diversi auttori illustri per cantar et sonar in concerti a sette, otto, nove, dieci, undeci, et duodeci voci, novamente raccolta, et non più stampata. Libro primo (Venice, 1584)

Ordini della compagnia del Santissimo Corpo di Christo (Mantua, 1576)

Pallavicino, B.: *Il secondo libro de madrigali a cinque voci* (Venice, 1606)

  Il terzo libro de madrigali a cinque voci (Venice, 1585)

Il quarto libro de madrigali a cinque voci (Venice, 1588)

Il primo libro de madrigali a sei voci con alcuni a otto (Venice, 1587)

Pavoni, G.: *Delle feste celebrate nelle solennissime nozze delli serenissimi sposi, il Sig. Don. Ferdinando Medici, & la Sig. Donna Christina di Loreno Gran Duchi di Toscana . . . Alli molto illustri & miei patroni osservandiss. li Signori Giasone & Pompeo fratelli de' Vizani* (Bologna, 1589)

Pellini, G. (ed.): *Missae dominicales quinis vocibus diversorum auctorum* (Milan, 1592)

Possevino, A.: *Vita et morte della Serenissima Eleonora Arciduchessa d'Austria et Duchessa di Mantova* (Mantua, 1594)

Possevino, A. the Younger: *Gonzaga. Calci operis addita genealogia totius familiae* (Mantua, 1628 [col. 1617])

Preti, A.: *Il primo libro de madrigali a cinque voci* (Venice, 1587)

(ed.): *L'amorosa caccia de diversi eccellentissimi musici mantovani nativi a cinque voci* (Venice, 1588)

Rime di diversi nobilissimi et eccellentissimi auttori, in lode dell'illustrissima signora, la signora donna Lucretia Gonzaga Marchesana (Bologna, 1565)

[Rossi, B. de]: *Descrizione dell'apparato e degli intermedi. Fatti per la commedia rappresentata in Firenze. Nelle nozze de' Serenissimi Don Ferdinando Medici e Madama Cristina di Loreno Gran Duchi di Toscana* (Florence, 1589)

Rossi, O.: *Elogi historici de bresciani illustri* (Brescia, 1620)

Rufilo, M.: *Il primo libro de madrigali a cinque voci* (Venice, 1561)

Sabino, I.: *Il settimo libro de madrigali a cinque, et a sei voci* (Venice, 1569)

Sacco, C.: *Vita e sante attioni dell'ill'mo . . . F. Francesco Gonzaga Vescovo di Mantova* (Mantua, 1624)

Li sontuosissimi apparecchi, trionfi, e feste fatti nelle nozze della Gran Duchessa di Fiorenza . . . et la descrittione de gl'intermedi rappresentati in una comedia nobilissima recitata da gl'Intronati senesi (Florence and Ferrara, 1589)

Soriano, F.: *Il primo libro de madrigali a cinque voci* (Venice, 1581)

Striggio, A.: *Madrigali a cinque voci . . . libro primo* (Venice, 1560)

Il terzo libro de madrigali a cinque voci (Venice, 1596)

Il quarto libro de madrigali a cinque voci (Venice, 1596)

Il quinto libro de madrigali a cinque voci (Venice, 1596)

Il primo libro de madrigali a sei voci (Venice, 1560)

Tasso, T.: *La Gierusalemme liberata overo il Goffredo del Sig. Torquato Tasso* (Parma, 1581)

Tesoro delle ninfe in lode di Agnese d'Argotte del Carretto Marchese di Grana (Mantua, 1593)

Testore, G.: *Il primo libro de madrigali . . . a cinque voci* (Venice, 1566)

Thomassin, L.: *Ancienne et nouvelle discipline de l'église . . . ,* 4 vols. (Paris, 1678–81)

Toscanella, O.: *Precetti necessarii sopra diverse cose* (Venice, 1562)

Troiano, M.: *Dialoghi* (Venice, 1569)

Ulloa, A. de: *La vita del valorosissimo capitano Don Ferrante Gonzaga* (Venice, 1563)

Wert, G. de: *Il primo libro delle canzonette villanelle a cinque voci* (Venice, 1589)

Il primo libro de' madrigali a quattro voci (Venice, 1561)

Il primo libro de madrigali a cinque voci (Venice, 1558)

Il quarto libro de madrigali a cinque voci (Venice, 1567)

Il sesto libro de madrigali a cinque voci (Venice, 1577)

Il settimo libro de madrigali a cinque voci (Venice, 1581)

L'ottavo libro de madrigali a cinque voci (Venice, 1586)
Il nono libro de madrigali a cinque voci (Venice, 1588)
Il decimo libro de madrigali a cinque voci (Venice, 1591)
L'undecimo libro de madrigali a cinque voci (Venice, 1595)
Il secondo libro de motetti a cinque voci (Venice, 1581)
(See also Bibliography: Works printed after 1700, MacClintock and Bernstein (eds.): *Giaches de Wert. Opera omnia*)

WORKS PRINTED AFTER 1700

Abstracts of papers read at the forty-fourth annual meeting of the American Musicological Society...Minneapolis, Minnesota October 19–22, 1978 (n.p., n.d.)

Ademollo, A.: *La bell'Adriana ed altre virtuose del suo tempo alla corte di Mantova* (Città di Castello, 1888)

Affò, I.: *Vita di Vespasiano Gonzaga* (Parma, 1780)

Alberì, E.: *Relazioni degli ambasciatori veneti al senato, raccolte, annotate, ed edite*, 15 vols. (Florence, 1839–63)

Alberigo, G.: *I vescovi italiani al Concilio di Trento* (Florence, 1959)

Amadei, F.: *Cronaca universale della città di Mantova*, 5 vols. (Mantua, 1954–7)
Il fioretto delle croniche di Mantova...ampliato [by F. Amadei] (n.p., [1741])

Arnold, D.: *Monteverdi*, 2nd rev. edn (London, 1975)
'Monteverdi: Some colleagues and pupils' in Arnold and Fortune (eds.): *The Monteverdi companion*
'Music at the Scuola di San Rocco', *Music and letters* XL (1959), p. 229
'"Seconda pratica": A background to Monteverdi's madrigals', *Music and letters* XXXVIII (1957), p. 34
and N. Fortune: 'The man as seen through his letters' in Arnold and Fortune (eds.): *The Monteverdi companion*
and N. Fortune (eds.): *The Monteverdi companion* (London, 1968)

Askew, P.: 'The question of Fetti as fresco painter: A reattribution to Andreasi of frescoes in the Cathedral and Sant'Andrea at Mantua', *Art bulletin* L/1 (1968), p. 1

Bandello, M.: *Novelle*, 9 vols. (London and Livorno, 1791–3)

Barocchi, P.: *Trattati d'arte del cinquecento fra manierismo e contrariforma*, vols. 1– (Bari, 1960–   )

Bautier-Regnier, A.-M.: 'Jachet de Mantoue (Jacobus Collebaudi), v. 1500–1559', *Revue belge de musicologie* VI (1952), p. 101
'Jacques de Wert (1535–1596)', *Revue belge de musicologie* IV (1950), p. 40

Baxandall, M.: *Giotto and the orators. Humanist observers of painting in Italy and the discovery of pictorial composition 1350–1450* (Oxford, 1971)

Becherini, B.: *Catalogo dei manoscritti musicali della Biblioteca Nazionale di Firenze* (Kassel, 1959)

Bellonci, M.: *Segreti dei Gonzaga*, 2nd rev. edn (Venice, 1974)

Belluzzi, A. and W. Capezzali: *Il palazzo dei lucidi inganni. Palazzo Te a Mantova* (Florence, 1976)

Bendiscioli, M.: 'Finalità tradizionali e motivi nuovi in una confraternità a Mantova del terzo decennio del cinquecento' in *Problemi di vita religiosa in Italia nel cinquecento* (Padua, 1960), p. 91

Benrath, K.: *Julia Gonzaga. Ein Lebensbild aus der Geschichte der Reformation in Italien*, Schriften des Vereins für Reformationsgeschichte XVI/4 (Halle, 1900)

Bercken, E. von der: *Die Gemälde des Jacopo Tintoretto* (Munich, 1942)

Berelà, G. G. and A. Petrioli Tofani: *Feste e apparati medicei da Cosimo I a Cosimo II* (Florence, 1969)

Bertolotti, A.: 'Architetti, ingegneri, matematici in relazione coi Gonzaga signori di Mantova nei secoli XV, XVI e XVII', *Giornale ligustico di archeologia, storia e letteratura* XV (1888), p. 417

    Lettres inédits de M.-A. Muret et documents les concernants transcrits aux archives de Mantoue et de Rome (Limoges, 1886)

    Musici alla corte dei Gonzaga in Mantova dal secolo XV al XVIII. Notizie e documenti raccolti negli archivi mantovani (Milan, [1890])

Birnbaum, E.: 'Musici ebrei alla corte di Mantova dal 1542 al 1628', *Civiltà mantovana* II/9 (1967), p. 185 (rev. version by V. Colorni of 'Jüdische Musiker am Hof von Mantua von 1542–1628' in *Kalendar für Israeliten für das Jahr 5654* (Vienna, 1893))

Blackburn, B. J.: 'Josquin's chansons: Ignored and lost sources', *Journal of the American Musicological Society* XXIX (1976), p. 30

Blunt, A.: *Artistic theory in Italy, 1450–1600* (Oxford, 1940)

Bohatta, H.: *Bibliographie der Breviere 1501–1850* (Leipzig, 1937)

Bonino, M.: *Archeologia e tradizione navale tra la Romagna e il Po* (Ravenna, 1978)

Bragard, A.-M.: *Étude bio-bibliographique sur Philippe Verdelot, musicien français de la renaissance* (Brussels, 1964)

Braghirolli, W.: 'Carteggio di Isabella d'Este Gonzaga intorno ad un quadro di Giambellino', *Archivio Veneto* XIII (1877), p. 370

    Sulle manifatture di arazzi in Mantova (Mantua, 1879)

Braudel, F.: *The Mediterranean and the Mediterranean world in the age of Philip II*, trans. S. Reynolds, 2 vols. (London, 1972–3) (transl. of *La Méditerranée et le monde méditerranéen...*, 2 vols. (Paris, 1966–7))

    and F. Spooner: 'Prices in Europe from 1540 to 1750' in E. E. Rich and C. H. Wilson (eds.): *The Cambridge economic history of Europe*, IV (Cambridge, 1967), p. 378

Braun, J.: *Die christliche Altar in seiner geschichtlichen Entwicklung*, 2 vols. (Munich, 1924)

Brinton, S.: *The Gonzaga. Lords of Mantua* (London, 1927)

Brown, C. M.: '"Lo insaciabile desiderio nostro de cose antique": New documents on Isabella d'Este's collection of antiquities' in C. H. Clough (ed.): *Cultural aspects of the Italian Renaissance. Essays in honour of Paul Oskar Kristeller* (Manchester, 1976), p. 324

Brown, P. M.: *Lionardo Salviati. A critical biography* (Oxford, 1972)

Brulez, W.: 'Les routes commerciales d'Angleterre en Italie au XVIᵉ siècle' in G. Barbieri (ed.): *Studi in onore di Amintore Fanfani* (Milan, 1962), IV, p. 121

Burke, P.: *Venice and Amsterdam. A study of seventeenth-century élites* (London, 1974)

Cadioli, G.: *Descrizione delle pitture, sculture ed architetture che si osservano nella città di Mantova, e ne' suoi contorni* (Mantua, 1763)

Cairns, C.: *Domenico Bollani, Bishop of Brescia: Devotion to Church and state in the Republic of Venice in the sixteenth century* (Nieuwkoop, 1976)

Canal, P.: *Della musica in Mantova* (Venice, 1881)

Canuti, F.: *Il Perugino* (Siena, 1931)

Cappellini, C.: 'Storia e indirizzi dell'Accademia Virgiliana', *Atti e memorie dell'Accademia Virgiliana di Mantova* 1877–8, p. 199

Carnevali, L.: 'Cenni storici sull'Accademia Virgiliana', *Atti e memorie dell'Accademia Virgiliana di Mantova* 1885–6, I, p. 5

Cartwright, J.: *Isabella d'Este Marchioness of Mantua, 1474–1539*, 2 vols. (London, 1923)

Casimiri, R. *et al.*: *Le opere complete di Giovanni Pierluigi da Palestrina*, 29 vols. (Rome, 1939–61)

Cavicchi, A.: 'Lettere di musicisti ferraresi: Lodovico Agostini', *Ferrara viva* IV (1962), p. 185

'La scenografia dell'*Aminta* nella tradizione scenografica pastorale ferrarese del secolo XVI' in M. T. Muraro (ed.): *Studi sul teatro veneto fra rinascimento ed età barocca* (Florence, 1971), p. 53

'Teatro monteverdiano e tradizione teatrale ferrarese' in R. Monterosso (ed.): *Claudio Monteverdi e il suo tempo* (Verona, 1969), p. 139

(ed.): *Luzzasco Luzzaschi ferrarese (1545–1607). Madrigali per cantare e sonare a uno, due e tre soprani (1601)* (Brescia, 1965)

Cerreta, F.: *Alessandro Piccolomini letterato e filosofo senese del '500* (Siena, 1960)

Chambers, D. S.: *Patrons and artists in the Italian Renaissance* (London, 1970)

Chiappini, L.: *Gli Estensi* (Milan, 1967)

Cian, V.: 'Una baruffa letteraria alla corte di Mantova (1513)', *Giornale storico della letteratura italiana* VIII (1886), p. 387

Cipolla, C. M.: 'The economic decline of Italy' in Pullan (ed.): *Crisis and change*, p. 127 (transl. of 'Il declino economico dell'Italia' in *Storia dell'economia italiana* (Turin, 1953))

Colorni, V.: 'Pressito ebraico e comunità ebraiche nell'Italia centrale e settentrionale con particolare riguardo alla comunità di Mantova', *Rivista di storia del diritto italiano* VIII (1935), p. 7

Coniglio, G.: *I Gonzaga* (Milan, 1967)

Conservatorio di musica 'Giuseppe Verdi', Milano. Catalogo della biblioteca, fondi speciali 1. Musiche della cappella di S. Barbara in Mantova (Florence, 1972)

Corpus iuris canonici. Editio Lipsiensis post A. L. Richteri curas ad librorum manu scriptorum et editionis Romanae fidem recognovit et adnotatione critica instruxit, ed. E. Friedberg, 2 vols. (Leipzig, 1879–81)

Cottafavi, C.: 'Palazzo ducale di Mantova, camerini Isabelliani di castello', *Bollettino d'arte* X (1930), p. 279

Cozzi, G.: *Il doga Nicolò Contarini* (Venice and Rome, 1958)

Crawford, D.: 'The Francesco Sforza manuscript at Casale Monferrato', *Journal of the American Musicological Society* XXIV (1971), p. 457

'A review of Costanzo Festa's biography', *Journal of the American Musicological Society* XXVIII (1975), p. 102

Sixteenth-century choirbooks in the Archivio Capitolare at Casale Monferrato (n.p., 1975)

D'Accone, F.: 'The musical chapels at the Florentine Cathedral and Baptistry during the first half of the sixteenth century', *Journal of the American Musicological Society* XXIV (1971), p. 1

'The performance of sacred music in Italy during Josquin's time, *c.* 1475–1525' in Lowinsky and Blackburn (eds.): *Josquin des Prez*, p. 601

D'Ancona, A.: *Origini del teatro italiano*, 2 vols., 2nd edn (Turin, 1891)

D'Arco, C.: *Delle arti e degli artefici di Mantova*, 2 vols. (Mantua, 1857–9)

   Notizie di Isabella d'Este moglie a Francesco Gonzaga (n.p., n.d.)

   Studi statistici sulla popolazione di Mantova (Mantua, 1839)

Davari, S.: *Cenni storici intorno al tribunale della inquisizione in Mantova* (Mantua, 1973)

   Federico Gonzaga e la famiglia Paleologa del Monferrato, 1515–1533 (Genoa, 1891)

   'La musica a Mantova. Notizie biografiche di maestri di musica, cantori e suonatori presso la corte di Mantova nei secoli XV, XVI, XVII tratte dai documenti dell'Archivio Storico Gonzaga', *Rivista storica mantovana* I (1884), p. 53 (reprinted, with appendixes, by G. Ghirardini (Mantua, 1975); but citations in my notes are of the orig. edn)

   Notizie storiche intorno allo studio pubblico ed ai maestri del secolo XV e XVI che tennero scuola in Mantova, tratte dall'Archivio Storico Gonzaga di Mantova (Mantua, 1876)

Davolio, V.: *Memorie storiche della contea di Novellara, e dei Gonzaghi che vi dominarono* (Milan, 1833)

De Gaetano, A.: 'The Florentine Academy and the advancement of learning through the vernacular: The *Orti Orcellari* and the *Sacra Accademia*', *Bibliothèque d'Humanisme et Renaissance* XXX (1968), p. 19

Delle Torre, A.: *Storia dell'Accademia Platonica di Firenze* (Florence, 1902)

De Maddalena, A.: *Le finanze del ducato di Mantova all' epoca di Guglielmo Gonzaga* (Milan, 1961)

   'L'industria tessile a Mantova nel '500 e all'inizio del '600', in G. Barbieri (ed.): *Studi in onore di Amintore Fanfani* (Milan, 1962), IV, p. 607

De Nolhac, P. and A. Solerti: *Il viaggio in Italia di Enrico III, re di Francia, e le feste a Venezia, Ferrara, Mantova e Torino* (Turin, 1890)

De' Paoli, D.: *Claudio Monteverdi: Lettere, dediche e prefazione* (Rome, 1973)

Di Ricaldone, G. A.: *Annali del Monferrato (951–1708)*, 2 vols. (Villanova, Monferrato, 1972)

Disertori, B.: 'Le canzoni strumentali da sonar a quattro di Claudio Merulo', *Rivista musicale italiana* XLVII (1943), p. 305

Doni, G. B.: *Lyra Barberina* αρφιχορδος. *Accedunt eiusdem opera, pleraque nondum edita. Collegit et in lucem proferri curavit Antonius Franciscus Gorius, distributa in tomus II. absoluta studio et opera Jo. Baptistae Passeri* (Florence, 1763)

Drei, G.: *La corrispondenza del cardinale Ercole Gonzaga presidente del Concilio di Trento (1562–1563)* (Parma, 1918)

   'La politica di Pio IV e del card. E. Gonzaga', *Archivio della società romana di storia patria* 1917–18, offprint

Dunning, A.: 'Josquini antiquos', *Acta musicologica* XLI (1969), p. 111

   Die Staatsmotette 1480–1555 (Utrecht, 1970)

Einstein, A.: *The Italian madrigal*, 3 vols. (Princeton, 1949; reprinted, with additional index, 1971)

Eitner, R.: 'Jachet da Mantua und Jachet Berchem', *Monatshefte für Musikgeschichte* XXI (1889), pp. 129 and 143

Engel, H.: *Luca Marenzio* (Florence, 1956)

Engel, J. (ed.): *Grosser historischer Weltatlas*, III (Munich, 1962)

Errante, V.: '"Forse che sì, forse che no". La terza spedizione del duca Vincenzo Gonzaga in Unheria alla guerra contro il Turco (1601) studiata su documenti inediti', *Archivio storico lombardo*, ser. v, vol. xlii (1915)

Fabbri, P.: *Gusto scenico a Mantova nel tardo rinascimento* (Mantua, 1974)

Fehl, P.: 'Veronese and the Inquisition', *Gazette des Beaux-Arts* lviii (1961), p. 348

Fenlon, D.: *Heresy and obedience in Tridentine Italy. Cardinal Pole and the Counter-Reformation* (Cambridge, 1972)

Fenlon, I.: 'A supplement to Emil Vogel's *Bibliothek der gedruckten weltlichen Vocalmusik Italiens, aus den Jahren 1500–1700*', *Analecta musicologica* 15 (1975), p. 402, and 17 (1976), p. 310

— and J. Haar: 'Fonti e cronologia dei madrigali di Constanzo Festa', *Rivista italiana di musicologia* xiii (1978), p. 212

Finscher, L.: 'Der Medici-Kodex – Geschichte und Edition', *Die Musikforschung* xxx (1977), p. 468

Flanders, P.: 'The madrigals of Benedetto Pallavicino', 2 vols. (Ph.D. diss., New York University 1971)

Forster, K. W.: 'Metaphors of rule. Political ideology and history in the portraits of Cosimo I de' Medici', *Mitteilungen des Kunsthistorischen Instituts in Florenz* xv (1971), p. 65

Frey, H.-W.: 'Regesten zur päpstlichen Kapelle unter Leo X und zu seiner Privatkapelle', *Die Musikforschung* viii (1955), pp. 58, 178 and 412, and ix (1956), pp. 46 and 139

Friedensburg, W.: 'Der Briefwechsel Gasparo Contarini's mit Ercole Gonzaga nebst einem Briefe Giovanni Pietro Carafa's', *Quellen und Forschungen aus italienischen Archiven und Bibliotheken* ii (1899), p. 161

Gallico, C.: *Un canzoniere musicale italiana del cinquecento (Bologna, Conservatorio di Musica 'G. B. Martini' MS. Q21)* (Florence, 1961)

— 'Guglielmo Gonzaga signore della musica', *Nuova rivista musicale italiana* xi (1977), p. 321

— 'Monteverdi e i dazi di Viadana', *Rivista italiana di musicologia* i (1966), p. 242

— 'Vita musicale in Sant'Andrea di Mantova' in *Il Sant'Andrea di Mantova e Leon Battista Alberti* (Mantua, 1974)

Gallo, A.: *La prima rappresentazione al Teatro Olimpico, con i progetti e le relazioni dei contemporanei* (Milan, 1973)

Gandolfi, R.: 'Lettere inedite scritte da musicisti e letterati, appartenenti alla seconda metà del secolo XVI, estratte dal R. Archivio di Stato in Firenze', *Rivista musicale italiana* xx (1913), p. 527

Garbelotto, G.: 'Codici musicali della Biblioteca Capitolare di Padova', *Rivista musicale italiana* liii (1951), p. 289, and liv (1952), pp. 218 and 289

Garin, E. (ed.): *Il pensiero pedagogico dello umanesimo* (Florence, 1958)

Gaye, G.: *Carteggio inedito d'artisti dei secoli XIV. XV. XVI, pubblicato ed illustrato con documenti pure inediti*, 3 vols. (Florence, 1839–40)

Gerola, G.: 'Transmigrazione e vicende dei camerini di Isabella d'Este', *Atti e memorie della Reale Accademia Virgiliana di Mantova* xxi (1929–30), p. 253

Ghisi, F.: *Feste musicali della Firenze medicea (1480–1589)* (Florence, 1939)

Gombrich, E. H.: 'An interpretation of Mantegna's *Parnassus*', *Journal of the Warburg and Courtauld Institutes* xxvi (1963), p. 196

'The Sala dei Venti in the Palazzo del Te' in *Symbolic images. Studies in the art of the Renaissance* (London, 1972), p. 109 (revised version of article in *Journal of the Warburg and Courtauld Institutes* XIII (1950), p. 180)

Gozzi, T.: 'La basilica palatina di Santa Barbara in Mantova', *Accademia Virgiliana di Mantova, atti e memorie* XLII (Mantua, 1974), p. 3

'Lorenzo Costa il Giovane' in *Saggi e memorie di storia dell'arte* (Florence, 1976), p. 31

Grendler, P. F.: *Critics of the Italian world. Anton Francesco Doni, Nicolò Franco, & Ortensio Lando* (Madison, Wis., 1969)

Gribaudi, P.: 'Questioni di precedenza fra le corti italiane nel secolo XVI. Contributo alla storia della diplomazia italiana', *Rivista di scienze storiche* I (1904), pp. 166 and 278, and II (1905), p. 347

Guerrini, P.: 'Giovanni Contino di Brescia', *Note d'archivio* I (1924), p. 130

Gundersheimer, W. L.: *Ferrara, the style of a Renaissance despotism* (Princeton, 1973)

Guthmüller, B.: 'Ovidübersetzungen und mythologische Malerei. Bemerkungen zur Sala dei Giganti Giulio Romanos', *Mitteilungen des Kunsthistorischen Instituts in Florenz* XXI (1977), p. 35

Haar, J.: 'A madrigal falsely ascribed to Lasso', *Journal of the American Musicological Society* XXVIII (1975), p. 526

Haberl, F. X.: 'Das Archiv der Gonzaga in Mantua', *Kirchenmusikalisches Jahrbuch* I (1886), p. 40

Die römische 'Schola Cantorum' und die päpstlichen Kapellsänger bis zur Mitte des 16. Jahrhunderts (Leipzig, 1888)

Review of A. Bertolotti: *Musici alla corte dei Gonzaga*, in *Kirchenmusikalisches Jahrbuch* VI (1891), p. 114

Hartmann, A.: 'Battista Guarini and "Il pastor fido"', *Musical quarterly* XXXIX (1953), p. 415

Hartt, F.: *Giulio Romano*, 2 vols. (New Haven, 1958)

'Gonzaga symbols in the Palazzo del Te', *Journal of the Warburg and Courtauld Institutes* XIII (1950), p. 151

Hay, D.: *The Church in Italy in the fifteenth century* (Cambridge, 1977)

Heers, J.: *L'occident au XIVe et XVe siècles. Aspects économiques et sociaux* (Paris, 1963)

Heydenreich, L. H. and W. Lotz: *Architecture in Italy 1400 to 1600* (Harmondsworth, 1975)

Hollander, J.: *The untuning of the sky. Ideas of music in English poetry, 1500–1700* (Princeton, 1961)

Huber, K.: 'Die Doppelmeister des 16. Jahrhunderts: Eine methodologische Skizze' in *Festschrift zum 50. Geburtstag Adolf Sandberger* (Munich, 1918)

Hudson, R.: Review of Kirkendale, *L'Aria di Fiorenza*, in *Journal of the American Musicological Society* XXVI (1973), p. 344

Iacometti, F.: 'L'Accademia degli Intronati', *Bollettino senese di storia patria* XLVIII (1941), p. 191

Intra, G. B.: 'Nozze e funerali alla corte dei Gonzaga, 1549–1550', *Archivio storico lombardo*, ser. III, vol. V (1896), p. 381

'Una pagina della giovinezza del principe Vincenzo Gonzaga', *Archivio storico italiano*, ser. IV, vol. XVIII (1886), p. 197

Jackson, P. T.: 'The masses of Jacquet of Mantua' (Ph.D. diss., University of North Carolina 1968)

'Two descendants of Josquin's "Hercules" Mass', *Music and letters* LIX (1978), p. 188

Jacobs, C. (ed.): *Miguel de Fuenllana. Orphénica Lyra (Seville 1554)* (Oxford, 1978)

Jaffé, M.: *Rubens and Italy* (Oxford, 1977)

Jedin, H.: *A history of the Council of Trent*, trans. E. Graf, 2 vols. (London, 1957–61) (transl. of *Geschichte des Konzils von Trient*, 2 vols. (Freiburg, 1949–51))

'Das Konzil von Trient und die Reform der liturgischen Bücher', *Ephemendes liturgicae* XLIX (1945), p. 5

Papal legate at the Council of Trent, Cardinal Seripando, trans. F. C. Eckhoff (St Louis, 1947) (transl. of *Girolamo Seripando: Sein Leben und Denken in Geisteskampf des 16. Jahrhunderts*, 2 vols. (Würzburg, 1937))

'Il significato del periodo bolognese per le decisioni dogmatiche e l'opera di riforma del Concilio di Trento' in *Problemi di vita religiosa in Italia nel cinquecento* (Padua, 1960), p. 1

Jeppesen, K.: 'Pierluigi da Palestrina, Herzog Guglielmo Gonzaga, und die neugefundenen Mantovaner-Messen Palestrinas', *Acta musicologica* XXV (1953), p. 147

'The recently discovered Mantova masses of Palestrina', *Acta musicologica* XXII (1950), p. 36

Johnson, E. J.: *S. Andrea in Mantua. The building history* (Philadelphia, 1975)

Kaufmann, H. W.: *The life and works of Nicola Vicentino (1511–c. 1576)* (n.p., 1966)

Kenton, E.: 'A faded laurel wreath' in J. LaRue (ed.): *Aspects of medieval and Renaissance music. A birthday offering to Gustave Reese* (London, 1966), p. 500

Kettering, A. McNeil: 'Rembrandt's *Flute player*: A unique treatment of pastoral', *Simiolus* 9 (1977), p. 19

Kinkeldey, O.: 'A Jewish dancing master of the Renaissance' in *A. S. Freidus memorial volume* (New York, 1929), p. 329

Kirkendale, W.: *L'Aria di Fiorenza, id est Il Ballo del Granduca* (Florence, 1972)

Kirschbaum, E.: *Lexicon der christlichen Ikonographie*, 8 vols. (Freiburg, 1968–76)

Kristeller, P. O.: 'The contribution of religious orders to Renaissance thought and learning' in E. P. Mahoney (ed.): *Medieval aspects of learning. Three essays by Paul Oskar Kristeller* (Durham, N.C., 1974), p. 95

Kümmel, W. F.: 'Ein deutscher Bericht über die florentinischen Intermedien des Jahres 1589', *Analecta musicologica* 9 (1970), p. 1

Lamberti, G. M.: *Raccolta degli obblighi, e prerogativi dei guardiani grandi, banca e zonta, ministri e serventi della venerando scola di San Rocco*, 2nd edn (Venice, 1765)

Lapini, A.: *Diario fiorentino dal 252 al 1596, ora per la prima volta pubblicato da Gius. Odoardo Corazzini* (Florence, 1900)

Lauts, J.: *Isabella d' Este, Fürstin der Renaissance* (Hamburg, 1952)

Lavin, I.: 'Lettres de Parme (1618, 1627–1628) et débuts du théâtre baroque' in J. Jacquot (ed.): *Le lieu théâtrale à la renaissance* (Paris, 1964), p. 105

Lea, K. M.: *Italian popular comedy. A study in the commedia dell'arte, 1560–1620, with special reference to the English stage*, 2 vols. (Oxford, 1934)

Ledbetter, S.: 'Luca Marenzio: New biographical findings' (Ph.D. diss., New York University 1971)
  'Marenzio's early career', *Journal of the American Musicological Society* XXXII (1979), p. 304
Lehmann, P. W.:'The sources and meaning of Mantegna's *Parnassus*' in P. W. Lehmann and K. Lehmann (eds.): *Samothracian reflections. Aspects of the revival of the antique* (Princeton, 1973), p. 58
Leuchtmann, H.: *Orlando di Lasso*, 2 vols. (Wiesbaden, 1976)
Levri, M.: 'La cappella musicale del Madruzzo e i cantori del concilio', *Il Concilio di Trento* II (1943), p. 393
  Gli organi di Mantova. Ricerche d'archivio (Trent, 1976)
Lippmann, F.:'Musikhandschriften und -Drucke in der Bibliothek des Fürstenhauses Massimo, Rom. Katalog, 1. Teil: Handschriften', *Analecta musicologica* 17 (1976), p. 254
Litta, P.: *Famiglie celebri italiane*, 15 vols. (Milan, 1816–96)
Llorens, J. M.: 'El Códice Casanatense 2.856 identificado como el cancionero de Isabella d'Este (Ferrara), esposa de Francesco Gonzaga (Mantua)', *Anuario musical* XX (1967), p. 161
Lockwood, L.: *The Counter-Reformation and the masses of Vincenzo Ruffo* (Venice, 1970)
  'Dufay and Ferrara' in A. W. Atlas (ed.): *Papers read at the Dufay Quincentenary Conference, Brooklyn College December 6–7, 1974* (New York, 1976), p. 1
  'Jean Mouton and Jean Michel: French music and musicians in Italy, 1505–1520', *Journal of the American Musicological Society* XXXII (1979), p. 191
  'Josquin at Ferrara: New documents and letters' in Lowinsky and Blackburn (eds.): *Josquin des Prez*, p. 103
  'Music at Ferrara in the period of Ercole I d'Este', *Studi musicali* I (1972), p. 101
  'Pietrobono and the instrumental tradition at Ferrara in the fifteenth century', *Rivista italiana di musicologia* X (1975) (*Studi in onore di Nino Pirrotta*), p. 115
Lowinsky, E. E.: *The Medici codex of 1518. A choirbook of motets dedicated to Lorenzo de' Medici, Duke of Urbino*, 3 vols. (Chicago, 1968)
  'A newly discovered sixteenth-century motet manuscript in the Biblioteca Vallicelliana in Rome', *Journal of the American Musicological Society* III (1950), p. 173
  'On the presentation and interpretation of evidence: Another review of Costanzo Festa's biography', *Journal of the American Musicological Society* XXX (1977), p. 119
  and B. J. Blackburn (eds.): *Josquin des Prez. Proceedings of the International Josquin Festival Conference held at Lincoln Center in New York City, 21–25 June 1971* (London, 1976)
Il luogo teatrale a Firenze. Spettacolo e musica nella Firenze medicea, documenti e restituzioni I (Milan, 1975)
Luzio, A.: 'Ercole Gonzaga allo studio di Bologna', *Giornale storico della letteratura italiana* VIII (1886), offprint
  and R. Renier: 'La coltura e le relazioni letterarie di Isabella d'Este Gonzaga', *Giornale storico della letteratura italiana* [part 1] XXXIII (1899), p. 1; [part 2] XXXIV (1899), p. 1; [part 3] XXXV (1900), p. 193; [part 4] XXXVI (1900), p. 325; [part 5] XXXVII (1901), p. 201; [part 6] XXXVIII (1901), p. 41; [part 7] XXXIX (1902), p. 193; [part 8] XL (1902), p. 289; and [part 9] XLII (1903), p. 75

(and Renier): *Mantova e Urbino. Isabella d'Este ed Elisabetta Gonzaga nelle relazioni famigliari e nelle vicende politiche. Narrazione storica documentata* (Turin, 1893)

and P. Torelli: *L'Archivio Gonzaga di Mantua*, 2 vols. (Ostiglia and Verona, 1920–2)

Luzzato, G.: *Studi di storia economica veneziana* (Padua, 1954)

MacClintock, C.: *Giaches de Wert (1535–1596). Life and works* (n.p., 1966)

'New light on Giaches de Wert' in J. LaRue (ed.): *Aspects of medieval and Renaissance music. A birthday offering to Gustave Reese* (London, 1966), p. 595

'New sources of Mantuan music', *Journal of the American Musicological Society* XXII (1969), p. 508

(trans.): *Le balet comique de la Royne, 1581* (n.p., 1971)

(trans.): *Hercole Bottrigari: Il desiderio...Vicenzo Giustiniani: Discorso sopra la musica* (n.p., 1962)

and M. Bernstein (eds.): *Giaches de Wert. Opera omnia* (n.p., 1961–   )

McGowan, M. M.: *L'art du ballet de cour en France 1581–1643* (Paris, 1963)

McMurty, W. M.: 'Ferdinand, Duke of Calabria and the Estensi. A relationship honored in music', *The sixteenth century journal* VIII (1977), p. 17

Maier, B. (ed.): *Torquato Tasso. Opere*, 5 vols. (Milan, 1963–   )

Malipiero, G. F.: *Claudio Monteverdi* (Milan, 1929)

Mantese, G.: *Storia musicale vicentina* (Vicenza, 1956)

Mantova. La storia. Le lettere. Le arti, 9 vols. in 11 (Mantua, 1958–65):

Mantova. La storia, ed. G. Coniglio, 3 vols.

Mantova. Le lettere, ed. E. Faccioli, 3 vols.

Mantova. Le arti, ed. G. Paccagnini, 5 vols. in 3

Marotti, F. (ed.): *Leone de' Sommi. Quattro dialoghi in materia di rappresentazioni sceniche* (Milan, 1968)

The Mary Flagler Cary music collection, Pierpont Morgan Museum (New York, 1970)

Masson, G.: *Courtesans of the Italian Renaissance* (London, 1975)

Mattioli, D.: 'Fiamminghi a Mantova tra cinque e seicento' in *Rubens a Mantova*, p. 68

Maylender, M.: *Storia delle accademie d'Italia*, 5 vols. (Bologna, 1926–30)

Mazzi, C.: *La congrega dei Rozzi di Siena nel secolo XVI* (Florence, 1882)

Meerseman, G.: 'La riforma delle confraternite laicali in Italia prima del concilio di Trento', *Italia sacra* II (1960), p. 17

Mérimée, P. and L. Lacour (eds.): *Pierre de Bourdeille [Seigneur de Brantôme]. Oeuvres complètes...publiées pour la première fois selon le plan de l'auteur*, 13 vols. (Paris, 1858–95)

Michel A.: 'The earliest dance manuals', *Medievalia et humanistica* III (1945, p. 117

Middeldorf, U.: 'On the dilettante sculptor', *Apollo* 1978, p. 310

Milano, A.: *Storia degli ebrei in Italia* (Turin, 1963)

Mischiati, O.: 'I cataloghi di tre organari bresciani: Antegnati, Bolognini, Tonolo', *L'organo* XII (1974), p. 47

Review of *Conservatorio di musica*, in *Rivista italiana di musicologia* XI (1976), p. 138

Mompellio, F.: *Lodovico Viadana – musicista fra due secoli (XVI–XVII)* (Florence, 1967)

Montesinos, J.: *Cartas inéditas de Juan de Valdes al cardenal Gonzaga* (Madrid, 1931)

Monti, G. M.: *Le confraternite medioevali dell'alta e media Italia*, 2 vols. (Venice, 1927)

Moro, S. M.: 'Mantova e la corte gonzaghesca alla fine del secolo XVI' in *Rubens a Mantova*, p. 18

Mousnier, R.: *Les hiérarchies sociales* (Paris, 1969)

Müller, G. (ed.): *Raccolta di cronisti e documenti storici inediti*, 2 vols. (Milan, 1857)

Muoni, G.: *Gli Antegnati organari insigni* (Milan, 1883)

Nagler, A. M.: *Theatre festivals of the Medici* (New Haven, 1964)

Neri, A.: 'Gli "intermezzi" del "Pastor fido"', *Giornale storico della letteratura italiana* IX (1888), p. 405

Newcomb, A.: 'The musica segreta of Ferrara in the 1580s' (Ph.D. diss., Princeton University 1970)

   'The three anthologies for Laura Peverara', *Rivista italiana di musicologia* X (1975) (*Studi in onore di Nino Pirrotta*), p. 329

Newman, J.: 'The madrigals of Salamon de' Rossi' (Ph.D. diss., Columbia University 1962)

Nugent, G.: 'The Jacquet motets and their authors' (Ph.D. diss., Princeton University 1973)

   Review of Tagmann: *Archivalische Studien*, in *Journal of the American Musicological Society* XXIV (1971), p. 474

Odorici, L.: *Barbara Sanvitale e la congiura del 1611 contro i Farnese* (Brescia, 1862)

Osthoff, W.: *Josquin Desprez*, 2 vols. (Tutzing, 1962–5)

   Theatergesang und darstellende Musik in der italienischen Renaissance (15. und 16. Jahrhundert), 2 vols. (Tutzing, 1969)

Paccagnini, G.: *Il palazzo ducale di Mantova* (Turin, 1969)

   Pisanello alla corte dei Gonzaga (Venice, 1972)

Paganuzzi, E.: 'Notizie veronesi su Marco Cara e Michele Pesenti', *Rivista italiana di musicologia* XII (1977), p. 7

Paolo, O. P.: *Primiceri di S. Andrea* (Mantua, 1887)

Pappotti, F. I.: 'Annali o memorie storiche della Mirandola, i: 1500–1673', *Memorie storiche della città e dell'antico ducato della Mirandola* III (1876), p. 1

Pasquazi, S.: *Rinascimento ferrarese* (Caltanisetta and Rome, 1957)

Pastor, L. F. von: *History of the Popes*, trans. F. I. Antrobus, R. F. Kerr, E. Graf, and E. F. Peller (London, 1891–   ) (transl. of *Geschichte der Päpste seit dem Ausgang des Mittelalters*, 40 vols. (Freiburg im Breisgau, 1886–9))

Pecchai, P.: *Roma nel cinquecento* (Bologna, 1948)

Pellicia, G.: *La preparazione ed ammissione dei chierici ai santi ordini nella Roma del secolo XVI* (Rome, 1946)

Perella, N. J.: *The critical fortunes of Battista Guarini's 'Il pastor fido'* (Florence, 1973)

Perina, C.: *La basilica di S. Andrea in Mantova* (Mantua, 1965)

Perkins, L. L.: Review of Lowinsky: *The Medici codex*, in *Musical quarterly* LV (1969), p. 255

   (ed.): *Johannes Lhéritier. Opera omnia* (n.p., 1969)

Pescasio, L.: *Rarità bibliografiche mantovane* (Mantua, n.d.)

Picard, C.: 'Andrea Mantegna et l'antique', *Revue archéologique*, ser. VI, vol. XXXIX (1952), p. 126

Pirrotta, N.: *Li due Orfei, da Poliziano a Monteverdi. Con un saggio critico sulla scenografia di Elena Povoledo*, 2nd rev. edn (Turin, 1975)

   'Temperaments and tendencies in the Florentine camerata', *Musical quarterly* XL (1954), p. 169

Prinzivalli, V.: *Torquato Tasso nella vita e nelle opere* (Rome, 1895)

Prizer, W. F. II: 'La cappella di Francesco II Gonzaga e la musica sacra a Mantova nel primo ventennio del cinquecento' in *Mantova e i Gonzaga nella civiltà del rinascimento* (Rome, 1978), p. 267

'Marchetto Cara and the north Italian frottola', 3 vols. (Ph.D. diss., University of North Carolina at Chapel Hill 1974) (all references in my notes are to vol. 1)

Prodi, P.: *Il Cardinale Gabrielle Paleotti* (Rome, 1959)

'Lineamenti dell'organizzazione diocesana in Bologna durante l'episcopato del Cardinale G. Paleotti' in *Problemi di vita religiosa in Italia nel cinquecento* (Padua, 1960), p. 323

'Ricerche sullla teorica delle arti figurative nella riforma cattolica', *Archivio italiano per la storia della pietà* IV (Rome, 1965), p. 123

Prunières, H.: *Le ballet de cour en France avant Benserade et Lully* (Paris, 1914)

Pullan, B.: *Rich and poor in Renaissance Venice: The Social institutions of a Catholic state to 1620* (Oxford, 1971)

(ed.): *Crisis and change in the Venetian economy in the sixteenth and seventeenth centuries* (London, 1968)

Putelli, R.: *Vita, storia ed arte mantovana nel cinquecento*, 2 vols. (Mantua, 1934–5)

Quazza, R.: 'Emanuele Filiberto di Savoia e Guglielmo Gonzaga (1559–1560)', *Atti e memorie della R. Accademia Virgiliana di Mantova*, new ser., XXI (1929), p. 1

Queller, D. E.: 'The development of ambassadorial relazioni' in J. R. Hale (ed.): *Renaissance Venice* (London, 1973), p. 174

Ramazzini, A.: 'I musici fiamminghi alla corte di Ferrara', *Archivio storico lombardo* VI (1879), p. 116

Reiner, S.: 'La vag'Angioletta (and others), Part I', *Analecta musicologica* 14 (1974), p. 26

Rolandi, U.: 'Emilio de' Cavalieri, il Granduca Ferdinando e l'*Inferigno*', *Rivista musicale italiana* XXXVI (1929), p. 26

Romano, G. (ed.): *Cronaca del soggiorno di Carlo V in Italia (dal 26 Luglio 1529 al 25 Aprile 1530). Documento di storia italiana estratto da un codice della regia biblioteca universitaria di Pavia* (Milan, 1892)

Ronchini, A.: 'Vita della contessa Barbara Sanseverina', *Atti e memorie del RR. deputazione di storia patria per le provincie modenesi e parmensi* I (1863), offprint

Rosand, E.: 'Music in the myth of Venice', *Renaissance quarterly* XXX (1977), p. 511

Rossi, V.: *Battista Guarini ed il Pastor fido. Studio biografico-critico con documenti inediti* (Turin, 1885)

Roth, C.: *The Jews in the Renaissance* (Philadelphia, 1946)

Rubens a Mantova (Venice, 1977)

Rubenstein, N.: 'Vasari's painting of "The foundation of Florence" in the Palazzo Vecchio' in D. Frazer (ed.): *Essays in the history of architecture presented to Rudolph Wittkower* (London, 1967), p. 66

Ruble, A. de: *Histoire universelle*, 10 vols. (Paris, 1886)

Rubsamen, W. H.: *Literary sources of secular music in Italy (ca. 1500)* (Berkeley and Los Angeles, 1943)

'Music research in Italian libraries: An anecdotal account of obstacles and discoveries', *Notes* VI (1948–9), pp. 220 and 543, and VIII (1950–1), pp. 70 and 513

Russell, J. C.: *Medieval regions and their cities* (Newton Abbot, 1972)

Samuels, R. S.: 'Benedetto Varchi, the Accademia degli Infiammati, and the origins of the Italian academic movement', *Renaissance quarterly* XXIX (1976), p. 599

Scherliess, V.: 'Notizien zur musikalischen Ikonographie (II). Die Musik-Impresa der Isabella d'Este', *Analecta musicologica* 15 (1975), p. 21

Schlosser, J.: *La letteratura artistica* (Florence, 1956)

Schmidt-Görg, J.: *Nicolas Gombert, Kapellmeister Kaiser Karls V: Leben und Werk* (Bonn, 1938)

Schrade, L.: 'Les fêtes du mariage de Francesco dei Medici et de Bianca Cappello' in J. Jacquot (ed.): *Les fêtes de la renaissance*, I (Paris, 1956), p. 107

    La représentation d'Edipo Tiranno au Teatro Olimpico (Vicence, 1585) (Paris, 1960)

Schroeder, H. J. (trans.): *Canons and decrees of the Council of Trent* (St Louis, 1941)

Segarizzi, A.: *Relazioni degli ambasciatori veneti al senato*, 4 vols. (Bari, 1912–16)

Segre, A.: 'Un registro di lettere del cardinale Ercole Gonzaga (1535–36) con un'appendice di documenti inediti (1520–48)', *Miscellanea di storia italiana*, ser. III, vol. XVI (1913), p. 275

Selfridge-Field, E.: *Venetian instrumental music from Gabrieli to Vivaldi* (Oxford, 1975)

Sella, D.: 'Crisis and transformation in Venetian trade' in Pullan (ed.): *Crisis and change*, p. 88 (revised transl. of 'Il declino dell'emporio realtino' in *La civiltà veneziana nell'età barocco* (Florence, 1959))

Sherr, R.: 'The publications of Guglielmo Gonzaga', *Journal of the American Musicological Society* XXXI (1978), p. 118

Shulvass, M.: *Haye ha-Yehudim be Italyah bi-tekufat ha-Renesans* (New York, 1955) (transl. as *The Jews in the world of the Renaissance* by E. I. Kose (Leiden, 1973))

Sickel, T. von: *Römische Bericht*, 5 parts (Sitzungsberichte der Kaiserlichen Akademie der Wissenschaften in Wien, philosophisch–historische Classe, CXXXIII–CXLIV) (Vienna, 1895–1901)

Simonsohn, S.: *Toledòt ha-Yehudìm bedukhasùt Mantova*, 2 vols. (Jerusalem, 1962–4)

Slim, H. C.: *A gift of madrigals and motets*, 2 vols. (Chicago, 1972)

Solerti, A.: *Gli albori del melodramma*, 3 vols. (Milan, 1904–5)

    Ferrara e la corte estense nella seconda metà del secolo decimosesto. I discorsi di Annibale Romei (Città di Castello, 1890)

    'Laura Guidiccioni Lucchesini ed Emilio de' Cavalieri, i primi tentativi del melodramma', *Rivista musicale italiana* IX (1902), p. 797

    Musica, ballo e drammatica alla corte medicea dal 1600 al 1637. Notizie tratte da un diario con appendice . . . (Florence, 1905)

    and D. Lanza: 'Il teatro ferrarese nella seconda metà del secolo XVI', *Giornale storico della letteratura italiana* XVIII (1891), p. 148

Stella, A.: 'La crisi economica veneziana nella seconda metà del secolo XVI', *Archivio Veneto* LVIII–LIX (1956), p. 17

Stevens, D.: Review of MacClintock and Bernstein (eds.): *Giaches de Wert. Opera omnia*, XI (n.p., 1969), in *Notes* XXXI (1975), p. 124

Straeten, E. van der: *La musique aux Pays-Bas avant le XIXᵉ siecle*, 8 vols. (Brussels, 1867–88)

Strunk, O.: 'Guglielmo Gonzaga and Palestrina's *Missa Dominicalis*' in *Essays on music in the Western world* (New York, 1974), p. 94 (reprinted from *Musical quarterly* XXXIII (1947), p. 228)

Gli studioli di Isabella d'Este. Documenti, vicende, restauri (Mantua, 1977)

Le studiolo d'Isabelle d'Este, Musée du Louvre: Les dossiers du département des peintures 10 (Paris, 1975)

Tadlock, R. J.: 'Alessandro Striggio madrigalist', *Journal of the American Musicological Society* XI (1958), p. 29

Tagmann, P. M.: *Archivalische Studien zur Musikpflege am Dom von Mantua (1500–1627)* (Bern, 1967)

'La cappella dei maestri cantori della basilica palatina di S. Barbara a Mantova (1565–1630): Nuovo materiale scoperto nelli archivi mantovani', *Civiltà mantovana* IV (1970), p. 376

Tedeschi, E.: 'La "Rappresentazione d'Orfeo" e la tragedia d'Orfeo', *Atti e memorie dell'Accademia Virgiliana di Mantova*, new ser., XVII–XVIII (1925), p. 47

Tesori d'arte nella terra dei Gonzaga (Venice, 1974)

Thieme, U. and F. Becker: *Allgemeines Lexicon der bildenden Künstler von der Antike bis zur Gegenwart*, 40 vols. (Leipzig, 1907–56)

Tietze, H. and E. Tietze-Conrat: *The drawings of the Venetian painters in the 15th and 16th centuries* (New York, [1944])

Tiraboschi, G.: *Storia della letteratura italiana*, 10 vols. (Rome, 1782–97)

Torri, L.: 'Nei parentali (1614–1914) di Felice Anerio e di Carlo Gesualdo Principe di Venosa', *Rivista musicale italiana* XXI (1914), p. 501

Turrini, G.: *Il patrimonio musicale della biblioteca capitolare di Verona dal sec. XV al XIX* (Verona, 1952)

Vaccaro, J.-M. (ed.): *Oeuvres d'Albert de Rippe I: Fantasies* (Paris, 1972)

Valdrighi, L. F.: 'Cappelle, concerti e musiche di casa d'Este dal secolo 15 al 18', *Atti e memorie delle RR. deputazione di storia patria per le provincie modenesi e parmensi*, ser. III, vol. II (1883 and 1884), pp. 416 and 517

Vandelli, D.: *Opusculi inediti di Tarquinia Molza modenese* (Bergamo, 1750)

Vasari, G. (ed. G. Milanesi): *Giorgio Vasari. Le opere. Le vite de' più eccellenti pittori scultori ed architettori. Con nuove annotazione e commenti*, 4 vols. (Florence, 1878–85)

Ventura, A.: 'Considerazioni sull'agricoltura veneta e sulla accumulazione originaria del capitale nei secoli XVI e XVII', *Studi storici* IX (1968), p. 674

Verheyen, E.: *The paintings in the 'studiolo' of Isabella d'Este at Mantua* (New York, 1971)

The Palazzo del Te in Mantua. Images of love and politics (Baltimore, 1977)

Vogel, E.: *Bibliothek der gedruckten weltlichen Vocalmusik italiens aus den Jahren 1500–1700*, 2 vols. (Berlin, 1892; reprinted with A. Einstein's supplements, 2 vols. (Hildesheim, 1962))

Walker, D. P. (ed.): *Les fêtes du mariage de Ferdinand de Médicis et de Christine de Lorraine (Florence 1589), I. Musique des intermèdes de 'La Pellegrina'*...notes critiques par *Federico Ghisi et D. P. Walker* (Paris, 1963)

Warburg, A.: 'I costumi teatrali per gli intermezzi del 1589', with addenda by G. Bing, in *Gesammelte Schriften*, I (Leipzig, 1932), pp. 259 and 394

Weinberg, B.: *A history of literary criticism in the Italian Renaissance*, 2 vols. (Chicago, 1961)

Widmaier, K.: 'Jachet von Mantua und sein Motettenschaffen' (Ph.D. diss., University of Freiburg 1953)

Wind, E.: *Bellini's 'Feast of the Gods', a study in Venetian humanism* (London, 1948)

Winternitz, E.: 'The knowledge of musical instruments as an aid to the art historian'
  in *Musical instruments and their symbolism in Western art* (London, 1967), p. 43
Woodward, W. H.: *Vittorino da Feltre and other humanist educators* (Cambridge, 1921)
Yates, F. A.: *The French academies of the sixteenth century* (London, 1947)
  The Valois tapestries, 2nd rev. edn (London, 1975)
Yriarte, C.: 'Isabella d'Este et les artistes de son temps', *Gazette des Beaux-Arts* XIII–XIV
  (1895), pp. 189, 382 and 394
Zanca, A.: *Notizie sulla vita e sulla opere di Marcello Donati da Mantova (1583–1602),
  medico, umanista, uomo di stato* (Pisa, 1964)

Index

Note: Of Appendixes II and III only the introductions and footnotes are indexed.

227